Advanced Applications in Osmotic Computing

G. Revathy
SASTRA University, India

A volume in the Advances in Systems Analysis, Software Engineering, and High Performance Computing (ASASEHPC) Book Series

IGI Global
PUBLISHER of TIMELY KNOWLEDGE

Published in the United States of America by
IGI Global
Engineering Science Reference (an imprint of IGI Global)
701 E. Chocolate Avenue
Hershey PA, USA 17033
Tel: 717-533-8845
Fax: 717-533-8661
E-mail: cust@igi-global.com
Web site: http://www.igi-global.com

Library of Congress Cataloging-in-Publication Data

Names: Revathy, G., 1987- editor.
Title: Advanced applications in osmotic computing / edited by G. Revathy.
Description: Hershey, PA : Engineering Science Reference, [2024] | Includes bibliographical references and index. | Summary: "This book is positioned to serve as a thorough compendium that will shed light on the most recent developments, tactics, and practical applications in IoT, Cloud, Edge, Fog, and Machine Learning"-- Provided by publisher.
Identifiers: LCCN 2023051949 (print) | LCCN 2023051950 (ebook) | ISBN 9798369316948 (h/c) | ISBN 9798369316955 (ebook)
Subjects: LCSH: Cloud computing. | Edge computing.
Classification: LCC QA76.585 .A36 2024 (print) | LCC QA76.585 (ebook) | DDC 004.67/82--dc23/eng/20240209
LC record available at https://lccn.loc.gov/2023051949
LC ebook record available at https://lccn.loc.gov/2023051950

This book is published in the IGI Global book series Advances in Systems Analysis, Software Engineering, and High Performance Computing (ASASEHPC) (ISSN: 2327-3453; eISSN: 2327-3461)

British Cataloguing in Publication Data
A Cataloguing in Publication record for this book is available from the British Library.

For electronic access to this publication, please contact: eresources@igi-global.com.

Advances in Systems Analysis, Software Engineering, and High Performance Computing (ASASEHPC) Book Series

ISSN:2327-3453
EISSN:2327-3461

Editor-in-Chief: Vijayan Sugumaran, Oakland University, USA

MISSION

The theory and practice of computing applications and distributed systems has emerged as one of the key areas of research driving innovations in business, engineering, and science. The fields of software engineering, systems analysis, and high performance computing offer a wide range of applications and solutions in solving computational problems for any modern organization.

The **Advances in Systems Analysis, Software Engineering, and High Performance Computing (ASASEHPC) Book Series** brings together research in the areas of distributed computing, systems and software engineering, high performance computing, and service science. This collection of publications is useful for academics, researchers, and practitioners seeking the latest practices and knowledge in this field.

COVERAGE

- Computer System Analysis
- Engineering Environments
- Storage Systems
- Virtual Data Systems
- Network Management
- Computer Networking
- Parallel Architectures
- Distributed Cloud Computing
- Performance Modelling
- Computer Graphics

IGI Global is currently accepting manuscripts for publication within this series. To submit a proposal for a volume in this series, please contact our Acquisition Editors at Acquisitions@igi-global.com or visit: http://www.igi-global.com/publish/.

The Advances in Systems Analysis, Software Engineering, and High Performance Computing (ASASEHPC) Book Series (ISSN 2327-3453) is published by IGI Global, 701 E. Chocolate Avenue, Hershey, PA 17033-1240, USA, www.igi-global.com. This series is composed of titles available for purchase individually; each title is edited to be contextually exclusive from any other title within the series. For pricing and ordering information please visit http://www.igi-global.com/book-series/advances-systems-analysis-software-engineering/73689. Postmaster: Send all address changes to above address.

Titles in this Series

For a list of additional titles in this series, please visit:
http://www.igi-global.com/book-series/advances-systems-analysis-software-engineering/73689

Quantum Computing and Cryptography in Future Computers
Shyam R. Sihare (Dr. APJ Abdul Kalam Govt. College, India)
Engineering Science Reference • © 2024 • 300pp • H/C (ISBN: 9781799895220) • US $270.00

Frameworks for Blockchain Standards, Tools, Testbeds, and Platforms
Yanamandra Ramakrishna (School of Business, Skyline University College, Sharjah, UAE) and Priyameet Kaur Keer (Department of Management Studies, New Horizon College of Engineering, India)
Engineering Science Reference • © 2024 • 300pp • H/C (ISBN: 9798369304051) • US $285.00

Enhancing Performance, Efficiency, and Security Through Complex Systems Control
Idriss Chana (ESTM, Moulay Ismail University of Meknès, Morocco) Aziz Bouazi (ESTM, Moulay Ismail University of Meknès, Morocco) and Husain Ben-azza (ENSAM, Moulay Ismail University of Meknes, Morocco)
Engineering Science Reference • © 2024 • 300pp • H/C (ISBN: 9798369304976) • US $300.00

Handbook of Research on Integrating Machine Learning Into HPC-Based Simulations and Analytics
Belgacem Ben Youssef (King Saud University, Saudi Arabia) and Mohamed Maher Ben Ismail (King Saud University, Saudi Arabia)
Engineering Science Reference • © 2024 • 400pp • H/C (ISBN: 9781668437957) • US $325.00

Machine Learning Algorithms Using Scikit and TensorFlow Environments
Puvvadi Baby Maruthi (Dayananda Sagar University, India) Smrity Prasad (Dayananda Sagar University, India) and Amit Kumar Tyagi (National Institute of Fashion Technology, New Delhi, India)
Engineering Science Reference • © 2024 • 453pp • H/C (ISBN: 9781668485316) • US $270.00

IGI Global
PUBLISHER of TIMELY KNOWLEDGE

701 East Chocolate Avenue, Hershey, PA 17033, USA
Tel: 717-533-8845 x100 • Fax: 717-533-8661
E-Mail: cust@igi-global.com • www.igi-global.com

Table of Contents

Detailed Table of Contents

Emotion recognition refers to the process of identifying the emotions expressed by an individual, typically through their facial expressions, speech, body language, and sometimes physiological signals like heart rate or skin conductance. In this chapter, facial expression is used to recognise. Emotions like happiness, sadness, anger, fear, surprise, and disgust are typically recognized. This chapter aims at developing a real-time approach to classification of facial emotions such as happy, normal, yawn, and sleep in a real-time context. For this, images are captured using sensors and stored in a cloud storage bucket in which the processing is done. The facial emotions are identified through the use of Haar cascade classifiers. The histogram-oriented gradients features are extracted in the detected facial emotion images, and the extracted features are classified by using machine learning models support vector machine and k-nearest neighbour classifiers as happy, normal, yawn, and sleep. The suggested system outperforms other current systems when tested with real-time datasets.

IoT is a trending technology, and it can be combined with various other technologies like cloud computing, machine learning, and deep learning to use it in versatile applications in real-time world for the past two decades. Usually, IoT sensors are used to collect data from the real-time environment, and the collected data from the sensors are usually large in volume. Here, cloud computing plays its vital role to store the collected data. Therefore, in IoT, the required data acquired from the sensors need to be scrutinized in real-time for providing quick control action for the industrial IoT devices.

In the digital IoT world, image watermarking has been determined as a solution of copyright problems and protecting the sensitive images from unauthorized access. A novel invisible watermarking technique which is secure against unapproved extraction of watermark and strong against different attacks has been proposed. Chaos-based image watermarking provides higher security than the traditional methodology. The proposed chaos-based watermarking involves three phases. In the first phase, a two-dimensional Henon chaos map is utilized to generate the chaotic series which act as keys for embedding the watermark. Before embedding the watermark, the image is encrypted by using Zig-Zag confusion process, and then in the last phase, the watermark image is converted into quaternary sequence, and by using random key of Henon map, each bit is embedded in the original image. The proposed model is applicable for both greyscale and colour images. Different performance analysis such as PSNR, SSIM will be used to identify the strength and quality of the proposed watermarking technique.

Rainfall prediction is a pivotal aspect of climate forecasting, influencing agriculture, water resource management, and disaster preparedness. This comprehensive review explores the integration of advanced algorithms and edge analytics within a fog computing framework to elevate the accuracy of rainfall predictions. The introduction outlines the significance of accurate rainfall predictions, the limitations of traditional methods, and the motivation for embracing fog computing, advanced algorithms, and edge analytics. A detailed examination of fog computing architecture underscores its decentralized nature and proximity to data sources, addressing challenges inherent in centralized models. The integration of edge analytics is discussed in depth, emphasizing its crucial role in preprocessing IMD data at the source. Insights gained from these implementations offer valuable perspectives on the practical implications, successes, and challenges associated with these methodologies.

In the evolving landscape of distributed computing, the integration of edge devices with traditional cloud infrastructures necessitates innovative approaches to harness their combined computational prowess. Osmotic computing, a paradigm that promises such integration, has transitioned from theoretical frameworks to tangible implementations. This chapter provides a comprehensive examination of osmotic computing, tracing its journey from conceptual underpinnings to its current real-world applications. Central to osmotic computing is the deployment of microservices—modular, autonomous units of computation—strategically positioned across the edge-cloud continuum based on immediate needs and resource availabilities. This review elucidates the foundational principles of osmotic computing, its distinguishing characteristics, the challenges encountered in its practical adoption, and its demonstrable benefits in current computing scenarios.

Speech emotion recognition is a critical component of human-computer interaction and affective computing. This chapter presents a comprehensive study on the application of deep learning techniques for the task of speech emotion recognition. Emotions conveyed through speech play a crucial role in understanding human behavior and are essential in various domains, including human-robot interaction, customer service, and mental health assessment. This chapter also investigates the impact of different feature extraction methods and data pre-processing techniques on the recognition accuracy. Basically, RNN algorithm is used for speech emotion recognition to identify the emotion through audio, but this chapter will accomplish this with CNN algorithm because the time complexity of RNN algorithm is high and to analyze the audio takes more time where CNN will be converted into spectrograms from each dimension of emotions, which will be recognized by augmenting it. And finally, it is used in the medical field, security, and surveillance management.

This study illustrates how electric car battery performance can be monitored using the internet of things (IoT). It is evident that an electric vehicle's only energy source is its battery. But the car's energy supply is steadily running out, which causes a drop in performance. This is a major source of concern for the battery industry. The chapter suggests using IoT techniques to monitor vehicle performance in order to perform the monitoring directly. The two primary elements of the suggested internet of things-based battery monitoring system are the monitoring device and the user interface. Test results indicate that the system may detect decreased battery life and alert the user to take appropriate action.

Health monitoring systems are designed to transform patient care by providing continuous monitoring and remote capabilities. Traditional healthcare often lacks constant monitoring, which can lead to delays in identifying issues. Wearable sensors, such as heart rate and eye blink sensors, collect real-time data that is transmitted to the cloud-based ThingSpeak platform. Non-intrusive eyeblink sensors aid in diagnosing conditions like dry eye syndrome, blepharospasm, and Parkinson's disease. Remote monitoring enables healthcare professionals to offer timely interventions with customizable alerts. IoT technology reduces hospital visits for chronic patients, potentially improving outcomes and reducing complications. The primary goal is to ensure seamless sensor connectivity to ThingSpeak, allowing users to access data from laptops and mobile devices. By empowering patients to actively manage their health, this system enhances health monitoring capabilities, paving the way for a more patient-centric and efficient healthcare landscape.

communications in public places. The corpus is trained by fine-tuning the pre-trained wav2vec2 XLSR model. This model captures the diverse acoustic features and patterns and even applied to multiple dialects, making it adaptable to real-world speech. The implemented model is evaluated on various noisy environments like markets, hospitals, shops, etc. In terms of various evaluation metrics such as word error rate (WER) and character error rate (CER), the designed model exhibits an optimal performance by achieving a lower error rate when compared to the baseline ASR models.

Preface

Dear Esteemed Contributors and Readers,

It is with great pleasure and anticipation that I present to you an unparalleled opportunity to embark on an extraordinary journey within the evolving realm of osmotic computing. *Advanced Applications in Osmotic Computing* stands as an ambitious endeavor to carve out new pathways in data-driven innovation, and your participation is pivotal in shaping this transformative narrative.

At its core, this book serves as a beacon illuminating the cutting-edge developments, innovative methodologies, and practical applications that define the landscape of IoT, Cloud, Edge, Fog, and Machine Learning. Authored by a collective force of visionaries, this compendium aims not just to document progress but to propel the industry forward, bridging the chasm between theory and practice, between possibility and implementation.

Our objectives are bold and purposeful:

Explore State-of-the-Art Techniques

Delve into the forefront of advancements in Osmotic Computing, unraveling the intricate tapestry of revolutionary techniques shaping decision-making through data.

Bridge Theory and Practice

We strive to seamlessly connect theoretical paradigms with their real-world applications, ensuring a comprehensive understanding that transcends conceptual boundaries.

Showcase Cross-Disciplinary Collaboration

Emphasize the collaborative essence of Osmotic Computing, showcasing how its prowess extends beyond siloed disciplines, fostering innovation across diverse industries.

Address Ethical and Responsible AI

Illuminate the ethical dimensions inherent in cutting-edge technology, advocating for responsible practices and equitable outcomes in Osmotic Computing.

Empower Researchers and Practitioners

Equip our readers with advanced tools and strategies, empowering them to push the boundaries of data analysis and smart connections.

Promote Interpretability and Transparency

Prioritize the interpretability of models and algorithms, ensuring that insights gained are not just accurate but also comprehensible.

Showcase Real-World Applications

Paint vivid portraits of successful implementations through diverse case studies, elucidating how Osmotic Computing transforms industries and sectors.

Predict Future Trends

Peer into the horizon of emerging trends, guiding our readers to anticipate challenges and seize opportunities in the ever-evolving landscape of Osmotic Computing.

Facilitate Lifelong Learning

Cultivate a culture of continuous learning, offering a timeless resource for readers to stay abreast of evolving methodologies and practices.

Encourage Collaboration and Dialogue

Forge a platform for knowledge exchange, fostering dialogue that ignites innovation and propels the field forward.

This compendium extends its reach to a diverse cohort of professionals, researchers, educators, students, and practitioners. Whether you seek foundational knowledge or aim to push the boundaries of expertise, this book is crafted to enrich your understanding and impact within the realms of data mining and machine learning.

We cordially invite contributions spanning a myriad of topics, from advanced IoT and machine learning algorithms to ethical considerations and future trends. Your insights will not only enrich this compendium but will also steer the course of Osmotic Computing's transformative journey.

Together, let us inscribe a new chapter in the annals of technological innovation.

ORGANIZATION OF THE BOOK

Within the pages of this edited reference book, *Advanced Applications in Osmotic Computing*, an array of chapters elucidate pioneering concepts and applications in diverse domains. Each chapter encapsulates innovative approaches, technologies, and insights, fostering a rich tapestry of knowledge within the realm of osmotic computing.

Facial Emotion Recognition Using Osmotic Computing

The chapter on Facial Emotion Recognition explores real-time classification techniques for emotions like happiness, sadness, anger, fear, surprise, and disgust through facial expressions. Leveraging Haar cascade classifiers and machine learning models like SVM and KNN, this work surpasses current systems in identifying emotions in real-time datasets.

Role of Osmotic Computing in Civil Engineering

This chapter delves into IoT's integration with cloud computing, emphasizing real-time data analysis for swift industrial IoT device control, marking a pivotal step in enhancing efficiency.

A Secure Image Protection for IoT Applications Using Watermarking Technique and Non-Linear Henon Chaos

Examining image watermarking for copyright protection, this chapter introduces a novel chaos-based watermarking technique, promising security against unauthorized access and various attacks.

Enhancing Rainfall Prediction Accuracy Through Fog Computing: Integration of Advanced Algorithms and Edge Analytics

The chapter reviews the integration of Fog Computing, advanced algorithms, and edge analytics to enhance rainfall prediction accuracy, crucial for agriculture, water resource management, and disaster preparedness.

From Theory to Practice: A Comprehensive Review of Osmotic Computing

Tracing the evolution of osmotic computing, this chapter navigates from theoretical underpinnings to real-world applications, emphasizing microservices and their role in edge-cloud computation.

Speech Emotion Recognition With Osmotic Computing

Focusing on deep learning techniques for speech emotion recognition, this chapter investigates feature extraction methods, emphasizing CNN for efficient analysis in medical, security, and surveillance domains.

Osmatic-Based Supervision of EV

The chapter focuses on the EV usage and the effects on advancements with Osmotic Computing.

Healthcare Monitoring and Analysis Using ThingSpeak IoT Platform: Capturing and Analyzing Sensor Data for Enhanced Patient Care

This chapter emphasizes wearable sensors and ThingSpeak IoT platform, facilitating continuous patient monitoring and remote interventions, promising improved healthcare outcomes.

Cloud Computing and Machine Learning in the Green Power Sector: Harnessing Sustainable Innovations

Exploring the synergy between cloud computing, machine learning, and the green power sector, this chapter elucidates how these technologies optimize renewable energy production for a sustainable future.

Convergence of AI and Self-Sustainability: Ethical and Social Implications

This chapter probes the ethical considerations surrounding the fusion of AI and self-sustainability, emphasizing fair policies, inclusive strategies, and responsible AI development.

Image Enhancement Using Holistic Transformer Super Resolution

Detailing the Holistic Transformer Super-Resolution technique, this chapter aims to enhance image resolution, pivotal in medical imaging, satellite observations, and scientific research.

Cloud Based Offensive Code Mixed Text Classification using Hierarchical Attention Network

Addressing mixed-language text classification, this chapter introduces the Hierarchical Attention Network, showcasing its effectiveness in classifying offensive content.

Diabetes Prediction Model Using Stochastic Gradient Descent Logistic Regression Approach

With a focus on diabetes prediction, this chapter compares LR, RFECV-LR, and RFECV-SGDLR models, suggesting an IoT-based diabetes model for improved patient monitoring.

IoT's Role in Smart Manufacturing Transformation for Enhanced Household Product Quality

Examining the fusion of IoT and smart manufacturing, this chapter explores data-driven insights, predictive maintenance, and customized product quality for enhanced household products.

Visual Speech Recognition by Lip Reading Using Deep Learning

This chapter presents Visual Speech Recognition, utilizing image processing to extract voice data from facial features, applying the 3D-CNN model for optimal classification accuracy.

An Enhanced Real-Time Automatic Speech Recognition System for Tamil Language Using Wav2Vec2 Model

Detailing the development of an ASR system for Tamil language, this chapter leverages real-time spontaneous speech data, showcasing its efficacy in various noisy environments.

These chapters collectively illuminate the multifaceted landscape of osmotic computing, offering a diverse spectrum of insights and applications across domains. We invite you to delve into these chapters, each a testimony to the dynamic intersection of technology and innovation.

IN SUMMARY

As we draw to a close in this compilation, *Advanced Applications in Osmotic Computing*, it is with a sense of fulfillment that we reflect on the wealth of knowledge, innovative insights, and pioneering applications encapsulated within these chapters.

From Facial Emotion Recognition and Speech Emotion Recognition leveraging osmotic computing to the profound implications in civil engineering, healthcare, agriculture, and beyond, each chapter stands as a testament to the transformative potential of this evolving field. We've navigated through the integration of IoT, cloud computing, machine learning, and edge analytics, witnessing their collective power in reshaping industries and driving sustainable innovations.

The pursuit of excellence in image enhancement, offensive code-mixed text classification, healthcare monitoring, and the convergence of AI and self-sustainability has illuminated the path toward more inclusive, ethical, and impactful technological advancements. Through comprehensive reviews, predictive models, and real-time applications, the book threads a tapestry of possibilities across various domains, empowering practitioners, researchers, educators, and enthusiasts alike.

The collaborative efforts of our esteemed authors have not only broadened our understanding but have also sparked curiosity, innovation, and dialogue. Their contributions have paved the way for cross-disciplinary collaboration, enabling us to envision a future where osmotic computing transcends boundaries, creating a synergy between technology and human progress.

As we conclude this volume, we extend our deepest gratitude to the contributors whose expertise, dedication, and insights have enriched this book. We also express our heartfelt appreciation to the readers whose curiosity and thirst for knowledge drive the continual exploration of the frontiers of osmotic computing.

May the knowledge shared within these pages inspire further exploration, innovation, and collaboration, propelling us toward a future where osmotic computing continues to redefine possibilities and create a positive impact on society.

I hereby give me great thanks to the almighty, dignitaries of SASTRA university, SRC Dean and Associate Dean, my CSE department faculty and all my academic and personal friends. Not but not least I thank my parents, my husband and my kids for their moral support in bringing this volume of book as a great success.

Warm Regards,

G. Revathy
SASTRA University, India

Chapter 1
Facial Emotion Recognition Using Osmotic Computing

P. Aurchana
Malla Reddy University, India

R. Indhumathi
Idhaya College for Women, India

G. Revathy
https://orcid.org/0000-0002-0691-1687
SASTRA University, India

A. Ramalingam
Sri Manakula Vinayagar Engineering College (Autonomous), India

ABSTRACT

Emotion recognition refers to the process of identifying the emotions expressed by an individual, typically through their facial expressions, speech, body language, and sometimes physiological signals like heart rate or skin conductance. In this chapter, facial expression is used to recognise. Emotions like happiness, sadness, anger, fear, surprise, and disgust are typically recognized. This chapter aims at developing a real-time approach to classification of facial emotions such as happy, normal, yawn, and sleep in a real-time context. For this, images are captured using sensors and stored in a cloud storage bucket in which the processing is done. The facial emotions are identified through the use of Haar cascade classifiers. The histogram-oriented gradients features are extracted in the detected facial emotion images, and the extracted features are classified by using machine learning models support vector machine and k-nearest neighbour classifiers as happy, normal, yawn, and sleep. The suggested system outperforms other current systems when tested with real-time datasets.

DOI: 10.4018/979-8-3693-1694-8.ch001

1. INTRODUCTION

A Latin verb "movere," which meaning to provoke, arouse, disturb, or elicit a response, is where the term "emotion" begins. According to psychology, emotion is a perplexing state of feeling that alters both the body and the mind and has an effect on behaviour and cognition. Emotions are made up of: cognition, feeling, and behaviour. Cognitive component primarily functions to shape our assessment of a given situation, leading us to experience emotions in various ways or not at all. In our everyday existence, we contemplate and take into account. When someone is stimulated, their emotions alter quickly and visibly. Vocal, facial, postural, and gestural reactions are all part of the behavioral component (Social Work Education BD, n.d.). Paul Eckman, a psychologist, identified six emotions that he felt all human societies shared in the 1970s. He named the emotions of happiness, sorrow, disgust, fear, surprise, and rage. He then included pride, dishonour, shame, and enthusiasm in his list of extra main emotions (Very Well Mind, n.d.). these feelings had been used as research subjects by numerous scholars. Mixed feelings are also employed in study. Artificial intelligence is given the ability to recognize emotions. The emotions are applied to other computer vision applications to generate interactive apps (Indhumathi & Geetha, 2019). Fig 1 depicts the range of emotions collected for this suggested project.

Figure 1. Emotions for the proposed work

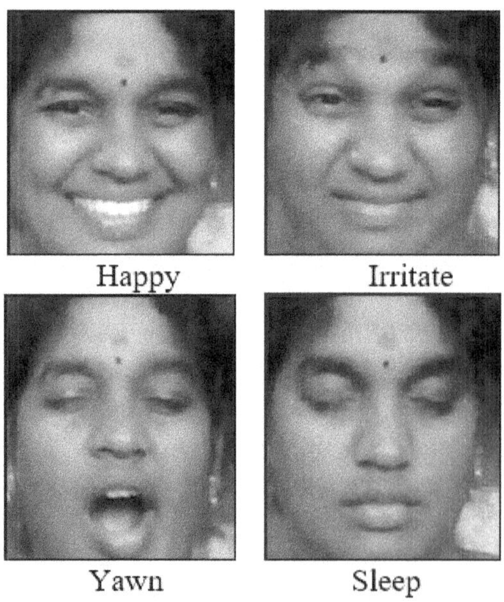

Figure 2. Overall block diagram of the proposed work

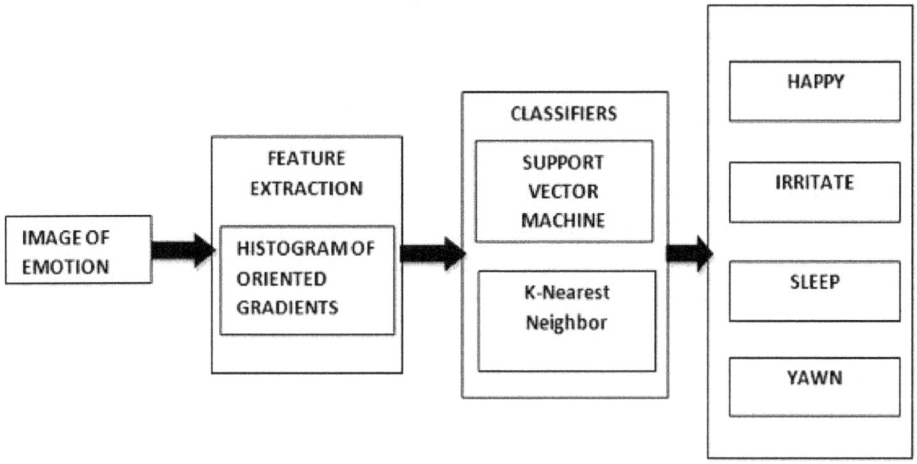

In the proposed work the images the emotion are captured and stored in cloud bucket storage and the training is done where the features are extracted using HOG, the derived features are fed into KNN and SVM which classes the emotions into four classes mainly happy, irritate, sleep and yawn.

2. LITERATURE SURVEY

In Sun & Li, (2017), deep learning is one kind of which the proposed convolutional neural network (CNN) is. Three datasets, CK, JAFFE, and NVIE, were chosen in order to train and verify the model. The 10-overlap Cross Validation technique was employed. In T et al. (2015), E-Learning Framework for Support Vector Machine-Performed Multiuser Face Detection-Based E-Learning. A multi-user e-learning framework to enhance learning with webcams and microphones (Bahreini et al., 2014). Provides quick actualresponse based on the student's facial and verbal expression. They presented a framework designed to detect and monitor student emotions in an online learning environment (Krithika & Lakshmi Priya, 2016). This system too offers a real-time input component to improve e-learning assets for moved forward. By recognizing eye and head movements, it becomes possible to gauge the students' level of concentration.For a remote learning platform, Salma Boumiza and her coworkers (Boumiza & Bekiarski, 2017) developed an automated tutor that makes use of both facial recognition and emotion identification technologies.SL Happy and others. Happy (2013) introduced a non-invasive, self-contained model designed for the intelligent assessment of emotions, alertness states, and even the appropriateness of feedback based on the user's age. This system employs unobtrusive visual cues to assess the user's emotional and alertness states, providing appropriate feedback based on the recognized cognitive state. It takes into account facial expressions, visual parameters, body postures, and gestures to make these assessments.

For emotion detection in facial images, an efficient Deep Learning (DL) neural network (DCNN) using TensorFlow (TL) with pipeline adjustment strategy has been proposed.Proposed method has a very high It has detection accuracy (Akhand et al., 2021). In the current study, experiments conducted in a general environment without a pre-trained DCNN model resulted in misclassification along with some confusing face images (mostly profiles).

In Sarvakar et al. (2023), people have always found it easy to express their emotions, but computer programming is a much more difficult task. Recent advances in computer vision and machine learning have the potential to detect emotions in images. This article introduces a new method for recognizing facial emotions. FERC is based on the CNN network and is spit into two parts. Initially removes the image background, and then removes the face vectors. The FERC model uses expression vectors (EVs) to recognize four different types of canonical facial expressions. A two-stage For emotion detection in facial images, an efficient Deep Learning (DL) neural network (DCNN) using TensorFlow (TL) with pipeline adjustment strategy has been proposed. FERC differs from Widespread in that it improves accuracy. Furthermore, EV generation prevents many problems from occurring before using the new background removal process.

Recently, the research project has become popular due to the many applications (Dalal & Triggs, 2005). Handcraft methods (HCF) and deep learning (DL) methods are two FER approaches. HCF methods rely on the performance of manual feature extractors. Convolutional neural networks (CNNs), excel at image classification. The disadvantage of Deep Learning methods requires a large amount of data to train and recognize efficiently.

3. FEATURE EXTRACTION

3.1 Histogram of Gradients

It is used for object detection in computer vision and machine learning (Sekaran et al., 2021). Shape and texture are quantified and represented using HOG descriptors. HOG is divided into five stages.

- Images are determined before description.
- Calculate gradients in the x and y directions.

- Get weighted votes for cell layout and spacing.
- In contrast, overlapping space cells are normalized.
- Collect and combine histograms of oriented gradients (HOG) to generate the optimal feature vector.

The orientations, pixels_per_cell, and cells_per_block are the main factors that significantly affect the HOG descriptor. These three variables ultimately control how many dimensions the resulting feature vector has, along with the size of the original image. In practical applications, HOG is typically employed alongside a Linear Support Vector Machine (SVM) for object detection.

4. CLASSIFICATION

The extracted HOG features are classified by using the following models.

4.1 Support Vector Machine

It follows the minimization of structural risk as a standard. SVM uses support vectors to handle non-linear class boundaries in addition to building a continuous model to compute the resolution function (Analytics Vidhya, 2017). SVM trains a linear machine to identify that divides the data cleanly, minimizes error, and maximizes the length between the hyperplane and the nearest training point if data is linearly separable. These closest training points are support vectors. The architecture of a support vector machine (SVM) is depicted in Fig 3. SVM transforms the input

Figure 3. Structure of the support vector machine

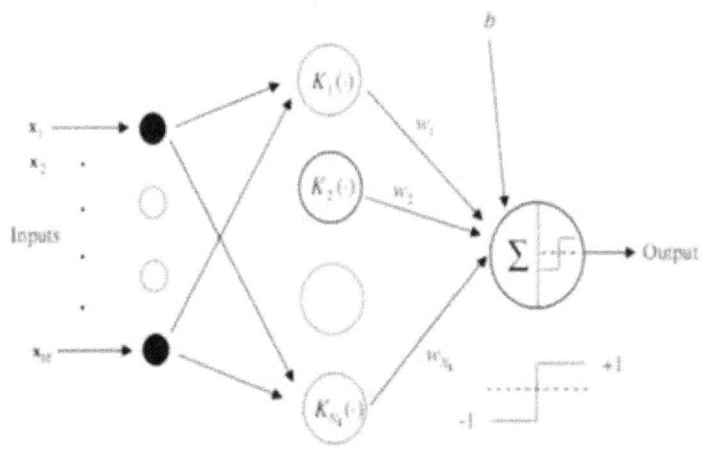

Figure 4. (a) Nonlinear problem, (b) linear problem

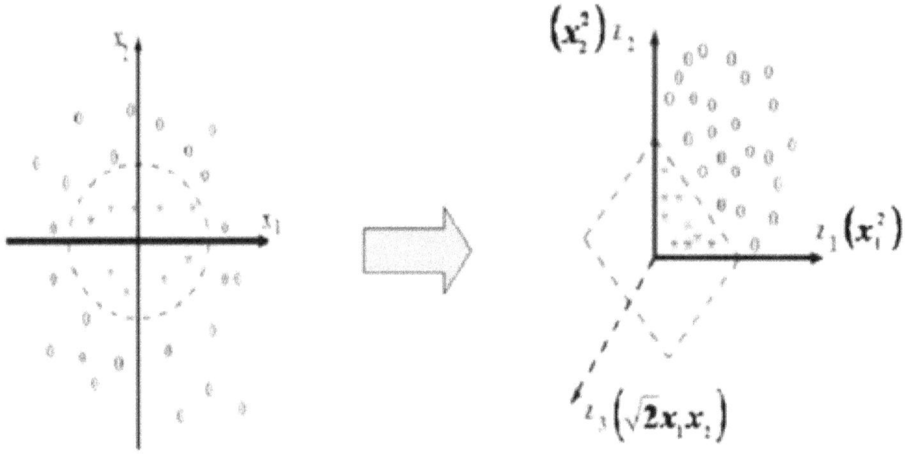

samples into a high-dimensional image space using a non-linear mapping. It is used to create a linear decision surface. Because of this, SVM can act as a linear classifier in the parameter space.

SVM locates a separating hyperplane that maximises the margin between the data points on either side when working with linearly separable data. However, for data that is not linearly separable, SVM employs a kernel function ϕ(x) to translate the data from the input space x∈R^I to a higher-dimensional space ϕ(x)∈R^H. This transformation allows SVM to find an effective dividing hyperplane in the higher-dimensional feature space. A kernel function, ϕ(x), is depicted in Fig. 3, illustrating how it maps a 2-dimensional input space to a higher 3-dimensional feature space. Originally, SVM was created to solve two class classification issues. Each SVM (one-vs-rest technique) isolates a single class from every other class. SVM typically works with boundaries that are linear. SVMs can map input vectors to a large-scale image space if linear boundaries are not required. Fig 4 shows how SVM chooses a nonlinear map to generate the best segmentation plane in this high-resolution space. The K function is defined as a kernel function to generate internal results that can be used to build various types of machines. Non-deterministic display in input field.

Table 1 illustrates the variety of SVM kernel functions available. The dimension of the feature space vector is given by: Here the polynomial kernel index is p and the input sample size is d

Table 1. Types of SVM kernel

Types of kernels	Inner Product Kernel $K(x^T, x_i)$
Polynomial	$(x^T x_i + 1)^p$
Gaussian	$exp\left[-\frac{\|x^T - x_i\|^2}{2\sigma^2}\right]$
Sigmoidal	$tanh\left(\beta_0 x^T x_i + \beta_1\right)$

$$\frac{(p+d)!}{p!d!} \tag{1}$$

The shape of the spatial component has been proven to be infinite for both Gaussian and sigmoid kernels. To determine the optimal speed for the face and non-face regions, feature vectors are extracted from the face and non-face regions and fed as input to the SVM.

4.2 K-Nearest Neighbors

It assesses the resemblance of two points based on the distance between them in a given area, typically using a metrics. The algorithm chooses the k data points that are closest to the new observation and finds the most frequent class among them in order to determine which points from the training set are similar enough to affect prediction for a new observation (Lkozma, n.d.; Math, n.d.):

1. Enter a positive integer value for k and a new sample.
2. Define the k entries from the database that are nearer to the current sample.
3. Determine the usual classification among the selected entries.
4. Assign classification to the latest sample.

5. EXPERIMENTAL RESULTS

5.1 Training

Web cameras are used to record face emotions, which are then sorted into four categories—happy, annoyed and yawning. 300 training samples from each class total about 1200 for the training process. For better performance, every frame is downsized to 200 x 100.

5.2 Testing

There are about 200 samples evaluated, with 50 samples per class. Grayscale images are created by downscaling the video frames to 200 x 100. The models categorize the frames as cheerful, annoyed, yawning, or sleeping.

5.3 Confusion Matrix

A confusion matrix with 200 emotions (50 per class) with KNN and SVM are formed as presented in Tables 2 and 3.

Table 2. Confusion matrix for KNN

ACTUAL CLASS		PREDICTED CLASS			
		Happy	Irritate	Yawn	Sleep
	Happy	38	0	5	7
	Irritate	2	44	0	4
	Yawn	10	3	27	10
	Sleep	0	1	0	49

Table 3. Confusion matrix for SVM

ACTUAL CLASS		PREDICTED CLASS			
		Happy	Irritate	Yawn	Sleep
	Happy	40	4	3	3
	Irritate	1	41	4	4
	Yawn	2	3	35	10
	Sleep	2	2	0	46

5.4 Classification Report

The purpose of evaluating a model with test datasets is to assess its effectiveness based on specific metrics. Various performance metrics are employed to assess the performance. These metrics give you an idea of how well the model is doingin terms of its precision, ability to recall relevant information, balance between precision and recall, and overall correctness.

5.5 Precision

This calculation can be derived from the confusion matrix using the following formula:

$$P = \frac{TP}{TP + FP} \tag{2}$$

5.6 Recall

The calculation for Recall is as follows, derived from the confusion matrix:

$$R = \frac{TP}{TP + FN} \tag{3}$$

Recall is an important metric because it evaluates the model's ability to find all instances of a positive class minimizing the number of false negatives and ensuring that as few positive instances as possible are missed.

5.7 F1 Score

This score is especially useful when both accuracy and recall are to be taken into account in a balanced way, equating their relative importance.

$$F1 - score = \frac{2PR}{P + R} \tag{4}$$

5.8 Classification Accuracy

The accuracy is one of the most commonly used performance metrics for classification algorithms. It is calculated as follows:

$$Accuracy = \frac{TP + TN}{TP + FP + FN + TN} \quad (5)$$

Tables 4 and 5 show the classification reports for KNN and SVM.

RESULT AND DISCUSSION

The classifier is fed pre-processed training samples. The hog feature is used to extract features. The extracted feature was compatible with the SVM and KNN models. The labels are predicted by the classifier. The SVM classifier achieves 91% accuracy, while the KNN classifier achieves 90% accuracy. Head-left and head-right gestures

Table 4. KNN classification report

	Precision (%)	Recall (%)	F1-Score (%)	Accuracy (%)
Happy	76.0	76.0	76.0	88.0
Irritate	88.0	91.0	89.0	95.0
Yawn	54.0	84.0	66.0	86.0
Sleep	98.0	70.0	82.0	89.0
Average	79.0	80.0	78.0	90.0

Table 5. Classification performance of SVM

	Precision (%)	Recall (%)	F1-Score (%)	Accuracy (%)
Happy	80.0	80.0	88.0	93.0
Irritate	82.0	82.0	82.0	91.0
Yawn	70.0	83.0	76.0	89.0
Sleep	92.0	73.0	81.0	90.0
Average	81.0	82.0	82.0	91.0

Figure 5. Classification of happy emotion

Figure 6. Classification of irritate emotion

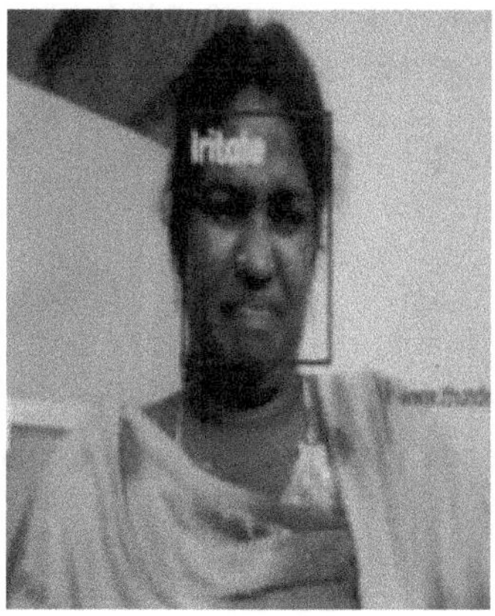

Figure 7. Classification of yawn emotion

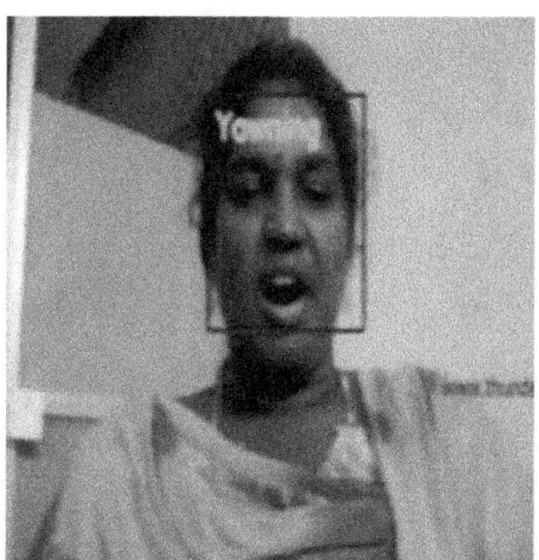

Figure 8. Classification of sleep emotion

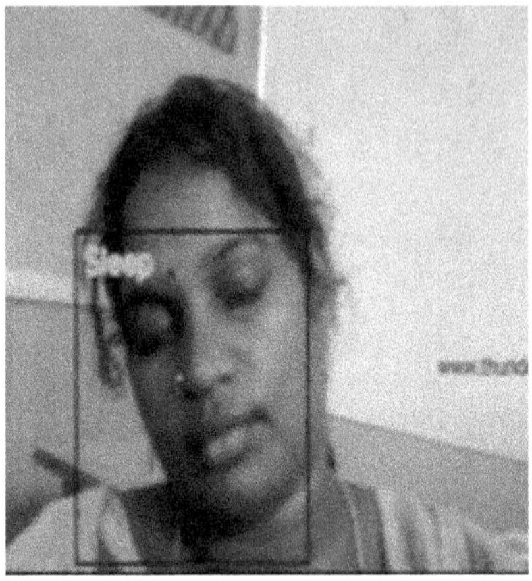

are recognized better than head-origin and head-down gestures by the proposed method. The proposed system and its performance are evaluated.

6. CONCLUSION

The facial emotion recognition is performed by using Hog feature with KNN and SVM. The machine learning models classify the facial emotion into Happy, Irritate, Yawn and Sleep. Both KNN and SVM produce good accuracy. The SVM outperforms the KNN in classifying the facial emotions. Other models and features for facial emotion recognition may be considered in the future.

REFERENCES

Akhand, M. A. H., Roy, S., Siddique, N., Kamal, M. A. S., & Shimamura, T. (2021). Facial emotion recognition using transfer learning in the deep CNN. *Electronics (Basel)*, *10*(9), 1036. doi:10.3390/electronics10091036

Analytics Vidhya. (2017). https://www.analyticsvidhya.com/blog/2017/09/understaing-support-vector-machine-example-code

Bahreini, K., Nadolski, R., & Westera, W. (2014). Towards Multimodal Emotion Recognition in E-learning Environment. *Interactive Learning Environments*, *24*(6), 1375–1391.

Boumiza, S., & Bekiarski, A. (2017). Development of Model for Automatic Tutor in E-learning Environment based on Student Reactions Extraction using Facial Recognition. In *IEEE 15-th International Conference on Electrical Machines, Drives and Power Systems (ELMA)*. IEEE.

Dalal, N., & Triggs, B. (2005). Histogram of Oriented Gradients for Human Detection. In *Proceedings of the 2005 IEEE Computer Society Conference on Computer Vision and Pattern Recognition (CVPR)* (pp. 63-69). IEEE. 10.1109/CVPR.2005.177

Happy, S. L. (2013). Automated Alertness and Emotion Detection for Empathic Feedback During E-Learning. IEEE.

Indhumathi, R., & Geetha, A. (2019). Emotional Interfaces for Effective E-Reading using Machine Learning Techniques. *International Journal of Recent Technology and Engineering*, *8*(4), 4443–4449.

Krithika, L. B., & Lakshmi Priya, G. G. (2016). *Student Emotion Recognition System (SERS) for E-learning Improvement on Learners Concentration Metric*. Elsevier B.V. doi:10.1016/j.procs.2016.05.264

Lkozma. (n.d.). http://www.lkozma.net/knn2.pdf

Math. (n.d.). http://www.math.le.ac.uk/people/ag153/homepage/KNN/KNN3.html

Revathy, G., & … . (2022). Investigation of E-voting system using face recognition using convolutional neural network (CNN). *Theoretical Computer Science*, *925*, 61–67.

Sarvakar, K., Senkamalavalli, R., Raghavendra, S., Kumar, J. S., Manjunath, R., & Jaiswal, S. (2023). Facial emotion recognition using convolutional neural networks. *Materials Today: Proceedings*, *80*, 3560–3564. doi:10.1016/j.matpr.2021.07.297

Sekaran, S. A. R., Lee, C. P., & Lim, K. M. (2021, August). Facial emotion recognition using transfer learning of AlexNet. In *2021 9th International Conference on Information and Communication Technology (ICoICT)* (pp. 170-174). IEEE. 10.1109/ICoICT52021.2021.9527512

Social Work Education BD. (n.d.). https://socialworkeducationbd.blogspot.com/2017/08/definition-of-emotion-and-its.html

Sun, A., & Li, Y.-J. (2017). Using facial expression to Detect Emotion in E-learning System: A Deep Learning Method. Springer International Publishing AG.

T, S. A., Jose, J., G, R., & Reddy, R. M. (2015). An E-learning System with Multiracial Emotion Recognition using Supervised Machine Learning. *International Journal of Recent Technology and Engineering, 8*(4), 4449.

Very Well Mind. (n.d.). https://www.verywellmind.com/an-overview-of-the-types-of-emotions4163976

Chapter 2
Role of Osmotic Computing in Civil Engineering

B. Kumaravel
Annamalai University, India

G. Indirani
Independent Researcher, India

ABSTRACT

IoT is a trending technology, and it can be combined with various other technologies like cloud computing, machine learning, and deep learning to use it in versatile applications in real-time world for the past two decades. Usually, IoT sensors are used to collect data from the real-time environment, and the collected data from the sensors are usually large in volume. Here, cloud computing plays its vital role to store the collected data. Therefore, in IoT, the required data acquired from the sensors need to be scrutinized in real-time for providing quick control action for the industrial IoT devices.

INTRODUCTION

Osmatic computing is a new trending technology to efficiently support and execute the Programmable object interface services and applications at the boundary network. Osmotic computing promotes digital transformation. Cyber–Physical Systems (CPSs) combined calculative, atmosphere, and man-kind mechanisms together to execute, dominate, and regularize complicated procedures in the existing environment. Here the main aim of using IoT is that real-time data is processed and remedial action will be taken immediately without any delay. So many lives will be saved from

DOI: 10.4018/979-8-3693-1694-8.ch002

dangerous situations. This process will also be automated continuously so there will be continuous monitoring.

IoT sensors will collect data from the real world by communicating with the environment. Here Environment implies the place which to be monitored for a particular purpose. In this Environment, the IoT sensors are located at various places. Each type of sensor has its own purpose. For example, the temperature sensor will quantify the temperature of the environment and the humidity sensor will measure the humidity of the environment. Usually, the data gathered from the sensors will be large in volume and it is also based on the number of sensors. That is why, it is required to go for cloud storage where all the details gathered from the detectors will be stored. Hereafter the processing will take place based on the application. Here we can make use either python code if Raspberry Pi board is used or we can use Arduino based C if Arduino Uno board is used. Once the processing is over, any action which has to be triggered or alarming is done to help the society. This book chapter will concentrate on Structural health monitoring(SHM), agricultural monitoring, Pollution monitoring and water management in Civil Engineering.

LITERATURE SURVEY

The paper titled "Challenges and opportunities for structural health monitoring for PVP applications" (Giurgiutiu, 2014) elaborates that the confrontation with events of utilizing the fitness discovering of buildings ideas and mechanisms in force liner penetrating uses. Here the structural health detecting experienced a dramatic increase by two factors. First is, our commercial fittings, jet caravans, civilian framework, etc. become extremely old and need increasingly costly care taking activities and mending. This costly maintenance and inspection can be reduced to some extent and can be done only when it is required with the continuous monitoring of the structures; and (b) the SHM concepts can be practically implemented with the emergence of modern methods, e.g., energetic things-dependent detectors, selectors, and photocells and also new details gathering, fact calculations, and fact archaeology mechanisms.

This paper indicates up to date, that the research on SHM has been concentrated mostly on the areas namely astrinics, guarding, and non-military framework uses bug only very little research, is performed. It is only because of the challenges faced by the PVP applications when compared to some other applications which used SHM concepts that have been tried so far. The current work discusses both the claiming which have to be overcome and the chances for using SHM in PVP applications.

The Paper titled "A review of structural health monitoring methods for composite materials" (Metaxa et al., 2019) explains that all the researchers worldwide are very interested in giving the important and critical information related to the damage of the structures and producing the expected performance. It is also required that they should be able to work with optimal performance and also against the commonly occurring disasters. In many applications related to SHM, composite materials are used. But as the result of that failure is more and complex. So, structures health monitoring systems have to be continuously monitored by keeping in mind the current status, benefits and limitations and the future enhancements have to be decided.

The Paper titled "Real-time prediction of mechanical behaviors of underwater shield tunnel structure using machine learning method based on structural health monitoring data" (Tan et al., 2023) states that the automatic behaviors of the structures prediction and the difficulties and problems are identified in advance to have the safe health of the structures eventually. The forecasting duration of the previous works is irregular even though the influencing factors are incomplete in nature. So this paper implements a real-time prediction model which is dependent on the SHM facts by combining both the space and time relationship with the exterior bundle by an auto encoder system. An auto associator technique is employed to collect the main depiction of uncooked discovering of facts at various geographical locations, and the repeated machine learning is employed to understand the time relationship from the episode. After this, the calculated time and space based details is combined with changing burden via a dense layer to identify the building presentation performance for the coming 12 h. Here, the newly developed model is made on the facts obtained from the structures a characteristic submerged target mine. The strength of the proposed study is performed to verify its reliability and the prediction capability. At the end, the auto associator method is also contrasted with some standard models, and the outputs show that it provides the greatest execution. A self-moving method is having a good value to detect the current-time growth of dig arrangement.

The Paper titled "Probabilistic data self-clustering based on semi-parametric extreme value theory for structural health monitoring" (Sarmadi et al., 2023) elaborates that many Engineering applications employ Clustering technique because of its popularity and its unsupervised learning principle. But due to the use of a few hands-on and applied problems namely critical changeability in nameless details, indispensability of identifying the number of bunches, and the use of some extra method for doorsill identification in the issue of abnormality identification restricts the uses of grouping code to SHM. These summons can be overcome by proposing a new likelihood based facts identity-bunches technique to identify the destructions of wide ranging civilian buildings through receiving a plan from near-parallelism end constant hypothesis. The essence of this model is that it considers every faceless fact as a localized bunch. So, it is also feasible to perform with the great practical issue of identifying the number of bunches related to almost all of the modern bunching methods. By employing an unruled adjacent search, every confined bunch has farthest quantities as a reverse lowest interval regarding main details and omits immaterial details delicate to deviation and any origin of changeability. So, this approach can be able to solve the most issues of surroundings and/or operative flexibility in the health of the structures. Here a newly discovered abnormality result is also mentioned to estimate both a decision threshold and also to differentiate an anomaly control from a common one.

This Paper titled on “Large-scale Structural Health Monitoring using Composite Recurrent neural networks and grid environments” (Eltouny & Liang, 2022) discusses that Nowadays the requirement for strong and intelligent structures have been varying in the forward manner. Sine because of the big data arrival, fact driven SHM has got friction in the civil Engineering field. Unruled learning can very well be applied purely using acquired facts from the area under study. But most of the unconquered learning work gives importance for identifying the harm in easy constructions. This work provides a new spotting foundation for identifying and constraining destruction in far-reaching layouts. This new work also depends on a 5D, time-sensitive mesh surroundings and also the modern space and time-based diabolo network. This system is a combination of auto associator based intricacy most powerful neural network and lengthy temporary systems. This newly developed work’s efficiency is also verified with 10 – story, 10-bay organization.

This Paper titled on “Agricultural monitoring System: A study” (Hashim et al., n.d.) gives a detailed study for monitoring temperature and soil moisture using the Arduino device to report the problems of resilient and usefulness based on Android based agriculture monitoring system. In future it has been planned to implement a less expensive and bendable agriculture supervising structure with less cost elements namely high-end computer machines. The advantage of this system is that it may be connected from anywhere and at any time. So, this study involves various plan of intelligent supervising arrangement by applying an implanted mini-mesh waiter, with IP connectedness for retrieving. The three primary elements used in this work are an electric gadgets appliance, package design (eclipse), and model IP layer. Here, the objective is to construct the mesh association and to merge these three elements together. At last, this paper will help the farmers to come with a dependable quality product with the help of an application using an electronic device.

The Paper titled “IoT based Agriculture (Ag-IoT): A detailed study on Architecture, Security and Forensics” (Rudrakar & Rughani, 2023) IoT based agriculture (Ag-IoT) is a trending transmission mechanism which is mostly employed by cultivational business person and agronomists to do cultivational farm-activities in the field to progress yield, better supervising, and to decrease work price. But by the application of the net in Intelligent-Ag, present fitness is incorporated in a farming arrangement, and at the same time it can improve the danger of safety violation and cyber-warfare that will make the Intelligent-Ag system to go wrong and may disturb its benefits. This makes cultivational-IoT is neglected in cyber safety parameters, and its impacts are more on its reliability and assumption by cultivational groups. To fill this slot, this paper provides an organized work of the written works printed during the period between 2001 and 2023 and also the advancements in Ag-Universal Object Interaction mechanism. The topics mentioned in the work on Ag-IoT are appearing applications, various UOI constructions, mistrust digital-intrusions and Cybercrimes, and summons in occasion reactions and online moot. It also discusses about the future research works related to the security risks in Intelligent cultivational technology. The primary intention is that it wants to maintain the security in Ag-UOI surroundings to provide continuous solutions and also to cope up with unexpected security problems.

The Paper titled “Advanced contribution of IoT in agricultural production for the development of smart livestock environments” (Mishra & Sharma, 2023) elaborates the various parts of fashionable life which require the application of Expert system, Machine Learning(ML), and the Universal Object Interaction(UOI) for investigation and summarization. Livestock farming is a very trending field using which various activities namely ethology and difficulties, the avoidance and handling of health issues, and the planning of the cultivator’s profitable options can be better understood by the use of AI and ML. Device shadow (DS) mechanism is especially an encouraging area that constructs on AI and is hitherto being employed to improve efficiency and reduce costs in boviness creature cultivation. This DS is a continuous modification print of smart livestock environments. The combination of both the IoT and Digital twin technology will achieve precision Livestock Farming (PLF) by developing more new technologies and tools used to monitor the well-being of the animals. Global Positioning Satellite (GPS), Radio Frequency IDentification (RFID), AI, and even ML are few of the recent mechanisms to keep track the whereabouts of the individual animals automatically. Even though many new techniques are employed to evaluate and monitor the animal welfare, there is a difficulty in achieving it. By the application of the DT technique illness investigation detection for single grange is improved by an element of 92%. The willingness of DTLF will be a 92% reaction rate in examining the pulsate, a 94% success rate in monitoring the heat span, and a 94% universal success in evaluating the moisture span.

The Paper titled “IOT Based Monitoring System in Smart Agriculture” (Prathibha et al., 2017) explains that the Internet of Things (IoT) plays a major role in Intelligent cultivational field. Intelligent farming is a growing idea\, since IoT detectors are proficient at giving details related to their cultivational fields. The main intention of this work is to employ growing mechanism i.e. Universal Object Interaction and Intelligent cultivation by employing mechanization. The yield of the well-organized crops can be improved by supervising its environmental factors. In this work, the heat and moisture level of cultivational land are monitored by using detectors namely CC3200 single chip. Polaroid is connected with CC3200 to collect pictures and transmit those images by using MMS to growers cell numbers using Wi-Fi.

Paper titled on "IoT Based Smart Agriculture Monitoring System" (Pendyala et al., n.d.) discusses that in all countries farming is performed from era which are measured to be science and art of taming vegetation. In our everyday life, mechanism is changing from time to time and in the same way there should be a change in the cultivation. IoT becomes a major role in an Intelligent cultivation. IoT sensors are employed to collect the required facts related to cultivational lands. The important benefit of IoT is to supervise the cultivation by applying the wireless detector networks and gather the details from various detectors that are situated at different nodes and transmit them by wireless agreement. In Universal Object Interaction system, the Intelligent cultivation is activated by Node MCU. It uses the humidity sensor, temperature sensor and DC motor. This framework operates to verify the heat and steam level. Here the detectors are applied to monitor the level of liquid and the system automatically starts watering when the level is below the range. UOI also displays the details of heat, moisture level in addition to date and time.

The Paper titled "A smart air pollution monitoring system" (Okokpujie, 2018) elaborates about the air pollution postures strand to the ecosystem and the standard of natural living beings of the planet. Air quality monitoring needs to understand the effects and which is the root cause of these problem for a long period. Consumers must know to some extent which activities are the reason for the deprived air quality. This study proposed and established a system for monitoring air quality with Arduino microcontroller. By bring up-to-date and care the data through the internet, air pollution can be monitor and analyse the air quality in real-time basis through a remote server data log. The measurements of air quality in metrices (PPM) and analysis with Microsoft Excel is conceivable. This study also organized a hardware's display interface to present the output, further cloud is retrieved over cloud at all nifty mobile devices.

The Paper titled "IoT Based Air Pollution Monitoring System" (Naik, 2023) explains that Mankind are being severely affected when they are exposed to pollutants in the ambient air (Metaxa et al., 2019). Therefore, setting up of air quality standards for health should be established by observing and detecting the air pollutants in the atmosphere by the respective countries are fetching progressively vital. Thus, cautious preparation of quantities is important. The main factors which stimulate the depiction of data observed in the place of observing stations. Hence, identification and establishments of observing station locations are composite and acquires a large amount of money. Furthermore, Air quality monitoring needs to understand the effects and which is the root cause of these problem for a long period. Consumers must know to some extent which activities are the reason for observing the deprived air quality. Therefore, air contamination supervising using an Universal Object Interaction is suggested to observe the pollutant concentrations of several contaminants in the ambient environment. Topographical zone is divided as various zones namely industrial, Residential, and traffic areas. As a result of this work an IoT system which can be installed at the desired location and can stock the observed concentrations in a cloud database. Then the analysis of pollutant levels is performed and display the same.

The Paper titled "Spatial-Temporal Graph Attention Fuser for Calibration in IoT Air Pollution Monitoring Systems" (Niresi et al., 2023) significantly increased air pollution monitoring using sensors, which gives the distribution of affordable sensors. In spite of this progressiveness, there is a challenge in standardizing the values precisely in the unrestrained atmosphere. To discourse this, this study planned a novel tactics which controls graphical representation using neural networks, particularly the graph considers network elements, to augment the standardization procedure with mingling data from various sensors. By this study it came know, the effectiveness of the standardization correctness of sensors meaningfully enlightening in IoT air pollution monitoring podiums. Hence this approach can be considered in air contamination supervising by applying IoT.

The Paper titled "Multi sensor data fusion calibration in IoT air pollution platforms" (Ferrer-Cid et al., 2020) discuss about the use of more than one detector usage for facts combination mechanisms using expert system and packed aggregating procedure in air contamination supervising programmes. This newly proposed study established the efficiency of conventional machine learning algorithms, including support vector regression (SVR), random forest (RF), and k-nearest neighbors (KNN), in blending detector data and evaluation is performed by comparing weighted averaging.

The Paper titled "Low-cost sensors for the measurement of atmospheric composition: overview of topic and future applications" (Lewis et al., 2018) explains that the dust contamination supervising plans come out with the rapid use of Universal Object Interaction

(UOI), making to gather the present data through various detectors located in different places. Here we concentrate on the precision trioxygen detectors.

The Paper titled "Use of electrochemical sensors for measurement of air pollution: correcting interference response and validating measurements" (Cross et al., 2017) discuss that the Manufacturers mostly omit the measurement operation and also to verify the surrounding conditions namely heat and moisture can disturb the detector's execution. The dependability and usefulness of pellistors can be improved in air quality supervising programmes by incorporating both less expensive heat detectors, wetness detectors and catalytic bead detectors. This duplication of monitoring contaminant application supports to increase the evaluation feature of gas detectors.

This paper titled "IoT-based water distribution system" (Devasena et al., 2019) has approached to supervise the wastage of water in pipe network system using IoT. Most of the water distribution system operated by manually in urban and rural areas. Meanwhile, the monitoring of water level in tanks, quantity of running water, quality and point of water leakage in pipe network system are difficult to find manually. This study proposed an IoT based water distribution system approach to supervise all the needs. The leakage of water in the water distribution system are monitored by implementing IoT technology using wirelessly. Necessary data is collected from the houses individually to process the real time monitoring system with sensors. Finally, all the collected data are presented in the web.

This paper titled “IoT Enabled Water Distribution system” (Krishna et al., 2019) has explained the importance of managing, monitoring the efficient distribution of water. Urbanization is being increased due to the rapid growth of population in urban areas. Hence, domestic water supply system became a vital one to meet the demand with proper distribution, water conservation and water consumption by the people. To fulfil the raised demand by the population growth, it is indispensable to supply required quantity of water to everyone in each area uniformly. Using IoT can manage the water supply system up to that entire scale such as from small colonies to mega townships, Intelligent cities buildings and sometimes for managing irrigation water. The proper and continuous monitoring of water supply system leads to proper distribution of water. This can be achieved by record the information about the available quantity of water at sources, supply amount, and faults in the network system. The IoT physical objects are rooted with sensors, automated measuring devices, software and networks. This study concluded the monitoring can be done at anywhere in the network by receiving the shortages as short messages and notification of water supply timing to the communities.

The paper titled “IoT-Based Water Management Systems: Survey and Future Research Direction” (Ismail et al., 2022) has suggested IoT are sustainable solutions for monitoring and managing the valuable natural resources for the next generation. This study focused on design of smart water management and monitoring system for many applications such as drinking water supply, industrial, agriculture purpose and oil exploration system in sometimes using IoT. Though sufficient paper not available, this study focused on four sectors, primarily on oilfield processes which is need certain amount of water to stimulate oil productivity along with agriculture, residential and industrial water supply systems. A new water optical management system was addressed, which is an improved technique for identifying and communicating the information. Hence, this approach acts as a pivotal manual for further research activities integrated with IoT.

The paper titled “Automated water Distribution System in Metro’s using IOT” (Suresh Kumar et al., 2019) mainly focused on water theft which occur of superfluity water to a particular client. The water supply system provides a stable amount of water to home and commercial sector in urban areas in a specified time. But the water discharging to the consumers are unceremoniously and is considered as water theft. This work proposed a remote based water observation and action against the robbery by forming a frame work by build inserted sensors between consumers and suppliers. This study utilized PIC16F877A as a controller and the variety of sensors are investigated to differentiate the proximity of water in that exact pipeline. IR sensors are utilized to differentiate the watercourse. Thus, this study achieved the general goal by framing the proper conveyance network, supply well water to the consumer at particular area and insufficient amount and achieve evaluation and most exciting presence with low nominal cost and advanced working strategies.

The paper titled "IoT technology for Smart water system" (Radhakrishnan & Wu, 2018) particularly makes sure that the condition of the water in the dissemination system which drops seriously. Colour changes and odour in water can leads to intensify the both bio and non-biological things, which create a hazardous to the entire water system and community. The analysis of water quality needs much labour and more time in conventional methods. Thus, it is necessary to monitor and save the water by reducing the contamination in the present time monitoring of pure aqua method. IoT has helped in many ways to solve the series problems by develop efficient methods in real time. This study focused on design of planning, uses and IoT in the liquid quality supervision method.

Structures Health Monitoring (SHM)

It is the procedure of supervising the health of the important structures such as bridges, tunnels, dams and wind turbines to verify whether they are in a good condition or not. It is one of the very much required applications to be done in the civil Engineering field. IoT sensors can be used to take the measurements of different parameters of structures such a strain, crack width, vibration, moisture, and others. structural vibration can also be observed by using sensors. The various sensors used for SHM are load cells, transducers, strain gauges, thermistors, thermocouples, integrated temperature circuits, accelerometer, anemometer, microphone, internet camera technology. The purpose of these sensors is shown in Table 1.

SHM is a continuous process of monitoring and evaluating the fitness of the existing constructions. It also helps to provide alternative solutions to ensure the safety of structures against early detection of failures. Here detectors are employed to gather facts from the existing structures to know whether they are in a proper condition or not. The collected data are then analyzed so that it can avoid any damage or failure of structures that may occur in its life span. It can be applied for various important structures such as bridges, skyscrapers, airports, dams, stadiums, tunnels, hospitals, schools and many others.

Table 1. Various sensors used for structural health monitoring

S.No.	Sensor Name	Parameters Measured
1.	Accelerometer	Structures vibration is measured
2.	Thermocouples	To measure the temperature
3.	Acoustic emission sensors	To measure high frequency energy signals
4.	Tiltmeter	To monitor a very small changes in the inclination of the structures
5.	Inclinometer	To monitor subsurface movements and deformations.
6.	Strain Gauge Rosette	To measure strains along different directions of the component
7.	Linear Variable Differential Transformer (LVDT)	To measure linear displacement
8.	Strain sensors	To monitor loads, compression, tension, bending, and torsion in a structure.
9.	Crack detection sensors	To monitor the position and length of cracks in concrete structures
10.	Load cells	To verify whether the loads are as per the standards and also to check how they are distributed on the structure

Role of Internet of Things (IoT) Technology in Smart Health Monitoring (SHM)

Internet of Things is an Intelligent wireless technique that can be used in various types of industries as well as buildings and structures. IoT sensors can be used for data collection from the structures. As a result, IoT sensors can collect some important parameters from the sensors. Based on the data collection, the processing can be performed using either Arduino uno or Raspberry Pi board. Now if the collected parameters are as per the required standard of the structures, no need to take any immediate action otherwise it has to take an immediate action and alert message has to be sent to the concerned personnel regarding the abnormal condition of the structures.

Components of Structural Health Monitoring (SHM)

The various components of the SHM are

1) Structures
2) Data Acquisition System
3) Data Transfer
4) Digital Processing

5) Storage of data and
6) Data Diagnostics

Structures:

The actual structure to be monitored is the first component of the SHM. It may be any of the structures such as Bridges, hospitals, schools, tunnels, etc. Ususally the structures to be supervised will be a critical one and also of large in size.

Data Acquisition System (DAS):

This system addresses both the number and types of sensors chosen for the actual structure to be monitored. The fixation of the sensors in the structures should not affect the actual operation of the structures. This system should also cover when each sensor in the structure is activated to collect the data from the structures and how and where to save the collected data. The number and type of sensors used is directly proportional to the size of the structures to be supervised. Each sensor is meant for collecting a particular parameter from the structures such as strain, vibration, crack, displacement, etc.

Data transfer:

Now the data from the structures have been collected using DAS. Actual processing need not take place in the same place where details acquisition took place. Suppose if the processing of facts take place at the same place as the data collection place no need to do the data transfer. But actually, it is not always possible practically. So data transfer has to take place either wired manner or wireless manner. Wired form is not suitable for large structures. Then only wireless form has to be chosen but it has its own disadvantages such slower and more expensive.

Digital Processing:

Actual processing of data takes place only after performing the preprocessing operation. The preprocessing involves removal of noises, removal of duplicates and finding the missing data. Once the processing is over, it will find out whether the structures are in a good condition or not. Now the processed data has to be stored somewhere safely for future purposes.

Storage of data:

Here only the computed facts can be saved for a lengthy period of hour and received later for further inspection and explication.

Data Diagnostics:

It means converting the actual facts to the valuable statistics related to the construction's current status.

Advantages of SHM

1) Field structural behaviors can be easily understood

2) Damages in the structures can be detected at an advance stage of issue occurrence itself
3) Both examination and restore times are reduced
4) Encouragement in the application of creative things
5) SHM helps to create logical supervision and preservation plans

Disadvantages of SHM

1) Pre-opening charges are more
2) Sensitive to environment sound doctoring
3) Susceptible to earth tremor situations
4) Manipulation the large amount of data generated by the sensors itself is a challenging task
5) As the size of the structures is large, correspondingly large number of sensors are required to be installed.

Agricultural Monitoring System (AMS)

Agriculture monitoring system is the process of monitoring the agriculture fields with a collection of sensors connected in a wireless manner. These detectors can gather details from different locations that are located at the various positions of the field. The collected data from the sensors are then processed or analyzed by the IoT experts. Various types of sensors that are used to collect the data from the agriculture field are shown in Table 2.

Importance of an AMS

Usually, the farmers are involved in the agriculture. They have to manually monitor the fields. Since the size of the agricultural field is very large, monitoring it is not that much easy. The type of crops used in the cultivational fields will also be varying from one field to another. The soil moisture, temperature and water level of the fields are also varying among the fields. Checking whether all the fields are in the proper condition or not can be made easy by incorporating the concept of IoT in the cultivational field. So, the work tension of the farmers is reduced very much. Hence the manual farming becomes the smart farming by using sensors of different types at various places of the fields. As a result of smart farming, the daily challenges of the farmers are well solved. It includes watering, gathering of crops, planting, pest control, etc.

AMS is a collection of wireless sensors. Each sensor is meant for collecting a particular type of data from the fields. The collected data are then analyzed by specialist or confined agronomist. Different deductions can be obtained from the details by the experts namely style of ambient conditions, the nourishment of the soil, cultivated plant standard, etc. If necessary proper information can be immediately sent to the farmers to take the required action.

Components of AMS

The various components of AMS are

- Arduino or Raspberry Pi
- Sensors
- Cloud storage

Types of Sensors Used in an AMS

Mostly farmers may want to monitor some key parameters from the cultivational field. For this he has to employ the corresponding types of sensors. If the manual method is used for monitoring these key parameters, it will be time-consuming and error-prone. These limitations can very well be overcomed by using sensors. Here the sensors are implanted in many places of the cultivational land. These sensors have some important properties such as reliability, accuracy and portable data aggregators. These sensors form a basic part as well as an integral part of an agricultural monitoring system. Each sensor is for a particular purpose. The different types of sensors used in AMS can include:

- Temperature sensor
- Humidity sensor
- Air Quality Sensor
- Gas sensor
- Light sensor
- Soil moisture sensor
- Barometric pressure sensor
- Water-level sensor, etc.

Advantages of an AMS

1) Reduce water usage.
2) Improve productivity
3) Improved pest control
4) Limited use of pesticides and fertilizers

Table 2. Sensors used in agriculture monitoring system

Sensor Names	Parameter Measured
Optical sensors	Measures light intensity
Electro chemical sensors	Nutrient of the soil levels
Mechanical soil sensors	Soil compression
Soil moisture sensors	Moisture levels
Soil ec sensor	To measure the conductivity of different types of soil
Location sensors	They determine location information in terms of latitude and longitude.
Airflow sensors	Soil air penetration
Soil pH meters	To identify the acidity or alkalinity of the soil

5) Based on the soil moisture content, the different types of crops can be grown
6) Cultivation yield can happen based on the weather forecasting.

Disadvantages of AMS

1) Initial Investment cost is more
2) Set up and maintenance of IoT systems for AMS is complex
3) AMS requires a reliable internet connection and network infrastructure

Challenges of AMS

1) The process of connecting the various sensors involved in AMS and the data gathered from them should be sent to the analysis operation for processing is not that much easy.
2) Triggering the particular events or alarming require software expertise.
3) All the three things namely Software, sensors and agricultural equipment should be integrated together is also a dull activity
4) Seasonal conditions should also be taken into account during agricultural monitoring system

Air Pollution Monitoring Using IoT Techniques

Air pollution causes a warning to the environs and the calibre of life on the world, which affects everyday life standard. Monitoring of air quality is inevitable, due to rapid growth of urbanization, industrial and anthropogenic activities over the past decays. The presence of air pollutant in the atmosphere is either in the form of gaseous or suspended particulate matter. The pollutant which is directly emitted in to the atmosphere is termed as primary pollutant, but that pollutant produced when the main contaminants react with the other climatic synthetic known as subordinate impurities. The effect of air pollution on human health is ranges from difficulty in breathing, coughing, asthma and emphysema. Sometimes giddiness, headache which leads to heart attacks. Air pollution is a prime cause of increasing death rate and premature death annually and globally. Recent decays Childrens are at high risk of respiratory problems when exposed to dust contamination. Various prototypes have been implemented by many analysts to supervise the gaseous contaminations such as Sulfurous oxide (SO2), Carbon Monoxide gas (CO), Carbonic acid (CO2), Nitric Oxide (NO) etc. globally. Though various models available, real time gaseous contamination supervising prototype is needed to monitor and analyze.

Monitoring of gaseous contamination is quite difficult to measure and understanding the process from the sources to the need points or areas. The sources of air pollutions are mainly categorized as point, line and area sources. Based on the sources of air pollution only can decide the methods of measurement of that pollution. Every source has its own methodology to observe the pollutant from the sources which is vary from source to source. Air pollution measurement methods are available at different ways and according to the objectives of the study can choose the best one.

Air quality monitoring consists of the following steps:

1. Objective of Air Sampling
2. Method of sampling procedures including procedures for analysis the samples
3. locations of Sampling Points
4. Period of sampling, frequency of sampling and duration
5. Supplementary measurements (like meteorological parameters)
6. Data Processing

Manual process is very difficult because it requires suitable site should be available for long time. The site should be an easily accessible in any time throughout the year. Require power supply of sufficient rating should be available. Sampling stations may need to be protected from extreme of temperature. It also needs skilled knowledge and special techniques. When analyzing the gaseous contaminants manually, both spectroscopy, atomic assimilation, ICP discharge methods and Gas chromatography are mostly used. Though all region air pollutants are measured manually, the intensity of air pollutant measurements are difficult to find at the particular time. Thus, incarnate of advanced methods or automated are essential, now a days lots of advanced techniques are available.

Internet of Things (IoT) is a trending and recent mechanism with the combination of detectors connected through wireless communications. IoT can be applied for a large range of uses in atmospheric supervising and controlling contaminants. Here, sensor nodes in a wireless sensor network can very well be used for both environmental gaseous contaminants supervising and gaseous controlling of quality. Hence, air pollutant which contains in the ambient air could be easily found and can be forecasted to the public too. Furthermore, Node MCU ESP32 module, can very well be used to supervise the gaseous contamination remotely with its Wi-Fi facility.

PROBLEM DEFINITION

In the existing systems, gaseous pollutants monitoring are costlier and many models need software skills and learning and understanding of the model is very difficult and time-consuming processes. So it is neither possible to measure how much pollutants are available in the air nor possible to monitor them. The primary pollutants Sulphur dioxide, nitrogen oxide and ozone level are dangerous to the living world, secondary pollutants like airborne particles, carbonic acid gas, NOX, SOX, volatile organic compounds are dangerous to the fitness of the human beings. It is purely because of the insufficient of devices air pollution neither can be measured and Environmental department nor be able to do about the pollution. Hence, the presence of air borne illness have increased. Hence, it is essential to make the planning of measurements as careful as possible. Gaseous contamination supervising system based on IoT is projected to supervise the levels of contamination of various contaminants that is organized anywhere and stock the monitored quantities in a fog storage, to perform pollution examination and make view of the contamination level at any given place.

METHODOLOGY

As the company emerges, different contaminants have to be supervised by the smart system over the Internet and should also be able to display the quality limit of the gas amidst the traffic. Here, the MQ135 sensor monitors CO2, SO2, CH4, NH3; the MQ9 sensor monitors CO and Propane (C3H8) and MQ2 sensor detects any escape of gases is available or not. This system can use ESP32 Microcontroller (Node MCU), to get all detector's details. Node MCU ESP32 will transfer all these sensor data to the Cloud through wireless connectivity. Therefore, all the real time data can be viewed with the mobile phone. If MQ2 sensor identifies any Gas Leakage then the system will immediately specify the alert through the mobile phone For this just

Table 3. Pollutants specifications

Pollutants	Time	Concentration in Air	
		Industrial Area	Residential Area
Carbon Dioxide(CO2)	Average 24 Hour	Below 5000 ppm	Below 1000 ppm
Sulphur Dioxide(SO2)	Average 24 Hour	Below 45 ppm	Below 30 ppm
Ammonia(NH3)	Average 24 Hour	Below 0.56 ppm	Below 0.56 ppm
Methane(CH4)	Average 24 Hour	Below 1.7 ppm	Below 1.7 ppm
Carbon Monoxide(CO)	Average 24 Hour	Below 8.44 ppm	Below 3.38 ppm
Propane(C3H8)	Average 24 Hour	Below 15 ppm	Below 15 ppm

wi-fi access point is required and it is also uncomplicated to manage. If there is any problem in this model means it is only because of the connectivity.

Water Distribution System

Water is a precise element in the world for all living being and their activities. Fresh water availability is decreasing continuously and rapidly every year due to anthropogenic behavior. The recent research articles reveal the increased demand of water at a high-rate scarcity globally which leads world economic war. Thus, conservation of water is playing a major role to meet the demand and minimize the losses during its storages and transportation which is difficult in practice.

The water dropping is mostly because of the connection of the lines, gaps and breaches in the line network, leakages/overfill in the head containers/second containers, drop in force and obstacle is because of the deposits in the tubes. The recommendations of International Water Association (IWA) have suggested recently developed techniques for tailoring efflux spotting and dropping handling elements.

Hence, the design and establishment of an Intelligent aqua dissemination method of planning is essential for a city which is to be carried out with storehouse containers, supporter push stops, blaze faucets, distribution main and user assistance channels and duplicate webbing through quick-witted greenish mesh and spiral. In the early days, the liquid discharging methods utilized the confusion dependent conclusions for the determination of the rate of flow of the liquid.

Though many water distribution network methods are available to monitor the drinking water distribution, EPANET were used in many cities to identify the leakage, pressure loss, cracks in pipe during transportation of water and alternate main to supply the water for the demand area. Thus, the aqua requirement detection is needed for day-to-day usage in a span of time. The water demand estimation can

Figure 1. Flowchart of the proposed system

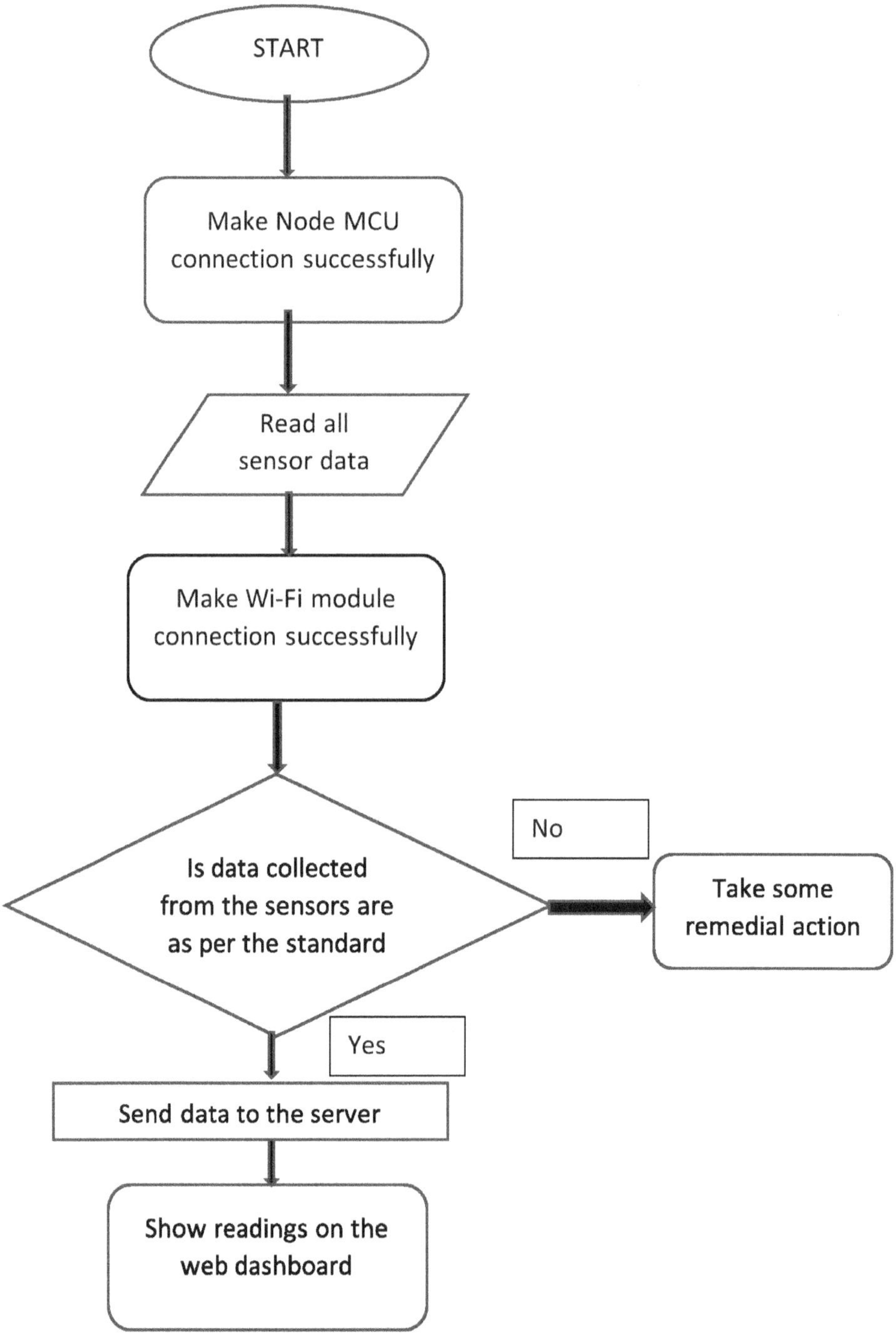

Table 4. Sensors used for environmental monitoring

Sensor Names	Parameter Measured
Temperature sensors	Measures light intensity
Humidity sensors	Nutrient of the soil levels
PM 2.5 sensors	Soil compression
PM 10 sensors	Moisture levels
Wind sensors	These sensors measure the wind horizontal, vertical speed and wind direction.
Solar radiation sensors	It measures the intensity of the sun's radiation reaching a horizontal surface.
PAR sensor	To measure the light intensity at frequencies associated with photosynthesis
Common gas sensors include CO2 sensor, CO sensor, CH4 sensor, NH3 sensor, O3 sensor, SO2 sensor, NO2 sensor, H2S sensor, HCHO sensor, etc.	To measure the corresponding type of gas

be computed using non-stationary combined with mean and line like reversion analysis methods.

In Recent decades, Universal object interaction based below the surface water dissemination construction combined with Fog computing and Cloud has been proposed where the current operation occurs. Here, sensor-based data apprehended from network of underground pipes for regulating the substation. All historical data and other appropriate information are stored as cloud data for the data analyses. For Universal object interaction based below the surface water dissemination network design aimed at developed town through minimum fatalities, it is required, to know town pattern and type of consumers with the amount of consumption can be obtained from the historical data.

To resolve problems related with water distribution, an intelligent water distribution network system has been designed which is essential based on the demand, and consists of: (1) water consumption data and demand. (2) To forecast demand using statistical model (3) IoT-based water distribution design and planning using EPANET.

Problems:

The existing system has more problems that's why it will not face the challenges mentioned above. They are listed as:

1 Improper Management; 2 Wasting of water; 3 Improper Maintenance; 4 Less Quality of Water; 5 Water Leakage

1 Improper Management:

Generally, the municipal corporation is supplying the water to the public without proper management. The amount of not distributed sufficiently to the people who are having the water resources they only get more amount of water. Thus, need to maintain proper management for the distribution of the equal amount of water to each and every area.

2 Wasting of water:

Recent days the people are wasting the water without knowing the awareness of availability of water at the public taps and home etc., particularly where the sources of water available plenty in amount. So, the people/consumers must realize about the wasting of water at the time of usage. It is the responsibility of the people to preserve the water while using.

3 Improper Maintenance:

Water discharge in the network of tube arrangement may occur because of the improper fixing of taps, installation of pipes and using fewer quality materials which cause damage and wastages. This is also due to the improper maintenance and monitoring by the municipal corporation.

4 Less Quality of Water:

Now a days the water distribution is carryout without any primary treatment to the clients. By adding the bleaching powder in the water is not purification process, it just kills the germs only which harmful to the people's health. So, have to ensure quality water with advanced treatment methods.

5 Water Leakage:

Water leakage is inevitable, when it is supplied through the network of pipeline from the municipal supply tank. Due to the improper installation of pipes and tapes, breaking of the pipes and joints water is leaked from the system. The proper monitoring and identification of leakages are difficult by maintenance people in the underground network system. This is the reason for wasting more amount of water unnecessarily.

Advantages:

The water distribution system is mainly affected by various factors including longevity, cheap, avoiding against deluge and support issues. So, IoT based water

Table 5. Sensors used for measuring the water quality

Sensor	Aqua Standard Feature
Spectro:lyser	Opacity, heat, force, hue, dissolved ions, UV254
Smart Coast	pH, Dissolved oxygen (DO), conductivity, temperature, turbidity, phosphate and level of aqua
Kapta 3000 AC4	Chlorine, heat, force, conductivity
Smart water (Libelium)	pH, Dissolved oxygen (DO), conductivity, temperature, oxidation-reduction potential (ORP), turbidity, dissolved ions
Lab-on-chip	Any specific bio-chemical
I:scan	Color, turbidity, UV254

distribution network keeps away from large amount of utilization of water, demolition of water and pledges structured water handling network with good quality of water.

CONCLUSION

This chapter provides the important role of IoT in four different civil engineering field applications such as structural health monitoring, water supply management, agricultural monitoring system and air pollution monitoring system. The various sensors that are used in all the above-mentioned applications are also discussed. The advantages and disadvantages of using IoT in the aforementioned applications are also given. This work clearly mentioned the methodology used to implement all the specified applications. By using IoT in the civil engineering field the wastage of time, money can very well be reduced. The death rate can also be decreased in the structural health monitoring. But the area of the study is continuously monitored and the failure in the area of study will be informed as early as possible. So, the remedial action will be performed to avoid the problems in the area under observation. Wherever possible the machine learning algorithms can be applied to do the tasks such as classification, clustering and regression. The future scope of this work is to use the IoT to implement the other civil engineering field applications.

REFERENCES

Cross, E. S., Williams, L. R., Lewis, D. K., Magoon, G. R., Onasch, T. B., Kaminsky, M. L., Worsnop, D. R., & Jayne, J. T. (2017). Use of electrochemical sensors for measurement of air pollution: Correcting interference response and validating measurements. *Atmospheric Measurement Techniques*, *10*(9), 3575–3588. doi:10.5194/amt-10-3575-2017

Devasena, Ramya, Dharshan, Vivek, & Darshan. (2019). IoT based water distribution system. *International Journal of Engineering and Advanced Technology, 8*(6), 132-135.

Eltouny & Liang. (2022). Large-scale Structural Health Monitoring using Composite Recurrent neural networks and grid environments. Academic Press.

Ferrer-Cid, P., Barcelo-Ordinas, J. M., Garcia-Vidal, J., Ripoll, A., & Viana, M. (2020). Multi sensor data fusion calibration in IoT air pollution platforms. *IEEE Internet of Things Journal*, *7*(4), 3124–3132. doi:10.1109/JIOT.2020.2965283

Giurgiutiu. (2014). Challenges and opportunities for structural health monitoring for PVP applications. *Proceedings of the ASME 2014 Pressure vessels and piping conference, vol. 6A: Materials and Fabrication.*

Hashim, Zarifie, Abd Aziz, Zoinol, Salleh, & Najmiah. (n.d.). Agriculture monitoring system: A study. *Journal Technologies, 77*. doi:10.11113/jt.v77.4099

Ismail, Dawoud, Ismail, Marsh, & Alshami. (2022). IoT-Based Water Management Systems: Survey and Future Research Direction. *IEEE Access, 10*, 35942 – 35952.

Krishna, Gopinath, Lakshmanudu, Prasad, & Kuma. (2019). IoT Enabled Water Distribution system. *Journal of Emerging Technologies and Innovative Research*, 351-355. www.jetir.org

Lewis, Peltier, & von Schneidemesser. (2018). *Low-cost sensors for the measurement of atmospheric composition: overview of topic and future applications*. Academic Press.

Metaxa, S., Kalkanis, K., Psomopoulos, C. S., & Stavros, D. (2019). A review of structural health monitoring methods for composite materials. *Procedia Structural Integrity, 22*, 369-375.

Mishra, S., & Sharma, S. K. (2023). Advanced contribution of IoT in agricultural production for the development of smart livestock environments. *Internet of Things : Engineering Cyber Physical Human Systems*, *22*, 100724. Advance online publication. doi:10.1016/j.iot.2023.100724

Naik. (2023). Iot Based Air Pollution Monitoring System. *International Journal of Scientific Research & Engineering Trends, 9*(3).

Niresi, Zhao, Bissig, Baumann, & Fink. (2023). *Spatial-Temporal Graph Attention Fuserfor Calibration in IoT Air Pollution Monitoring Systems*. Intelligent Maintenance and Operations Systems (IMOS) Lab, EPFL.

Okokpujie. (2018). A smart air pollution monitoring system. *International Journal of Civil Engineering and Technology, 9*(9), 799–809.

Pendyala, Rodda, Mamidi, & Vangala. (n.d.). *IoT-Based Smart Agricultural Monitoring System*. Academic Press.

Prathibha, S. R., Hongal, A., & Jyothi, M. P. (2017). IoT Based Monitoring System in Smart Agriculture. *2017 International Conference on Recent Advances in Electronics and Communication Technology (ICRAECT)*, 81-84. 10.1109/ICRAECT.2017.52

Radhakrishnan, V., & Wu, W. (2018). IoT Technology for Smart Water System. *2018 IEEE 20th International Conference on High Performance Computing and Communications; IEEE 16th International Conference on Smart City; IEEE 4th International Conference on Data Science and Systems (HPCC/SmartCity/DSS)*, 1491-1496. 10.1109/HPCC/SmartCity/DSS.2018.00246

Rudrakar, S., & Rughani, P. (2023). IoT based Agriculture (Ag-IoT): A detailed study on Architecture, Security and Forensics. *Information Processing in Agriculture*, 1–18. doi:10.1016/j.inpa.2023.09.002

Sarmadi, H., Entezami, A., & De Michele, C. (2023, March). Probabilistic data self-clustering based on semi-parametric extreme value theory for structural health monitoring. *Mechanical Systems and Signal Processing, 187*, 109976. doi:10.1016/j.ymssp.2022.109976

Suresh Kumar, Subhash, Tamilselvan, Sudhakar, & Vignesh. (2019). Automated water Distribution System in Metro's using IOT. *International Journal of Innovative Technology and Exploring Engineering, 8*(6), 207-211.

Tamilselvan, G. M., Ashishkumar, V., Jothi Prasath, S., & Mohammed Yusuff, S. (2018). IoT Based Automated Water Distribution System with Water Theft Control and Water Purchasing System. *International Journal of Recent Technology and Engineering, 7*(4).

Tan, X., Chen, W., Zou, T., Yang, J., & Du, B. (2023). Real-time prediction of mechanical behaviors of underwater shield tunnel structure using machine learning method based on structural health monitoring data. *Journal of Rock Mechanics and Geotechnical Engineering, 15*(4), 886-895. doi:10.1016/j.jrmge.2022.06.015

Chapter 3
A Secure Image Protection for IoT Applications Using Watermarking Technique and Non-Linear Henon Chaos

Sujarani Rajendran
SASTRA University, India

Manivannan Doraipandian
SASTRA University, India

ABSTRACT

In the digital IoT world, image watermarking has been determined as a solution of copyright problems and protecting the sensitive images from unauthorized access. A novel invisible watermarking technique which is secure against unapproved extraction of watermark and strong against different attacks has been proposed. Chaos-based image watermarking provides higher security than the traditional methodology. The proposed chaos-based watermarking involves three phases. In the first phase, a two-dimensional Henon chaos map is utilized to generate the chaotic series which act as keys for embedding the watermark. Before embedding the watermark, the image is encrypted by using Zig-Zag confusion process, and then in the last phase, the watermark image is converted into quaternary sequence, and by using random key of Henon map, each bit is embedded in the original image. The proposed model is applicable for both greyscale and colour images. Different performance analysis such as PSNR, SSIM will be used to identify the strength and quality of the proposed watermarking technique.

DOI: 10.4018/979-8-3693-1694-8.ch003

1. INTRODUCTION

In this modern era everything become digitalized. In this digital IoT world data lost is not a big issue, even if it is lost, we have option called backup but If an original sensible data is modified by some unknown person it leads to false information. To overcome it watermark is injected into every digital documents. Now cryptography techniques are used to protect the data, modification of data is in lesser chance but illegal use of same data may happen. To avoid it digital watermarking is used. Two types of watermarking are available visible and invisible. This work subjects to injection of invisible watermark in colour images. If invisible watermark is embedded in corresponding images copyright is protected. The two main challenges in invisible watermarking are imperceptibility and robustness. Numerous work has been done for providing solution for these challenges some of the state of the art are discussed below.

2. LITERATURE REVIEW

In the present era, various types of data are easily shared, including multimedia content on public platforms that are accessible to the public (S. Kumar et al., 2020). Consequently, copyright assumes a crucial role in safeguarding such data from unauthorized access, and it can be implemented through means such as text or logos. A notable method for this purpose is watermarking, and different approaches to watermarking are explored. Fragile watermarking stands out as a method for safeguarding copyright information, primarily focused on detecting tampering and unauthorized alterations (Sreenivas & Kamkshi Prasad, 2018). As implied by its name, the "fragile" nature of this technique makes it susceptible to various attacks. Consequently, researchers are actively exploring more robust alternatives to enhance the level of protection. In the identification process, discrepancies between the original and mined pictures may arise, attributed to synchronization errors and potential attacks (Xu et al., 2019). To counteract these issues, the polar harmonic transform (PHT) is employed as a protective measure. Rectangular perpendicular moments are extracted from the PHT, and the embedding of the watermark occurs by choosing stable moments from the derived set. This approach has proven effective in withstanding a range of signal processing attacks. Ingular value decomposition is utilized to protect watermarks, yet it faces vulnerabilities when subjected to puzzle attacks (Najafi & Loukhaoukha, 2019). To address this limitation, researchers have explored an alternative approach by integrating SFLCT. The fusion of these two techniques offers enhanced security, particularly in defending against puzzle attacks. In order to fortify the security measures against potential attacks, the proposal introduces the integration of contourlet transform and Hessenberg fragmenting (Su et al., 2017). A pseudo-random algorithm based on MD5 hash is employed to select coefficient blocks derived from the low-frequency sub-band. The author suggests that the combination of these two techniques enhances the robustness and imperceptibility of the watermarking process. Preserving image quality poses a significant challenge, necessitating a proposed method to be both robust and non-detrimental to image quality (Mehta et al., 2018). The exploration of various transforms is undertaken, with the host image decomposed using the DWT to acquire the low-frequency sub-band. Subsequently, this sub-band undergoes further decomposition. Fares et al. (2020) Yamni et al. (2020) introduced a method named FrCPs. This technique involves algebraically deriving discrete moments of FrCPs through the spectral fragmenting of Charlier polynomials. The Lagrange interpolation formula is employed to obtain a peculiar projector. Following the decomposition by SVD, the result is inferred with the aid of Fractional Charlier Moment Sequences (FrCMS). Kazemivash & Moghaddam (2018) used relapse tree as prognosticate model and metaheuristic algorithms as an enhance model. The author used LWT to divide the figure into quadrate subordinate bands. Small reoccurrence is used to derive non overlaying blocks. The chunks are arranged in increasing order. Security is achieved by Fibonacci-Q transforms. A.K. J. Kumar et al. (2018) has employed a regression tree as a predictive model and metaheuristic algorithms as an enhancement model. Additionally, the author utilized the LWT (Lapped Wavelet Transform) to partition the image into square subordinated bands, with small recurrence guiding the derivation of non-overlapping blocks. These blocks are then organized in increasing order, and security is bolstered through the application of Fibonacci-Q transforms. During the process of capturing and printing photos, watermarks are printed alongside for security reasons. Despite their presence, there exists a potential risk of extracting them from the images (Guo & Prasetyo, 2014). To address this, various algorithms have been employed in the past, with earlier attempts using Singular Value Decomposition (SVD) proving ineffective. The author has introduced a new SVD-based image watermarking approach. In this method, the primary component of the watermark is embedded into the carrier image using the spread spectrum concept. In the past, an older version of Polar Harmonic Fourier Moments (PHFM) was employed, but the computation process encountered numerical integration errors, leading to a degradation in accuracy (Anand & Singh, 2020). To address this issue, the present approach utilizes an improved version called accurate PHFM based on Gaussian Numerical Integration. This adjustment effectively eliminates numerical integration errors, resulting in an enhanced level of accuracy. Additionally, a chaotic process is incorporated in the initial stage to scramble the watermarking image. Balancing between imperceptibility and robustness presents a challenge (Ali et al., 2014). The optimization of these parameters is addressed using a technique known as differential evolution. The process involves applying the DCT to the image, followed by applying SVD. To guard against geometric attacks, a combined approach involving DWT, DCT, and SVD is employed (Fazli & Moeini, 2016). The initial step involves dividing the image into four non-overlapping segments, each of which is individually embedded with watermarks. An innovative synchronization technique is proposed to recover images that have undergone geometric attacks. Notably, these techniques demonstrate resilience against various signal processing attacks as well. In the medical domain, a combination of DWT, DCT, and SVD is applied (Zear et al., 2018). In this context, the doctor's signature and symptomatic information of patients serve as crucial elements. To bolster robustness, a Back Propagation Neural Network is incorporated. The certainty is enhanced through the application of the Arnold transform. Additionally, the watermark undergoes obfuscation via lossless mathematical constriction, and Hamming error correction is implemented to further refine the process. In the pursuit of achieving the dual objectives of imperceptibility and robustness, SVD was initially employed (Wafa' Hamdan Alshoura et al., 2021). However, it proved inadequate in withstanding various geometric attacks. Even a hybrid SVD scheme faced limitations and encountered failures in certain cases. While SVD is widely popular, it is not without its drawbacks, particularly the false alarm problem (Wafa'Hamdan H. Alshoura et al., 2020). To address this issue, SVD incorporates disorganized maps. The confidential key is derived from both the master and pinnacle images. This key is subsequently utilized to generate a confused matrix and puzzled-multiple-scaling factors, enhancing vulnerability. Notably, the secret key mined is distinct for both the host and watermark images. This approach is discussed by Alawida et al. (2019). A solution to the False Positive Problem (FPP) is proposed through the integration of Singular Value Decomposition (SVD), Integer Wavelet Transform, and chaotic maps. In this method, a grayscale image watermark is decomposed into eight-bit planes before undergoing encryption. The arrangement of these planes is further manipulated by a chaotic sequence. The obtained results generate hash values, which play a role in resolving the FPP issue. While numerous research works have focused on watermarking using grayscale images, there is a scarcity of studies on color image watermarking.

The focus of this work is to provide security for watermarking in colour images. In order to achieve this, the Henon chaotic map (Ismail et al., 2022) and the zig-zag permutation technique is utilised. The Henon chaotic map was employed in this work to generate a key for the watermarking process. It is considered an effective technique due to its ability to generate pseudo-random numbers and exhibit excellent chaotic behaviour. The generated key from the Henon chaotic map was used for randomly embedding the watermark image. In addition to the Henon chaotic map, the zig-zag permutation technique was utilized for the encryption and decryption process. The zig-zag permutation involves rearranging the elements of the watermark or the encrypted image in a zig-zag pattern. By combining the Henon chaotic map for key generation and the zig-zag permutation for encryption and decryption, this work aimed to enhance the security of watermarking in colour images. The Henon chaotic map provided strong and random key generation, while the zig-zag permutation added an additional layer of encryption to protect the watermark from unauthorized access or tampering.

This paper is organized like, section 3 designates the 2d Henon chaotic map mathematical description. Section 4 discoursed the proposed embedding and extraction model and Section 5 reflects the security study part and ends with section 6 which discourse the conclusion part.

3. MATERIALS AND METHODS

The advanced crypt model employs the 2D Henon chaotic system to generate two distinct chaotic series using various mathematical functions. These chaotic series are then employed to embed the content on each channel of the provided input color image. The subsequent subsection provides a detailed explanation of the Henon chaotic map.

3.1. Two-Dimensional Henon Map

Another prominent 2D discrete chaotic system is the Henon map (Li & Liu, 2013), which is defined by the following equation Eq(1). The Henon series exhibits a chaotic state only when the system parameter falls within the range of β = 0.3 and α = 1.4.

$$\begin{aligned} x_{i+1} &= 1 - \alpha x_i^2 + y_i \\ y_{i+1} &= \beta x_i mod 1 \end{aligned} \tag{1}$$

4. PROPOSED EMBEDDING AND EXTRACTION ARCHITECTURE

The proposed model is the combination of three process. At first, watermark image is encrypted using zig-zag permutation concept and the second is to generate random numbers using 2D hyper chaotic system and finally based on the random number the pixels of watermark image is embed into the cover image. The proposed embedding

Figure 1. Proposed model architecture of embedding and extraction process

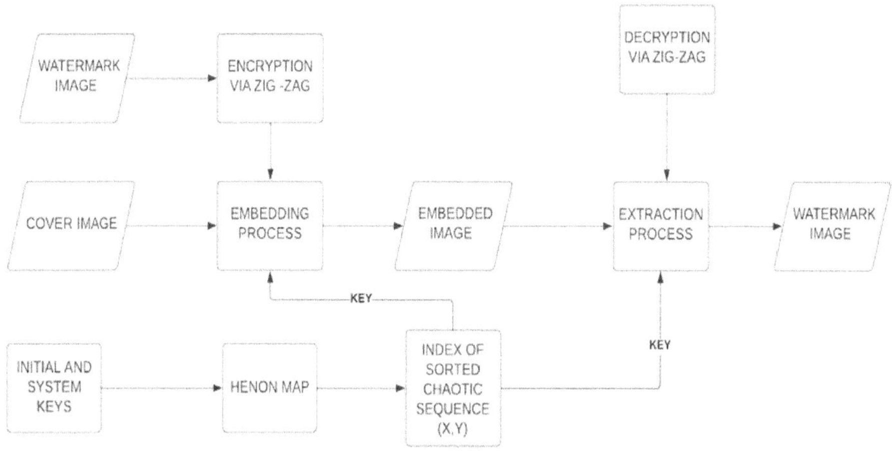

and extraction algorithms are discussed in details in the following section and the detailed diagrammatical representation is given in the following Figure 1.

4.1. Algorithm for Encryption End Embedding

Step1: select two images, cover image and watermark image.

Step2: Resize the respective images.

Step3: separate the images based on colour channels red, green and blue. RED [(:,:,1)], GREEN[(:,:,2)] and BLUE[(:,:,3)].

Step4: Encrypt the watermark image using zig-zag scrambling.

```
for l1 = 1:p
for l2= 1:p
nimr = mod(((l1-1) + (l2-1)),p) + 1;
nimc = mod(((l1-1) + 2*(l2-1)),p) + 1;
r1(nimr,nimc,:) = r(l1,l2,:);
end
end
```

Step5: Generate chaotic series using Henon chaotic map.

```
x(1)=0.15; y(1)=0.25;
alpha=1.40; bets=0.3;
for i=2:32
x(i)=1-(alpha*power(x(i-1),2)+y(i-1));
y(i)=bets*x(i);
```

end

Sort the chaotic series and the index value of sorted chaotic series is used to select pixel position from cover image.

[sortx,indexx]=sort(x);

[sorty,indexy]=sort(y);

Step6: Pixel position is selected and modification of LSB bit and finally watermark image is embedded.

4.2. Algorithm for Decryption and Extraction

Step1: Watermark embedded cover image is loaded.

Step2: separate the images based on colour channels red, green and blue.

RED [(:,:,1)], GREEN[(:,:,2)] and BLUE[(:,:,3)].

Step3: Generate chaotic series using Henon chaotic map.

```
x(1)=0.15;
y(1)=0.25;
alpha=1.40;
bets=0.3;
for i=2:32
x(i)=1-(alpha*power(x(i-1),2)+y(i-1));
y(i)=bets*x(i);
end
```

Sort the chaotic series and the index value of sorted chaotic series is used to find the pixel position from cover image in which the watermark is embedded.

[sortx,indexx]=sort(x);

[sorty,indexy]=sort(y);

Step4: Watermark is extracted and it is still in encrypted form.

Step5: Decrypt the watermark image using zig-zag scrambling.

```
for l1 = 1:p
for l2= 1:p
nimr = mod(((l1-1) + (l2-1)),p) + 1;
nimc = mod(((l1-1) + 2*(l2-1)),p) + 1;
r1(nimr,nimc,:) = r(l1,l2,:);
end
end
```

Step6: Watermark image is extracted.

Figure 2. Encryption and embedding of watermark image

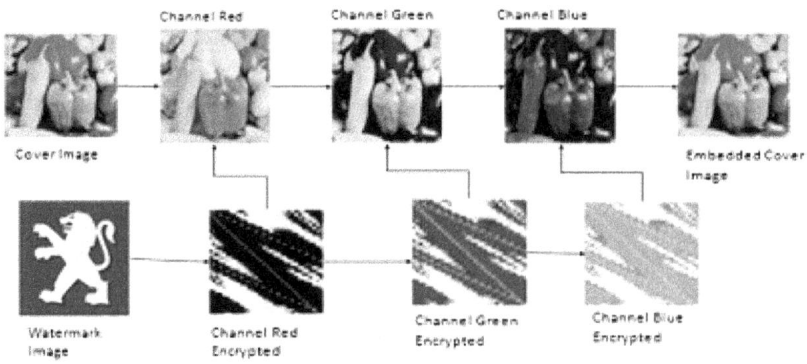

4.3. Experimental Outcome

The proposed technique is executed in MATLAB-R2022. MATLAB 2022 is installed in corresponding system. The system configurations are 8GB RAM, Windows OS-11th, 64-bit operating system, x64-based processor, intel i3 processor with version 22H2. The following Fig.2 shows the encryption and embedding and Fig.3 shows the extraction and decryption of the watermarked image.

5. PERFORMANCE ANALYSIS

An invisible watermarking technique is said to be more efficient when it achieves the two challenges namely imperceptibility and robustness. Imperceptibility in watermarking refers to the quality of a watermark being visually unnoticeable in the media content to which it is applied. Robustness refers to the ability watermark to withstand against various attacks. The proposed technique ensures imperceptibility and robustness with the help of Henon chaotic map and zig-zag scrambling techniques respectively.

5.1. SSIM Analysis

SSIM stands for Structural Similarity Index Measure (Rajendran et al., 2021). It is a widely used metric in image and video processing that quantifies the similarity between two images based on their structural information. SSIM compares the

Figure 3. Encryption and embedding of watermark image

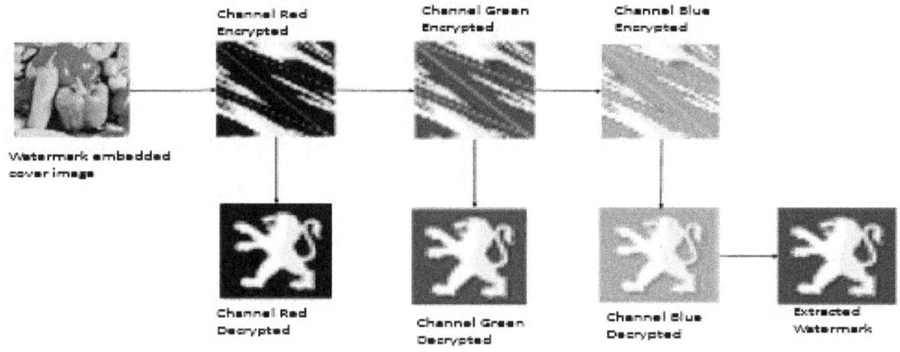

structural information, such as texture, edges, and luminance, between the original image and the watermarked image.

Assign parameters value. [k1, k2, L], Calculate mean value of two images. [muI, muK] and calculate standard deviation of two images. [sigmaI, sigmaK] then calculate the covariance, constants C1,C2 and C3. The following formula will be used for calculating SSIM

l = (2 * muI * muK + C1) / (muI^2 + muK^2 + C1).

c = (2 * sigmaI * sigmaK + C2) / (sigmaI^2 + sigmaK^2 + C2).

s = (sigmaIK + C3) / (sigmaI * sigmaK + C3).

Calculate ssim Index.

ssimIndex = l * c * s.

5.2. PSNR Analysis

Rajendran et al. (2020) measures the influence of the noise or distortion introduced by the watermarking process. It is a common metric used to assess the quality of a signal by comparing the strength of the signal to the level of unwanted elements (noise or distortion) present in it. In the context of watermarking, a higher SNR is generally desirable as it indicates a better balance between the strength of the embedded signal and the impact of any potential noise or distortion.

psnr = 10 * log10(1 / mse). (2)

5.3. BER Analysis

BER stands for Bit Error Rate. In the context of watermarking, BER (Norouzi et al., 2013) refers to the rate at which errors occur in the detection or extraction of the watermark bits from the watermarked signal. It quantifies the accuracy of the watermark retrieval process by measuring the discrepancy between the original watermark bits and the detected or extracted watermark bits. Evaluating the BER in watermarking helps determine the robustness and reliability of the watermarking algorithm.

threshold = 0.5.

- original_bw = original > threshold.
- processed_bw = processed > threshold.
- num_errors = nnz (original_bw ~= processed_bw).
- ber = num_errors / num_pixels.

5.4. MSE Analysis

MSE stands for Mean Squared Error. It provides a quantitative measure of the overall distortion or error introduced by the watermarking process. All the measures results of different image are shown in Table 1.

- num_pixels = numel(original).
- diff = abs (original - processed).
- mse = sum (diff (:). ^2) / num_pixels.

5.5 Histogram Analysis

In watermarking, the histogram of an image (Rajendran & Doraipandian, 2019) is often used to compare the cover image (original image) with the watermarked image (watermark embedded image). Comparing the histograms helps in assessing the perceptual impact of the watermarking process and evaluating the level of imperceptibility of the embedded watermark.

6. CONCLUSION

This work presents a novel watermarking technique that utilised the Henon chaotic map and zig-zag scrambling to achieve both imperceptibility and robustness. The

Table 1. Performance analysis results

S. No	Image	MSE	PSNR	BER	SSIM
1	Peppers	0.0066	22.82 db	0.0575	0.9442
2	Hello33	0.0047	23.24 db	0.0615	0.9422
3	Rose	0.0022	26.54 db	0.0116	0.9593
4	Dalia	0.0026	25.90 db	0.0176	0.9450
5	Flower	0.0031	25.02 db	0.0169	0.9266

Figure 4. Histogram analysis

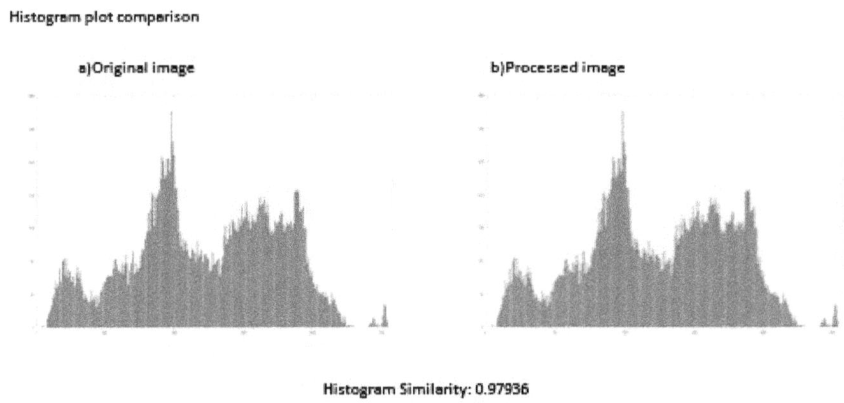

utilization of the Henon chaotic map allows for excellent chaotic behaviour. It has been observed that even a slight modification to the parameter values of the Henon chaotic map can result in the collapse of the retrieved watermark, highlighting the sensitivity of the proposed technique. To evaluate the performance of the algorithm, various quality assessment metrics including PSNR, BER, MSE, SSIM, and histogram analysis were employed. The obtained results demonstrate the robustness of the proposed algorithm, as it successfully resists common attacks while maintaining the imperceptibility of the watermarked images. This implies that the embedded watermark remains intact and unnoticeable to potential intruders. Hence, the proposed model can be utilized for any secure image transaction in IoT applications.

REFERENCES

Alawida, M., Samsudin, A., Sen, J., & Alkhawaldeh, R. S. (2019). A new hybrid digital chaotic system with applications in image encryption. *Signal Processing*, *160*, 45–58. doi:10.1016/j.sigpro.2019.02.016

Ali, M., Ahn, C. W., & Pant, M. (2014). A robust image watermarking technique using SVD and differential evolution in DCT domain. *Optik (Stuttgart)*, *125*(1), 428–434. doi:10.1016/j.ijleo.2013.06.082

Alshoura, W. H., Zainol, Z., Teh, J. S., & Alawida, M. (2020). A New Chaotic Image Watermarking Scheme Based on SVD and IWT. *IEEE Access, 8*, 43391–43406. doi:10.1109/ACCESS.2020.2978186

Anand, A., & Singh, A. K. (2020). An improved DWT-SVD domain watermarking for medical information security. *Computer Communications*, *152*(January), 72–80. doi:10.1016/j.comcom.2020.01.038

Fares, K., Amine, K., & Salah, E. (2020). A robust blind color image watermarking based on Fourier transform domain. *Optik (Stuttgart)*, *208*(February), 164562. doi:10.1016/j.ijleo.2020.164562

Fazli, S., & Moeini, M. (2016). A robust image watermarking method based on DWT, DCT, and SVD using a new technique for correction of main geometric attacks. *Optik (Stuttgart)*, *127*(2), 964–972. doi:10.1016/j.ijleo.2015.09.205

Guo, J. M., & Prasetyo, H. (2014). False-positive-free SVD-based image watermarking. *Journal of Visual Communication and Image Representation*, *25*(5), 1149–1163. doi:10.1016/j.jvcir.2014.03.012

Ismail, R., Fattah, A., Saqr, H. M., & Nasr, M. E. (2022). An efficient medical image encryption scheme for (WBAN) based on adaptive DNA and modern multi chaotic map. *Multimedia Tools and Applications*. Advance online publication. doi:10.1007/s11042-022-13343-8

Kazemivash, B., & Moghaddam, M. E. (2018). A predictive model-based image watermarking scheme using Regression Tree and Firefly algorithm. *Soft Computing*, *22*(12), 4083–4098. doi:10.1007/s00500-017-2617-4

Kumar, J., Singh, P., Yadav, A. K., & Kumar, A. (2018). Asymmetric Cryptosystem for Phase Images in Fractional Fourier Domain Using LU-Decomposition and Arnold Transform. *Procedia Computer Science*, *132*, 1570–1577. doi:10.1016/j.procs.2018.05.121

Kumar, S., Singh, B. K., & Yadav, M. (2020). A Recent Survey on Multimedia and Database Watermarking. *Multimedia Tools and Applications, 79*(27–28), 20149–20197. doi:10.1007/s11042-020-08881-y

Li, J., & Liu, H. (2013). Colour image encryption based on advanced encryption standard algorithm with two-dimensional chaotic map. *IET Information Security, 7*(4), 265–270. doi:10.1049/iet-ifs.2012.0304

Mehta, R., Rajpal, N., & Vishwakarma, V. P. (2018). Robust image watermarking scheme in lifting wavelet domain using GA-LSVR hybridization. *International Journal of Machine Learning and Cybernetics, 9*(1), 145–161. doi:10.1007/s13042-015-0329-6

Najafi, E., & Loukhaoukha, K. (2019). Hybrid secure and robust image watermarking scheme based on SVD and sharp frequency localized contourlet transform. *Journal of Information Security and Applications, 44*, 144–156. doi:10.1016/j.jisa.2018.12.002

Norouzi, B., Seyedzadeh, S. M., Mirzakuchaki, S., & Mosavi, M. R. (2013). A novel image encryption based on row-column, masking and main diffusion processes with hyper chaos. *Multimedia Tools and Applications, 74*(3), 781–811. doi:10.1007/s11042-013-1699-y

Rajendran, S. & Doraipandian, M. (2019). Construction of Two Dimensional Cubic-Tent-Sine Map for Secure Image Transmission. *Communications in Computer and Information Science, 1116 CCIS*, 51–61. doi:10.1007/978-981-15-0871-4_4

Rajendran, S., Krithivasan, K. & Doraipandian, M. (2020). *Fast pre-processing hex Chaos triggered color image cryptosystem*. Academic Press.

Rajendran, S., Krithivasan, K., & Doraipandian, M. (2021). A novel cross cosine map based medical image cryptosystem using dynamic bit-level diffusion. *Multimedia Tools and Applications, 80*(16), 24221–24243. doi:10.1007/s11042-021-10798-z

Alshoura, W. H., Zainol, Z., Teh, J. S., Alawida, M. & Alabdulatif, A. (2021). Hybrid SVD-Based Image Watermarking Schemes: A Review. *IEEE Access, 9*, 32931–32968. doi:10.1109/ACCESS.2021.3060861

Sreenivas, K., & Kamkshi Prasad, V. (2018). Fragile watermarking schemes for image authentication: A survey. *International Journal of Machine Learning and Cybernetics, 9*(7), 1193–1218. doi:10.1007/s13042-017-0641-4

Su, Q., Wang, G., Lv, G., Zhang, X., Deng, G., & Chen, B. (2017). A novel blind color image watermarking based on Contourlet transform and Hessenberg decomposition. *Multimedia Tools and Applications*, *76*(6), 8781–8801. doi:10.1007/s11042-016-3522-z

Xu, H., Kang, X., Chen, Y. & Wang, Y. (2019). Rotation and scale invariant image watermarking based on polar harmonic transforms. *Optik, 183*(December), 401–414. doi:10.1016/j.ijleo.2019.02.001

Yamni, M., Daoui, A., El ogri, O., Karmouni, H., Sayyouri, M., Qjidaa, H., & Flusser, J. (2020). Fractional Charlier moments for image reconstruction and image watermarking. *Signal Processing*, *171*, 107509. doi:10.1016/j.sigpro.2020.107509

Zear, A., Singh, A. K., & Kumar, P. (2018). A proposed secure multiple watermarking technique based on DWT, DCT and SVD for application in medicine. *Multimedia Tools and Applications*, *77*(4), 4863–4882. doi:10.1007/s11042-016-3862-8

Chapter 4
Enhancing Rainfall Prediction Accuracy Through Fog Computing:
Integration of Advanced Algorithms and Edge Analytics

P. Umamaheswari
https://orcid.org/0000-0003-2007-697X
SASTRA University, India

V. Ramaswamy
SASTRA University, India

ABSTRACT

Rainfall prediction is a pivotal aspect of climate forecasting, influencing agriculture, water resource management, and disaster preparedness. This comprehensive review explores the integration of advanced algorithms and edge analytics within a fog computing framework to elevate the accuracy of rainfall predictions. The introduction outlines the significance of accurate rainfall predictions, the limitations of traditional methods, and the motivation for embracing fog computing, advanced algorithms, and edge analytics. A detailed examination of fog computing architecture underscores its decentralized nature and proximity to data sources, addressing challenges inherent in centralized models. The integration of edge analytics is discussed in depth, emphasizing its crucial role in preprocessing IMD data at the source. Insights gained from these implementations offer valuable perspectives on the practical implications, successes, and challenges associated with these methodologies.

DOI: 10.4018/979-8-3693-1694-8.ch004

1. INTRODUCTION

In recent years, the world has witnessed a surge in extreme weather events, with unpredictable and intense rainfall being a significant contributor to natural disasters such as floods and landslides. As societies grapple with the increasing frequency and severity of these events, there is a growing need for advanced technological solutions to improve the accuracy of rainfall predictions. This article explores the promising convergence of Fog Computing, Advanced Algorithms, and Edge Analytics as a transformative approach to enhance the precision and reliability of rainfall forecasting.

Rainfall prediction plays a pivotal role in disaster preparedness, resource management, and overall climate resilience. Traditional methods, often reliant on centralized computing systems, face challenges in processing vast amounts of real-time data efficiently. Fog Computing, an emerging decentralized paradigm, shows promise as a solution to tackle these challenges by extending the capabilities of cloud computing to the network's edge.

By distributing computational tasks closer to the data source – in this case, meteorological sensors and devices Fog Computing minimizes latency and enhances the agility of data processing. This article delves into the integration of advanced algorithms into the Fog Computing framework, presenting a cutting-edge approach to optimizing rainfall prediction models. Utilizing sophisticated machine learning and data analytics algorithms at the network's edge enables the exploitation of real-time data streams, past trends, and meteorological factors to enhance computational capabilities. The synergy between Fog Computing and advanced algorithms enables more accurate and timely predictions, facilitating early warning systems and improving disaster response strategies.

Furthermore, the incorporation of Edge Analytics enhances the efficiency of data processing and decision-making at the edge devices. By enabling intelligent data filtering and analysis directly at the source, Edge Analytics reduces the need for transmitting large volumes of raw data to centralized servers, thereby conserving bandwidth and expediting response times. The article explores the implications of this integration on the scalability, cost-effectiveness, and overall performance of rainfall prediction systems.

As we navigate an era marked by climate uncertainty, this article aims to contribute to the discourse on leveraging Fog Computing, Advanced Algorithms, and Edge Analytics to revolutionize rainfall prediction. By fostering innovation at the intersection of meteorology and cutting-edge computing technologies, we endeavor to create a more resilient and adaptive infrastructure capable of mitigating the impacts of extreme rainfall events on communities worldwide.

Figure 1. Prediction models

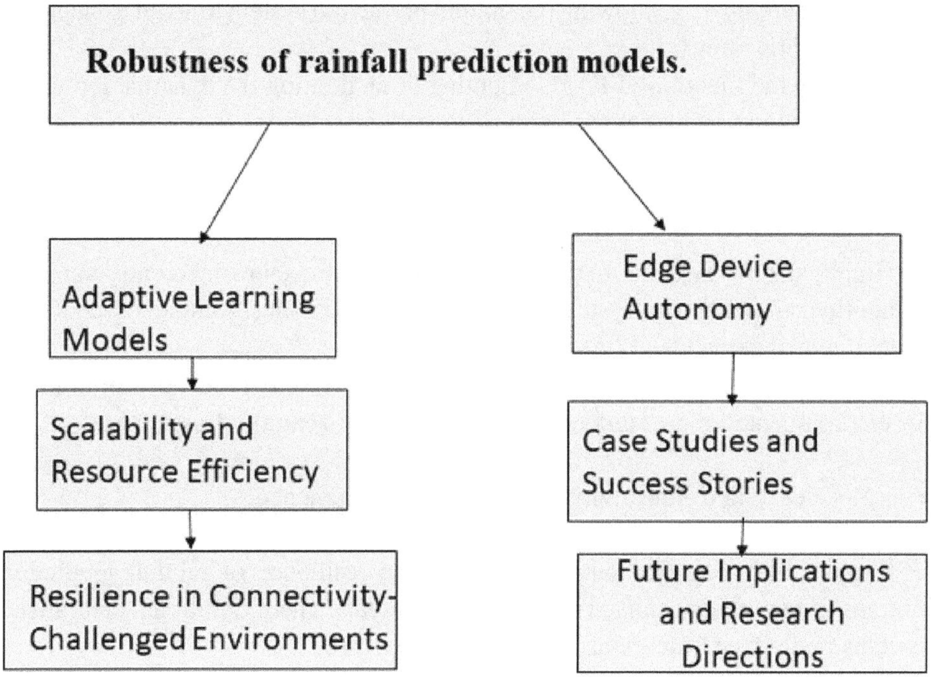

2. BACKGROUND

Fog Computing facilitates the seamless integration of diverse data sources, including satellite imagery, weather stations, and sensor networks, in real-time. The section explores how the fusion of these heterogeneous data sets at the edge enhances the accuracy and robustness of rainfall prediction models as shown in figure 1.

- Edge Device Autonomy:

Discuss the autonomy and self-sufficiency of edge devices empowered by Fog Computing, enabling them to make localized decisions based on analyzed data.

Emphasize the reduced dependency on central servers, making the system more resilient in the face of network disruptions.

- Adaptive Learning Models:

Explore the potential of adaptive learning algorithms that continuously evolve based on incoming data, allowing the rainfall prediction system to adapt to changing climate patterns over time.

Examine the function of Fog Computing in facilitating the dynamic retraining of models at the edge to enhance accuracy.

- Scalability and Resource Efficiency:

Highlight how Fog Computing's distributed architecture inherently supports scalability, allowing the system to handle an increasing volume of data and computational demands.

Discuss the resource efficiency gained by processing data locally, minimizing the environmental impact and reducing the strain on central infrastructure.

- Resilience in Connectivity-Challenged Environments:

Explore how Fog Computing enhances the resilience of rainfall prediction systems in remote or connectivity-challenged areas, where traditional centralized systems might face limitations.

Discuss the benefits of local decision-making during network outages or intermittent connectivity.

- Case Studies and Success Stories:

Integrate relevant case studies or success stories where Fog Computing, Advanced Algorithms, and Edge Analytics have been applied to improve rainfall prediction accuracy.

Highlight the measurable impact on disaster preparedness, response times, and overall community resilience.

- Ethical Considerations and Privacy:

Address ethical considerations related to data privacy and security when deploying advanced algorithms and Fog Computing in meteorological applications.

Discuss strategies for ensuring responsible data management and protecting sensitive information gathered from diverse sources.

- Future Implications and Research Directions:

Conclude by outlining potential future developments and research directions in the field, such as the integration of emerging technologies like artificial intelligence, blockchain, or quantum computing.

Encourage further exploration of interdisciplinary collaborations between meteorologists, data scientists, and computing experts to advance the field.

By incorporating these additional points, your article will provide a comprehensive overview of how the integration of Fog Computing, Advanced Algorithms, and Edge Analytics can revolutionize rainfall prediction accuracy and its implications for disaster mitigation and climate resilience.

3. CHALLENGES IN TRADITIONAL RAINFALL PREDICTION METHODS

3.1 Limitations of Statistical Methods

Statistical methods have long been employed in various fields, including weather prediction, due to their simplicity and interpretability. However, these methods come with inherent limitations that can impact their effectiveness in certain contexts. Some key limitations of statistical methods in the context of rainfall prediction include:

- Assumption of Linearity

Statistical methods often assume a linear relationship between variables. In the case of rainfall prediction, where the relationship between meteorological factors can be complex and nonlinear, this assumption may lead to inaccurate predictions.

- Limited Incorporation of Dynamic Factors

Traditional statistical models may struggle to capture dynamic and evolving relationships between variables. Weather patterns are influenced by a multitude of dynamic factors that change over time, and statistical methods might not adequately adapt to these changes.

- Difficulty in Handling Multivariate Relationships

Rainfall is influenced by a combination of multiple meteorological variables. Statistical methods might encounter challenges in handling complex multivariate relationships, leading to oversimplification or overlooking crucial interactions.

- Sensitivity to Outliers

Statistical models can be sensitive to outliers, which are often present in meteorological datasets. Anomalies or extreme values can disproportionately influence the model, potentially leading to skewed predictions.

- Limited Capacity for Non-Gaussian Distributions

Many statistical methods assume a normal distribution of data, which may not always hold true for meteorological variables. Rainfall data, for example, often exhibits a skewed or non-Gaussian distribution, challenging the assumptions of traditional statistical approaches.

- Inability to Capture Spatial Dependencies

Statistical models might struggle to account for spatial dependencies in weather patterns, as they often assume independence between observations. Weather phenomena, including rainfall, often exhibit spatial correlations that need to be considered for accurate predictions.

- Limited Adaptability to Seasonal Variations

Rainfall patterns can vary significantly across seasons. Statistical methods may face challenges in adapting to and capturing the nuances of seasonal variations, potentially leading to less accurate predictions during certain times of the year.

- Difficulty in Handling Missing Data

Meteorological datasets may have missing or incomplete data, which can pose challenges for statistical models. Traditional statistical methods might struggle to handle missing data effectively, potentially introducing biases into the predictions.

- Lack of Incorporation of Machine Learning Techniques

Traditional statistical methods may not fully leverage the power of modern machine learning techniques. Advanced algorithms, such as those based on artificial intelligence and deep learning, can often outperform traditional statistical approaches in capturing complex relationships in large and diverse datasets. Understanding these limitations underscores the need for more sophisticated and adaptive approaches, such as machine learning and data-driven models, in the field of rainfall prediction to improve accuracy and reliability.

3.2 Issues With Linear and Logistic Regression

Statistical methods have long been employed in various fields, including weather prediction, due to their simplicity and interpretability. However, these methods come with inherent limitations that can impact their effectiveness in certain contexts. Some key limitations of statistical methods in the context of rainfall prediction include:

- Assumption of Linearity

Statistical methods often assume a linear relationship between variables. In the case of rainfall prediction, where the relationship between meteorological factors can be complex and nonlinear, this assumption may lead to inaccurate predictions.

- Limited Incorporation of Dynamic Factors

Traditional statistical models may struggle to capture dynamic and evolving relationships between variables. Weather patterns are influenced by a multitude of dynamic factors that change over time, and statistical methods might not adequately adapt to these changes.

- Difficulty in Handling Multivariate Relationships

Rainfall is influenced by a combination of multiple meteorological variables. Statistical methods might encounter challenges in handling complex multivariate relationships, leading to oversimplification or overlooking crucial interactions.

- Sensitivity to Outliers

Statistical models can be sensitive to outliers, which are often present in meteorological datasets. Anomalies or extreme values can disproportionately influence the model, potentially leading to skewed predictions.

- Limited Capacity for Non-Gaussian Distributions

Many statistical methods assume a normal distribution of data, which may not always hold true for meteorological variables. Rainfall data, for example, often exhibits a skewed or non-Gaussian distribution, challenging the assumptions of traditional statistical approaches.

- Inability to Capture Spatial Dependencies

Statistical models might struggle to account for spatial dependencies in weather patterns, as they often assume independence between observations. Weather phenomena, including rainfall, often exhibit spatial correlations that need to be considered for accurate predictions.

- Limited Adaptability to Seasonal Variations

Rainfall patterns can vary significantly across seasons. Statistical methods may face challenges in adapting to and capturing the nuances of seasonal variations, potentially leading to less accurate predictions during certain times of the year.

- Difficulty in Handling Missing Data

Meteorological datasets may have missing or incomplete data, which can pose challenges for statistical models. Traditional statistical methods might struggle to handle missing data effectively, potentially introducing biases into the predictions.

- Lack of Incorporation of Machine Learning Techniques:

Traditional statistical methods may not fully leverage the power of modern machine learning techniques. Advanced algorithms, such as those based on artificial intelligence and deep learning, can often outperform traditional statistical approaches in capturing complex relationships in large and diverse datasets. Understanding these limitations underscores the need for more sophisticated and adaptive approaches, such as machine learning and data-driven models, in the field of rainfall prediction to improve accuracy and reliability.

3.3 Need for Advanced Approaches

The need for advanced approaches in the field of rainfall prediction arises from the inherent complexities and challenges associated with meteorological data. Traditional methods, such as statistical models and simple regression techniques, may struggle to capture the intricate patterns and dynamic interactions present in weather-related datasets. Several factors underscore the necessity for more sophisticated and advanced approaches:

- Non-Linearity of Meteorological Relationships

Meteorological phenomena, including rainfall, often exhibit non-linear relationships between variables. Advanced approaches, such as machine learning algorithms and nonlinear regression models, are better equipped to capture these complex and non-linear dependencies compared to traditional linear methods.

- Spatial and Temporal Dependencies

Meteorological data frequently displays spatial and temporal dependencies, where conditions in one location or at one time point influence those in nearby locations or subsequent time points. Advanced models, including those based on neural networks and spatial-temporal analysis, can better account for these dependencies.

- Multivariate and Multidimensional Nature of Data

Meteorological datasets involve numerous variables, each contributing to the overall weather patterns. Advanced approaches, particularly those capable of handling high-dimensional data, provide a more comprehensive and accurate representation of the interplay between multiple meteorological factors influencing rainfall.

- Handling of Missing or Noisy Data

Meteorological datasets often suffer from missing or noisy data due to various factors such as sensor malfunctions or measurement errors. Advanced approaches, including ensemble methods and imputation techniques, can effectively handle missing data and mitigate the impact of noise on predictions.

- Dynamic Nature of Weather Patterns:

Weather conditions are dynamic, evolving over time due to various atmospheric and environmental factors. Sophisticated models employing adaptive learning, including recurrent neural networks (RNNs) and Long Short-Term Memory (LSTM) networks, can adjust to evolving weather patterns, leading to more precise predictions.
Prediction of Extreme Events:

Traditional models may struggle to predict extreme weather events, including heavy rainfall leading to floods or drought conditions. Advanced approaches, such as decision trees, random forests, and support vector machines, can better capture the complex patterns associated with extreme events.

- Integration of Multiple Data Sources:

Cutting-edge methods enable the smooth incorporation of data from diverse origins, such as satellite images, remote sensing, and ground-based sensors. This integration enhances the richness of input features and contributes to more robust rainfall predictions.

- Adaptability to Climate Change:

With the changing climate, traditional models may become less effective in predicting rainfall patterns. Advanced approaches, particularly those employing adaptive learning mechanisms and considering long-term climate trends, offer more robust tools for predicting rainfall under changing climatic conditions. In summary, the complexities inherent in meteorological data, including non-linearity, spatial-temporal dependencies, and dynamic nature, necessitate the adoption of advanced approaches for accurate and reliable rainfall prediction. These approaches leverage the power of modern machine learning and data-driven techniques to overcome the limitations of traditional methods and provide more insightful and actionable predictions for weather-related applications.

4. TAXONOMY OF FOG APPROACHES IN WEATHER FORECASTING

Figure 2. Fog approaches in weather forecasting

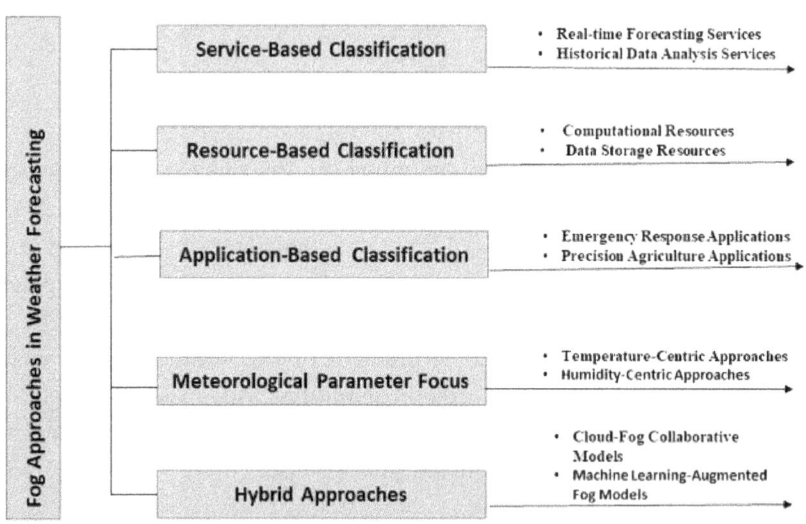

5. RELATED WORK

In this section, we delve into the realm of weather forecasting, specifically focusing on the intersection of fog and edge computing. The discussion aims to elucidate the central theme surrounding the integration of fog and edge computing in the context of weather prediction. Additionally, we explore the various factors that exert influence on the performance of weather forecasts, providing a comprehensive understanding of the intricacies involved in this field. The increasing importance of the Internet of Things (IoT) and its influence on the global landscape. Recognizing the pivotal role of cloud computing in addressing the constraints of processing and storage within the realm of IoT, the abstract highlights, as articulated by Fernandez et al. (2018), the formidable challenges stemming from the escalating proliferation of IoT devices and data. This surge not only leads to network bottlenecks but also precipitates latency issues in cloud communications. In light of these challenges, it becomes imperative to explore solutions that can alleviate the strain on networks and enhance the efficiency of cloud-based communication systems, ensuring seamless integration and optimal performance within the expanding landscape of the Internet of Things. To address these challenges, the paper introduces an edge computing architecture, leveraging the λ-CoAP architecture. This comprehensive architecture spans from IoT devices through edge Smart Gateways to cloud infrastructure, offering a holistic solution to enhance processing efficiency and reduce latency in IoT deployments.

The concept of Vehicular Edge Computing (VEC)(Raza, S et al,2019) and its significance in augmenting vehicular network computing capacity has been introduced. However, it might benefit from a clearer statement regarding the specific goals or objectives of the research. While this work claims to shed light on future research challenges and provide new directions in VEC, it could be more explicit about the potential impact of the research and the novelty of the proposed solutions.

The integration of machine learning (ML) within fog computing systems has become increasingly vital due to the surge in data production. With the proliferation of fog computing applications, machine learning has achieved notable advancements in fields such as speech recognition robotics, computer graphics, natural language processing (NLP), decision-making and neuromorphic computing. Despite the growing importance, there is a notable gap in the literature regarding the exploration of ML's role in the fog computing paradigm. This literature review attempts (Abdulkareem, K. H., et al., 2019) to address this gap by providing a thorough summary of machine learning functionalities in the context of fog computing. The application of ML not only strengthens end-user experiences but also enhances high-level services, facilitating profound analytics and intelligent responses for various tasks. The review focuses on three critical aspects: resource management, accuracy, and security, outlining the latest improvements in ML techniques.

Additionally, the role of ML in edge computing is emphasized, encompassing diverse perspectives such as application support, techniques employed, and datasets used. To provide a well-rounded understanding, the literature review also addresses research challenges and open issues, contributing to a holistic comprehension of the current landscape at the intersection of ML and fog computing. The utilization of machine learning not only improves end-user interactions but also elevates advanced services, enabling in-depth analytics and intelligent feedback across a range of tasks. The review concentrates on three crucial elements—resource management, precision, and security—highlighting recent enhancements in machine learning methodologies. Moreover, the literature emphasizes the role of machine learning in edge computing, covering diverse aspects such as application support, employed techniques, and utilized datasets. In order to offer a comprehensive understanding, the literature review also discusses existing research challenges and unresolved issues, contributing to a thorough comprehension of the current landscape where machine learning intersects with fog computing.

The transition from conventional Cloud Computing to Fog Computing in the context of Vehicular Ad-Hoc Networks (VANETs) has been presented by Gaba, P., & Raw, R. S. (2020). Within this transformation, ANET, a specific category of Mobile Ad-Hoc Network (MANET), plays a crucial role in establishing connections between vehicles, serving as a platform for the exchange of essential data for both safety and non-safety features among drivers and passengers. Initially introduced to enhance VANETs with computation, storage, and networking capabilities, the integration of Cloud Computing with vehicles, referred to as Vehicular Cloud Computing (VCC), faced challenges due to the centralized nature of Cloud Computing, prompting a shift towards the more adaptable Fog Computing.

Fog computing, extending cloud functionality to the network edge, emerges as a compelling solution for real-time applications in VANETs. This literature review systematically explores the drawbacks of Cloud Computing, emphasizing the need for high-speed processing, low latency, and enhanced security in vehicular environments. The evolution to Fog Computing is examined in detail, showcasing its efficacy in meeting the demands of real-time applications, conserving network bandwidth, and ensuring reliability and security. Special attention is given to the application of Fog Computing in vehicles, leading to the conceptualization of Vehicular Fog Computing (VFC).

A critical aspect of the review involves an in-depth comparative analysis between VCC and VFC, highlighting the strengths and weaknesses of each paradigm. Furthermore, the literature review discusses various applications of Fog Computing in vehicular contexts and explores the security and forensic challenges associated with this evolving technology. By synthesizing existing knowledge and research findings, this chapter aims to provide a nuanced understanding of the transition from Cloud to

Fog Computing in the context of vehicular networks. Some researchers (Tabrizchi, H., & Kuchaki Rafsanjani, M. 2020) delve into the escalating significance of cloud computing, highlighting its advantages such as simplified IT infrastructure, global accessibility, and cost efficiencies. However, it recognizes the pressing security and privacy challenges associated with cloud adoption.

Drawing on research from academia, industry, and standards organizations, the paper comprehensively examines security issues, requirements, threats, and vulnerabilities in cloud computing. It not only analyzes various components of cloud systems but also introduces a novel classification of recent security solutions. The survey goes further to identify and discuss diverse types of security threats jeopardizing cloud services, outlining open issues and proposing future directions. With a focus on cloud entities like service providers, data owners, and users, this paper aims to provide a detailed exploration of the evolving landscape of security challenges in the realm of cloud computing.

Various authors, including Qiu, T., et al., investigate the crucial intersection between the Industrial Internet of Things (IIoT) and edge computing with the aim of optimizing industrial processes and services. Through the interconnection of industrial equipment via networks, facilitating data acquisition, exchange, and analysis, IIoT aims to reduce costs and improve productivity. The integration of edge computing into IIoT is emphasized as a significant advancement, notably reducing decision-making latency, conserving bandwidth, and enhancing privacy. The paper delves into the concepts of IIoT and edge computing, providing insights into research advancements and suggesting a future architecture. Critical technical aspects such as routing, task scheduling, data storage, analytics, security, and standardization are thoroughly examined. This survey also explores opportunities and challenges in 5G-based edge communication, data offloading, edge intelligence, load balancing and data sharing security. It concludes by presenting typical application scenarios of edge computing in IIoT, encompassing prognostics, smart grids, manufacturing coordination, intelligent connected vehicles, smart logistics and health management.

This study by Mahmud et al. (2020) delves into the increasing adoption of the Internet of Things (IoT) for the development of intelligent environments across various sectors, including smart cities, healthcare, Industry 4.0, and Agtech. The conventional approach of executing IoT applications in a Cloud-centric manner encounters challenges arising from the multi-hop distance between datacenters and IoT devices. In response to this, Fog computing, serving as an extension of the Cloud at the edge, emerges as a viable solution. Fog computing executes applications in proximity to data sources, thereby reducing service delivery time and alleviating network congestion.

However, the efficacy of Fog computing is contingent upon overcoming challenges associated with the distributed and heterogeneous nature of Fog nodes, which are often constrained in terms of resources. This necessitates the implementation of efficient application management strategies to optimize the performance of IoT applications in diverse and resource-limited Fog environments. Hence, the study underscores the significance of addressing these intricacies for the seamless integration of Fog computing in the broader landscape of IoT applications.

This research delves (Sadeeq, M.et al 2021) into an in-depth examination of existing strategies for managing applications in Fog computing, conducting a thorough review based on architectural considerations, placement, and ongoing maintenance. Introducing a comprehensive taxonomy, the study systematically identifies gaps within the realm of Fog-based application management. To address these gaps, the research proposes a perspective model, presenting valuable insights and paving the way for future research directions aimed at augmenting the efficiency of application management in Fog computing environments.

The focus of this report is squarely on the formidable challenges posed by the exponential growth of the Industrial Internet of Things (IIoT) and the imperative for effective handling of the vast volume of generated data. Acknowledging the inherent limitations of energy and storage in IIoT devices, the study underscores the pivotal role of outsourced data and cloud computing. This is facilitated through the principles of self-organization and short-range IoT networking.

A crucial aspect highlighted in the report is the escalating efficiency of cloud computing delivery, coupled with the evolving trend of transitioning data from in-house records to hubs managed by Cloud Computing Vendors. Emphasizing the significance of this shift, the research underscores unfamiliar safeguards necessary for seamless integration between IoT and cloud systems. Furthermore, the study explores innovative computing techniques designed to facilitate the smooth transition of IoT applications to the cloud, effectively addressing challenges associated with intensive workloads and data management. This comprehensive analysis contributes to the ongoing discourse on optimizing the synergy between Fog computing, IIoT, and cloud integration.

Another work addresses (Mantri, R et al., 2021) the perennial challenges in weather forecasting due to the intricate and dynamic nature of the atmosphere. It acknowledges the limitations of current physical models, notably in terms of computing time. The study explores the promising role of supervised machine learning methods in improving weather predictions by employing artificial neural networks (ANNs), support vector machines (SVMs), random forest (RF), and k-nearest neighbors (KNN). Three diverse datasets from the Weather stack database are used for training and evaluation, revealing that ANNs outperform other methods across all datasets. Notably, all machine learning methods exhibit substantial improvements compared to Weather stack's existing model. The study also highlights the impact of data uncertainty on model performance, particularly in datasets with predicted input features. Overall, it provides valuable insights into leveraging machine learning for more accurate weather forecasting, offering a significant contribution to the advancement of precision prediction models. In the year 2021, researchers underscored the myriad advantages presented by the Internet of Things (IoT) and highlighted the rapid expansion of its ecosystem. The study emphasizes the crucial contribution of various computing domains, including cloud, fog, edge, and dew computing, in tackling challenges encountered within the burgeoning IoT landscape, as articulated by Ahammad et al. (2021). Delving into a comprehensive exploration, the research thoroughly investigates the intricate interactions, benefits, and limitations inherent in these computing domains within the broader IoT ecosystem. This examination not only sheds light on the evolving dynamics of IoT technologies but also provides valuable insights into the nuanced relationships among different computing paradigms, thereby contributing to a deeper understanding of their collective impact on the IoT landscape.

Additionally, a concise comparative analysis of cloud, fog, edge, and dew computing is presented. The document delves into the influence of internet and offline computing on these domains, offering a thorough examination. Ultimately, it provides strategic suggestions for the adoption of appropriate computing domains in optimizing IoT ecosystems, contributing valuable insights to the evolving field of IoT technology. Another set of researches (Vuyyuru, V. A.,et al.,2021) address the burgeoning growth of future weather data and explores the potential of machine learning advancements, particularly in artificial intelligence (AI), to leverage this wealth of information. Recognizing the inherent challenges in flawless weather prediction, the document proposes a novel hybrid mechanism integrating a multi-layer perceptron (MLP) and a variational auto-encoder (VAE) with a fire-fly optimization mechanism. Acknowledging the diverse nature of weather-related data, the paper argues that a single mechanism may not effectively extract both global and local features. Consequently, the hybrid approach utilizes VAE to extract global features and integrates MLP to extract local features, aiming to enhance the accuracy and consistency of weather data classification. The study contributes to the evolving field of AI-driven weather prediction methodologies.

Some Authors (Umamaheswari, P., & Ramaswamy, V., 2022) focused on the vital role of rainfall prediction in meteorology, emphasizing its impact on global manufacturing and service sectors. Acknowledging the challenges in accurate rainfall prediction, the document introduces a novel algorithm, the Moving Average-Probabilistic Regression Filtering (MV-PRF), for preprocessing historical weather data. This method effectively eliminates unwanted samples with low amplitude. The Time Variant Particle Swarm Optimization (TVPSO) model is then applied to optimize the preprocessed rainfall data. The optimized data is subsequently employed in various classification processes, enhancing the accuracy of rainfall forecasts.

Machine Learning (ML) techniques are utilized for classifying weather parameters to predict rainfall on a daily or monthly basis. Experimental results demonstrate the efficiency and accuracy of the proposed methods in rainfall analysis, showcasing their potential for advancing the field of rainfall prediction in meteorology.

Various industries have embraced IoT to enhance efficiency, security, and predictive maintenance. This paper focuses on improving the Quality of Service (QoS) by identifying anomalies in predictive maintenance, which can adversely affect production. A multi-agent-based anomaly detection scheme is proposed, leveraging fog computing infrastructure to reduce communication latency. Multiple agents are deployed in fog nodes to conduct various operations related to anomaly detection. The scheme utilizes a multi-step prediction technique and applies a Gated Recurrent Unit (GRU) model for time series prediction. An Artificial Bee Colony algorithm is employed to fine-tune the hyperparameters of the GRU model, enhancing accuracy. The proposed model, evaluated using Google Colab and TensorFlow's Keras library, demonstrates increased accuracy compared to existing approaches, making it a promising solution for anomaly detection in the fog computing environment.

Over the last two decades, there has been a widespread adoption of the Internet of Things (IoT) due to its numerous benefits, including flexibility, autonomy, cost-effectiveness, and improved productivity (Bulla, C., & Birje, M. N., 2022). Various industries have embraced IoT to enhance efficiency, security, and predictive maintenance. This research paper is dedicated to enhancing the Quality of Service (QoS) by identifying anomalies in predictive maintenance, which can have adverse effects on production. To achieve this, a novel multi-agent-based anomaly detection scheme is proposed, making use of fog computing infrastructure to minimize communication latency. Multiple agents are deployed in fog nodes to perform various operations related to anomaly detection. The scheme employs a multi-step prediction technique and utilizes a Gated Recurrent Unit (GRU) model for time series prediction. The hyperparameters of the GRU model are fine-tuned using an Artificial Bee Colony algorithm, thereby improving accuracy. The effectiveness of the proposed model is evaluated using Google Colab and TensorFlow's Keras library, demonstrating a notable increase in accuracy compared to existing approaches. This establishes it as a promising solution for anomaly detection in the fog computing environment.

The economic significance of rainfall prediction (Umamaheswari, P., & Ramaswamy, V., 2023) and its potential benefits for society, particularly in water conservation and agricultural yield improvement. While traditional methods like linear and logistic regression have been used in the past, they face inefficiencies in handling various influencing parameters. To address this, the paper introduces a deep learning model with three phases, focusing on data preprocessing, including missing value estimation, irrelevant data removal, and data transformation. The proposed model employs a novel modified Long Short-Term Memory (M-LSTM) approach to enhance predictive accuracy. Comparative analysis with several techniques, including Naive Bayes, Support Vector Machines, Genetic Algorithms, and Random Forest, is conducted. Utilizing data from the Indian Meteorological Department spanning 1901 to 2015, the study concludes that the M-LSTM approach offers more efficient qualitative rainfall predictions. Some of the study aims to forecast fog using a diagnostic method that relies on the outputs of a global Numerical Weather Prediction (NWP) model.

The diagnostic method involves (Singh, A., et al 2022) establishing thresholds for meteorological variables associated with fog formation, derived from observations during foggy conditions. These thresholds are then applied to the global NWP model output for fog prediction. Focusing on the winter season over the northern plains of India, where fog is a common occurrence, the diagnostic method is employed to predict fog events at three stations in northern India. The results indicate that the proposed method effectively predicts both occurrences and non-occurrences of fog at these stations, with a notable 94% accuracy in forecasting observed fog events. The diagnostic approach performs particularly well over Delhi, exhibiting the highest accuracy (0.61) and probability of detection (0.60). The study concludes that a diagnostic approach using global model output serves as a valuable tool for fog prediction at specific locations.

Another researcher (Umamaheswari, P., 2022) addresses the significant issue of water wastage resulting from irregular heavy rainfall and dam water releases. Traditional statistical methods for predicting water levels are deemed approximate, prompting the use of the gradient descent algorithm for enhanced accuracy and performance. The K-means algorithm is employed for clustering, iteratively assigning data points to groups based on attributes. This clustering is refined for year-wise and month-wise data extraction, achieving a clustering accuracy of 90.22%. The gradient descent algorithm is then applied to reduce errors and facilitate precise water level predictions. The study suggests that this approach aids in effective watershed development, contributing to groundwater recharge and benefiting both farmers and domestic water usage. Overall, the combination of clustering and gradient descent algorithms presents a promising strategy for optimizing water resource management.

The increasing importance of health monitoring, particularly in the context of rising instances of diabetes due to factors like work pressure and unhealthy eating habits are discussed in another paper (Kumar et al, 2023) . Recognizing the significance of early diabetes prediction, the study proposes a fog-based diabetes prediction model leveraging cloud and fog computing. Sensor data from remote devices are gathered and processed using fog computing, ensuring real-time communication. The hybrid ANFIS-PSO-WOA algorithm is applied in the cloud layer for diabetes level detection, achieving high accuracy. Processed data is stored in the fog layer for further analysis by healthcare professionals. The proposed framework, evaluated with UCI repository diabetes data, demonstrates a remarkable accuracy of 92%, outperforming SVM, ANN, and ANFIS. The nature-based algorithm contributes to superior accuracy, making the framework efficient for early diabetes detection, thereby enabling prompt treatment and potentially saving lives.

The research conducted by Songhorabadi, M., et al. in 2023 explores the crucial role of advanced computing paradigms, particularly fog computing, in the advancement of smart cities, focusing on applications that require location awareness, low latency, and high security. While cloud-based approaches are commonly used in smart cities, this study emphasizes their drawbacks, including compromised security and limited flexibility. To tackle these challenges, the paper suggests a comprehensive examination of cutting-edge fog-based approaches in smart cities, classifying them into three categories: service-based, resource-based, and application-based. The research investigates evaluation criteria, tools, methodologies, advantages, disadvantages, and the types of proposed algorithms for each category. Additionally, it discusses open issues and challenges, categorizing future trends and concerns into practical sub-categories, providing a comprehensive overview of the landscape for fog-based solutions in smart cities.

This research focuses (Swetha, K., et al 2023) on image classification, specifically addressing the challenges posed by degraded image data due to weather conditions like haze, smoke, fog, rain, or snow. The study introduces the concept of de-weathering, a preprocessing phase aimed at removing weather effects to enhance image quality and usability. The proposed deep learning-based weather image recognition model considers 11 distinct weather situations, including dew, fog/smog, frost, glazing, hail, lightning, rain, rainbow, rime, snow, and sandstorm. The research aims to develop a comprehensive solution that can effectively recognize and categorize images under various weather conditions, providing a valuable tool for image analysis and classification.

REFERENCES

Abdulkareem, K. H., Mohammed, M. A., Gunasekaran, S. S., Al-Mhiqani, M. N., Mutlag, A. A., Mostafa, S. A., Ali, N. S., & Ibrahim, D. A. (2019). A review of fog computing and machine learning: Concepts, applications, challenges, and open issues. *IEEE Access : Practical Innovations, Open Solutions*, *7*, 153123–153140. doi:10.1109/ACCESS.2019.2947542

Ahammad, I., Khan, A. R., & Salehin, Z. U. (2021). A review on cloud, fog, roof, and dew computing: IoT perspective. *International Journal of Cloud Applications and Computing*, *11*(4), 14–41. doi:10.4018/IJCAC.2021100102

Bulla, C., & Birje, M. N. (2022). Anomaly detection in industrial IoT applications using deep learning approach. *Artificial Intelligence in Industrial Applications: Approaches to Solve the Intrinsic Industrial Optimization Problems*, 127-147.

Fernández, C. M., Rodríguez, M. D., & Muñoz, B. R. (2018, May). An edge computing architecture in the Internet of Things. In *2018 IEEE 21st international symposium on real-time distributed computing (ISORC)* (pp. 99-102). IEEE.

Gaba, P., & Raw, R. S. (2020). Vehicular cloud and fog computing architecture, applications, services, and challenges. In *IoT and cloud computing advancements in vehicular ad-hoc networks* (pp. 268–296). IGI Global. doi:10.4018/978-1-7998-2570-8.ch014

Kumar, D., Mandal, N., & Kumar, Y. (2023). Fog-based framework for diabetes prediction using hybrid ANFIS model in cloud environment. *Personal and Ubiquitous Computing*, *27*(3), 909–916. doi:10.1007/s00779-022-01678-w PMID:33815032

Mahmud, R., Ramamohanarao, K., & Buyya, R. (2020). Application management in fog computing environments: A taxonomy, review and future directions. *ACM Computing Surveys*, *53*(4), 1–43. doi:10.1145/3403955

Mantri, R., Raghavendra, K. R., Puri, H., Chaudhary, J., & Bingi, K. (2021, July). Weather prediction and classification using neural networks and k-nearest neighbors. In *2021 8th International Conference on Smart Computing and Communications (ICSCC)* (pp. 263-268). IEEE. 10.1109/ICSCC51209.2021.9528115

Qiu, T., Chi, J., Zhou, X., Ning, Z., Atiquzzaman, M., & Wu, D. O. (2020). Edge computing in industrial internet of things: Architecture, advances and challenges. *IEEE Communications Surveys and Tutorials*, *22*(4), 2462–2488. doi:10.1109/COMST.2020.3009103

Raza, S., Wang, S., Ahmed, M., & Anwar, M. R. (2019). A survey on vehicular edge computing: Architecture, applications, technical issues, and future directions. *Wireless Communications and Mobile Computing*, *2019*, 2019. doi:10.1155/2019/3159762

Sadeeq, M. M., Abdulkareem, N. M., Zeebaree, S. R., Ahmed, D. M., Sami, A. S., & Zebari, R. R. (2021). IoT and Cloud computing issues, challenges and opportunities: A review. *Qubahan Academic Journal*, *1*(2), 1–7. doi:10.48161/qaj.v1n2a36

Singh, A., Maheskumar, R. S., & Iyengar, G. R. (2022). A Diagnostic Method for Fog Forecasting Using Numerical Weather Prediction (NWP) Model Outputs. *Journal of Atmospheric Science Research*, *5*(4), 10–19. doi:10.30564/jasr.v5i4.5068

Songhorabadi, M., Rahimi, M., MoghadamFarid, A. M., & Haghi Kashani, M. (2023). Fog computing approaches in IoT-enabled smart cities. *Journal of Network and Computer Applications*, *211*, 103557. doi:10.1016/j.jnca.2022.103557

Swetha, K., Kumari, E. V., Reddy, V. A., & Gupta, K. G. (2023, August). Visual Weather Analytics-Leveraging Image Recognition for Weather Prediction. In *2023 Second International Conference on Augmented Intelligence and Sustainable Systems (ICAISS)* (pp. 800-804). IEEE. 10.1109/ICAISS58487.2023.10250605

Tabrizchi, H., & Kuchaki Rafsanjani, M. (2020). A survey on security challenges in cloud computing: Issues, threats, and solutions. *The Journal of Supercomputing*, *76*(12), 9493–9532. doi:10.1007/s11227-020-03213-1

Umamaheswari, P. (2022). Water-Level Prediction Utilizing Datamining Techniques in Watershed Management. In *Handbook of Research on Evolving Designs and Innovation in ICT and Intelligent Systems for Real-World Applications* (pp. 261–275). IGI Global.

Umamaheswari, P., & Ramaswamy, V. (2022). Optimized preprocessing using time variant particle swarm optimization (TVPSO) and deep learning on rainfall data. *Journal of Scientific and Industrial Research*, *81*(12), 1317–1325.

Umamaheswari, P., & Ramaswamy, V. (2023, March). A Novel Modified LSTM Deep Learning Model on Precipitation Analysis for South Indian States. In *International Conference on Deep Sciences for Computing and Communications* (pp. 189-201). Cham: Springer Nature Switzerland. 10.1007/978-3-031-27622-4_15

Vuyyuru, V. A., Rao, G. A., & Murthy, Y. S. (2021). A novel weather prediction model using a hybrid mechanism based on MLP and VAE with fire-fly optimization algorithm. *Evolutionary Intelligence*, *14*(2), 1173–1185. doi:10.1007/s12065-021-00589-8

Chapter 5
From Theory to Practice:
A Comprehensive Review of Osmotic Computing

P. Umamaheswari
https://orcid.org/0000-0003-2007-697X
SASTRA University, India

ABSTRACT

In the evolving landscape of distributed computing, the integration of edge devices with traditional cloud infrastructures necessitates innovative approaches to harness their combined computational prowess. Osmotic computing, a paradigm that promises such integration, has transitioned from theoretical frameworks to tangible implementations. This chapter provides a comprehensive examination of osmotic computing, tracing its journey from conceptual underpinnings to its current real-world applications. Central to osmotic computing is the deployment of microservices—modular, autonomous units of computation—strategically positioned across the edge-cloud continuum based on immediate needs and resource availabilities. This review elucidates the foundational principles of osmotic computing, its distinguishing characteristics, the challenges encountered in its practical adoption, and its demonstrable benefits in current computing scenarios.

1. INTRODUCTION

In today's digital era, the proliferation of devices, from smartphones to IoT sensors, has radically transformed the computational landscape. Traditional cloud-based processing models, while powerful, are increasingly challenged by the sheer volume of

DOI: 10.4018/979-8-3693-1694-8.ch005

data generated at the edge of the network, raising concerns about latency, bandwidth consumption, and data privacy. Enter osmotic computing, a paradigm shift aiming to seamlessly blend the capabilities of edge devices with cloud infrastructures.

The capacity to shift computational processes from the Cloud to IoT devices positions. Osmotic Computing as an ideal fit for rapidly changing environments like smart cities. Industry 5.0 represents the next phase in manufacturing where humans and advanced technology (Rani, S., & Srivastava, G., 2024) work together to transform workflows. It's crucial for the evolution of the next-generation smart cities. Designing and operating smart infrastructure for Industrial Internet of Things (IIoT) involves various decision-making processes across different domains. Today, complex systems can be thought of as a network of serverless services (or workflows) distributed across the Cloud and Edge layers. However, implementing applications in this complicated context while still assuring built-in security remains difficult. Osmotic Computing has recently emerged as a novel computational method. It may provide a solid foundation for improving security in serverless programs throughout the Cloud-Edge spectrum. Osmotic Computing concepts to modify the structure of OpenWolf, a novel serverless engine, resulting in a 65% reduction in the execution time of encrypted data. In such settings, intelligent services, attuned to specific contexts, frequently manage environmental variables and discern patterns in people's actions.

At its core, osmotic computing envisions a dynamic computational environment where tasks are efficiently distributed across the edge-cloud continuum. This is achieved through the strategic deployment of microservices, which are self-contained units of computation that can be easily migrated based on contextual needs and resource availabilities. While the theoretical foundations of osmotic computing promise a revolution in distributed computing, it's in the practical implementations that its true potential is being rigorously tested. Many Cloud providers are already embracing serverless computing via the Function as a Service (FaaS) concept. This strategy, which is based on (Morabito, Get et al., 2023) dynamically allocating serverless services, has significantly altered how Cloud applications are constructed.

There are numerous studies in the literature that address naming geographical regions in a manner easily understood by humans. However, some of these methods result in geocode conflicts, while others don't support the designation of areas of varying sizes. Additionally, some solutions are proprietary, limiting their widespread adoption or integration into open-source initiatives. This review seeks to traverse the journey of osmotic computing from its early conceptualizations to its current real-world applications.

By merging consortium blockchain (also known as supervisory blockchain) and fog computing, the authors have produced a novel approach. This suggested system is divided into three layers: the application layer, the fog layer, and the blockchain security layer. The authors (Almaiah, M. A., & Alkdour, T., 2023). present a new consensus technique dubbed the Proof of Enhanced Concept (PoEC) to successfully implement this concept. This method secures transactions before delegating them to the fog layer or fog devices via homomorphic encryption. This method aids in the mitigation of numerous security risks such as collusion attacks, phishing attacks, and replay attacks, while also increasing the resilience of each layer against such intrusions. The model presented by the authors uses a hybrid-deep learning approach to protect electronic medical records against potential breaches. Additionally, by employing a decentralized fog computing system (Kochovski, P, et al.,2023) it reduces latency and enhances security measures.

Load balancing is essential for enhancing fog computing performance by evenly distributing the workload across available Virtual Machines (VMs) within a segment. Given the complexity introduced by numerous users in a fog computing environment, distributing this load becomes challenging. To address this, a new method named Mutated Leader Algorithm (MLA) is introduced for efficient load balancing. Initially, the fog computing (Shruthi, G, et al., 2023) structure consists of three layers: fog, cloud, and end-user. Tasks are submitted from the end-user to the fog layer, which contains clusters of nodes. In these clusters, load balancing occurs, and the Deep Residual Network (DRN) predicts the resources for each VM. Using MLA, tasks from users are allocated and reallocated to VMs in the cloud based on resource constraints. This balancing aims to optimize both resources and objectives. If a VM becomes overloaded, tasks are removed and shifted to less burdened VMs. With this approach, MLA has achieved an execution time of 1.472ns, a cost of $69.448, and a load of 0.0003%.Traditional centralized models, though efficient for large-scale computations, are not always equipped to cater to the latency-sensitive requirements of applications like autonomous vehicles, smart cities, and telemedicine. These challenges can be addressed through the effective use of osmotic computing, an emerging approach that integrates edge-cloud and both public and private infrastructure. However, the present state of osmotic computing is still in its infancy and needs additional development to tackle the array of issues outlined in the subsequent section.

An IoT-centered monitoring system designed for quarantine and isolation is non-contact, offering a means to mitigate the risk of exposure to contagious pathogens, particularly for healthcare personnel. The authors of this paper (Arif, A. M., et al., 2023) have examined essential physiological indicators in humans that wearable biomedical sensors can detect and oversee through IoT technology. Their focus lies in monitoring the well-being, stability, and recuperation of COVID-19-positive individuals and frontline healthcare workers. Ultimately, this article aims to motivate healthcare professionals and biomedical engineers alike to develop digital health platforms for the surveillance and management of similar pandemic situations.

Osmotic computing emerges as a response to these challenges, offering a distributed approach that capitalizes on the strengths of both edge devices and cloud systems. The idea of "osmosis" in this context alludes to the natural, bidirectional flow of computational tasks and data between the edge and the cloud, much like the biological process where molecules move across a membrane. Furthermore, the modularity of microservices in osmotic computing makes it inherently scalable and adaptable. This granularity allows for precise control over where and how each computational task is executed, enabling systems to adapt to changing conditions and demands in real-time. A contactless IoT-based monitoring system (Kaushik, K.et al., 2023) for quarantine and isolation has the potential to reduce the risk of healthcare professionals' exposure to infectious pathogens. The present manuscript outlines the clinically significant physiological parameters in humans that can be assessed using wearable biomedical sensors and monitored using IoT technology. It explores how these parameters contribute to tracking the health, stability, and recovery of individuals with COVID-19 and frontline healthcare workers. The authors of this paper aim to encourage frontline healthcare workers and biomedical engineers to initiate the development of digital healthcare platforms for monitoring and effectively managing pandemics of this nature. Another notable aspect is the potential for enhanced data security and privacy. By processing sensitive data locally at the edge there's a reduced need to transmit it across potentially vulnerable networks, offering an additional layer of protection against breaches and unauthorized access. However, the journey from conceptualizing osmotic computing to its tangible realization hasn't been devoid of challenges. From ensuring seamless interoperability between edge and cloud systems to managing the complexities introduced by microservices architectures, the path has been both intriguing and demanding.

2. THEORETICAL FOUNDATIONS

5G technology has become popular in smart transportation systems, with vehicles often communicating in open environments, making them susceptible to security and privacy issues. Although some have suggested pseudonym authentication methods for these 5G vehicular networks (Ren, J, et al., 2023) many are complex and time-consuming. This paper introduces a fog computing-based pseudonym authentication (FC-PA) solution to reduce performance overhead in 5G vehicular networks. This scheme (Mohammed, B. A.et al., 2023) uses just one elliptic curve cryptography multiplication operation for information verification. Our security evaluation confirms that this method ensures both privacy and pseudonym authentication and can withstand typical security threats. Furthermore, our approach offers a better balance between efficiency and security compared to other recent solutions.

5G-supported vehicular fog computing continues to spearhead innovations, especially in intelligent transport, by enabling traffic data sharing and collaborative urban operations. However, ensuring the security of messages has been a major hindrance (Almazroi, A, et al, 2023). While several researchers have put forward certificateless authentication techniques using pseudonyms and traceability to sidestep conventional certificate management and key escrow issues, challenges such as high communication costs, potential security risks, and computational complexity remain. In light of these challenges, this paper presents the ECA-VFog, a streamlined certificateless authentication solution tailored for fog computing within 5G-assisted vehicular networks. The ECA-VFog strategy capitalizes on elliptic curve cryptography operations, aided by a fog server through a 5G base station. The authors then offer a security evaluation to underscore the efficiency and advantages of the ECA-VFog system.

The notion of fog computing entails the usage of a variety of devices located at the network's edge, which are diverse in type and frequently have limited resources. The Fog computing paradigm deploys latency-critical and bandwidth-hungry IoT application services to the network's edge using scattered, heterogeneous, and resource-constrained devices. Furthermore, several writers discovered (Pallewatta, S .et al., 2023) that the MicroService Architecture (MSA) is increasingly being used to meet the rapid development and deployment requirements of rapidly growing IoT applications. MSA has considerable promise in leveraging Fog and Cloud resources due to its fine-grained modularity and independently deployable and scalable nature, giving rise to novel paradigms such as Osmotic computing.

Understanding the trajectory of osmotic computing from its theoretical inception to its real-world applications is paramount for several reasons:

- Historical Context: Every technological paradigm is rooted in a set of problems it aims to solve. By tracing osmotic computing's theoretical underpinnings, we gain a holistic view of the challenges it was conceived to address. This historical context offers invaluable insights into its foundational principles and allows us to appreciate its evolutionary arc.
- Bridging the Gap: Transitioning from theory to practice is riddled with unforeseen challenges. Recognizing these challenges aids in refining the paradigm, making it more adaptable and robust. By understanding this transition, we can more effectively navigate the complexities that arise during real-world implementation.
- Evolving Needs: The theoretical basis of any computational model often arises from abstract, ideal conditions. However, practical scenarios introduce variables that might not have been originally considered. Observing how

osmotic computing adapts to these real-world demands provides a roadmap for its future refinements and highlights its adaptability.

- Value Proposition: The real test of a computational paradigm lies in its tangible benefits in practical applications. By comparing the theoretical promises of osmotic computing against its practical outcomes, we can assess its true value proposition and potential for widespread adoption.
- Future Innovations: The journey from theory to practice is a continuous feedback loop. Practical implementations often feedback into the theory, leading to new insights and innovations. By understanding this journey, we pave the way for future iterations and enhancements of osmotic computing.

The surge in Internet coverage globally has led to an increased reliance on cloud computing, which operates on a pay-as-you-use basis using shared computational resources. The Internet of Things (IoT), a rapidly evolving technology, employs various applications and inherently leans on cloud computing. However, the physical distance between cloud resources and IoT's endpoint can result in significant delays, especially problematic for applications requiring immediate responses. Fog computing serves as an intermediary layer between the cloud and the endpoint, ensuring reduced latency for these delay-sensitive IoT applications. In this setup, managing and distributing workload, or load balancing, is crucial for ensuring optimal quality of service (QoS), user experience (QoE), and overall system performance. Different metrics, including response time, throughput, and energy consumption, and utilization, drive load balancing decisions. Research papers (Ebneyousef, S., & Shirmarz, A., 2023) from renowned publishers like Elsevier, ACM, IEEE, Springer, and Wiley spanning 2018 to 2022 have been explored. These studies delve into various load-balancing algorithms, system blueprints, tools, applications, along with their respective merits and demerits. This review serves as a valuable resource for those looking to enhance load balancing performance.

Osmotic computing, at its core, is inspired by the biological process of osmosis, where molecules pass through a semi-permeable membrane from a region of low concentration to a region of high concentration until equilibrium is achieved. This natural phenomenon offers a vivid analogy for the dynamic and adaptive allocation of computational resources and tasks.

- Biological Analogy: The osmotic process is all about balance and efficient resource allocation. In osmotic computing, tasks and resources flow between cloud and edge environments, much like molecules through a membrane, seeking an equilibrium that ensures optimal performance and efficiency. This bio-inspired model lays the groundwork for how tasks can be dynamically allocated and executed in the most suitable environment.

- Decentralization and Autonomy: One of the primary theoretical tenets of osmotic computing is decentralization. Unlike traditional cloud-based models, where a central entity oversees and manages tasks, osmotic computing pushes for decision-making processes to be distributed across the network. This autonomy ensures that decisions about where a task should be executed are made closer to the data source, resulting in reduced latency and increased responsiveness.
- Dynamic Resource Allocation: Osmotic computing thrives on adaptability. Theoretically, it's designed to respond in real-time to changing workloads, data locations, and application requirements. This dynamic allocation ensures that resources are utilized optimally, leading to improved efficiency and cost-effectiveness.
- Fluidity in Task Migration: At a foundational level, osmotic computing emphasizes seamless and adaptive migration of tasks between the edge and the cloud. The goal is to ensure that tasks are executed where they can achieve the best performance, whether that's closer to the data source on the edge or in a more powerful cloud environment.
- Integration of Environments: The theoretical model of osmotic computing doesn't favor one environment over another but instead promotes an integrated approach. Edge and cloud are seen as complementary entities, each offering unique advantages, and the osmotic model ensures they work in tandem to deliver the best results

3. KEY PRINCIPLES OF OSMOTIC COMPUTING

The key principles of osmotic computing define its foundational concepts and guide its application in real-world scenarios. The authors (Ghobaei-Arani, M., & Shahidinejad, A. 2022) pinpointed an evolutionary-driven method that uses both throughput and energy consumption as objective measures to determine the optimal placement of IoT services while ensuring the Quality of Service (QoS) needs of each IoT service are met. In addition, they crafted a self-sufficient service placement framework, aligned with a tri-layered architecture of the fog ecosystem, to illustrate how key components from both the IoT device and fog layers collaborate for the deployment of IoT applications. When tested, our proposed method showcased improved resource utilization and a higher rate of service acceptance. It also led to decreased service delays and energy usage when compared to other strategies based on metaheuristic mechanisms. The table emphasizes the core aspects of the "Integration of Environments" principle in osmotic computing and how it translates to operational advantages.

Figure 1. Key principles of osmotic computing

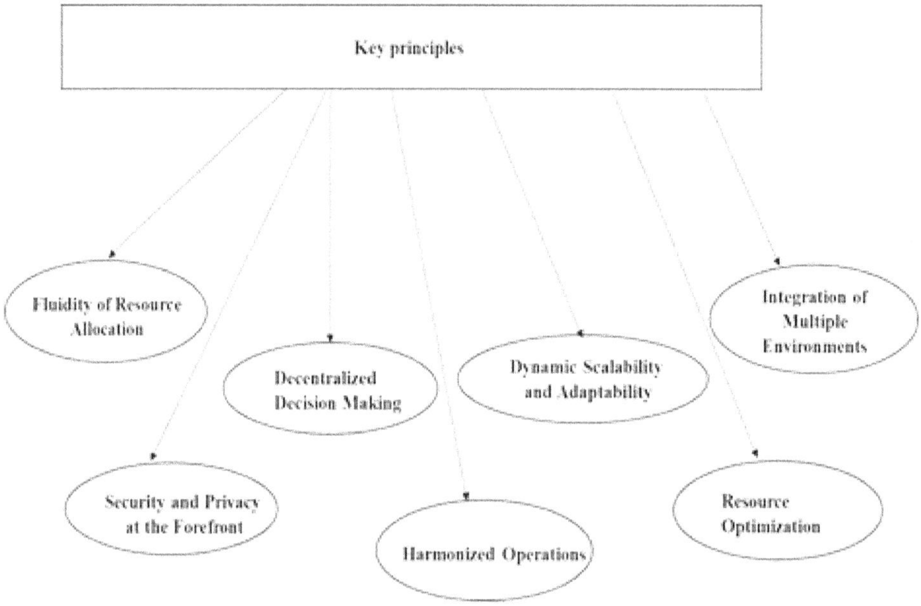

4. TRANSITION FROM THEORY TO IMPLEMENTATION

Fog computing presents a decentralized approach, providing services similar to cloud computing but closer to the network's edge. This ensures reduced latency and increased bandwidth, making it suitable for various IoT application contexts. For tapping into the full potential of this computational model, there's a need for scheduling methods and algorithms that are not only scalable and adaptable but also precise. Such mechanisms should efficiently account for the changing needs of users, specifics of IoT applications, environmental conditions, and optimization goals. The authors have (Goudarzi, M., et al., 2022) outlined a comprehensive review of recent studies related to scheduling IoT applications within the realm of Fog computing. Through their unique classification system, they have scrutinized existing literature, highlighted areas that need further investigation, and suggested potential avenues for future research.

The journey of osmotic computing from its theoretical foundations to real-world implementations has been marked by both challenges and successes. This transition is pivotal to assess the practical implications and effectiveness of this computational paradigm.

- Early Conceptions (Carnevale, L. et al., 2019)

Table 1. Description and operational relevance of osmotic computing principles

Principle	Description	Operational Relevance
Fluidity of Resource Allocation	Inspired by biological osmosis, it ensures balanced distribution and seamless migration of tasks between edge and cloud.	Ensures tasks are executed in environments most suited for them, considering factors like latency and data proximity.
Decentralized Decision Making	Promotes decision-making at the edge, allowing tasks and processes to be executed close to the data source.	Enhances system responsiveness, especially crucial for real-time processing scenarios.
dynamic Scalability and Adaptability	Systems can dynamically scale resources based on workload, ensuring optimal utilization of both edge and cloud.	Provides adaptability during peak times and data-intensive operations, ensuring cost and energy efficiency.
Integration of Multiple Environments	Views edge and cloud as integrated components of a larger ecosystem, harmoniously shifting tasks between the two based on various parameters.	Applications can leverage both the computational power of the cloud and the low latency advantages of the edge.
Security and Privacy at the Forefront	By processing data closer to its source, better data privacy is achieved. Only necessary information is sent to the cloud.	Offers a framework where data exposure is minimized, addressing the challenges of security in an increasingly interconnected world.
Harmonized Operations	Osmotic computing doesn't prioritize either the edge or the cloud exclusively. Instead, it seeks a harmonized operation between the two.	Allows for a balanced computational approach, where tasks can shift between environments based on need, ensuring optimal performance.
Task Fluidity	Tasks and services are not bound rigidly to one environment. They fluidly transition between edge and cloud depending on real-time requirements.	Enables dynamic response to changing conditions, such as network congestion, peak load times, or specific latency requirements.
Resource Optimization	Resources from both edge and cloud environments are utilized in an integrated manner to ensure efficient processing and minimal wastage.	Prevents resource underutilization or over allocation, leading to energy and cost savings.
Unified Management Framework	Osmotic computing provides a unified framework where both edge devices and cloud servers are managed as part of a cohesive ecosystem.	Simplifies administration, monitoring, and management tasks, ensuring seamless operation across diverse hardware and infrastructure.
Interoperability and Compatibility	Prioritizes creating a system where different devices, platforms, and cloud solutions can interact and work together without friction.	Reduces challenges and complexities associated with integrating diverse technologies, allowing for more flexibility in designing and deploying solutions.

 - The theoretical conception of osmotic computing was rooted in addressing the inefficiencies of traditional cloud-centric models, especially with the surge in IoT devices. Inspired by the biological osmosis process, the idea was to balance the computational load between the cloud and the edge dynamically.
- Challenges in Transition:
  - Technical Limitations: Implementing a fluid model of task distribution in real-world environments introduced complexities. Addressing the heterogeneous nature of edge devices, their varying computational capabilities, and the inherent instability of some edge environments posed challenges.
  - Security Concerns: As data processing became more decentralized, ensuring data security and integrity across various points became a considerable concern.
  - Interoperability: Ensuring seamless task migration and interoperability among diverse edge devices and cloud platforms was another hurdle.
- Practical Implementations:
  - Despite challenges, various sectors began to see the benefits of osmotic computing. Smart cities started leveraging it for traffic management, energy consumption optimization, and infrastructure monitoring. Healthcare saw applications in real-time patient monitoring, with data processed immediately at the edge for timely interventions.
- Learning from Implementations:
  - Real-world applications offered feedback loops. Successes highlighted the strengths of osmotic computing, such as reduced latency and bandwidth efficiency. On the other hand, challenges faced during implementations provided insights into areas needing refinement.
- The Feedback Loop:
  - As osmotic computing found its way into practical applications, the feedback from these real-world scenarios began to inform and refine the theory. This iterative process ensures that osmotic computing remains adaptable, evolving based on actual needs and challenges.

The transition of osmotic computing from theory to practice is emblematic of the trajectory many technological paradigms undergo. The iterative process of theory, implementation, feedback, and refinement ensures that osmotic computing remains poised to address the future challenges of an increasingly interconnected digital landscape. The authors (Kumari, N., et al., 2022) commence by delving into the concept of fog computing and the nuances of the task offloading procedure. They explore multiple factors instrumental in decision-making related to task

Figure 2. Osmatic in other paradigms

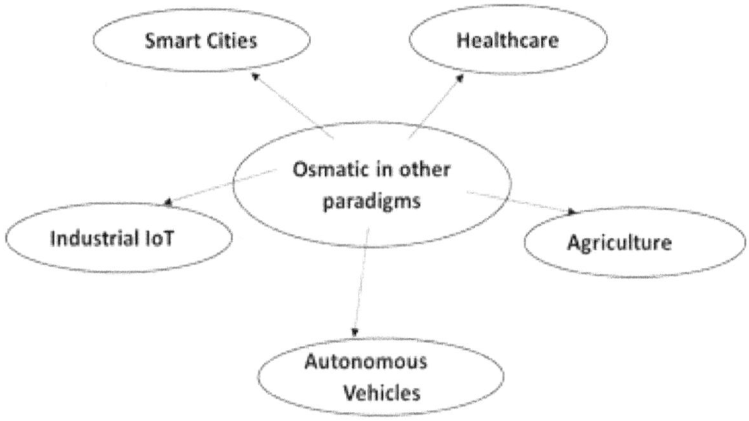

offloading and review various surveys on the topic. An entire section is devoted to a comprehensive review of offloading objectives, complete with examples. They also discuss numerous optimization techniques employed in task offloading. The concluding segment focuses on the challenges and prospective trajectories in fog computing. This survey is instrumental for readers, offering insights into optimization in task offloading and equipping them with a structured approach to designing offloading strategies with distinct goals.

5. COMPARISON WITH OTHER PARADIGMS

Healthcare and smart cites: The authors reviewed (Kamruzzaman, M.et al., 2022) that storage plays a vital role in enabling healthcare providers to maintain data interoperability. Furthermore, they assert that fog computing has emerged as a catalyst for enhancing efficiency in the healthcare sector. Fog computing empowers care providers to integrate cost-effective remote monitoring with swift operations and reduced latency (Ahuja, K., et al., 2021). Developing Smart Cities Using Internet of Things.

Agriculture: A predominant challenge in agriculture involves cultivating and delivering farm (Shenoy, J., & Pingle, Y., 2016) produce to the final consumers at optimal prices and top quality. Globally, roughly 50% of farm products don't make it to the end consumers because of waste and less-than-ideal pricing. The authors present a solution that leverages IoT to cut down transportation costs, forecast prices based on historical data analytics and current market trends, and minimize intermediaries between the farmer and the end user.

Figure 3. General vehicular environment - urban scenario
Source: Feroz, B., et al. (2021)

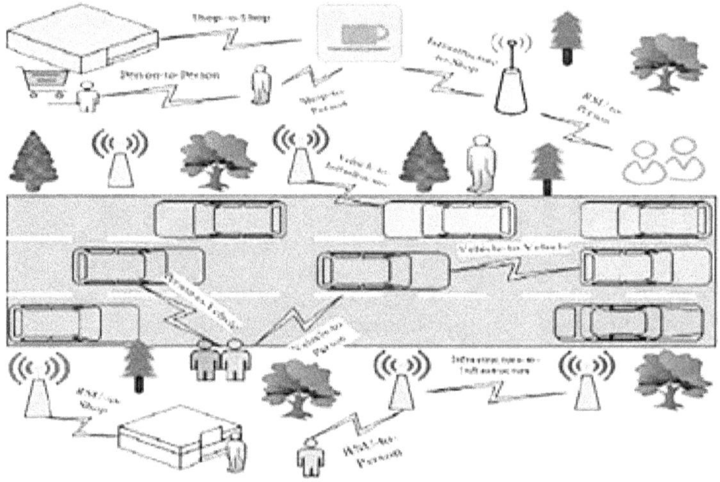

Indusrial IOT: Software has evolved to play a pivotal role in manufacturing and company-wide systems. The advent of internet connectivity has revolutionized monitoring and control protocols. Additionally, the adoption of public standards and personal computing devices (like PCs, tablets, and smartphones) has delivered substantial advantages for end-users and manufacturers alike. This evolution birthed the concept of Industry 4.0, which integrates the Internet of Things (IoT) into industrial practices. The authors (Ungurean et al., 2014) delve into an IoT framework that relies on OPC.NET specifications, applicable in both industrial settings and smart building environments.

Autonomous vehicles:

The authors introduced an advanced protocol tailored for scenarios involving connected and autonomous vehicles (Feroz, B., et al., 2021) in Intelligent Transportation Systems (ITS). This design aims to swiftly provide emergency services, thereby aiming to lower mortality rates from accidents. The protocol seamlessly communicates with all essential entities during emergencies, ensuring uninterrupted traffic flow to expedite ambulance arrivals. Additionally, it effectively curbs excessive message broadcasts across the network for tasks where delays can be detrimental. When evaluated on metrics such as channel collision, average packet delay, packet loss, and routing overhead, this protocol showcases superior performance over earlier protocols like Emergency Message Dissemination for Vehicular (EMDV), Contention Based Broadcasting (CBB), and Particle Swarm Optimization Contention-based Broadcast (PCBB).

6. POTENTIAL AND FUTURE DIRECTIONS

Osmotic Computing is a new methodology that focuses primarily on the automatic distribution of microservices across cloud and edge settings. The term “osmotic” is used metaphorically to indicate the natural flow of these microservices between the two ecosystems, which depends on the current conditions, similar to how osmosis works in biology.

- Potential of Osmotic Computing

Efficiency: Osmotic computing can be more energy and bandwidth efficient. It reduces the amount of data that needs to be sent to the cloud, saving both energy and bandwidth.

Latency Reduction (Goudarzi, M et al., 2022): Critical for applications like autonomous vehicles, healthcare, and industrial automation, where decisions need to be made in real-time.

Flexibility: Automatically deploying tasks based on the local environment and current conditions ensures that the system can adjust as necessary without manual intervention.

Enhanced Privacy and Security: Data can be processed locally, reducing the amount of raw data that needs to be sent to the cloud, which can help with data protection concerns.

- Future Directions in Osmotic Computing

Advanced Algorithms: (Ebneyousef, S., et al., 2023): The development of more sophisticated algorithms to determine where and when to deploy services, considering factors like power consumption, available resources, and network conditions.

Interoperability Standards: As osmotic computing integrates various devices and platforms, establishing robust interoperability standards will be crucial.

Security and Trust Protocols (Sicari, S., et al., 2022): Insights into security and privacy towards fog computing Addressing the security and trust concerns when shifting between edge devices and the cloud.

Dynamic Resource Allocation (Tran-Dang et al., 2022): Mechanisms to allocate and reallocate resources in real-time as conditions change, ensuring the most efficient use of the infrastructure.

Integration with 5G and Beyond: The rise of 5G and subsequent generations of mobile technology offer enhanced bandwidth and lower latencies. Osmotic computing can benefit from these improvements, allowing even better decision-making about where to deploy microservices.

Application Development Frameworks (Villari, et al., 2016): Tools and frameworks specifically designed for osmotic computing, assisting developers in creating applications that make the most of this new paradigm.

Holistic Management Solutions: As osmotic computing environments can be highly dynamic, tools for managing, monitoring, and maintaining these environments will be crucial.

Hardware Innovations: New types of devices designed specifically for osmotic computing. These devices might optimize for tasks like data processing at the edge or offer enhanced connectivity options.

7. CONCLUSION

The thorough assessment emphasizes the promise of osmotic computing in tackling urgent issues in present computational models, such as latency, bandwidth use, and energy efficiency. As the volume of data we generate grows dramatically, so does the need for real-time processing and decision-making. Osmotic computing presents a framework that adheres to these requirements, stressing proximity-based processing, automatic task distribution, and resource judiciousness. However, the path from theoretical frameworks to actual application is fraught with difficulties. Key concerns to be solved include interoperability, dynamic resource allocation, and the implementation of security mechanisms. Furthermore, to properly negotiate the subtleties of this hybrid paradigm, there is an inherent requirement for holistic management solutions, cutting-edge hardware, and powerful algorithms.

To summarize, osmotic computing, while yet in its infancy, has sown the seeds of a computational revolution. The integration of theory and practice examined in this review reveals a horizon rich in prospects and problems, urging the global tech community to join forces and usher in a new era of distributed computing.

REFERENCES

Ahuja, K., Gour, S., & Vaishnav, K. (2021). Developing Smart Cities Using Internet of Things. *International Journal of Engineering Trends and Applications*, *8*(4), 15–19.

Almaiah, M. A., & Alkdour, T. (2023). Securing Fog Computing Through Consortium Blockchain Integration: The Proof of Enhanced Concept (PoEC) Approach. In Recent Advancements in Multimedia Data Processing and Security: Issues, Challenges, and Techniques (pp. 107-140). IGI Global.

Almazroi, A. A., Aldhahri, E. A., Al-Shareeda, M. A., & Manickam, S. (2023). ECA-VFog: An efficient certificateless authentication scheme for 5G-assisted vehicular fog computing. *PLoS One*, *18*(6), e0287291. doi:10.1371/journal.pone.0287291 PMID:37352258

Alwasel, K., Jha, D. N., Habeeb, F., Demirbaga, U., Rana, O., Baker, T., Dustdar, S., Villari, M., James, P., Solaiman, E., & Ranjan, R. (2021). IoTSim-Osmosis: A framework for modeling and simulating IoT applications over an edge-cloud continuum. *Journal of Systems Architecture*, *116*, 101956. doi:10.1016/j.sysarc.2020.101956

Arif, A. M., Hamad, A. M., & Mansour, M. M. (2023). Internet of (Healthcare) Things Based Monitoring for COVID-19+ Quarantine/Isolation Subjects Using Biomedical Sensors, A Lesson from the Recent Pandemic, and an Approach to the Future. *Journal of Electronics, Electromedical Engineering, and Medical Informatics*, *5*(1), 1–12. doi:10.35882/jeeemi.v5i1.267

Carnevale, L., Celesti, A., Galletta, A., Dustdar, S., & Villari, M. (2019). Osmotic computing as a distributed multi-agent system: The body area network scenario. *Internet of Things : Engineering Cyber Physical Human Systems*, *5*, 130–139. doi:10.1016/j.iot.2019.01.001

Ebneyousef, S., & Shirmarz, A. (2023). A taxonomy of load balancing algorithms and approaches in fog computing: A survey. *Cluster Computing*, *26*(5), 1–22. doi:10.1007/s10586-023-03982-3

Feroz, B., Mehmood, A., Maryam, H., Zeadally, S., Maple, C., & Shah, M. A. (2021). Vehicle-life interaction in fog-enabled smart connected and autonomous vehicles. *IEEE Access : Practical Innovations, Open Solutions*, *9*, 7402–7420. doi:10.1109/ACCESS.2020.3049110

Ghobaei-Arani, M., & Shahidinejad, A. (2022). A cost-efficient IoT service placement approach using whale optimization algorithm in fog computing environment. *Expert Systems with Applications*, *200*, 117012. doi:10.1016/j.eswa.2022.117012

Goudarzi, M., Palaniswami, M., & Buyya, R. (2022). Scheduling IoT applications in edge and fog computing environments: A taxonomy and future directions. *ACM Computing Surveys*, *55*(7), 1–41. doi:10.1145/3544836

Ilyas, A., Alatawi, M. N., Hamid, Y., Mahfooz, S., Zada, I., Gohar, N., & Shah, M. A. (2022). Software architecture for pervasive critical health monitoring system using fog computing. *Journal of Cloud Computing (Heidelberg, Germany)*, *11*(1), 84. doi:10.1186/s13677-022-00371-w PMID:36465318

Kalajdjieski, J., Stojkoska, B. R., & Trivodaliev, K. (2020, November). IoT based framework for air pollution monitoring in smart cities. In *2020 28th Telecommunications Forum (TELFOR)* (pp. 1-4). IEEE. 10.1109/TELFOR51502.2020.9306531

Kamruzzaman, M. M., Yan, B., Sarker, M. N. I., Alruwaili, O., Wu, M., & Alrashdi, I. (2022). Blockchain and fog computing in IoT-driven healthcare services for smart cities. *Journal of Healthcare Engineering*, *2022*, 2022. doi:10.1155/2022/9957888 PMID:35126961

Kaushik, K. (2023). Smart Agriculture Applications Using Cloud and IoT. *Convergence of Cloud with AI for Big Data Analytics: Foundations and Innovation*, 89-105.

Kochovski, P., Gec, S., Stankovski, V., Bajec, M., & Drobintsev, P. D. (2019). Trust management in a blockchain based fog computing platform with trustless smart oracles. *Future Generation Computer Systems*, *101*, 747–759. doi:10.1016/j.future.2019.07.030

Kumari, N., Yadav, A., & Jana, P. K. (2022). Task offloading in fog computing: A survey of algorithms and optimization techniques. *Computer Networks*, *214*, 109137. doi:10.1016/j.comnet.2022.109137

Mohammed, B. A., Al-Shareeda, M. A., Manickam, S., Al-Mekhlafi, Z. G., Alreshidi, A., Alazmi, M., Alshudukhi, J. S., & Alsaffar, M. (2023). FC-PA: Fog computing-based pseudonym authentication scheme in 5G-enabled vehicular networks. *IEEE Access : Practical Innovations, Open Solutions*, *11*, 18571–18581. doi:10.1109/ACCESS.2023.3247222

Morabito, G., Sicari, C., Ruggeri, A., Celesti, A., & Carnevale, L. (2023). Secure-by-design serverless workflows on the Edge–Cloud Continuum through the Osmotic Computing paradigm. *Internet of Things : Engineering Cyber Physical Human Systems*, *22*, 100737. doi:10.1016/j.iot.2023.100737

Pallewatta, S., Kostakos, V., & Buyya, R. (2022). QoS-aware placement of microservices-based IoT applications in Fog computing environments. *Future Generation Computer Systems*, *131*, 121–136. doi:10.1016/j.future.2022.01.012

Pallewatta, S., Kostakos, V., & Buyya, R. (2023). Placement of Microservices-based IoT Applications in Fog Computing: A Taxonomy and Future Directions. *ACM Computing Surveys*, *55*(14s), 1–43. doi:10.1145/3592598

Rani, S., & Srivastava, G. (2024). Secure hierarchical fog computing-based architecture for industry 5.0 using an attribute-based encryption scheme. *Expert Systems with Applications*, *235*, 121180. doi:10.1016/j.eswa.2023.121180

Ren, J., Zhang, D., He, S., Zhang, Y., & Li, T. (2019). A survey on end-edge-cloud orchestrated network computing paradigms: Transparent computing, mobile edge computing, fog computing, and cloudlet. *ACM Computing Surveys*, *52*(6), 1–36. doi:10.1145/3362031

Seo, J. M., Yoo, H., Yun, K., Kim, H., & Choi, S. I. (2018, September). Behavior recognition of a person in a daily video using joint position information. In *2018 IEEE First International Conference on Artificial Intelligence and Knowledge Engineering (AIKE)* (pp. 172-174). IEEE. 10.1109/AIKE.2018.00040

Shenoy, J., & Pingle, Y. (2016, March). IOT in agriculture. In *2016 3rd International Conference on Computing for Sustainable Global Development (INDIACom)* (pp. 1456-1458). IEEE.

Shruthi, G., Mundada, M. R., Supreeth, S., & Gardiner, B. (2023). Deep learning-based resource prediction and mutated leader algorithm enabled load balancing in fog computing. *International Journal of Computer Networks and Information Security, 15*(4), 84-95.

Sicari, S., Rizzardi, A., & Coen-Porisini, A. (2022). Insights into security and privacy towards fog computing evolution. *Computers & Security*, *120*, 102822. doi:10.1016/j.cose.2022.102822

Talaat, F. M. (2022). Effective prediction and resource allocation method (EPRAM) in fog computing environment for smart healthcare system. *Multimedia Tools and Applications*, *81*(6), 8235–8258. doi:10.1007/s11042-022-12223-5

Tran-Dang, H., Bhardwaj, S., Rahim, T., Musaddiq, A., & Kim, D. S. (2022). Reinforcement learning based resource management for fog computing environment: Literature review, challenges, and open issues. *Journal of Communications and Networks (Seoul)*, *24*(1), 83–98. doi:10.23919/JCN.2021.000041

Ungurean, I., Gaitan, N. C., & Gaitan, V. G. (2014, May). An IoT architecture for things from industrial environment. In *2014 10th International Conference on Communications (COMM)* (pp. 1-4). IEEE. 10.1109/ICComm.2014.6866713

Villari, M., Fazio, M., Dustdar, S., Rana, O., Jha, D. N., & Ranjan, R. (2019). Osmosis: The osmotic computing platform for microelements in the cloud, edge, and internet of things. *Computer*, *52*(8), 14–26. doi:10.1109/MC.2018.2888767

Villari, M., Fazio, M., Dustdar, S., Rana, O., & Ranjan, R. (2016). Osmotic computing: A new paradigm for edge/cloud integration. *IEEE Cloud Computing*, *3*(6), 76–83. doi:10.1109/MCC.2016.124

Chapter 6
Speech Emotion Recognition With Osmotic Computing

T. Manoj Praphakar
Sri Shakthi Institute of Engineering and Technology, India

D. S. Dhenu
Sri Shakthi Institute of Engineering and Technology, India

D. Gavash
Sri Shakthi Institute of Engineering and Technology, India

M. Mega Shree
Sri Shakthi Institute of Engineering and Technology, India

S. Divesh
Sri Shakthi Institute of Engineering and Technology, India

ABSTRACT

Speech emotion recognition is a critical component of human-computer interaction and affective computing. This chapter presents a comprehensive study on the application of deep learning techniques for the task of speech emotion recognition. Emotions conveyed through speech play a crucial role in understanding human behavior and are essential in various domains, including human-robot interaction, customer service, and mental health assessment. This chapter also investigates the impact of different feature extraction methods and data pre-processing techniques on the recognition accuracy. Basically, RNN algorithm is used for speech emotion recognition to identify the emotion through audio, but this chapter will accomplish this with CNN algorithm because the time complexity of RNN algorithm is high and to analyze the audio takes more time where CNN will be converted into spectrograms from each dimension of emotions, which will be recognized by augmenting it. And finally, it is used in the medical field, security, and surveillance management.

DOI: 10.4018/979-8-3693-1694-8.ch006

INTRODUCTION

Speech of the human beings is most important in our daily lives to make other people to understand about the emotions. As emotions play a very important role in our daily life because every human being has an emotion to make others to understand about their emotion. Emotions can be easily understood by humans but digital computers cannot understand the emotions easily (Chen et al., 2017; Hossain & Muhammad, 2019; Schuller, 2018). So, we use deep learning techniques to classify the emotions by the computer. These systems aim to improve the interaction with machines through facilitating direct voice engagement, foregoing the use of conventional devices for input. This approach seeks to simplify the comprehension of verbal content and facilitates more effortless response from human listeners. Identifying the emotional state of individual is a unique endeavor and can serve as a benchmark for any emotion recognition model. It encompasses a range of emotions including anger, boredom, disgust, surprise, fear, joy, happiness, neutrality, and sadness. Deep Learning approaches for the Sentiment and Emotion Recognition (SER) offers numerous benefits compared to the conventional methods. These advantages include the abilities to discern the intricate structures and the features without requiring any manual extraction and tuning. The speech emotion recognition is detected by using exploring deep learning architectures like Convolution Neural Networks (CNNs), Recurrent Neural Networks (RNNs) and Long Short-Term Memory (LSTM) within the domain of speech emotion recognition (SER) highlighting the applications of advanced learning methods. Has ushered in a new era of sophistication and accuracy. One of the prominent deep learning models is employed for this purpose is Convolution Neural Network (CNN) stands out of its proficiency in recognizing the spatial patterns and has proved the effective in capturing intricate features within speech signals (Chen et al., 2017). By leveraging the hierarchical learning capabilities of CNNs, the model's ability to discern complex structures in audio data without the need for explicit manual feature extraction improves the efficiency of emotion classification. Complementing CNNs are Recurrent Neural Networks (RNNs), which bring a temporal aspect to emotion recognition. RNNs are capable of capturing the sequential dependencies in speech data due to their recurrent connections, which are often associated with emotions unfolding over a time. This makes them well-suited for tasks where the understanding context and progression of emotions is crucial. Furthermore, Long Short-Term Memory (LSTM) networks, a distinctive variant of recurrent neural network, offers an advantage of mitigating and vanishing the gradient problem and enables the model to retain the information over a long time spans (Lane & Georgiev, 2015). The incorporation of these deep learning models in SER not only enhances the accuracy but also eliminates the need of manual fine-tuning features, making the process more automated and adaptable to diverse the datasets. The ability of these models is to discern subtle nuances in speech which will enables the classification of the wide range of emotions, including anger, boredom, disgust, surprise, fear, joy, happiness, neutral, and sadness. This versatility makes the deep learning based SER systems invaluable for the applications ranging from human-computer interaction to sentiment analysis in various fields. As technology continues to become advanced, the synergy between deep learning techniques and emotion recognition in speech holds an great promise which paves the way for more natural and nuanced interactions between humans and machines. These developments not only contribute to the field of artificial intelligence but also to the improvement of the systems that are designed to comprehend and reacts to the intricate array of human emotions expressed through the language spoken (Lane & Georgiev, 2015).

LITERATURE SURVEY

In recent times, there has been a surge in interest in researching emotional speech signals within human-machine interfaces, attributed to the increased computational capabilities now accessible. Numerous systems have been put forth in scholarly works aiming to discern emotional states through speech. The primary challenges in speech emotion recognition systems revolve around the judicious selection of feature sets, the formulation of effective classification methods, and the creation of pertinent datasets. This manuscript critically examines existing approaches in speech emotion recognition, focusing on three evaluative parameters: the chosen feature set, feature classification methods, and their precise utilization. B. W. Schuller et. al. (Schuller, 2018) proposed A setup was established to collect audio samples encompassing Short-Term Energy (STE), Pitch, and MFCC coefficients representing emotions of frustration, happiness, and sadness. The audio samples were sourced from freely available North American English datasets. Served as expression and as feedback was used to record natural speech. Thus, only three emotions i.e., anger, happiness and sadness were recognized. In the year of 2018, he tested the accuracy and measured it and also, he improved the accuracy. They also identified the speaker's detailed features, such as sound, energy, pitch. Accuracy he tested was 65.36%. The complete Ryerson Audio-Visual Database of Emotional Speech and Song (RAVDESS) dataset undergoes a manual partitioning into training and testing sets. Feature vectors serve as input for the multi-class Support Vector Machine (SVM), generating a distinct model for each emotion. Hossain et al. (Hossain & Muhammad, 2019). In the year of 2019, he recognized the accuracy and published the paper the investigation into emotion recognition spans various studies, each contributing unique methodologies and achievements. In a study by M. Chen et al. (Chen et al., 2017), the Ryerson

Audio-Visual Database of Emotional Speech and Song (RAVDESS) dataset was utilized, employing CNN and DBN with multiple layers, including LSTM, achieving notable accuracies of 91.6% and 92.9%. The model's adaptability to multimodal emotion recognition was highlighted. N. D. Lane et al. (Lane & Georgiev, 2015), in 2015, focused on the IEMOCAP database, employing 2D CNN with phoneme data input. The achieved accuracy in Speech Emotion Recognition (SER) was 4% above average, showcasing potential applications beyond emotion recognition, such as conversational chat bots. J. G. Razuri et al. (Razuri, Sundgren, Rahmani, Moran, Bonet, & Lars-son, 2015), also in 2015, employed RNN and CNN on the IEMOCAP database, combining them into an RNN-CNN model for the I Club robot. The model demonstrated an impressive 83.2% accuracy and hinted at future work involving generative models for real-time data input D. Le et al. (Le & Provost, 2013), in the same year, utilized the Emotes (EMO-Tional Sensitivity Assistance System for people with disabilities) dataset, employing a combination of CNN and RNN with ResNet. Although achieving 45.12% improvement dataset accuracy and 42.27% on the test dataset, the study proposed future enhancements in feature learning and A. B. Nassif Lee et al. (Nassif et al., 2019), in 2019, focused on the CMU-MOSEI dataset, employing LSTM-based CNN. The proposed model demonstrated an impressive 83.11% accuracy in SER, with potential future exploration in multi-modality testing S. Sahu et al., utilizing OpenSmile features on the IEMOCAP database, employed adversarial auto-encoders (AAE), achieving an accuracy with Unweighted Average Recall (UAR) of approximately 57.88%. The study hinted at potential extensions to recognize additional emotions. Lastly, J. G. Razuri et al. (Razuri, Sundgren, Rahmani, Moran, Bonet, & Lars-son, 2015), in 2015, explored the CAS emotional speech database, employing feature fusion with SVM and Deep Belief Network (DBN) for SER. DBN provided a remarkable accuracy of 94.6%, outperforming SVM at 84.54%. Future directions may involve training DBN with a combination of lexical and audio features.

DEEP LEARNING

Within machine learning deep learning sets itself as a part of specialized domain that leverages the capabilities of artificial neural networks to address the complex problems often achieving the state of the art performance levels (Lane & Georgiev, 2015; Razuri, Sundgren, Rahmani, Moran, Bonet, & Lars-son, 2015). A distinctive capability of deep learning lies in its seamless conversion of images and audio into spectrograms a feat often unattainable by the conventional machine learning algorithms. The ability to automatically generate and process spectrograms signifies a technological leap and underscores the efficiency and versatility of deep learning in handling diverse types of data. Moreover deep learning models exhibit a remarkable trait in their capacity to analyze the data continuously providing a dynamic and adaptive approach for the information processing. This inherent flexibility allows these models to evolve and improve over a time ensuring that they effectively address the evolving intricacies of complex tasks. This adaptability is particularly crucial in the real time of speech and image recognition where frequencies and variations demand a sophisticated understanding that the deep learning models are excel at delivering. The impact of deep learning extends across a myriad of industries leaving an indelible mark on fields such as healthcare where diagnostic accuracy has been augmented through image recognition applications, finance with enhanced fraud detection systems retail through improved customer experience and personalized recommendations, logistics an optimizing supply chain operations and robotics enabling machines to perceive and respond to their environments more intelligently (Razuri, Sundgren, Rahmani, Moran, Bonet, & Lars-son, 2015). The transformative influence of deep learning underscores its pivotal role in reshaping how we approach addressing the challenges and making the decisions in the world are characterized by growing the complexity and reliance on data.

CNN

A convolution neural network is a grid topology is commonly used to analyze the given input. It is also called a convolution network (Chen et al., 2017; Lane & Georgiev, 2015; Le & Provost, 2013; Razuri, Sundgren, Rahmani, Moran, Bonet, & Lars-son, 2015). Convolution neural networks detects and classifies the objects in image such as spectrograms. A spectrogram visually illustrates how the frequency components of a signal vary over a time. Typical CNN architecture has many layers such as Convolution layers which use filters to extract features from the input image. Each filter is a small matrix of weights placed on the image to detect the certain features. Pooling layers: These layers reduce the dimensionality of feature maps through down sampling. This helps to control the size of the mesh and prevents over fitting. Activation layers introduce nonlinearity into the network using nonlinear activation function such as rectified linear units (ReLU) (Nassif et al., 2019). Final layers utilize the extracted features for a conclusive classification or additional processing. The CNN training process includes the following steps: Data preparation: Prepare the input data by preprocessing it such as normalizing the pixel values and resizing the image. Model definition define the CNN architecture and specify the number of layers, filter size, and hyperparameters. Loss of calculation calculates a function measuring the difference between estimated and actual output. Back propagation: Use back propagation to calculate the slope of the loss function based on the network parameters. Parameter update: Use an optimized method to update the parameters such as stochastic gradient descent (SGD) (Nassif et al., 2019; Razuri, Sundgren, Rahmani, Moran, Bonet, & Lars-son, 2015). Evaluation: The effectiveness of the training model was evaluated based on separate evidence sets. In addition to their widespread use in image analysis CNN has demonstrated remarkable effectiveness in various applications due to their grid like input processing. One notable application is the natural language processing where CNN's have proven adept at sentiment analysis and text classification tasks. By treating words or characters as grid like structures CNN's can capture local patterns and dependencies making them versatile tools for understanding sequential data. The distinctive architecture of a CNN with its convolution layers, pooling layers, activation layers and fully connected layers contribute to its success in feature extraction and hierarchical representation learning (Scherer, 2005). The convolution layers play a pivotal role in identifying critical features through filter operations. In contrast, pooling layers contribute to down-sampling by reducing the dimensionality of feature maps and enhancing computational efficiency. Activation layers introduce nonlinearity enabling the network to model complex relationships within the data. Beyond static image recognition CNN's have also demonstrated prowess in dynamic tasks such as video analysis. They excel in discerning temporal patterns and spatial relationships within consecutive frames, enabling applications like action recognition and scene understanding (Scherer, 2005). This adaptability showcases CNN's ability to extend its utility beyond still images making it a valuable tool in multimedia analytics. As outlined in the original description the training process of a CNN underscores the

Figure 1. Architecture of convolution neural network (Gupta et al., 2020)

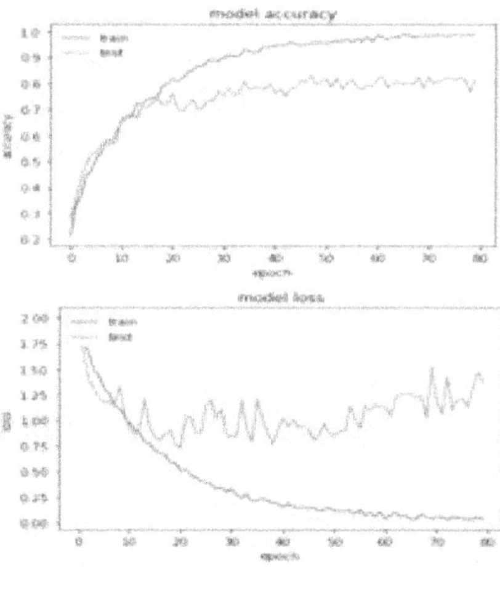

	precision	recall	f1-score	support
angry	0.94	0.77	0.85	39
calm	0.85	0.92	0.89	38
disgust	0.78	0.86	0.82	37
fearful	0.82	0.74	0.78	38
happy	0.85	0.80	0.82	35
neutral	0.76	0.79	0.78	24
sad	0.63	0.76	0.69	38
surprised	0.92	0.85	0.88	39
accuracy			0.81	288
macro avg	0.82	0.81	0.81	288
weighted avg	0.82	0.81	0.81	288

importance of meticulous data preparation, thoughtful model definition, and rigorous evaluation. As deep learning continues to evolve researchers and practitioners are exploring the ways to enhance the CNN architectures further incorporating attention mechanisms, transfer learning and other innovations to push the boundaries of what these networks can achieve. The ongoing advancements in CNN's refine their performance in existing domains and open doors to novel applications promising a future where these networks continue to play a central role in advancing artificial intelligence across the diverse domains (Razuri, Sundgren, Rahmani, Moran, Bonet, & Lars-son, 2015; Scherer, 2005).

EDA (Evolutionary Data Analysis)

EDA is to analyze the data which tells the nature of the data and also provides valuable information (Lalitha, Madhavan, Bhushan, & Saketh, 2014). EDA is used to uncover and address data quality issues such as rectifying missing entries, eliminating duplicates, correcting inaccuracies, identifying anomalies and ensuring proper data types. EDA generally conveys the data summary. EDA will analyze the audio files that contain 1440 files of 24 actors where 12 audios are of men and the remaining 12 are of women. The audio signal will be analyzed based on frequency amplitude, latitude, and duration. After analysis, the audio will be normalized and the quality of the audio will be checked. The emotions will be classified and plotted in a waveform visualization which helps to understand the characteristics of emotions (Balomenos et al., 2001; Cowie et al., n.d.; Lalitha, Madhavan, Bhushan, & Saketh, 2014). The emotions that have been identified will be manifested in time and frequency. The wave plots will not directly identify the emotion through the patterns. The audio files can be identified as the specific emotion. In the wave plot the x-axis denotes time and the y-axis denotes amplitude. Time is an essential factor in analyzing the audio signals which gives the structure of the waveform. The y-axis of amplitude indicating the signal's strength or loudness. Through the wave plot we can identify the structure or pattern. The anomalies like noise, air and background noise will be identified in the wave plot in the EDA (Balomenos et al., 2001; Batliner et al., 2011; Cowie et al., n.d.; Lalitha, Madhavan, Bhushan, & Saketh, 2014). To waveform visualization another crucial aspect of exploratory data analysis (EDA) for audio files involves extracting spectrogram features. Spectrograms provide a detailed representation of the frequency content of audio signals over time. By applying techniques such as Short Time Fourier Transform (STFT) the spectrogram unveils the distribution of energy across different frequency bands offering insights into the tonal characteristics of the audio. Analyzing the spectrogram can reveal patterns and variations that may not be immediately apparent in the waveform enriching the understanding of the audio's acoustic properties. Furthermore during the EDA process statistical metrics such as mean, median and standard deviation of the audio features can be computed to quantify the central tendency and variability within the dataset (Anagnostopoulos et al., 2015). This statistical analysis contributes to a more comprehensive understanding of the distribution and dispersion of vital audio characteristics aiding in identifying outliers or unusual patterns that may require further investigation. As part of the normalization process mentioned in the original paragraph techniques like z-score normalization or min-max scaling can be applied to standardize the amplitude levels across different audio files. Normalization ensures a consistent basis for comparison and analysis which is particularly important when dealing with diverse emotional expressions that may exhibit varying intensity levels. In addition to waveform and spectrogram visualizations, statistical summaries, and normalization, employing machine learning techniques for feature extraction and dimensionality reduction can enhance the efficiency of EDA (Anagnostopoulos et al., 2015). Utilizing techniques like Principal Component Analysis (PCA) or t-distributed Stochastic Neighbor embedding (t-SNE) allows for extracting crucial features and representing interrelationships among various emotions within a condensed dimensional framework. The insights gained from this comprehensive EDA aid in understanding the inherent characteristics of the audio dataset but also lay the groundwork for building robust emotion classification models. By addressing data quality issues normalizing audio signals and extracting meaningful features, the EDA process becomes a critical precursor to developing accurate and reliable

Figure 2. EDA wave plot and spectrogram

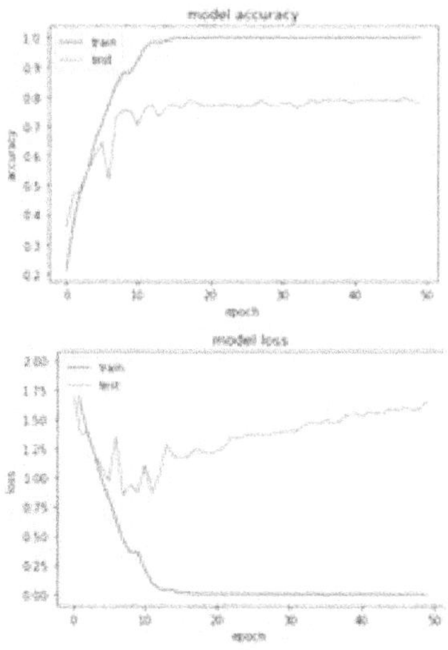

	precision	recall	f1-score	support
angry	0.82	0.79	0.81	39
calm	0.75	0.95	0.84	38
disgust	0.70	0.76	0.73	37
fearful	0.81	0.55	0.66	38
happy	0.86	0.86	0.86	35
neutral	0.82	0.75	0.78	24
sad	0.68	0.66	0.67	38
surprised	0.83	0.90	0.86	39
accuracy			0.78	288
macro avg	0.78	0.78	0.77	288
weighted avg	0.78	0.78	0.77	288

emotion recognition systems for diverse applications including human computer interaction and affective computing (Anagnostopoulos et al., 2015).

Baseline and Initial Model:

The baseline provides references for complex problems. It will be easily used to analyze the complex problem (Hu, 2008; Razuri, Sundgren, Rahmani, Moran, Bonet, & Lars-son, 2015). The initial model is a starting point to develop the model. The Initial model defines the initial architecture and chooses the activation functions, number of layers, neurons etc. In the baseline model the MFCC (Mel et al.) might be extracted from the speech signal. These signals may be fed into the SVM or decision trees to classify emotions from audio signals (Razuri, Sundgren, Rahmani, Moran, Bonet, & Lars-son, 2015). In the baseline model metrics such as accuracy, precision, recall and F1-score are computed. In the preliminary model an analysis of the speech data is conducted. It will be segmented and converted into spectrograms or frequencies and it will help handle the imbalanced dataset. The initial model will be used to validate the emotion of the audio signals. The x-axis will be considered as the Epoch which will be used to train the dataset. Each Epoch has one iteration where the model sees the entire training dataset undergone during training. Accuracy in the Y-axis will validate and predict the accurate emotion from the speech signal. The accuracy will be determined by the proportion of the correctly predicted samples to the overall size of the dataset. The accuracy is expected to be minimal as the model embarks on the learning process to discern patterns within the data (Hu, 2008).

The plot might show the fluctuations indicating the frequency of the speech. The feature engineering process plays a crucial role in developing an initial model for emotion recognition from speech signals. Beyond extracting MFCC's in the baseline model other relevant features such as spectral contrast, chrome features, and rhythm patterns can be explored to capture a more comprehensive representation of the emotional content in the audio. This diversification of features can contribute to a richer dataset for training and refining the model. To address the imbalanced dataset challenge strategic techniques like oversampling minority classes or under sampling majority classes can be applied during the data preprocessing phase in the initial model (Dimmita & Siddaiah, 2019). This ensures that the model is exposed to a balanced representation of different emotions preventing biases toward dominant classes and promoting more accurate emotion classification across the spectrum. In the visualization plotting additional metrics such as loss of functions alongside accuracy can offer a more nuanced understanding of the model's performance. The loss function graph provides insights into how well the model converges during the training which helps in identifying the potential over fitting or under fitting issues.

Moreover incorporating transfer learning from pre-trained models, such as using a pre-trained CNN for extracting features from spectrograms can expedite the training process and enhance the model's ability to discern complex patterns in speech data (Chen et al., 2016; Dimmita & Siddaiah, 2019; Hossain & Muhammad, 2019; Hu, 2008). Monitoring the learning curves can reveal necessary information about the model's convergence and generalization capabilities as the model iterates through epochs during training. Early stopping techniques can be implemented to prevent overtraining and achieve an optimal tradeoff between bias and variance in the model. In addition to traditional evaluation metrics like accuracy, precision, recall, and F1-score, exploring the confusion matrix gives a more detailed look at how well the model performs across different emotion classes. This can highlight specific areas where the model may need further refinement or where certain emotions might be more challenging to distinguish. The iterative nature of model development starts from a baseline and evolving through an initial model which allows for continuous refinement and improvement (Hu, 2008). Regularly updating the model architecture, experimenting with hyper parameters and incorporating advanced techniques are the understanding of the dataset depends on all contribute to build a more robust and effective emotion recognition model for diverse application (Dimmita & Siddaiah, 2019). Although loss is minimal between the train and test set the accuracy score is low (38%).

Figure 3. Baseline and initial models

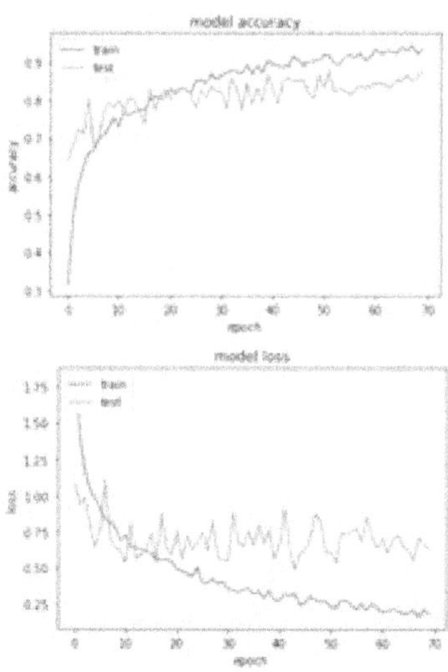

	precision	recall	f1-score	support
angry	0.95	0.95	0.95	39
calm	0.82	0.95	0.88	38
disgust	0.81	0.92	0.86	37
fearful	0.86	0.82	0.84	38
happy	0.92	0.94	0.93	35
neutral	0.81	0.88	0.84	24
sad	0.83	0.66	0.74	38
surprised	1.00	0.90	0.95	39
accuracy			0.88	288
macro avg	0.87	0.88	0.87	288
weighted avg	0.88	0.88	0.87	288

DATA AUGMENTATION

We can use methods to make the training data more diverse and robust. This involves artificially making the dataset larger by applying changes to the existing data. For speech samples here Noise Injection is used which introduces background noise or other environmental sounds to make the model more resilient to real world acoustic conditions. As part of the data augmentation process, a noise injection is the method that involves introducing background noise or ambient sounds into the speech samples (Lakkhanawannakun, 2019). The noise injection is for speech emotion recognition and the objective is to fortify the model against the challenges posed by real world acoustic conditions. This involves artificially integrating background noise or environmental sounds into the training dataset (Lakkhanawannakun, 2019). The model applies to diverse acoustic environments ensuring it can discern emotional cues in speech amidst varying audio settings. In real world noise scenarios during training process that the model becomes more robust and adaptable and better equipped to handle the inherent variability in acoustic conditions encountered in the practical applications. This method aims to enhance the model's capacity to recognize and classify emotions in speech accurately (Raghib et al., 2018). In addition to noise injection time stretching is another powerful data augmentation technique employed in speech emotion recognition. This technique involves in manipulating the temporal aspects of the speech signal either compressing or expanding the duration of the utterance. Time stretching introduces variability in the pacing of speech making the model more adapt at handling the different speaking rates and speech cadences. Exposing the model to a spectrum of temporal variations during training makes it more resilient to fluctuations in speech delivery commonly encountered in the real world scenarios. Furthermost pitch shifting is another valuable augmentation method that involves altering the pitches of the speech signal. This technique is particularly effective in addressing variations in vocal pitch and tonal nuances across speakers (Lakkhanawannakun, 2019; Raghib et al., 2018). The model can generalize its understanding of emotional expressions across a diverse range of voices and pitch registers by artificially introducing pitch variations during training. This proves instrumental in ensuring that the speech emotion recognition model remains accurate and reliable despite of the natural diversity in human speech characteristics. The combination of noise injection, time stretching and pitch shifting contributes to creating a training dataset that reflects the rich diversity of acoustic conditions encountered in real world settings. These augmentation techniques equip's the model with the adaptability required to effectively recognize and classify the emotions in speech across a broad spectrum of environmental and contextual challenges. In the study of recognizing emotions in speech using the intelligent ways to make more varied

Figure 4. Data augmentation

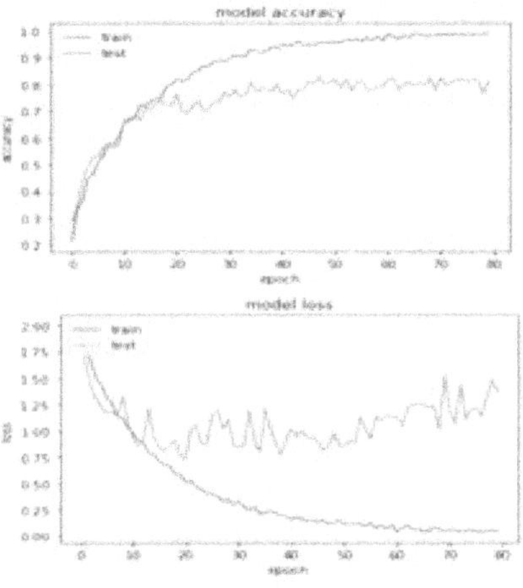

	precision	recall	f1-score	support
angry	0.94	0.77	0.85	39
calm	0.85	0.92	0.89	38
disgust	0.78	0.86	0.82	37
fearful	0.82	0.74	0.78	38
happy	0.85	0.80	0.82	35
neutral	0.76	0.79	0.78	24
sad	0.63	0.76	0.69	38
surprised	0.92	0.85	0.88	39
accuracy			0.81	288
macro avg	0.82	0.81	0.81	288
weighted avg	0.82	0.81	0.81	288

data becomes essential. This helps the models becomes more robust and work better in real life situations (Raghib et al., 2018). Achieved better accuracy score is 81%.

VGG16

A ready to use CNN with 16 layers, well-known for doing a great job on Image Net, a large image classification dataset. It captures intricate features from images at a higher abstraction level encompassing fundamental patterns such as edges, textures and shapes (Poorjam, 2019). A process where you leverage the pre-trained weights of VGG16 but adapt it to your specific task. Freezing the early convolution layers adding new layers at the end will specify to your task and training the entire network (including the frozen layers) on your smaller dataset. The VGG-16 model consists of 13 layers that do the convolution five layers that do max-pooling and three layers that are fully connected. These layers are organized into five groups (Poorjam, 2019). The CNN contains a max pooling layer which reduces the dimensionality spaces. This layer will convert the audio files into the spectrogram through the CNN network. These layers contain filters that will detect the emotions from the input spectrograms. The audio will be sent and will connect highly to the high-level feature which will quickly detect the emotion. The layers will function as the map which will map the audio to the generated emotion. The audio will be sent for every layer and there will be a mapping mechanism where the audio will be matched with the correct CNN spectrogram. Then at the final layer the classification will begin. The emotions will be classified and the audio will be mapped with the emotion and the accuracy will be predicted (Benkerzaz et al., 2019; Philipos, n.d.; Poorjam, 2019). The powerful pre-trained VGG16 model with fine-tuning its weights and adapting it for speech emotion recognition and transfer learning can further be enhanced by employing feature extraction and fine-tuning specific layers. Feature extraction involves utilizing the learned representations from intermediate layers of VGG16 that extracting these features and extracted them into a customized set of layers tailored to the nuances of speech emotion patterns. This process enables the model to capture more intricate and task-specific characteristics present in the audio data. Furthermore the application of transfer learning with VGG16 can be extended to explore other preprocessing technique like data augmentation (Philipos, n.d.). By artificially generating variations in the input spectrograms the model becomes more resilient to pitch, tone and cadence variations in different emotional expressions. This augmentation process contributes to a more robust and generalized model by improving its performance on diverse datasets. Additionally integrating attention mechanisms into the CNN structure can improve the model's concentration on essential parts of the spectrogram when categorizing emotions. Attention mechanisms enable the model to dynamically weigh on the importance of different temporal and frequency components allowing for more nuanced emotion detection. To address potential class imbalances in the dataset for the weighted loss functions or ensemble learning approaches can be explored (Philipos, n.d.). Weighted loss functions assign higher importance to the underrepresented classes during training that ensuring the model which learns to recognize emotions across all categories more effectively. As part of model evaluation exploring and analyzing the Receiver Operating Characteristic (ROC) curve and the Area under the Curve (AUC) metrics offers valuable insights into how the model balances between correctly identifying positives and incorrectly identifying negatives. This provides a thorough grasp of the model's ability to distinguish. Additionally performing the ablation studies by selectively deactivating specific layers or components of the model helps to uncover the impact of different architectural elements on the overall performance (Benkerzaz et al., 2019). This ongoing cycle of experimentation and improvement contributes to a nuanced understanding of the model's capabilities and areas for enhancement in speech emotion recognition. The accuracy level is 0.78%.

VGG16 Fine Tuning

Adjusting a ready to use VGG16 model with added data variations is a standard method to make a deep learning model work better for a particular job (Dimmita & Siddaiah, 2019; Hu, 2008). VGG16 is a well-known CNN already trained on the Image Net dataset. When using a pre-trained model like VGG16 it is crucial to grasp its structure, layers, and intended purpose. Since pre-trained models are usually designed for different tasks, you might need to change the last layer to fit the number of classes or categories in your dataset. The pre-trained model's layers freeze and can be updated during fine-tuning. During fine-tuning lower layers that capture low level features are frozen and higher layers that capture more abstract features are fine-tuned. During fine-tuning make sure that the model stays within the pre-trained weights. Apply data augmentation techniques to increase the size of your training dataset artificially. Train the model on the new dataset (Dimmita & Siddaiah, 2019). Monitor performance on a validation dataset of the fine-tuned model on a separate test set to assess its performance. Fine-tuning is a powerful technique that enables knowledge transfer from one domain to another. Fine-tuning a pre-trained VGG16 model with data augmentation is a widely adopted strategy to enhance the effectiveness of a deep learning model for a specific task. VGG16 is known for its success in image classification on the Image Net dataset it is a robust starting point due to its ability to capture intricate image patterns and features. The initial layers of the VGG16 model focus on low-level features like edges and textures, while the later layers specialize in more abstract and complex representations (Hu, 2008). When adapting a pre-trained model to a new task, it is crucial to tailor the architecture to the characteristics of the target dataset. This involves modifying the output layer to align with the number of classes or categories in the new dataset. Careful consideration is given to freezing lower layers during fine-tuning ensuring that low-level features remain intact while allowing higher layers to be updated to capture task specific nuances better. To prevent the model from diverging too far from the pre-trained weights during fine-tuning a balance is struck between retaining prior knowledge and adapting to the nuances of the new dataset (Hossain & Muhammad, 2019). Data augmentation techniques such as rotation, flipping, and zooming are applied to artificially expand the training dataset artificially that promoting robustness and generalization. Throughout the fine-tuning process monitoring the model's performance on a validation dataset is essential, adjusting hyperparameters and fine-tuning strategies as needed. The ultimate evaluation takes place on a separate test set to objectively assess the fine-tuned model's proficiency in handling the specific characteristics of the target task. Fine-tuning is a powerful and efficient mechanism for transferring knowledge from a pre-trained model to a domain-specific task leveraging the representational power encapsulated in the pre-trained weights (Hossain & Muhammad, 2019). This approach expedites the training process and capitalizes on the learned features that are transferrable across different datasets demonstrating the adaptability and versatility of the deep learning models. The accuracy score is high compared to the baseline and initial model (78%).

Figure 5. VGG16 fine tuning

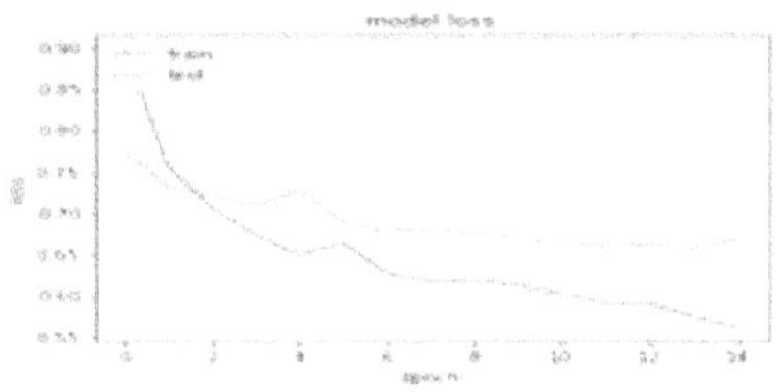

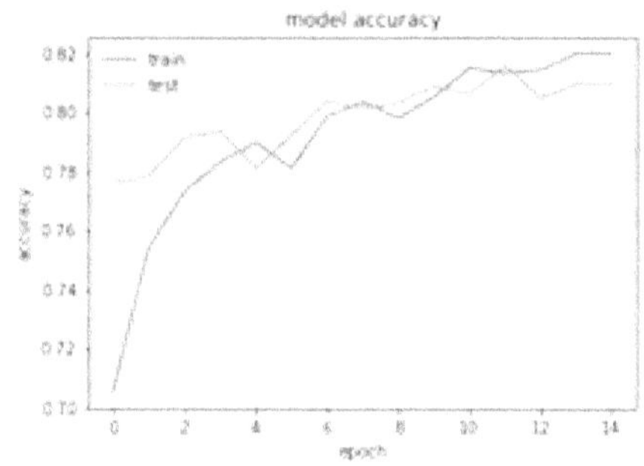

	precision	recall	f1-score	support
angry	0.85	0.84	0.85	192
calm	0.86	0.83	0.85	192
disgust	0.91	0.88	0.89	192
fear	0.87	0.78	0.82	192
happy	0.76	0.73	0.75	192
neutral	0.64	0.82	0.72	96
sad	0.79	0.74	0.76	192
surprise	0.75	0.85	0.80	192
accuracy			0.81	1440
macro avg	0.80	0.81	0.80	1440
weighted avg	0.82	0.81	0.81	1440

VGG16 FINETUNING WITH IMAGE AUGMENTATION

Using pre-trained models such as VGG16 offers a promising solution to leverage knowledge from broader datasets. Data augmentation addresses the scarcity of labeled data and enhances model generalization. VGG16 architecture emphasizes its strengths in capturing hierarchical features through deep convolution layers (Chen et al., 2016). VGG16 a pre-trained on Image Net, is a powerful feature extractor for image classification tasks. VGG16 adapts to the specific image classification task and concentrate on modifying the final layer to match the number of categories in the intended dataset. Augmentation techniques such as rotation and flipping are employed. They are fine-tuning VGG16 on the target dataset. Clarify which layers were frozen and which were allowed to be updated during training. Current baseline results compare them with fine-tuned models with data augmentation to interpret them emphasizing how using data augmentation affects how well the model can work with new and unfamiliar data. VGG16 with data augmentation for image classification tasks (Chen et al., 2016). VGG16 is a pre-trained model excels in efficiently extracting hierarchical features from images. Leveraging these pre-learned features allows the model to capture the patterns and complexities within the images even with limited labeled data. The scarcity of labeled data is a common challenge in many machine learning tasks. Data augmentation techniques like rotation and flipping are pivotal in mitigating the challenge. By artificially expanding the dataset with varied instances of the same images this model becomes more robust and adaptable to diverse patterns present in the data. Fine-tuning

Figure 6. VGG16 fine tuning with image augmentation

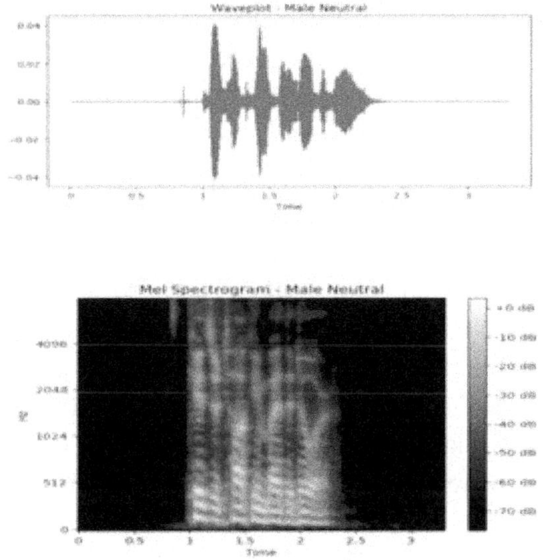

VGG16 on the target dataset involves a delicate balance between preserving the knowledge that is captured in pre-trained weights and adapting to the nuances of the specific image classification task. Presenting baseline results and comparing them with the fine-tuned models provides a comprehensive evaluation of the impact of data augmentation (Chen et al., 2016; Koolagudi & Rao, 2012; Lalitha, Madhavan, Bhushan, & Saketh, 2014; Scherer, 2005). Analyzing how the model performs both with and without the augmentation sheds light on its ability to generalize the previously of unseen data, showcasing the effectiveness of the transfer learning approach in conjunction with augmentation techniques. The fine-tuning process involves considerations of hyperparameter adjustments, including learning rates, batch sizes and regularization techniques. Highlighting how these hyperparameters were optimized during the adaptation phase adds another layer of transparency to the model development process (Chen et al., 2016). The accuracy score is higher than VGG16 with Fine-tuning (81%).

VGG19

VGG19 initially designed for images can be adapted for analyzing spectrograms representing speech signals (Koolagudi & Rao, 2012). Spectrograms capture audio signal's frequency and temporal characteristics that transforming the raw audio data into a format suitable for CNNs. Preparing the speech signals includes turning the original audio into spectrograms which are then used as the input for the customized VGG19 model. This stage is crucial to make sure that the format of the input data corresponds to the expectations of the neural network structure. Unlike images, speech data is inherently one-dimensional emphasizing the temporal sequence of audio features. Adapting the VGG19 model to accommodate this temporal aspect is essential. Consideration should be given to reshaping or adjusting the input layer to handle the one-dimensional nature of speech signals appropriately. The adapted VGG19 model is trained on a labeled dataset containing speech signals categorized into emotion classes (Koolagudi & Rao, 2012). The model learns to recognize patterns and features associated with different emotional expressions within the spectrograms. Align with the emotion classes in the specific speech emotion recognition task, adjustments are made to the output layer of the VGG19 model. The number of nodes is changed in the output layer to match the total number of emotions. This makes sure that the model can predict across all the different emotion categories. The final layer of the adapted VGG19 model typically employs a soft max activation function. This function converts the model's raw output into probability distributions over different emotion categories providing a probabilistic representation of the predicted emotions (Schmidhuber, 2015). The performance of the adapted VGG19 model is assessed by evaluating an independent test set. Commonly used measurements like accuracy, precision, recall, and F1-score are employed to assess how well the model can correctly categorize the speech into emotions.

VGG19 Fine Tuning

Implementing data augmentation techniques during training artificially expands the dataset's diversity. Techniques such as rotation, flipping and zooming can contribute to a more robust model that generalizes well to variations in speech signals (Schmidhuber, 2015). Experiment with different hyperparameters, adjusting factors like learning rates and batch sizes is essential for improving the fine-tuned VGG19 model's performance. Fine-tuning these parameters helps the model converge effectively while undergoing training. Implement regularization techniques like dropout to prevent overfitting. Adjust the dropout rate to balance exploiting the pre-trained weights and allowing the model to learn from the new dataset (Demircan & Kahramanlı, 2014). Explore various transfer learning strategies including feature extraction and fine-tuning of specific layers. Different strategies may yield better results depending on the dataset size and task complexity. Implement learning rate scheduling to adjust the learning rate during training dynamically. This can be particularly useful for fine-tuning allowing the model to adapt more efficiently to the new dataset (Pathak & Arun, 2011). Monitor additional metrics during training such as validation loss and

Figure 7. VGG19 fine tuning

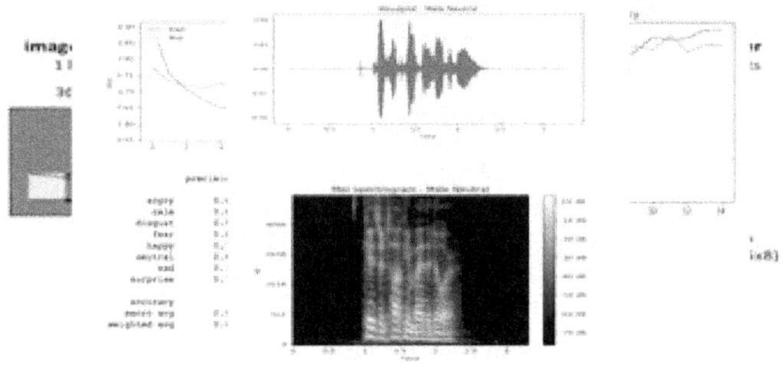

accuracy. These measurements offer valuable information about how well the model performs at various points that helps to determine the best time to end the training process. Explore ensemble techniques by merging predictions from various fine-tuned VGG19 models. Ensemble learning can improve the model's overall resilience and generalization ability. Incorporate techniques for model interpretability such as visualizing activation maps or attention mechanisms (Demircan & Kahramanlı, 2014; Gilke et al., 2012; Pathak & Arun, 2011). Understanding which parts of the input contribute most to the model's decisions can provide valuable insights. Address class imbalance issues in the dataset and significantly if certain emotion classes are underrepresented. Techniques like class weighting or oversampling can help balance the contribution of different classes during training. Post-processing steps such as threshold tuning or smoothing techniques will refine the model's predictions and enhance its robustness in real world scenarios. The accuracy score is high compared to the baseline initial model (82%).

VGG19 FINETUNING WITH IMAGE AUGMENTATION

VGG19 has already learned low-level features like edges and textures from the massive image net dataset (Bandela & Kumar, 2017; Demircan & Kahramanlı, 2014; Gilke et al., 2012; Pathak & Arun, 2011; Reddy & Kishore Kumar, 2018; Sharma et al., 2016). This pre-trained knowledge can be transferred to your task by saving training time and improving performance. The top layers of VGG19 are replaced with new layers specific to your classification dataset. Achieving a better accuracy with less training data, the high level features relevant to your data increases the training data size. It introduces robustness to variations in the real world. Resize and normalize your images to match the VGG19 input format. Initialize the model with pre trained weights from ImageNet. Freeze the weights of the lower layers in VGG19 to prevent them from being updated during training add new layers on top of the frozen base and assess the model's effectiveness by evaluating its performance on a distinct validation set. Adjustments to the learning rate or the number of frozen layers may be necessary based on the obtained results during this evaluation phase. Tailor the pre-trained VGG19 model to your specific classification task by replacing its top layers with new ones. This fine-tuning process hones the high-level features learned from Image Net to be more relevant to your dataset that ultimately enhancing the accuracy and performance. Capitalize on the pre-trained knowledge of low level features to overcome the limitations in training data (Gilke et al., 2012). Leveraging the pre-existing and understanding of edges and textures allows your model to achieve an notable accuracy even with a smaller training dataset. By increasing the training data size can introduce robustness to your model enabling it to handle the better variations encountered in real world scenarios. This dataset augmentation contributes to the model's adaptability to diverse conditions. Prepare the input data by resizing and normalizing images to align with the VGG19 input format. Consistent preprocessing ensures that the model receives input in a standardized manner facilitating the effective knowledge transfer. To preserve the pre-trained knowledge in lower layers freeze their weights during training (Reddy & Kishore Kumar, 2018). This prevents them from being updated allowing the model to retain the foundational features learned from the Image Net dataset while adapting to the higher layers to the specific task. Assess the model's effectiveness by evaluating its performance on a distinct validation set. This step provides insights into how well the fine-tuned VGG19 generalizes to new data guiding any necessary adjustments for optimal results. Consider making iterative adjustments based on the results obtained during the evaluation phase. This may involve fine-tuning the learning rate or modifying the number of frozen layers to balance leveraging pre-trained knowledge and adapting to the intricacies of your classification task. Regularly monitor the model's training progress and performance metrics to detect the potential issues or challenges. This iterative approach ensures a dynamic fine-tuning process that optimizes the model for your classification requirements (Zamil, 2019). The accuracy score is high compared to VGG16 with Fine-tuning (88%).

CONCLUSION

The successful implementation of an automated method for extracting key parameters from speech signals underscores it's robustness and reliability. By seamlessly integrating cutting edge technologies, this approach showcases the potential for broader applications in signal processing tasks. The synergy between CNN and

Figure 8. VGG19 fine tuning with image augmentation

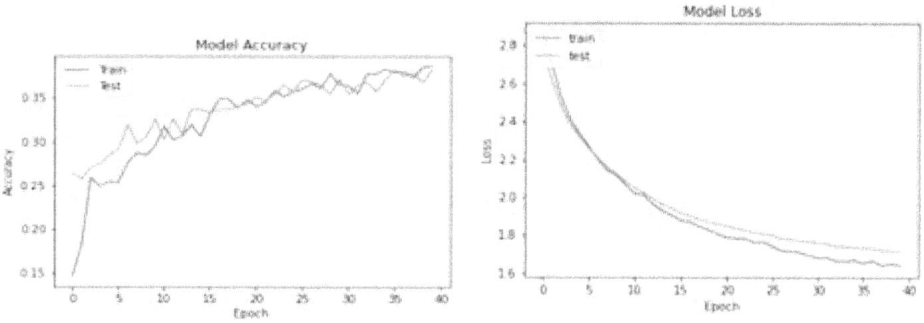

Table 1. Table of comparison

Algorithms used	Accuracy
VGG16 FINE TUNING	78%
VGG16 FINE TUNING WITH IMAGE AUGMENTATION	81%
VGG19 FINE TUNING	82%
VGG19 FINE TUNING WITH IMAGE AUGMENTATION	88%

Exploratory Data Analysis (EDA) proved in achieving the remarkable results. This results in a powerful framework for efficient parameter extraction. The fusion of VGG16 and VGG19 architectures in the proposed classifier model demonstrated exceptional performance. The highest is accuracy is predicted by the VGG19 fine tuning with image augmentation. The accuracy is 88% is achieved by VGG19 with image augmentation during practical training serves as a testament to the effectiveness of the innovative fusion approach. The accurate extraction of emotion characteristic parameters signifies a breakthrough in understanding and processing emotional cues embedded within speech signals. This approach effectively and accurately extracts emotion characteristic parameters causing a substantial enhancement in the recognition rate for emotional speech. With its high accuracy and robust performance this SER holds a real world application, such as emotion analysis which helps in mental health assessment through speech analysis.

REFERENCES

Anagnostopoulos, C.-N., Iliou, T., & Giannakos, I. (2015). Features and classifiers for emotion recognition from speech: A survey from 2000 to 2011. *Artificial Intelligence Review*, *43*(2), 155–177.

Balomenos, T., Raouzaiou, A., Ioannou, S., Drosopoulos, A., Karpouzis, K., & Kollias, S. (2001). Emotion analysis in man-machine interaction systems. In *International Workshop on Machine Learning for Multimodal Interaction*. Springer.

Bandela, S. R., & Kumar, T. K. (2017). Stressed speech emotion recognition using feature fusion of teager energy operator and MFCC. *2017 8th International Conference on Computing, Communication and Networking Technologies (ICCCNT),* 1-5.

Batliner, A., Schuller, B., Seppi, D., Steidl, S., Devillers, L., Vidrascu, L., Vogt, T., Aharonson, V., & Amir, N. (2011). *The automatic recognition of emotions in speech. In Emotion-Oriented Systems*. Springer.

Benkerzaz, Elmir, & Dennai. (2019). *A Study on Automatic Speech Recognition*. Academic Press.

Chen, M., Zhou, P., & Fortino, G. (2016). Emotion communication system. *IEEE Access : Practical Innovations, Open Solutions*, *5*, 326–337.

Chen, M., Zhou, P., & Fortino, G. (2017). Emotion communication system. *IEEE Access : Practical Innovations, Open Solutions*, *5*, 326–337.

Cowie, R., Douglas-Cowie, E., Tsapatsoulis, N., Votsis, G., Kollias, S., Fellenz, W., & Taylor, J. G. (n.d.). Emotion recognition in human-computer interaction. *IEEE Signal Processing Magazine*, *18*(1), 32–80.

Demircan, S., & Kahramanlı, H. (2014). Feature extraction from speech data for emotion recognition. *J. Adv. Comput. Netw.*, *2*(1), 28–30.

Dimmita, N., & Siddaiah, P. (2019, September). Speech Recognition Using Convolutional. *Neural Networks*.

Gilke, Kachare, Kothalikar, Rodrigues, & Pednekar. (2012). MFCC-based Vocal Emotion Recognition Using ANN. *International Conference on Electronics Engineering and Informatics, 49*.

Gupta, Fahad, & Deepak. (2020). Pitch-synchronous single frequency filtering spectrogram for speech emotion recognition. *International Journal of Multimedia Tools and Applications*. doi:10.1007/s11042-020-09068-1

Hossain, M. S., & Muhammad, G. (2019). Emotion recognition using deep Learning approach from audio-visual emotional big data. *Information Fusion, 49*, 69-78.

Hu. (2008). *Evaluation of Objective Quality Measures for Speech Enhancement.* Academic Press.

Koolagudi, S. G., & Rao, K. S. (2012). Emotion recognition from speech: A review. *International Journal of Speech Technology, 15*(2), 99–117.

Lakkhanawannakun. (2019). *Speech Recognition using Deep Learning*. Academic Press.

Lalitha, S., Madhavan, A., Bhushan, B., & Saketh, S. (2014a). Speech emotion recognition. In *Advances in Electronics, Computers and Communications (ICAECC), International Conference on*. IEEE.

Lalitha, S., Madhavan, A., Bhushan, B., & Saketh, S. (2014b). Speech emotion recognition. *Proc. Int. Conf. Adv. Electron. Comput. Commun. (ICAECC)*, 1-4.

Lane, N. D., & Georgiev, P. (2015). Can deep learning revolutionize mobile Sensing? In *Proceedings of the 16th International Workshop on Mobile Computing Systems and Applications*. ACM.

Le, & Provost. (2013). Emotion recognition from spontaneous speech using hidden markov models with deep belief networks. In *2013 IEEE Workshop on Automatic Speech Recognition and Understanding*. IEEE.

Nassif, Shahin, Attili, Azzeh, & Shaalan. (2019). Speech recognition using deep neural networks: A systematic review. *IEEE Access, 7*(19), 143-165.

Pathak, S., & Arun, K. (2011). Recognizing emotions from speech. *Electronics Computer Technology (ICECT), 3rd International Conference on, 4*.

Philipos. (n.d.). *Loizou Speech Quality Assessment*. Academic Press.

Poorjam. (2019). *Quality Control in Remote Speech Data Collection*. Academic Press.

Raghib, Sharma, Ahmad, & Alam. (2018). *Emotion Analysis and Speech Signal Processing*. Academic Press.

Razuri, J. G., Sundgren, D., Rahmani, R., Moran, A., Bonet, I., & Lars-son, A. (2015). Speech emotion recognition in emotionafeedback for human-robot interaction. *International Journal of Advanced Research in Artificial Intelligence, 4*(2), 20–27.

Reddy, S. B., & Kishore Kumar, T. (2018). Emotion Recognition of Stressed Speech using Teager Energy and Linear Prediction Features. *IEEE 18th International Conference on Advanced Learning Technologies.*

Scherer, K. R. (2005). What are emotions? and how can they be measured? *Social Sciences Information. Information Sur les Sciences Sociales*, *44*(4), 695–729.

Schmidhuber, J. (2015, January). Deep learning in neural networks: An overview. *Neural Networks*, *61*, 85–117.

Schuller, B. W. (2018). Speech emotion recognition: Two decades in a nutshell, Benchmarks, and ongoing trends. *Communications of the ACM*, *61*(5), 90–99.

Sharma, P., Abrol, V., Sachdev, A., & Dileep, A. D. (2016). Speech emotion recognition using kernel sparse representation based classifier. *2016 24th European Signal Processing Conference (EUSIPCO),* 374-377.

Vogt, T., & André, E. (2005). Comparing feature sets for acted and spontaneous speech in view of automatic emotion recognition. *Multimedia and Expo. ICME 2005. IEEE International Conference on. IEEE*, 474-477.

Zamil, A. A. A. (2019). Emotion Detection from Speech Signals using Voting Mechanism on Classified Frames. In *2019 International Conference on Robotics, Electrical and Signal Processing Techniques (ICREST).* IEEE.

Chapter 7
Osmatic-Based Supervision of EV

R. Mathi
SASTRA University, India

V. Sundaravazhuthi
SASTRA University, India

A. Sanjai
SASTRA University, India

ABSTRACT

This study illustrates how electric car battery performance can be monitored using the internet of things (IoT). It is evident that an electric vehicle's only energy source is its battery. But the car's energy supply is steadily running out, which causes a drop in performance. This is a major source of concern for the battery industry. The chapter suggests using IoT techniques to monitor vehicle performance in order to perform the monitoring directly. The two primary elements of the suggested internet of things-based battery monitoring system are the monitoring device and the user interface. Test results indicate that the system may detect decreased battery life and alert the user to take appropriate action.

INTRODUCTION

One of the main issues facing today's major cities is air pollution. The primary source of the haze problem, which affects even Delhi, the capital of India, is internal combustion engine cars. The even and odd car number policy, which permits cars with those numbers to operate within the city on alternate days, either had no impact

DOI: 10.4018/979-8-3693-1694-8.ch007

or greatly decreased the amount of pollutants in the air. Similar issues are being faced by other cities across the globe, which has paved the road for electric cars to become more widely available. Tesla makes automobiles. The market for electric vehicles was completely transformed by the first business to adopt an induction motor for manufacture, which is more reliable and less expensive than permanent magnet machines. When designing an electric car, estimating the parameters of several parts—like the gear ratio, battery rating, motor rating, and so on—is essential. The choice of motor type is influenced by various criteria such as cost, performance, longevity, stability, torque capacity, and so on. Depending on how the vehicle is being used, such as if a long range or fast speed is needed, the battery composition should be evaluated. Lithium titanate batteries are an example of a Li-ion chemistry that has fire safety, but other chemistries have fast discharge rates. A precise estimate of the state of charge (SOC) is crucial for an electric car, and range anxiety is an essential concern. The primary limitation for EV charging duration is with existing AC chargers, which impedes implementation and uptake. To address these issues, EV manufacturers have produced DC charging stations. The issues with DC chargers are related to battery pack health and safety vulnerabilities to rapid charging. To overcome the roadblocks, IoT integrated facilities must alter efficiency and safety, resulting in a new paradigm shift. Existing chargers are upgraded to include a monitoring procedure for charging EVs, in which EV vehicle characteristics are articulated with a smartphone device assisted cloud (Bharathi et al., 2022).

Architecture of Electric Vehicle

Figure 1 shows how EV is generally configured. These are the EV subsystems:

- Auxiliary system
- Energy source
- Electric propulsion.

In Figure 1, the system diagram delineates the mechanical link denoted by the black line, the electrical link by the green line, and the transfer of control information by the blue line. Predicated on inputs received from the brake and accelerator pedals, the electronic controller transmits requisite control signals to activate or deactivate the power converter. Subsequently, this regulates the quantity of power traversing between the electric motor and the energy source. The regenerative braking mechanism induces the backward flow of power. In order to control refuelling and track the energy source's consumption, it also interfaces with the energy-refuelling apparatus. The power required for all EV accessories is supplied by the auxiliary power supply at different voltage levels, including the air conditioning and steering systems ().

Figure 1. Layout of electric vehicle

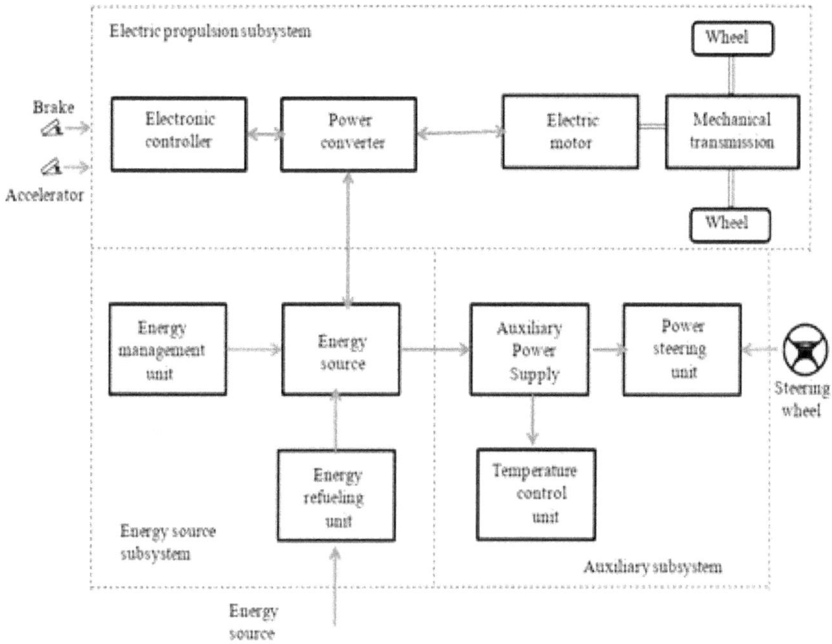

Dynamics of Electric Vehicle

Newton's second law, a cornerstone in vehicle design, asserts that an object's acceleration is directly proportional to the net force acting upon it. Thus, when the net force on an object is non-zero, it experiences acceleration. In the context of vehicles, various forces come into play, and it's the resultant force that determines motion in accordance with Newton's second law. The propulsion system of a vehicle is responsible for producing the requisite force to propel the vehicle in a forward direction. This propulsion unit force aids the vehicle in overcoming gravitational, air, and tyre resistance forces (Vempalli et al., 2018).

Rolling Resistance

The overall rolling resistance of a vehicle encompasses the impedance arising from tire deformation, tire slippage, and aerodynamic interactions encircling the wheel. The quantification of the rolling resistance force is articulated as (Jadhav, 2017; NPTEL, n.d.; Nugraha et al., n.d.; Perez-Pinal et al., 2006; Singh et al., 2014):

Figure 2. Forces on an ascending vehicle

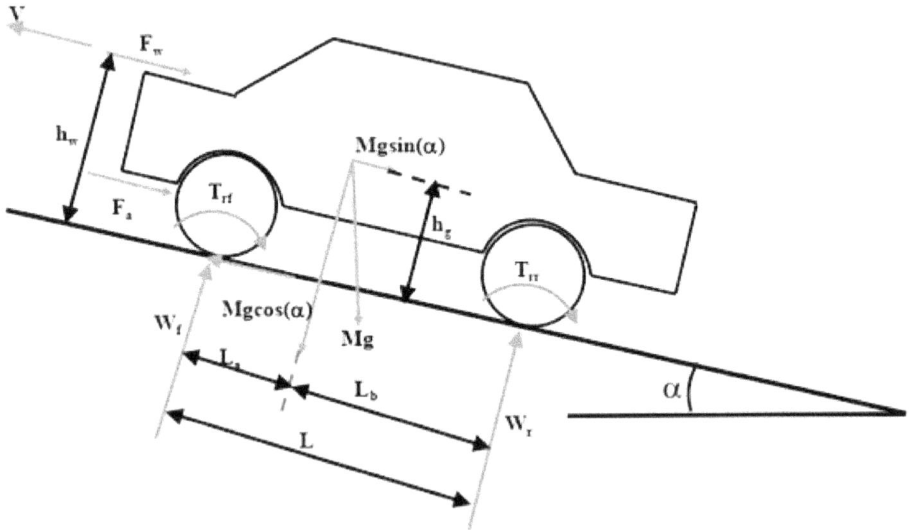

$$F_r = C_R mg$$

Where m is the mass of the Vehicle
g is the acceleration due to gravity, nominally 9.8 m/ s^2
C_R is the coefficient of rolling resistance

Aerodynamic Drag

When a vehicle moves against the direction of the wind, it encounters aerodynamic drag. This force is nullified when the vehicle moves in the same direction as the wind. Consequently, traction force is heightened in such conditions .

$$F_d = \frac{\rho}{2} * C_d * A_f * V^2$$

Where ρ is the density of air
C_d is the aerodynamic drag coefficient
A is the cross-sectional area of the vehicle
V is the vehicle speed in m/s

Figure 3. An automobile ascending an incline

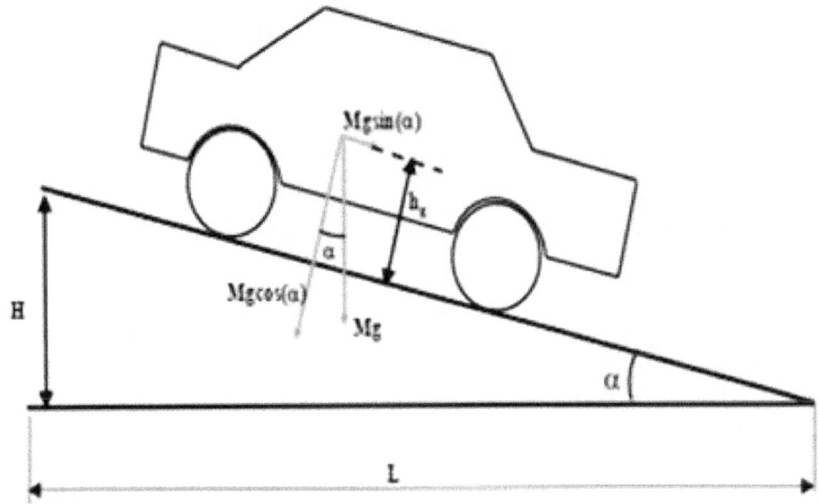

Grading Resistance

During incline or decline traversal, a force component, stemming from the vehicle's weight, persistently exerts itself in a downward direction. This force component serves to counteract the forward motion, particularly noticeable during gradient ascents. Conversely, when the vehicle descends the slope, this force component assists its movement. The representation of the resistance encountered during grading is denoted by

$$F_g = Mgsin\left(\alpha\right)$$

Where M is the mass in *kg*
g is the acceleration due to gravity, nominally 9.8 m/ s^2
α is the road angle in *radians*

Acceleration Resistance

Apart from the driving resistance experienced during steady-speed movement, inertial forces manifest during both acceleration and braking. Elements contributing to the resistance during acceleration involve the total vehicle mass and the inertial mass of rotating elements within the drive system experiencing acceleration or deceleration.

$$F_a = \lambda M \frac{dV}{dt}$$

Where λ is the rotational inertia constant
M is the mass of the vehicle in *kg*
V is the speed of the vehicle in m/s

Total Driving Resistance

The net force demanded at the drive wheels is characterized as the summation of resisting components impeding the vehicle's motion, outlined as follows:

$$\boldsymbol{F}_{resistance} = \boldsymbol{F}_r + \boldsymbol{F}_w + \boldsymbol{F}_g + \boldsymbol{F}_a$$

Substituting the values of all forces we get

$$F_{resis\tan ce} = C_R mg + \frac{\rho}{2} * C_d * A_f * V^2 + Mg\sin\left(\alpha\right) + \lambda M \frac{dV}{dt}$$

Dynamic Equation

The forces operating on a two-axle vehicle in the longitudinal direction include (Vempalli et al., 2018):

- Rolling resistance of the front and rear tires
- Aerodynamic drag
- Grade climbing resistance
- Acceleration resistance

The differential equation governing the vehicle's longitudinal motion dynamics is expressed as:

$$\boldsymbol{M}\frac{\boldsymbol{dV}}{\boldsymbol{dt}} = \left(\boldsymbol{F}_{tf} + \boldsymbol{F}_{tr}\right) - \left(\boldsymbol{F}_{rf} + \boldsymbol{F}_{rr} + \boldsymbol{F}_w + \boldsymbol{F}_g + \boldsymbol{F}_a\right)$$

The upper limit of tractive effort achievable at the tire-ground interface is defined by the multiplication of the normal load and the coefficient representing road adhesion (m).The maximum tractive force is supplied for front wheel drive vehicles.

IOT AND THINGSPEAK

The Internet of Things (IoT) represents a contemporary trend focused on interconnecting numerous embedded devices, commonly referred to as "things," to the Internet. These interconnected devices engage in communication, regularly transmitting sensor data to cloud storage and cloud computing resources. Within these cloud environments, data undergoes processing and analysis to derive valuable insights. The progression of cost-effective cloud computing capabilities and heightened device interconnectivity stands as pivotal factors propelling the expansion of the IoT. This technological domain spans multiple sectors, encompassing domains such as environmental telemetry, health telemetry, vehicular fleet orchestration, industrial telemetry and management, alongside domiciliary automation. The illustration below serves as a high-level representation that can elucidate many IoT systems (Thingspeak, n.d.).

The smart devices, known as "things" in the context of IoT, are depicted on the left side of the network. These devices encompass wearables, wireless temperature sensors, heart rate monitors, hydraulic pressure sensors, and manufacturing floor equipment, all situated at the edge of the network. In the central position is the cloud, serving as a hub where data from diverse sources is collected and assessed in real-

Figure 4. Data transfer

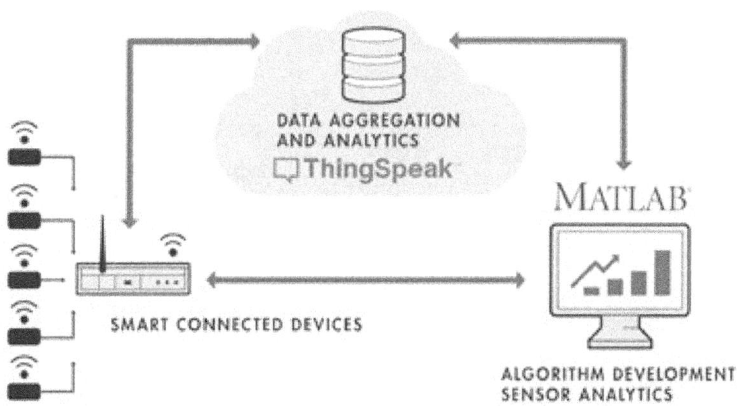

time, typically through a dedicated IoT analytics platform. On the right side of the diagram, the process involves developing algorithms for IoT applications. Engineers and data scientists aim to extract insights from gathered data through historical analyses. In this scenario, information is fetched from the Internet of Things (IoT) platform and channelled into a desktop software environment, facilitating engineers or scientists in the prototyping of algorithms. These algorithms could potentially be implemented either in the cloud or directly onto intelligent devices. These components collectively form the integral constituents of an IoT system. Particularly noteworthy is the inclusion of ThingSpeak within the cloud segment of the diagram, serving as a platform to efficiently aggregate and interpret data originating from internet-connected sensors. ThingSpeak excels in consolidating, visualizing, and analysing real-time data streams in the cloud. Its primary capabilities include easily configuring devices to transmit data to ThingSpeak via popular IoT protocols (Ravi et al., 2020).

- Instantaneous Visualization of Sensor Data in Real Time
- Flexible Data Aggregation from External Sources as Needed.
- Utilize MATLAB's Power to Extract Meaning from Your IoT Data.
- Develop IoT Solutions Without the Need for Server Setup or Web Application Development.
- Automate Immediate Responses to Data Insights and Connect with External Services such as Twilio® or Twitter®.

Simulation Model

The EV model is constructed using MATLAB powertrain block set and the outputs are monitored using the ThingSpeak platform.

Figure 5. Simulation model

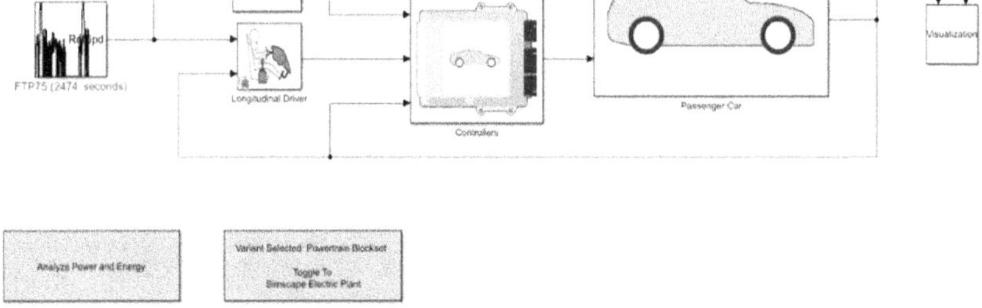

RESULTS AND DISCUSSION

The Figure 4.1 shows discharging profile of a battery. The SOC value varies from 75 percentage to 72.5 percentage during the driving mode and the different slope represents the difference in the driving and other environmental factors. The corresponding battery discharge current, motor torque and speed are shown in Figure 4.2, 4.3, 4.4.

Figure 6. Battery SOC

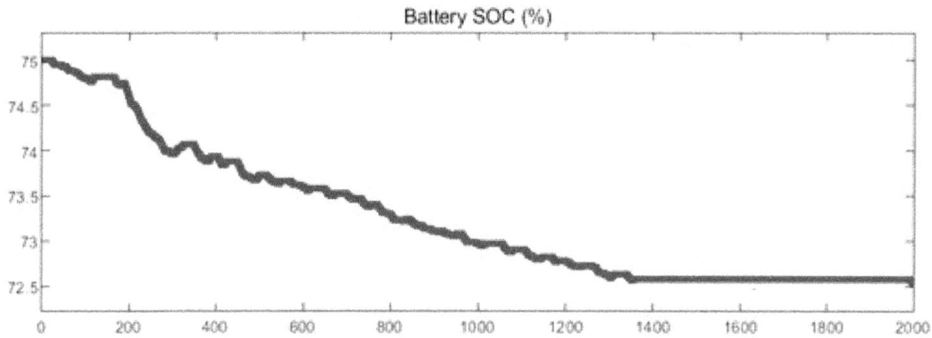

Figure 7. Battery current

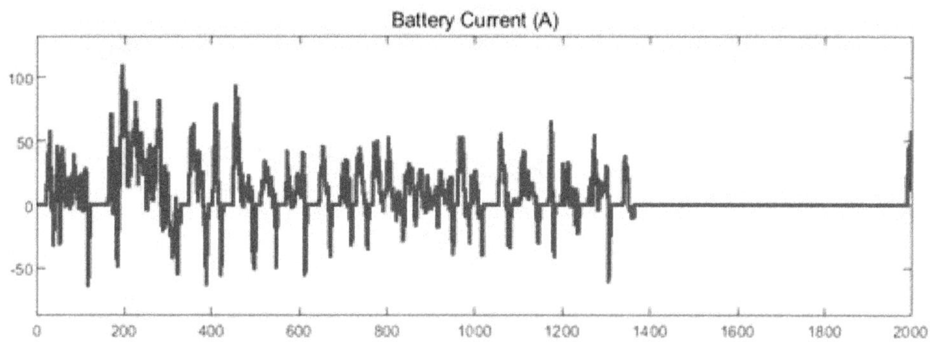

Figure 8. Motor torque

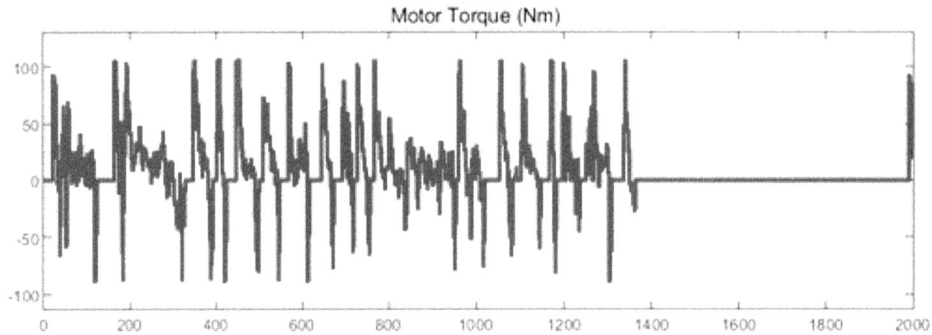

Figure 9. Motor speed

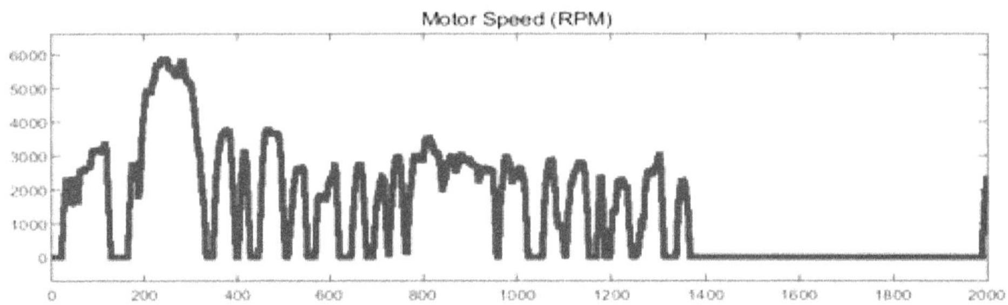

Figure 10. Thing speak output of battery SOC

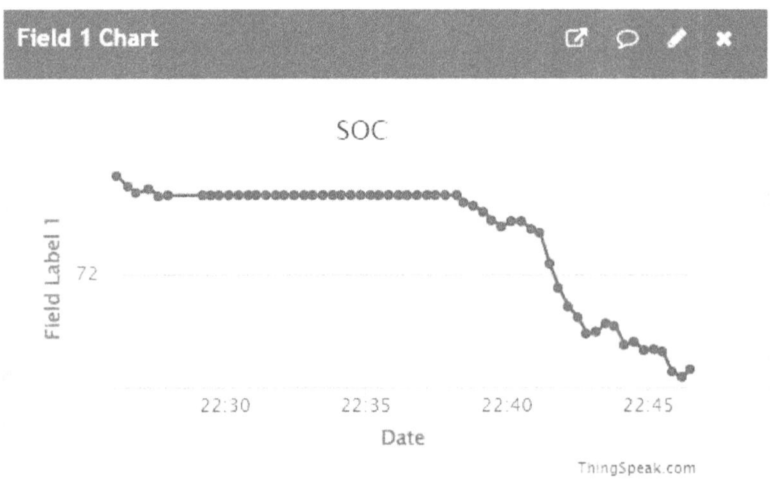

Figure 11. Thing speak output of motor torque

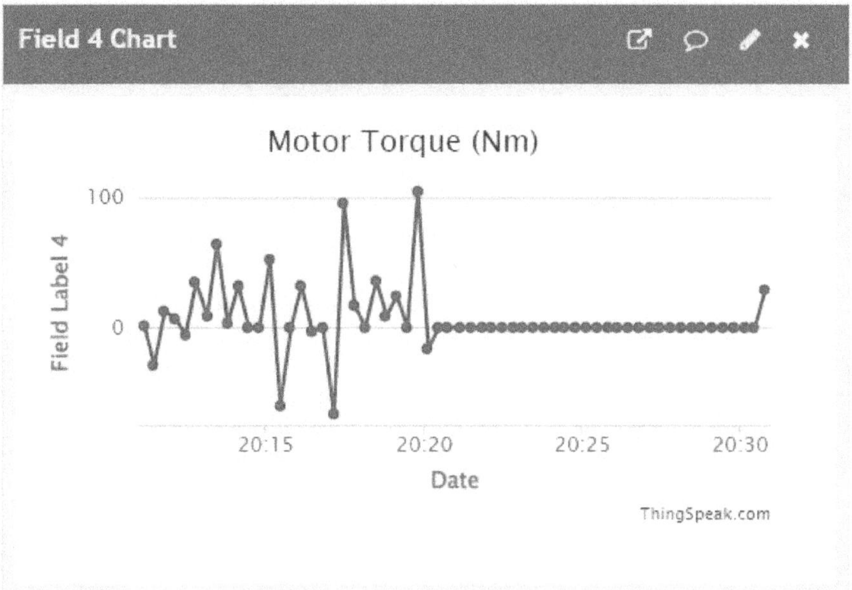

Figure 12. Thing speak output of motor speed

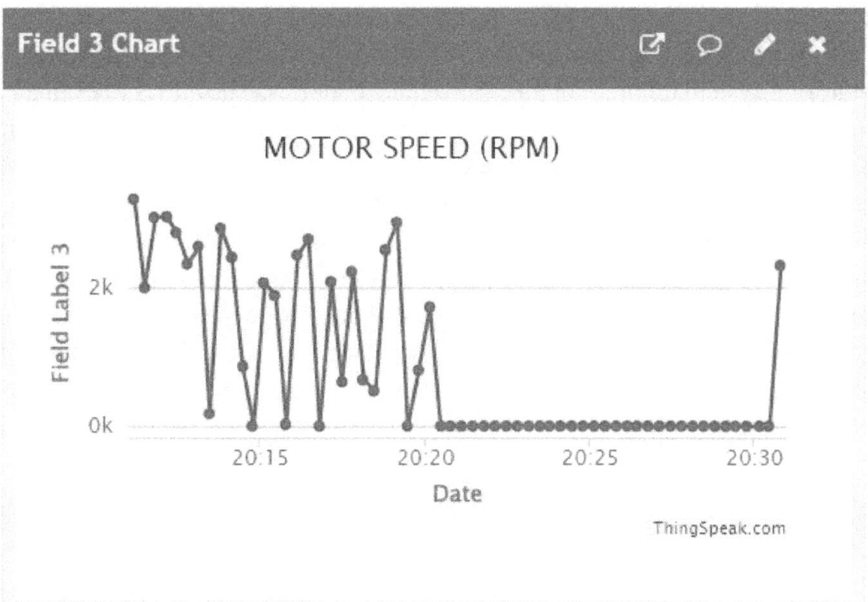

Figure 13. Thing speak output of battery current

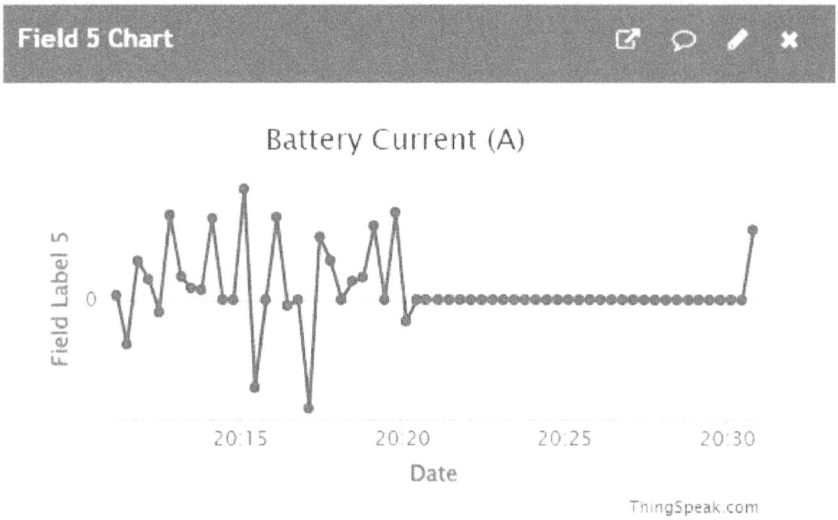

CONCLUSION

The research endeavor focused on real-time monitoring of battery degradation by investigating the development and execution of an Internet of Things (IoT) integrated monitoring system tailored for electric vehicle batteries. The aim is to evaluate the foundational feasibility of this concept. Presently, efforts are concentrated on crafting the hardware components for the battery monitoring apparatus and constructing a web-based interface as integral facets of the system's establishment. The device is capable of displaying data via the internet, providing information such as time and battery life. The system can be developed further by integrating new capabilities. The concept can be implemented in smartphones by developing a smartphone application that assists users in battery monitoring and serves as a reminder for battery degradation. Ethernet can be used to improve internet connections and make them superior to GPRS.

REFERENCES

Bharathi, M., Geetha, K., & Mani, P. K. (2022). AI and IoT-based Electric Vehicle Monitoring System. Academic Press.

Ehsani. (2005). *Hybrid Electric and Fuel Cell Vehicles: Fundamentals, Theory and Design*. Academic Press.

Jadhav, A. R. (2017, July). Drive Cycle Analysis for Electric Vehicle using MATLAB. *International Journal of Engineering Science.*

NPTEL. (n.d.). *Introduction to Hybrid and Electric Vehicles*. Academic Press.

Nugraha, F. A., Purwadi, A., Haroen, Y., & Heryana, N. (n.d.). The calculation of electric motor and Lithium battery capacity on Cikal Cakrawala ITB electric car. *Power Engineering and Renewable Energy (ICPERE), IEEE International Conference on*, 1-6.

Perez-Pinal, F. J., Nunez, C., Alvarez, R., & Gallegos, M. (2006). Step by step design procedure of an Independent-Wheeled Small EV applying EVLS. *IEEE Industrial Electronics, IECON 2006-32nd Annual Conference on*, 1176-1181.

Ravi, R., Surendra, U., & Shreya, N. (2020). *Comparative analysis of various techniques of IOT in Electric vehicle (No. 4500)*. Easy Chair.

Singh, A. K., Dalal, A., & Kumar, P. (2014). Analysis of induction motor for electric vehicle application based on drive cycle analysis. In *Power Electronics, Drives and Energy Systems (PEDES), IEEE International Conference* (pp. 1-6). IEEE.

Thingspeak. (n.d.). https://thingspeak.com/pages/learn_more

Vempalli, S. K., Ramprabhakar, J., Shankar, S., & Prabhakar, G. (2018). Electric Vehicle Designing. *Modelling and Simulation (Anaheim)*, 1–6.

Chapter 8
Healthcare Monitoring and Analysis Using ThingSpeak IoT Platform:
Capturing and Analyzing Sensor Data for Enhanced Patient Care

D. Sivabalaselvamani
https://orcid.org/0000-0002-3373-7610
Kongu Engineering College, India

K. Nanthini
Kongu Engineering College, India

Bharath Kumar Nagaraj
Revature LLC, Reston, USA

K. H. Gokul Kannan
Kongu Engineering College, India

K. Hariharan
Kongu Engineering College, India

M. Mallingeshwaran
Kongu Engineering College, India

ABSTRACT

Health monitoring systems are designed to transform patient care by providing continuous monitoring and remote capabilities. Traditional healthcare often lacks constant monitoring, which can lead to delays in identifying issues. Wearable sensors, such as heart rate and eye blink sensors, collect real-time data that is transmitted to the cloud-based ThingSpeak platform. Non-intrusive eyeblink sensors aid in diagnosing conditions like dry eye syndrome, blepharospasm, and Parkinson's disease. Remote monitoring enables healthcare professionals to offer timely interventions with customizable alerts. IoT technology reduces hospital visits for chronic patients, potentially improving outcomes and reducing complications. The primary goal is to ensure seamless sensor connectivity to ThingSpeak, allowing users to access data from laptops and mobile devices. By empowering patients to actively manage their health, this system enhances health monitoring capabilities, paving the way for a more patient-centric and efficient healthcare landscape.

DOI: 10.4018/979-8-3693-1694-8.ch008

1. INTRODUCTION

The healthcare sector has been transformed by the creation of health monitoring systems, which provide new opportunities for remote patient care and continuous monitoring of vital signs and health parameters. These systems use wearable sensors, data processing algorithms, and cloud-based platforms to offer real-time monitoring and analysis of patients' health conditions. This overview highlights the significance and potential benefits of health monitoring systems in improving patient care and outcomes. Traditional healthcare practices rely on sporadic visits to healthcare facilities, which limits the ability to monitor patients continuously and detect early signs of health issues. With the advancement in technology, health monitoring systems have emerged as a solution to bridge this gap. These systems allow for the collection of real-time data on vital signs and other health parameters, empowering healthcare providers with valuable information for proactive intervention and personalized care. Wearable sensors are a crucial component of health monitoring systems, as they can record vital indications such as heart rate, blood pressure, respiration rate, temperature, and physical activity levels. They are integrated into devices like biosensors, activity trackers, and smart watches. These sensors are non-invasive, comfortable to wear, and designed to seamlessly integrate into individuals' daily lives, enabling continuous monitoring without disrupting their routines. The collected data from wearable sensors undergoes sophisticated data processing algorithms, which leverage advanced signal processing techniques and machine learning algorithms to extract meaningful insights and identify abnormal patterns or trends. By analyzing the data, these algorithms can detect irregular heart rhythms, fluctuations in blood pressure, abnormal sleep patterns, and other indicators of potential health risks. Early detection and timely alerts can significantly improve patient outcomes by enabling healthcare providers to intervene promptly and prevent the escalation of health issues. To facilitate the seamless transmission and storage of data, health monitoring systems rely on cloud-based platforms. These platforms securely store and manage the collected data, enabling healthcare providers to access and review patient information remotely. Real-time alerts and notifications can be sent to healthcare professionals in cases of critical events or deviations from normal health parameters, enabling immediate responses and personalized care. Furthermore, the cloud-based platform allows patients to actively engage in their healthcare by providing them with access to their health data, personalized recommendations, and self-management tools. The benefits of health monitoring systems are manifold, as they enable continuous monitoring of patients' health conditions, even outside healthcare facilities, offering a comprehensive understanding of their well-being. By facilitating remote patient care, these systems reduce the need for frequent hospital visits, particularly for individuals with chronic conditions or those requiring long-term monitoring.

Amutha S. and Murali M. (2019) researched providing a smart hospital system through IoT. The integration of IoT technologies into the healthcare domain is a crucial research area. It promises uninterrupted continuous monitoring of human health conditions and provides optimal services during emergencies. The paper presents a novel framework for smart healthcare systems, introducing an enhanced methodology that incorporates intelligent decision-making, data fusion, and prediction algorithms based on machine learning concepts. Ester et al. (2022) introduced an integrated health monitoring system that combines IoT-based wearable medical devices with advanced safety features on the ThingSpeak platform. The wearable device is equipped with sensors for temperature, ECG, EEG, and collision detection, and communicates in real-time through Wireless Sensor Network technology. With an FPGA controller and built-in Wi-Fi ensuring secure data transmission, the system uses ThingSpeak's cloud-based platform for storage and analysis, enabling immediate responses to critical health events. Incorporating an OLED display and buzzer alerts for user feedback, the system seamlessly notifies healthcare professionals through ThingSpeak, providing timely intervention. The research also integrates non-intrusive sensors, such as heartbeat pulse and eye blink sensors, enhancing the system's holistic approach to healthcare and empowering patients to actively manage their health remotely. Majida Khan et al. (2023) proposed research that delves into the escalating concerns surrounding user privacy in the rapidly expanding Internet of Things (IoT) landscape, projected to see a threefold increase in connected devices from 2020 to 2030. With over 29 billion devices expected to be part of the global network, the substantial transmission of sensitive user information poses a significant privacy risk. The paper underscores the vulnerability of IoT systems, particularly cyber-physical systems reliant on sensors collecting data from the environment. Given the potential malicious use of this data, user privacy issues such as password theft, information and identity pilfering, intrusion, and data corruption are on the rise. Against this backdrop, privacy experts and researchers have ardently addressed these challenges by devising Privacy Enhancing Technologies (PETs). These technologies, encompassing blind signatures, group signatures, attribute-based credentials (ABCs), anonymous and pseudonymous data authentication, onion routing, and encrypted communications, among others, aim to mitigate user privacy risks in IoT. The paper synthesizes the evolving landscape of IoT-driven privacy concerns and the proactive measures taken to safeguard user information through cutting-edge PETs. The above articles introduce an integrated health monitoring system that leverages wearable devices for real-time communication and immediate response to critical health events. Additionally, they highlight the critical issue of user privacy in IoT. The groundbreaking work on a smart healthcare system lays the foundation for seamless IoT integration, promising continuous health monitoring and optimized emergency services.

2. LITERATURE REVIEW

Kishori Kasat et al. (2022) proposed a healthcare data security framework that uses IoT sensors to encrypt data with a unique key on the client's end and decrypt it at the recipient's end. Texas Instruments TI Launchpads were used to simulate sensors, facilitating digital information transfer and long-distance communication. The system collects data using sensors connected to a person's blood and merges it with a patient-specific code to enhance security. This approach demonstrated promising results for secure IoT healthcare data transfer, despite increasing system costs. Areej A. Malibar et al. (2023) introduced an IoT-based AI disease prediction system, EO-LWAMCNet, utilizing a lightweight CNN for healthcare. Sensors implanted in patients collect data, which is then transmitted to the cloud via a gateway. EO-LWAMCNet classifies chronic health states based on this sensor data. The system uses datasets for chronic kidney disease (CKD) and heart disease (HD), training the model with LWADCNet. Cloud and perception layers enable hierarchical disease data processing. Testing with MSSO-ANFIS, T-RNN, and DLMNN showed accuracy rates of 93.5% and 94% on separate datasets, proving its effectiveness in predicting chronic ailments, including renal and heart conditions. Mohd Javaid et al. (2021) proposed an IoT-enabled healthcare system to address COVID-19 challenges. The system emphasizes real-time monitoring via IoT, preventing fatalities from various conditions. Smart medical devices connect to smartphones for efficient data transmission to doctors, tracking vital parameters such as oxygen levels, blood pressure, and sugar levels. Big data is utilized for data collection, storage, and analysis, with cloud computing enabling rapid data sharing in emergencies. Smart sensors in healthcare networks yield reliable results, supported by specialized software for patient care and data management. Artificial intelligence aids in data evaluation and prediction. Actuators guide system behavior in specific environments, facilitating real-time data integration with technology. Overall, IoT has enhanced medical equipment and networks, reducing manual record-keeping and errors, and improving healthcare efficiency during the COVID-19 pandemic. Ninni Singh et al. (2022) discuss the critical need for an IoT-enabled helmet to protect the health of underground mine workers facing real-time hazards. The proposed solution introduces a real-time monitoring helmet equipped with IoT sensors to provide early warnings about fire, silicosis dust, temperature, and hazardous gases, reducing health risks and fatalities. Evaluation across different work settings reveals impressive accuracy rates: 96 percent in coal mines, 99 percent indoors, and 97 percent in industrial environments. The helmet integrates various sensors, RFID technology, and an LCD display to convey real-time data, while its three-tier structure ensures effective communication and alerting for worker safety in mines.

Amjad Rehman et al. (2022) presented a research paper that introduced a smart health analysis system for IoT networks. The system efficiently manages vast data while reducing communication overhead by utilizing regression analysis and intelligent hashing. It provides quality-aware services by employing regression prediction and delay-tolerant communication while prioritizing data security via cryptographic techniques. The system is made up of mobile sensors and operates through different phases like network initialization, data collection, relay, and security. The system is capable of enhancing learning, traffic prediction, and cost-effective e-health services. However, energy-hole problems in communication hubs remain a challenge. Jaeho Baek et al. (2023) proposed a research paper on a multi-sensor IoT system, introduced to manage diapers and the well-being of bedridden elderly patients. The system utilizes a movement tracking model and a predictive analytics watch to monitor diaper conditions and the mobility of elderly individuals confined to bed. Various sensors, including touch, temperature, moisture, VOC, and acceleration detectors, are integrated into the design to collect time-series data on mobility and diaper status. The authors developed models to predict urine, feces, flatulence, and the position of bedridden patients using this time-series data. The proposed system underwent impartial evaluation by accredited institutions. The system aims to track the posture, movement, and diaper status of elderly patients and can predict their condition and posture length, enhancing care monitoring. Data integrity and privacy in healthcare IoT are emphasized, necessitating robust encryption schemes. Rajkumar Ettiyan et al. (2023) presented a research paper that introduces a novel DNA-based hybrid logistic encryption system. This system enhances security in Internet of Things (IoT) patient monitoring systems, addressing the need for improved security in healthcare IoT. The innovative approach integrates 3D logistic chaotic charts and DNA operations into the widely used Advanced Encryption Standard (AES) system to provide added protection against IoT security breaches. The paper focuses on securing IoT devices, specifically in medical applications like fetal monitoring. Performance assessment involves simulations and trials on a testbed evaluating network characteristics, employing NIST statistical tests for randomness. The research's significant contribution lies in DNA calculations, generating translated bits and complex details for the proposed S-DAC security scheme, bolstering IoT security in healthcare operations. Sharda Tiwari et al. (2023) proposed a research paper that introduces a real-time, secure IoT-based medical management system that addresses privacy and security concerns in electronic healthcare. The system utilizes blockchain technology to protect patient data, comprising various sensors and medical equipment. Instead of conventional cloud storage, it employs Ethereum-based smart contracts, enabling doctors to monitor patients individually. The process involves Ethereum account creation, blockchain construction, IoT node deployment, data encryption, cloud storage, preprocessing, and doctor access via private keys. Access rights are time-limited for security purposes, and the system offers flexibility for incorporating additional sensors in the future, enhancing patient tracking and data security in healthcare IoT.

Andreas P. Plageras et al. (2023) introduced an IoT-based healthcare and emotional care system that aims to enhance patient-physician communication and overall healthcare quality. The system establishes a direct network for real-time data exchange between doctors and patients, facilitating the transmission of health and emotional data. It integrates various sensors such as heartbeat, blood volume, skin conductance, temperature, humidity sensors, and a camera device for capturing facial expressions. These sensors monitor the patient's physical health and assess emotional states such as anxiety, irritability, fear, upset, and panic. The system uses the TensorFlow framework for machine learning-based facial and lip movement analysis to extract key features for emotion recognition. A "Smart Healthcare Room" operates within a wireless sensor network (WSN) and employs data analysis and efficient algorithms to predict emotions. The system promotes collaboration and resource sharing between healthcare and emotional care components, offering comprehensive care for patients' physical and emotional well-being. Alhammari Hamoud H et al. (2023) present an IoT-based healthcare monitoring system using the MQTT protocol for real-time remote patient monitoring with an emphasis on accuracy and reduced signal transmission latency. The system uses vital sign sensors, a microcontroller (Arduino or Raspberry Pi), an MQTT broker for communication, and a receiver (a mobile app or website) to collect vital signs data. Data from various sensors is transmitted via Wi-Fi to the MQTT broker, which subsequently publishes the readings to a web server or mobile application. The study addresses security aspects, including MQTT authentication, user and device registration, and access control. The trial demonstrates error-free data package transfer, making the system valuable for hospitals. Doctors and nurses can monitor patients' vital signs remotely using computers or smartphones, reducing costs and travel time, particularly benefiting patients in suburban or rural areas. Nagendra Singh et al. (2022) proposed a novel approach for enhancing e-healthcare systems through the integration of deep learning and IoT technologies. The primary objective was to enable autonomous diagnosis and health condition prediction for patients in their homes. The MQTT protocol was recommended for IoT communications, facilitating the seamless transmission of patient data and emergency information to healthcare professionals. The study emphasized the need for standardized and interoperable sensors in e-health care to foster smarter healthcare services. The research highlighted the importance of sensor selection based on healthcare parameters and system specifications, including temperature sensors, accelerometers, glucose meters, heart rate monitors, and blood pressure monitors. Performance evaluation in a laboratory setting showcased the system's capabilities, promoting remote patient monitoring to reduce hospital visits, particularly during virus epidemics. Future research directions include the categorization of brain strokes through brain tissue analysis, further enhancing the potential of this hybrid e-healthcare model.

Nizar Al Bassam et al. (2021) have developed an IoT-based wearable device specifically designed to monitor COVID-19 symptoms in remote quarantined patients. The device has three key functionalities: an Android web interface for mobile accessibility, a pall subcaste featuring an operational API, and a wearable Internet of Things (IoT) detector subcaste. The device leverages sensors such as temperature, GPS, acceleration, and PPG to detect vital signs related to COVID-19. It can monitor body temperature, a crucial indicator of infection, in real-time, and the device can continuously track heart rate and pulse using algorithms based on finger-based data. Additionally, the system incorporates an artificial intelligence-based algorithm for cough detection. Real-time testing in a sanitarium has demonstrated the device's effectiveness in managing and controlling implicitly infected COVID-19 cases. The researchers recommend using this wearable device as a prototype for users entering and exiting vehicles, enhancing safety during the pandemic. Jarkko Hyysalo et al. (2022) have introduced an innovative IoT solution in the form of a Smart Mask that provides enhanced protection and personal health during the COVID-19 pandemic. This wearable ecosystem integrates sensing, AI, wireless connectivity, and software to collect vital health-related data both inside and outside the user. The Smart Mask has key sensors, including ambient light sensors (ALS) and an equivalent carbon dioxide (eCO2) sensor beneath the mask, to monitor light levels and air quality. Real-time communication with a user's smartphone enables data collection and analysis, facilitated by a dedicated mobile application. The Health AI backend supports data analytics, collaboration, data sharing, and long-term storage. This Smart Mask offers a comprehensive approach to combat respiratory viruses like COVID-19, aligning with the growing demand for intelligent respiratory protection equipment (RPE) in various sectors, including consumer, industrial, and medical applications. Fernanda Fama et al. (2022) present an innovative wireless biomonitoring system built on IoT technology for patient care, utilizing sensor patches adhered to the skin. These electronic skin patches, or bio stickers, collect a range of physiological and behavioral data and transmit it wirelessly to a smart bed IoT device. The Smart Bed acts as a hub, receiving data from bio stickers and relaying it over the Internet to the hospital information system for real-time patient monitoring. The system's core components include bio stickers as sensors, Smart Boxes within beds, and gateways linking to the hospital system. An edge/cloud platform employs AI, including machine learning, to process and analyze the collected data, enabling user profile identification and situational awareness. The system's use of FHIR standards, MQTT protocol, and BLE technology ensures seamless data collection, communication, and interoperability for effective wireless patient biomonitoring.

Rosario Morello et al. (2022) have developed an IoT-based ECG system which can be used to diagnose cardiac pathologies in smart city healthcare applications. The system customizes its processing algorithm for each patient, providing real-time data transmission to remote cardiologists or saving data for later analysis. It comprises an analog section for signal acquisition and a digital section that utilizes National Instruments MyRIO for real-time processing. The processing algorithm is developed using the LabVIEW environment. There are two memory systems which store patient-specific information and diagnostic parameters, which help improve accuracy. The system aims to provide reliable ECG monitoring for common cardiac diseases such as bradycardia, tachycardia, ischemia, and infarction, particularly in smart city settings. Naism Shaikh et al. (2023) have introduced an innovative IoT framework for healthcare applications that emphasizes real-time data analysis across diverse wireless networks. The proposed event-driven IoT architecture comprises event, context, and service layers, which enhance healthcare data analysis reliability. The study introduces cloud-based deep learning (CDN), leveraging deep learning standards and machine learning within an intelligent cloud system, resulting in improved healthcare parameters. The system utilizes accelerometer and ECG sensors for real-time data collection, processing through an event processing engine, and health prediction using deep learning. Rule-based systems ensure data accuracy and reliability. Extensive testing demonstrates its potential for remote healthcare monitoring, with high dependability and accuracy. Nisha Raheja et al. (2023) have presented a robust IoT-based healthcare framework for diagnosing heart diseases, particularly focused on remote ECG monitoring, which is crucial in rural areas during critical moments. The system preprocesses ECG data to enhance its quality, using noise reduction techniques. A deep-learning CNN classifier is trained to identify five arrhythmia types accurately. Security is ensured through the Triple Data Encryption Standard (TDES) algorithm. IoT functionality is incorporated via the ThingSpeak platform for secure data transmission to cardiologists. The system exhibits strong performance metrics, including high sensitivity, specificity, and accuracy in arrhythmia detection, paving the way for potential telecardiology applications and expanding its use beyond rural areas. Shivam Mishra et al. (2023) propose the use of non-invasive epidermal skin sensors for neonatal health monitoring, offering continuous monitoring of physiological parameters without invasive procedures. The article discusses the components of these sensors, including sensing units, data processing, and power sources, while addressing challenges like biocompatibility and data transmission. It emphasizes the importance of accurate measurements for parameters like body temperature, heart rate, and blood pressure in newborns.

The potential of machine learning for data analysis and the need for optimized data transmission are also highlighted. While epidermal sensors show promise, further research is essential to ensure their safety and effectiveness in real-time neonatal monitoring before widespread adoption.

Yeong Jun Jeon et al. (2023) have introduced a revolutionary wearable IoT solution designed to detect and manage sleep apnea in real-time, overcoming the limitations of earlier diagnostic and treatment approaches. The Sleepcare Kit and S-Pillow (SKP) form a wearable body-area network that monitors respiration, acceleration, and SpO2 to quickly and accurately identify episodes of sleep apnea. Additionally, the S-Pillow can adjust the patient's head position to ease sleep apnea symptoms. SKP uses a self-x-based closed-loop system to autonomously manage sleep apnea risk within the patient's home, significantly improving control frequency and reducing apnea time compared to previous pillow-based approaches. This innovation has the potential to enhance the comfort and efficacy of sleep apnea monitoring and management. When it comes to COVID-19 and dengue, two severe diseases that are prevalent in Bangladesh, Md. Siddikur Rahman et al. (2022) discuss the role of new technologies based on artificial intelligence and the Internet of Things (AI-IoT) in the fight against infectious diseases. Bangladesh is one of the world's poorest and most populous countries. A lack of a digital healthcare system, inadequate preparation, and poor public awareness pose unique challenges and a serious threat to the population, resulting in increasingly severe epidemics. This study suggests the implementation of a digital healthcare and surveillance system based on the Internet of Things (IoT) and artificial intelligence (AI) to enhance national prevention and control efforts by rapidly identifying COVID-19 and dengue cases. Numerous studies emphasize data security and privacy in IoT healthcare, utilizing encryption and blockchain for protection. Research is focused on AI-driven disease prediction and real-time patient monitoring. IoT-enabled remote patient monitoring is a major theme, reducing the need for hospital visits. IoT technology is integrated with medical equipment for various applications, and diverse sensors (e.g., ECG, temperature) play a crucial role in data collection. Research gaps in IoT-based healthcare include scalability, energy efficiency, human factors, cost-effectiveness, long-term studies, clinical integration, ethical considerations, and device diversity. Addressing these gaps can enhance the adaptability, usability, and ethical use of IoT healthcare systems.

3. PROPOSED METHODOLOGY

3.1 Proposed Work

The health monitoring system, shown in Figure 1, utilizes a Raspberry Pi as the central computing unit. It is responsible for gathering, processing, and analyzing data from non-intrusive heartbeat and eye blink sensors. These sensors measure heart rate and eye blink frequency, respectively, and send the data to the Raspberry Pi. The system prioritizes continuous monitoring, with the Raspberry Pi preparing and securely transmitting vital sign data to ThingSpeak, a cloud-based platform. ThingSpeak serves as a secure and scalable infrastructure for receiving, storing, and managing the data. It offers built-in visualization tools and programmable analytics algorithms for real-time monitoring of vital signs.

Healthcare practitioners can access patients' data remotely through the ThingSpeak dashboard, ensuring continuous monitoring and early identification of health issues. The system generates warnings and alarms based on pre-determined criteria, prompting a swift response to urgent changes in the patient's health. Additionally, the system may include a patient interface with a dashboard and notifications that enhance patient engagement and overall experience. This system aims to revolutionize healthcare by providing continuous, real-time monitoring, improving data accuracy, accessibility, and patient engagement while reducing the need for frequent hospital visits, especially for those with chronic diseases or requiring long-term monitoring.

Figure 1. Block diagram

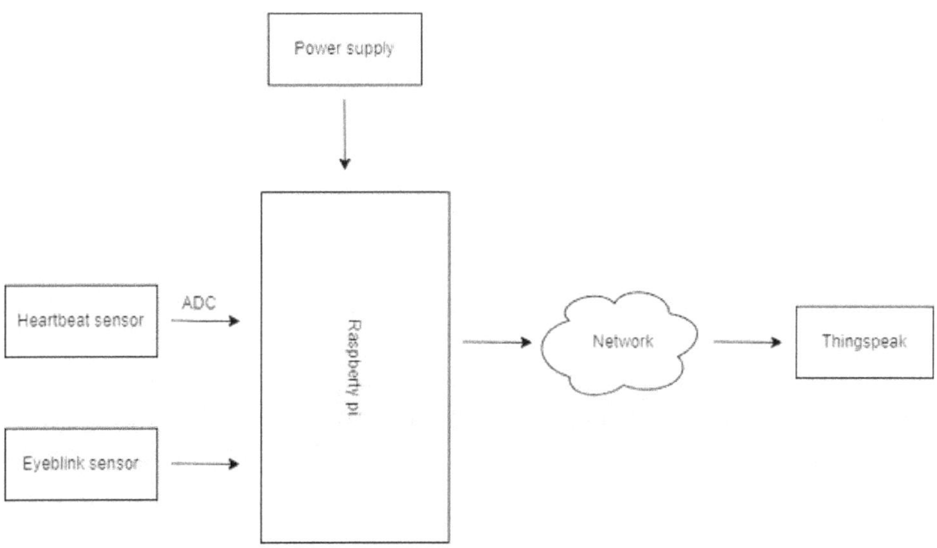

3.2 Proposed Model

ThingSpeak is a platform that provides powerful visualization tools to easily process and visualize data in real time. This enables us to perform sophisticated online analysis and gain valuable insights from the data as it streams in. The integration of an eye blink sensor is a novel addition that hasn't been extensively explored in previous studies. This sensor plays a pivotal role in detecting and monitoring abnormal blinking patterns, particularly in individuals with neurological disorders like blepharospasm. By incorporating the eye blink sensor, timely alerts and notifications are provided when abnormal eye blinks occur. The implications of this work are far-reaching. For instance, in the realm of driving, the eye-blink sensor can play a crucial role in identifying individuals with neurological conditions and monitoring their eye-blink patterns to ensure their safety on the road. In healthcare settings, the sensor can be invaluable for detecting and managing conditions related to abnormal blinking, providing early intervention, and improving patient care. This groundbreaking combination provides a cutting-edge solution for real-time data analysis and monitoring of abnormal blinking patterns. By harnessing the capabilities of ThingSpeak and leveraging the unique features of the eye blink sensor, it revolutionizes multiple domains, including healthcare, safety, and well-being. The aim is to enable timely detection and intervention, ultimately enhancing the quality of life for individuals with neurological disorders. Through this integration, it provides advancements in real-time data analysis and monitoring systems, setting a new standard in the field. This project represents a significant leap forward, showcasing the immense potential of combining technology.

3.3 Hardware Components

The hardware components used to monitor and store data in the cloud, which is used to analyze the data, are as follows:

i. Raspberry Pi Processor

The Raspberry Pi will act as the central control unit for the system, responsible for integrating sensors, processing data, and communicating with the cloud platform as shown in Figure 2. The Raspberry Pi is a microcontroller with the capabilities of a small computer. Its GPIO pins are used for input and output purposes, and can be customized to meet specific needs. It is widely used in development due to its ability to put the entire Linux server and peripheral devices on a single chip at a very low cost.

Figure 2. Raspberry Pi

ii. Eye-blink Sensor:

In Figure 3, the eye-blink sensor will be connected to either an optical or electrical eye-blink sensor to track when the driver blinks their eyes. This sensor module consists of a relay, an IR sensor, and an eye blink sensor frame. The driver needs to wear an eye-blink sensor frame that connects to the vibrator device. The vibrator will shake when a collision occurs or when the driver falls asleep. An IR transmitter emits IR rays towards the driver's eyes, and an IR receiver picks up reflected rays when the driver's eyes are closed. The frame is made up of these two components. The SST microcontroller board is connected to the relay to provide the additional current required by this module.

iii. Pulse Sensor:

To measure a person's heart rate accurately, a pulse sensor is necessary. The sensor has two sides: one with an LED and an ambient light sensor, and the other

Figure 3. Eye blink sensor

Figure 4. REES52 pulse sensor

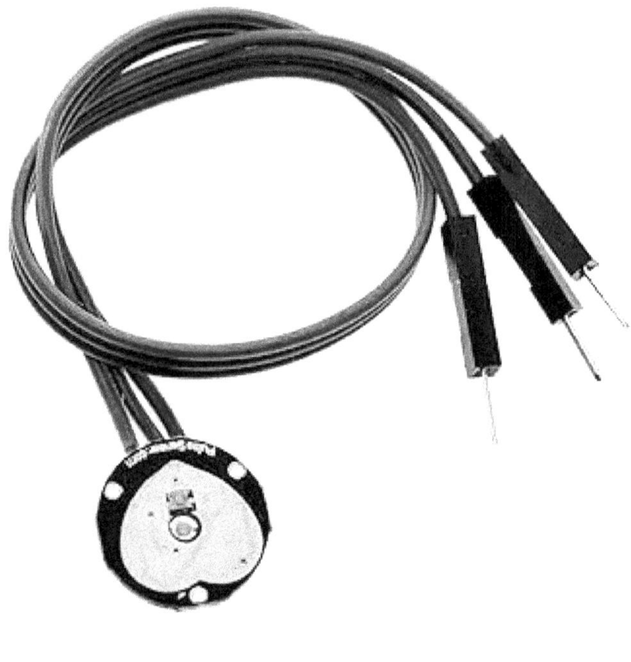

side with additional components that control the noise cancellation and amplification processes. The LED on the front of the sensor covers a vein in the human body. To get an accurate reading, you should place the sensor on the tip of your finger or ear directly over a vein. The LED emits light that reaches the vein, and blood only flows through veins when the heart is pumping. By monitoring the blood flow, you can easily measure the heartbeats, as shown in Figure 4.

iv. ADC

Figure 5 shows the usage of an 8-channel, 10-bit analog-to-digital converter for data acquisition and conversion, which is both affordable and reliable. This chip is an excellent option for reading simple analog signals, such as those from temperature or light sensors. ADCs provide high-precision and accurate measurement capabilities, enabling analog signals to be converted into digital values with exceptional resolution.

Figure 5. Raspberry Pi - ADC

3.4 Hardware Setup

The proposed system is designed to automatically measure the heart rate and movement of patients. It utilizes other health parameters and symptoms collected by the system to determine whether the patient is dealing with any chronic disorders or diseases. To provide real-time physiological monitoring and data storage, the suggested system integrates a Raspberry Pi, an eye blink sensor, a heartbeat sensor, and the ThingSpeak cloud platform. By storing and analyzing the data on a cloud platform, the system aims to provide precise and ongoing monitoring of heart rate and eye blink rate.

3.5 Implementation

The figure 6 above shows a Raspberry Pi connected to a breadboard, which interfaces with a heart rate sensor. This setup allows for real-time heart rate data collection for applications such as health monitoring and fitness tracking. Additionally, the Raspberry Pi is linked to an eye blink sensor, allowing the capture and analysis of blinking patterns. This integration opens up possibilities for projects related to

Figure 6. Overall experimental setup

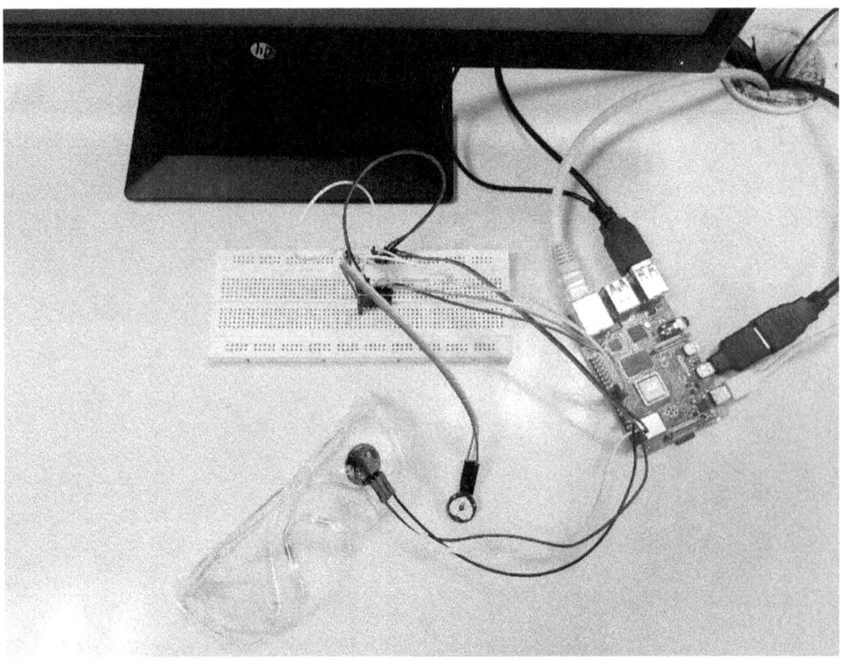

drowsiness detection and human-computer interaction, utilizing Raspberry Pi's capabilities for data processing and control. To set up the system, follow these steps:

- **Step 1:** Hardware Setup Connect a Raspberry Pi to the pulse sensor using its GPIO pins. Then, connect the eyeblink sensor to the GPIO pins of the Raspberry Pi.
- **Step 2:** Power and Connectivity Power the Raspberry Pi using a suitable power supply and connect it to the internet for communication with the cloud platform. Ensure that the power supply meets the power requirements of both the Raspberry Pi board itself and the connected sensors. The power supply should provide stable and sufficient power to avoid voltage drops or fluctuations that could affect sensor performance.
- **Step 3:** Raspberry Pi Setup Install the Raspberry Pi's operating system, Raspbian. Set up an Ethernet or Wi-Fi connection to the internet on the Raspberry Pi. Install the necessary libraries for the eyeblink and pulse sensors.
- **Step 4:** ThingSpeak Setup Create an account on the ThingSpeak platform (https://thingspeak.com). Create a new channel on ThingSpeak to store the health data. Note down the Write API Key of the channel.
- **Step 5:** Sensor Integration Interface the eye blink sensor and heartbeat sensor with the Raspberry Pi. This may involve using appropriate interfaces, such as GPIO pins or additional modules, to establish connections and ensure proper data acquisition from the sensors.
- **Step 6:** ThingSpeak Cloud Integration Transmit the processed physiological data from the Raspberry Pi to the ThingSpeak cloud platform. ThingSpeak provides an IoT analytics platform that allows storage, visualization, and analysis of sensor data.
- **Step 7:** Code Implementation Write a Python script to read data from the pulse sensor and eye blink sensor. Use Raspberry Pi's GPIO library to read the sensor values. Implement logic to process the sensor data and extract relevant health parameters. Use the ThingSpeak API to send the data to the created channel. Incorporate error handling and exception handling into the code.
- **Step 8:** Data Transmission in the Python script, establish a connection with ThingSpeak using the API key. Send the health data to the ThingSpeak channel by making HTTP POST requests to the ThingSpeak API endpoints. Include the relevant health parameters, such as pulse rate and eye blink monitoring count, in the data being sent.
- **Step 9:** Monitoring and Visualization Log in to your ThingSpeak account and navigate to the newly created channel. Configure the channel settings to display the received health data. Customize the visualization options, such as

graphs or gauges, to represent the data. Set up alerts or notifications based on specific health thresholds, if required.

- **Step 10:** Running the System Connect the Raspberry Pi to a power source and execute the Python script on the Raspberry Pi to start the health monitoring system. Monitor the ThingSpeak channel to view real-time health data. By following these steps, you can set up a health monitoring system using a Raspberry Pi, a pulse sensor, an eye blink sensor, and the ThingSpeak platform to collect, store, and visualize health data.
- **Step 11:** Experimental Evaluation Evaluate the system's performance through experiments conducted on a group of participants. Assess the accuracy and reliability of the eye blink rate and heart rate measurements by comparing them to reference values or established standards. Collect user feedback regarding the system's usability and overall effectiveness.

4. EXPERIMENTAL RESULTS

Our research study aimed to investigate the physiological responses of participants by utilizing data collected via the ThingSpeak cloud platform, specifically heartbeat sensor data and eye blink sensor data. The heartbeat sensor data provided valuable insights into the participants' cardiovascular health and their physiological reactions to various stimuli. The integration of the ThingSpeak cloud platform allowed for remote data collection, enabling us to analyze the data efficiently. Initially, we examined the correlation between heart rate and specific activities or stimuli. Participants were engaged in a range of activities, including exercise, stress-inducing tasks, and relaxation techniques. The heartbeat sensor data revealed distinct patterns of heart rate variation in response to these activities. For instance, heart rate increased significantly during high-intensity exercise, demonstrating the body's physiological response to physical exertion. Conversely, heart rate decreased during relaxation exercises, indicating a relaxation response. Moreover, we conducted an analysis of heart rate variability (HRV) using the collected sensor data. HRV is a measure of the variations in time intervals between successive heartbeats and is associated with autonomic nervous system function. Our findings showed that HRV varied across different activities and conditions. Higher HRV values were observed during periods of relaxation and low stress, indicating a state of overall well-being. Conversely, lower HRV values were observed during high-stress tasks, suggesting increased sympathetic nervous system activity and potential fatigue. Furthermore, the long-term monitoring capability provided by the ThingSpeak cloud platform allowed us to study trends and patterns in the heartbeat sensor data. By continuously collecting

Figure 7. Normal heartbeat detection

data over an extended period, we were able to analyze circadian rhythms and sleep quality.

Our results demonstrated diurnal variations in heart rate, with higher rates during the daytime and lower rates during nighttime rest. This analysis highlighted the potential of the ThingSpeak platform for monitoring and managing chronic conditions, as abnormal patterns could be identified and addressed. In conjunction with the heartbeat sensor data, the eye blink sensors provided additional insights into participants' visual attention, cognitive load, and fatigue levels. Analysis of blink rates revealed variations across different tasks and stimuli. Blink rates tended to decrease during periods of focused attention, indicating heightened concentration. Conversely, blink rates increased during relaxation or mind-wandering, suggesting a shift in attentional focus. Overall, the integration of heartbeat sensor data collected through the ThingSpeak cloud platform, combined with eye blink sensor data, enabled us to gain a comprehensive understanding of participants' physiological responses. These findings contribute to our understanding of human physiology and can have implications for various fields such as healthcare, sports performance, and stress management.

Figure 7 represents the Python code that likely involves importing the necessary modules, setting up a connection with the heartbeat sensor, reading sensor data, calculating the heart rate in BPM, and displaying the result. The output of the code you can run indicates a normal heart rate of 99 BPM.

Figure 8. Abnormal heartbeat detection

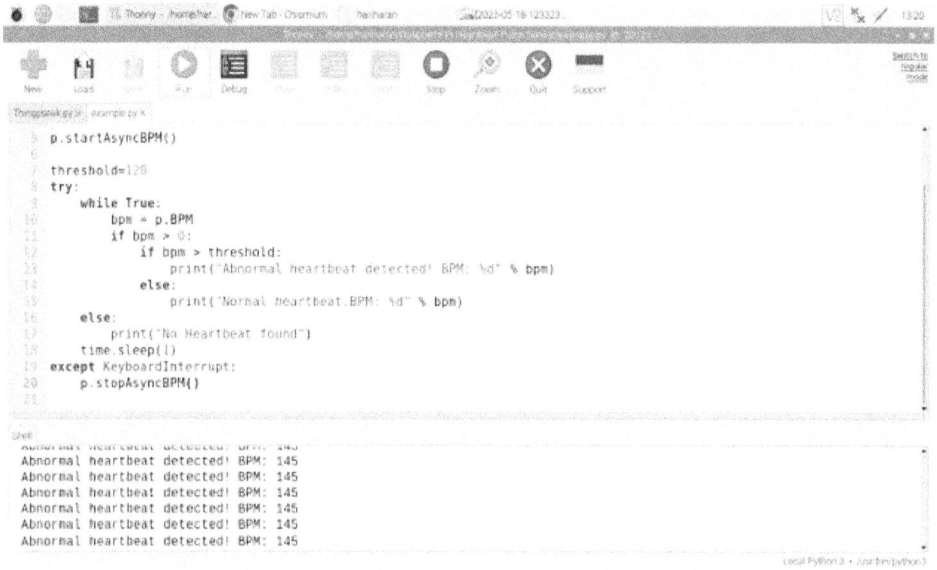

Figure 8 shows the output of a Python code for a heartbeat sensor, indicating an abnormal beat with a BPM of 145. Possible reasons for this could include physical exertion, anxiety or stress, equipment error, or an underlying health condition. Further evaluation and consultation with a healthcare professional would be necessary to determine the cause of the abnormal reading.

Figure 9 displays the output of a Python code for an eyeblink sensor, indicating an abnormal eyeblink detection. Possible causes for this abnormality could include eye fatigue, medical conditions affecting eye movement, or potential issues with the sensor or code.

Figure 10 represents the ThingSpeak visualization for heart rate data and would likely include a graph showing the heart rate measurements over time. The x-axis would represent time, while the y-axis would indicate the heart rate in BPM. The graph could reveal patterns, trends, and potential abnormalities in the individual's heart rate, providing valuable insights into their cardiovascular health. However, without a specific screenshot, it is challenging to provide a more detailed explanation.

Figure 11 displays the visualization of the Thing Speak app, displaying the output of the same visualization displayed on the ThingSpeak website. The ThingSpeak app and ThingSpeak visualization provide a user-friendly interface that simplifies the process of data analysis and enables users to harness the full potential of their IoT devices' data.

Figure 9. Abnormal eyeblink detection

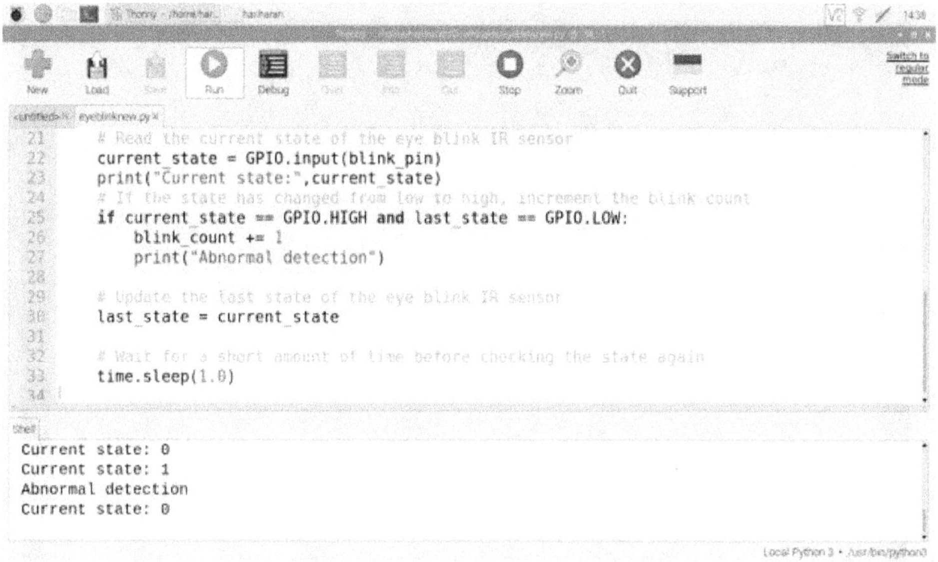

Figure 10. ThingSpeak visualization

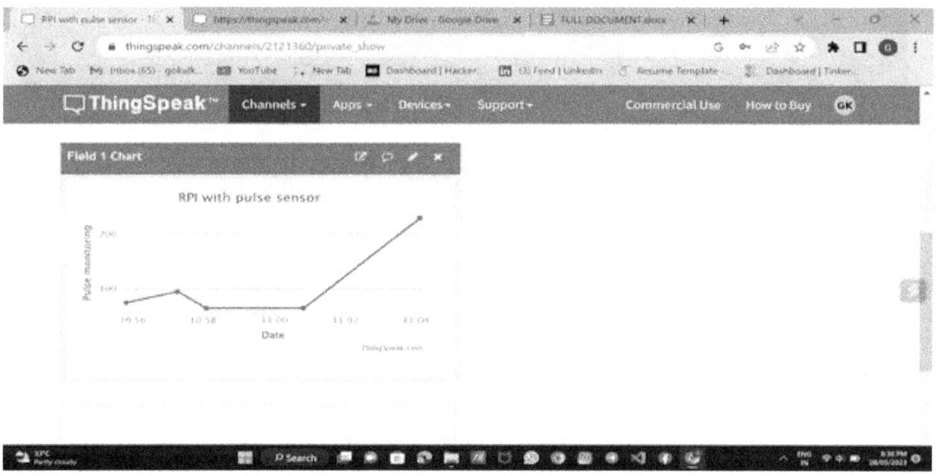

5. CONCLUSION AND FUTURE ENHANCEMENTS

Health monitoring systems have become an essential tool in modern healthcare. These systems are designed to provide numerous benefits and opportunities to enhance patient care and outcomes. Health monitoring systems utilize wearable sensors, advanced data processing algorithms, and cloud-based platforms to enable

Figure 11. Mobile visualization

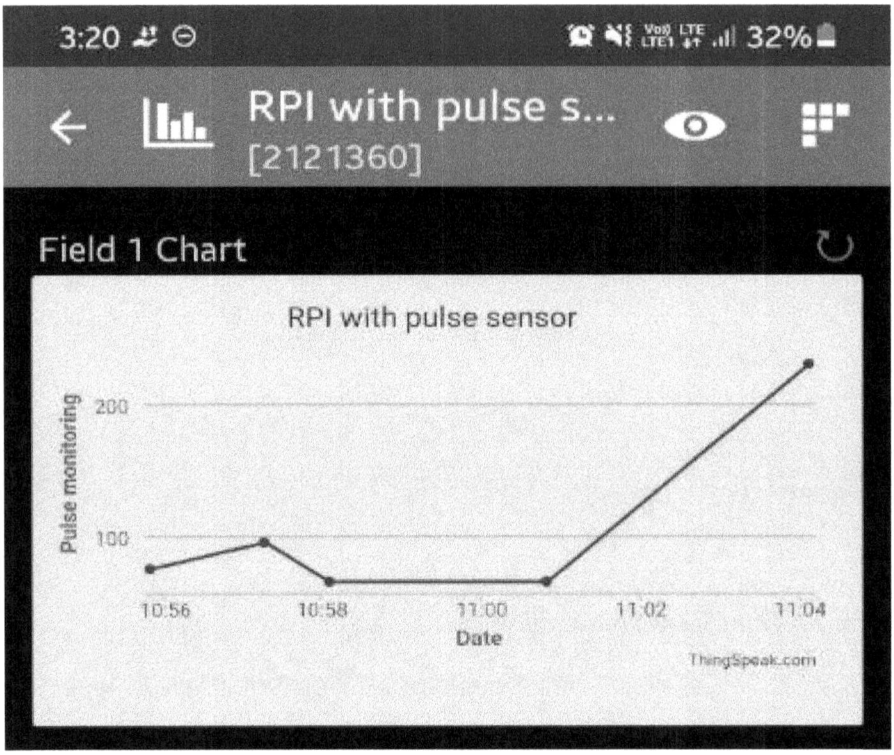

continuous monitoring, early detection of health issues, and personalized care. By leveraging wearable sensors, these systems can collect real-time data on vital signs and other health parameters, providing a comprehensive view of a patient's well-being. This continuous monitoring allows for early detection of abnormalities, such as irregular heart rhythms, abnormal blood pressure fluctuations, or sleep disorders, enabling timely intervention and preventive measures. Advanced data processing algorithms enable the extraction of meaningful insights from the collected data. Machine learning algorithms and signal processing techniques can identify patterns, trends, and anomalies, assisting healthcare professionals in accurate diagnosis, risk assessment, and personalized health recommendations. Real-time alerts and notifications enable healthcare providers to respond promptly to critical events and deviations from normal health parameters, ensuring timely interventions. Cloud-based platforms play a crucial role in health monitoring systems by securely storing and managing the collected data. These platforms enable remote access to patient information, facilitating seamless communication and collaboration between healthcare professionals and patients. Patients can actively engage in their healthcare by accessing their health data, receiving personalized recommendations, and utilizing self-management tools, promoting a patient-centric approach to care. Health monitoring systems enhance convenience, reduce costs, and improve patient satisfaction by reducing the need for frequent hospital visits, especially for patients with chronic conditions or those requiring long-term monitoring. Additionally, health monitoring systems empower individuals to take an active role in managing their health, promoting self-awareness and healthier lifestyle choices. While health monitoring systems have demonstrated significant potential, further choices and development are essential to enhancing their capabilities. Advancements in wearable sensor technology, data analytics, and machine learning algorithms will continue to refine and expand the functionalities of these systems. Collaboration between healthcare professionals, researchers, and technology experts is vital to driving innovation, addressing challenges, and maximizing the benefits of health monitoring systems. In summary, health monitoring systems hold great promise for revolutionizing healthcare by enabling remote patient care, continuous monitoring, and early detection of health issues. With their ability to provide real-time data analysis, personalized recommendations, and proactive interventions, these systems have the potential to improve patient outcomes, enhance patient-provider collaboration, and promote overall well-being in a rapidly evolving healthcare landscape.

REFERENCES

Al Bassam, N., Hussain, S. A., Al Qaraghuli, A., Khan, J., Sumesh, E. P., & Lavanya, V. (2021). IoT based wearable device to monitor the signs of quarantined remote patients of COVID-19. *Informatics in Medicine Unlocked*, *24*, 100588. doi:10.1016/j.imu.2021.100588 PMID:33997262

Alshammari, H. H. (2023). The internet of things healthcare monitoring system based on MQTT protocol. *Alexandria Engineering Journal*, *69*, 275–287. doi:10.1016/j.aej.2023.01.065

Baek, J. (2023). Smart predictive analytics care monitoring model based on multi sensor IoT system: Management of diaper and attitude for the bedridden elderly. *Sensors International*, *4*, 100213. doi:10.1016/j.sintl.2022.100213

Ettiyan, R., & Geetha, V. (2023). A hybrid logistic DNA-based encryption system for securing the Internet of Things patient monitoring systems. *Healthcare Analytics*, *3*, 100149. doi:10.1016/j.health.2023.100149

Famá, F., Faria, J. N., & Portugal, D. (2022). An IoT-based interoperable architecture for wireless biomonitoring of patients with sensor patches. *Internet of Things : Engineering Cyber Physical Human Systems*, *19*, 100547. doi:10.1016/j.iot.2022.100547

Hyysalo, J., Dasanayake, S., Hannu, J., Schuss, C., Rajanen, M., Leppänen, T., Doermann, D., & Sauvola, J. (2022). Smart mask–Wearable IoT solution for improved protection and personal health. *Internet of Things : Engineering Cyber Physical Human Systems*, *18*, 100511. doi:10.1016/j.iot.2022.100511 PMID:37521492

Javaid, M., & Khan, I. H. (2021). Internet of Things (IoT) enabled healthcare helps to take the challenges of COVID-19 Pandemic. *Journal of Oral Biology and Craniofacial Research*, *11*(2), 209–214. doi:10.1016/j.jobcr.2021.01.015 PMID:33665069

Jeon, Y. J., Park, S. H., & Kang, S. J. (2023). Self-x based closed loop wearable IoT for real-time detection and resolution of sleep apnea. *Internet of Things : Engineering Cyber Physical Human Systems*, *22*, 100767. doi:10.1016/j.iot.2023.100767

Kasat, K., Rani, D. L., Khan, B., Kirubakaran, M. K., & Malathi, P. (2022). A novel security framework for healthcare data through IOT sensors. *Measurement. Sensors*, *24*, 100535. doi:10.1016/j.measen.2022.100535

Malibari, A. A. (2023). An efficient IoT-Artificial intelligence-based disease prediction using lightweight CNN in healthcare system. *Measurement. Sensors*, *26*, 100695. doi:10.1016/j.measen.2023.100695

Mishra, S., Khouqeer, G. A., Aamna, B., Alodhayb, A., Ibrahim, S. J. A., Hooda, M., & Jayaswal, G. (2023). A review: Recent advancements in sensor technology for non-invasive neonatal health monitoring. *Biosensors & Bioelectronics: X*, *14*, 100332. doi:10.1016/j.biosx.2023.100332

Morello, R., Ruffa, F., Jablonski, I., Fabbiano, L., & De Capua, C. (2022). An IoT based ECG system to diagnose cardiac pathologies for healthcare applications in smart cities. *Measurement*, *190*, 110685. doi:10.1016/j.measurement.2021.110685

Nanthini, K., Sivabalaselvamani, D., Chitra, K., Mohideen, P. A., & Raja, R. D. (2023, March). Cardiac Arrhythmia Detection and Prediction Using Deep Learning Technique. In *Proceedings of Fourth International Conference on Communication, Computing and Electronics Systems: ICCCES 2022* (pp. 983-1003). Singapore: Springer Nature Singapore. 10.1007/978-981-19-7753-4_75

Plageras, A. P., & Psannis, K. E. (2023). IOT-based health and emotion care system. *ICT Express*, *9*(1), 112–115. doi:10.1016/j.icte.2022.03.008

Raheja, N., & Manocha, A. K. (2023). An IoT enabled secured clinical health care framework for diagnosis of heart diseases. *Biomedical Signal Processing and Control, 80*, 104368. doi:10.1016/j.bspc.2022.104368

Rahman, M. S., Safa, N. T., Sultana, S., Salam, S., Karamehic-Muratovic, A., & Overgaard, H. J. (2022). Role of artificial intelligence-internet of things (AI-IoT) based emerging technologies in the public health response to infectious diseases in Bangladesh. *Parasite Epidemiology and Control, 18*, e00266. doi:10.1016/j.parepi.2022.e00266 PMID:35975103

Rehman, A., Saba, T., Haseeb, K., Singh, R., & Jeon, G. (2022). Smart health analysis system using regression analysis with iterative hashing for IoT communication networks. *Computers & Electrical Engineering, 104*, 108456. doi:10.1016/j.compeleceng.2022.108456

Selvakarthi, D., Sivabalaselvamani, D., Wafiq, M. A., Aruna, G., & Gokulnath, M. (2023, March). An IoT Integrated Sensor Technologies for the Enhancement of Hospital Waste Segregation and Management. In *2023 International Conference on Innovative Data Communication Technologies and Application (ICIDCA)* (pp. 797-804). IEEE. 10.1109/ICIDCA56705.2023.10099836

Shaikh, N., Kasat, K., Godi, R. K., Krishna, V. R., Chauhan, D. K., & Kharade, J. (2023). Novel IoT framework for event processing in healthcare applications. *Measurement. Sensors, 27*, 100733. doi:10.1016/j.measen.2023.100733

Singh, N., Gunjan, V. K., Chaudhary, G., Kaluri, R., Victor, N., & Lakshmanna, K. (2022). IoT enabled HELMET to safeguard the health of mine workers. *Computer Communications, 193*, 1–9. doi:10.1016/j.comcom.2022.06.032

Singh, N., Sasirekha, S. P., Dhakne, A., Thrinath, B. S., Ramya, D., & Thiagarajan, R. (2022). IOT enabled hybrid model with learning ability for E-health care systems. *Measurement. Sensors, 24*, 100567. doi:10.1016/j.measen.2022.100567

Sivabalaselvamani, D., Nanthini, K., Selvakarthi, D., Niranchan, V. M., Kumar, L. S., & Swetha, P. (2023, September). Skin Melanoma Detection Using Image Augmentation. In *2023 4th International Conference on Smart Electronics and Communication (ICOSEC)* (pp. 1624-1630). IEEE. 10.1109/ICOSEC58147.2023.10275944

Sivabalaselvamani, D., Selvakarthi, D., Rahunathan, L., Eswari, S. N., Pavithraa, M., & Sridhar, M. (2021, January). Investigation on heart disease using machine learning algorithms. In *2021 International Conference on Computer Communication and Informatics (ICCCI)* (pp. 1-6). IEEE. 10.1109/ICCCI50826.2021.9402390

Sivabalaselvamani, D., Selvakarthi, D., Yogapriya, J., Thiruvenkatasuresh, M. P., Maruthappa, M., & Chandra, A. S. (2021, January). Artificial Intelligence in data-driven analytics for the personalized healthcare. In *2021 international conference on computer communication and informatics (ICCCI)* (pp. 1-5). IEEE.

Tiwari, S., Dhanda, N., & Dev, H. (2023). A real time secured medical management system based on blockchain and internet of things. *Measurement. Sensors*, *25*, 100630. doi:10.1016/j.measen.2022.100630

Toomula, S., Paulraj, D., Bose, J., Bikku, T., & Sivabalaselvamani, D. (2022). IoT and wearables for detection of COVID-19 diagnosis using fusion-based feature extraction with multikernel extreme learning machine. In *Wearable Telemedicine Technology for the Healthcare Industry* (pp. 137–152). Academic Press.

Chapter 9
Cloud Computing and Machine Learning in the Green Power Sector:
Harnessing Sustainable Innovations:

Anurag Vijay Agrawal
https://orcid.org/0000-0002-9753-1216
Department of Electronics and Communication Engineering, J. P. Institute of Engineering and Technology, India

G. Sujatha
Department of Electronics and Communication Engineering, Sri Venkateswara College of engineering (Autonomous), India

P. Sasireka
https://orcid.org/0000-0002-1660-1594
Department of Electronics and Communication Engineering, S.A. Engineering College, India

P. Ranjith
Department of Science and Humanity, Sri Sai Ram Institute of Technology, India

S. Cloudin
Department of Computer Science and Engineering, KCG College of Technology, India

B. Samp
Narasu's Sarathy Institute of Technology, India

ABSTRACT

The chapter explores the potential of cloud computing, machine learning, and the green power sector in promoting sustainable energy production and consumption. Cloud computing offers efficient data storage and processing, while machine learning algorithms optimize energy production, distribution, and consumption. It highlights how cloud-based infrastructure can enhance renewable energy forecasting, energy grid management, and demand response systems. Edge computing brings intelligence

DOI: 10.4018/979-8-3693-1694-8.ch009

closer to renewable energy sources, reducing latency and energy consumption. The chapter also addresses challenges like data privacy, security, and regulatory compliance in the green power sector. It reviews case studies and emerging trends to demonstrate how these technologies can optimize renewable energy production and contribute to a more sustainable power sector.

INTRODUCTION

The integration of cloud computing and machine learning technologies is a promising solution for the green power sector, as it can drive efficiency, reduce waste, and optimize resource utilization. As societies grapple with climate change and transition to renewable energy sources, this chapter explores the symbiotic relationship between these technologies and sustainable development in the green power sector. It delves into the ways in which these innovations are reshaping the landscape of energy production, distribution, and consumption, ultimately paving the way for a cleaner, more resilient, and environmentally responsible energy ecosystem. The chapter explores the potential of cloud-based infrastructure and intelligent machine learning algorithms in transforming energy management, renewable energy forecasting, and energy grid management. It highlights the potential for a greener, more sustainable future, highlighting the importance of optimizing energy consumption and minimizing carbon footprints, and the transformative journey towards a more sustainable future (Andronie et al., 2021).

The challenges posed by climate change and the finite nature of fossil fuel resources have galvanized a global movement towards renewable and sustainable energy solutions. The green power sector, comprising wind, solar, hydro, geothermal, and other forms of clean energy generation, has emerged as a linchpin in our quest to mitigate the impacts of climate change and transition towards a low-carbon economy. However, realizing the full potential of green power requires not only the harnessing of renewable energy sources but also the intelligent orchestration of these resources to meet the ever-growing energy demands of a rapidly advancing world (Mustapha et al., 2021).

Enter cloud computing and machine learning, two disruptive technologies that have, individually, revolutionized industries across the board. When integrated into the green power sector, these technologies bring a convergence of unprecedented computational power and data-driven intelligence, enabling the optimization of energy production, the enhancement of grid resilience, and the reduction of environmental footprints. This study explores the roles and impacts of cloud computing, a scalable infrastructure for data storage and processing, and machine learning algorithms, which uncover intricate patterns within data, for real-time energy management decisions (Murugesan, 2008).

This text explores the benefits of cloud computing, machine learning, and edge computing in sustainability. It discusses cloud computing models, deployment options, and their role in renewable energy forecasting, grid management, and demand response systems. Edge computing brings computational power closer to renewable energy sources, reducing latency and energy consumption. The text also examines the industry's evolution towards sustainability, emphasizing energy-efficient data centers, renewable energy-powered cloud services, and eco-friendly hardware design (Buyya et al., 2023). It also discusses the environmental impact of these technologies and strategies for reducing their carbon footprint.

This chapter explores the integration of cloud computing and machine learning in the green power sector, focusing on data privacy, security, and regulatory compliance. It provides real-world case studies and best practices to illustrate the success of this integration. The chapter also explores future trends and emerging technologies, such as the Internet of Things (IoT) and advanced artificial intelligence (AI), which are expected to further revolutionize the green power sector (Fan et al., 2023). The goal is to ensure sustainability without compromising privacy or integrity. This chapter provides a comprehensive guide on the relationship between cloud computing and machine learning, emphasizing their potential in the green power sector. It urges decision-makers, innovators, and researchers to adopt sustainable innovations for a more efficient, resilient, and environmentally responsible energy landscape, ensuring future challenges and planet protection (Shaw et al., 2022).

The backdrop against which this chapter unfolds is one characterized by increasing concerns about the environmental consequences of traditional energy production methods and the urgency to transition towards sustainable alternatives. Climate change, resource depletion, and the need to reduce greenhouse gas emissions have spurred a global shift towards renewable energy sources, forming the cornerstone of the green power sector (Pandey et al., 2023). However, while renewable energy offers tremendous promise, it also introduces complexities related to intermittency, variability, and efficient utilization. In response to these challenges, cloud computing and machine learning have emerged as technological saviors, offering the promise of smart, data-driven solutions to optimize energy production, distribution, and consumption. The motivation for this chapter lies in exploring how these two transformative technologies can be harnessed to drive sustainable development within the green power sector (Xu et al., 2020). Our goal is to improve clean energy efficiency and sustainability by combining cloud computing's predictive and scalability capabilities with machine learning's adaptive capabilities.

Objectives of the Chapter

This chapter aims to explore the relationship between cloud computing, machine learning, and the green power sector. It explains the foundational principles of cloud computing, its various service and deployment models, and how it forms a robust infrastructure for integrating machine learning in sustainable energy systems. It also explores the multifaceted landscape of machine learning applications in the green power sector, including renewable energy forecasting, energy grid management, and demand response systems. The chapter emphasizes the seamless synergy between cloud computing and machine learning, highlighting their combined capabilities for optimizing renewable energy generation and consumption. It also discusses the sustainability aspects of cloud computing, including energy-efficient data centers, renewable-powered cloud services, and eco-friendly hardware design.

The chapter explores the environmental impact of cloud computing and machine learning technologies, addressing ethical and regulatory aspects, and offers a comprehensive resource for green power sector stakeholders.

Overview of Cloud Computing, Machine Learning, and Green Power Sector

Cloud computing and machine learning are interconnected technologies that provide on-demand access to scalable infrastructure, platforms, and software services over the internet. Cloud computing is a paradigm shift in computing resources delivery, while machine learning is a subfield of artificial intelligence that enables systems to learn from data and make predictions without explicit programming. Understanding these domains is crucial for advancing sustainability in the green power sector (Pandey et al., 2023; Shaw et al., 2022).

FOUNDATIONS OF CLOUD COMPUTING

Cloud computing is a fundamental aspect of modern IT infrastructure, providing scalable and flexible resources that have significantly transformed the way businesses manage their data, applications, and services (Agrawal et al., 2024; Satav et al., 2024; Syamala et al., 2023).

Cloud Service Models (IaaS, PaaS, SaaS):

- **Infrastructure as a Service (IaaS):** IaaS provides virtualized computing resources over the internet. Users can access and manage virtual machines, storage, and networking infrastructure on a pay-as-you-go basis. This model offers maximum flexibility, allowing users to build, configure, and manage their own software stacks and applications (Srinivas et al., 2023).

- **Platform as a Service (PaaS):** PaaS provides a platform and environment for developers to build, deploy, and manage applications without worrying about the underlying infrastructure. It offers tools, services, and development frameworks to streamline the application development process. PaaS is well-suited for developers aiming to focus on coding and innovation rather than infrastructure management (Agrawal et al., 2024).
- **Software as a Service (SaaS):** SaaS delivers software applications over the internet on a subscription basis. Users can access these applications via web browsers, eliminating the need for installation or local software maintenance. Common examples include email services like Gmail and productivity suites like Microsoft Office 365.

Cloud Deployment Models (Public, Private, Hybrid):

- **Public Cloud:** Public clouds are owned and operated by third-party cloud service providers, offering computing resources to multiple organizations on a shared infrastructure. They are highly scalable and cost-effective, making them suitable for various applications and services. However, public clouds may raise data security and compliance concerns (Satav et al., 2024).
- **Private Cloud:** Private clouds are dedicated to a single organization and can be hosted on-premises or by a third-party provider. They provide greater control, customization, and security over infrastructure and data. Private clouds are ideal for organizations with strict regulatory requirements or specialized computing needs (Venkateswaran et al., 2023).
- **Hybrid Cloud:** Hybrid clouds combine elements of both public and private clouds, allowing data and applications to move seamlessly between them. This model provides flexibility and scalability, enabling organizations to leverage the benefits of both cloud types while maintaining control over critical data (Hema et al., 2023).

Cloud Computing Benefits for Sustainable Development:

Cloud computing plays a pivotal role in advancing sustainable development within the green power sector and beyond (Hema et al., 2023; Rahamathunnisa, Sudhakar, et al., 2023; Srinivas et al., 2023; Venkateswaran et al., 2023):

- **Resource Optimization:** Cloud computing allows organizations to scale their infrastructure up or down as needed, reducing wasteful over-provisioning and energy consumption.
- **Data Insights:** Cloud-based analytics and machine learning enable organizations to gain deeper insights into energy usage, facilitating better decision-making and resource allocation.
- **Collaboration and Remote Work:** Cloud-based collaboration tools support remote work, reducing the need for physical office space and commuting, which can contribute to reduced carbon emissions.
- **Disaster Recovery and Resilience:** Cloud services offer robust disaster recovery and backup capabilities, ensuring data and applications remain accessible even in adverse conditions, enhancing overall system resilience.
- **Energy-Efficient Data Centers:** Cloud providers are investing in energy-efficient data centers, often powered by renewable energy sources, contributing to reduced environmental impact.

The study aims to explore the potential of cloud computing and machine learning in promoting sustainable innovation in the green power sector.

MACHINE LEARNING IN THE GREEN POWER SECTOR

Applications of Machine Learning in Renewable Energy

Machine learning is revolutionizing the renewable energy sector by offering data-driven solutions to various challenges, with key applications in renewable energy(Syamala et al., 2023). The applications of machine learning in renewable energy is illustrated in Figure 1.

- **Renewable Energy Forecasting:** ML models can predict renewable energy generation from sources like solar panels and wind turbines with high accuracy. By analyzing historical weather data, sensor readings, and other relevant information, these models enable better resource planning, grid integration, and energy trading (Nishanth et al., 2023).
- **Energy Production Optimization:** ML algorithms can optimize the operation of renewable energy systems. For instance, they can adjust the angles of solar panels to maximize sunlight absorption or control the pitch of wind turbine blades to optimize power generation in varying wind conditions.

Figure 1. Applications of machine learning in renewable energy

- **Load Forecasting:** ML can predict energy demand patterns, allowing utilities to adjust supply accordingly. This helps prevent energy wastage and ensures a more efficient use of renewable energy resources.
- **Predictive Maintenance:** ML can predict when renewable energy equipment, such as wind turbines or solar inverters, is likely to fail. This proactive approach to maintenance reduces downtime and extends the lifespan of these assets.
- **Grid Integration:** ML can enhance the integration of renewable energy sources into the grid by predicting fluctuations in supply and demand. This enables utilities to balance the grid more effectively and minimize the need for backup fossil fuel power generation.
- **Energy Storage Optimization:** ML can optimize the use of energy storage systems (e.g., batteries) in conjunction with renewable sources. Algorithms can determine when to charge and discharge storage units to maximize cost savings and grid stability (Satav et al., 2024; Venkateswaran et al., 2023).

- **Microgrid Management:** ML can manage microgrids efficiently by analyzing real-time data from renewable energy sources, energy storage, and local demand. This ensures reliable power supply in isolated or remote areas.
- **Fault Detection and Diagnosis:** ML can detect anomalies and faults in renewable energy systems, allowing for quicker identification and resolution of issues. This improves system reliability and reduces maintenance costs.
- **Market Price Prediction:** ML can forecast energy market prices, helping renewable energy producers and consumers make informed decisions about when to buy or sell electricity, thus optimizing financial returns.

Renewable Energy Forecasting:

Machine learning is crucial in renewable energy forecasting, analyzing historical weather data, satellite imagery, and sensor readings to predict the generation of renewable energy sources like solar and wind power, enabling efficient green power generation (Agrawal et al., 2024; Kumara et al., 2023; Nishanth et al., 2023; Samikannu et al., 2022; Vanitha et al., 2023).

- **Grid Integration:** Utilities can better integrate variable renewable energy sources into the grid by anticipating energy fluctuations and adjusting supply accordingly.
- **Energy Trading:** Renewable energy producers can optimize energy trading by knowing when to sell excess energy or purchase additional power from the grid.
- **Resource Planning:** Energy providers can plan for maintenance and optimize resource allocation based on predicted energy generation.
- **Energy Efficiency:** Consumers can adjust their energy consumption patterns in response to renewable energy availability, reducing reliance on fossil fuels during peak demand periods.

Machine learning techniques like time series forecasting, neural networks, and ensemble methods significantly enhance the accuracy and reliability of renewable energy forecasts, thereby promoting more efficient and sustainable energy systems.

Energy Grid Management and Optimization:

Advanced machine learning algorithms are utilized in energy grid management and optimization to ensure efficient and reliable distribution of renewable energy within the grid (Boopathi, Kumar, et al., 2023; Domakonda et al., 2022; Kumara et al., 2023; Samikannu et al., 2022).

- **Grid Stability:** ML models can predict grid stability issues and take preventive measures to mitigate voltage fluctuations and frequency imbalances caused by intermittent renewable energy sources.
- **Demand Response:** ML can facilitate demand response programs by predicting peak demand periods and incentivizing consumers to reduce energy consumption during these times, thus reducing strain on the grid.
- **Energy Routing:** ML algorithms can optimize the routing of electricity within the grid, ensuring that renewable energy is distributed to areas with the highest demand and minimizing transmission losses.
- **Grid Reinforcement:** ML can identify areas of the grid that require reinforcement to handle increased renewable energy capacity and prevent overloads.
- **Real-time Monitoring:** ML-powered sensors and data analytics can provide real-time insights into the health and performance of the grid, allowing for proactive maintenance and issue resolution.

Machine learning applications in energy grid management and optimization improve grid reliability, reduce energy waste, and accelerate the transition to a greener, more sustainable energy infrastructure.

Demand Response Systems:

Demand response systems, utilizing machine learning and advanced analytics, are crucial in optimizing energy consumption patterns in response to supply fluctuations, particularly in renewable energy, and their significance is significant (B et al., 2024; Dhanya et al., 2023; Satav et al., 2024).

- **Real-time Demand Forecasting:** Demand response systems use machine learning algorithms to forecast energy demand patterns accurately. These forecasts consider factors such as weather conditions, time of day, and historical usage data.
- **Load Shifting:** Based on demand forecasts, demand response systems encourage consumers to shift their energy-intensive activities to times when renewable energy generation is high. For example, running large appliances during daylight hours when solar power production peaks.
- **Dynamic Pricing:** Machine learning helps establish dynamic pricing models, where electricity rates vary based on supply and demand conditions. Consumers can make informed choices to reduce energy consumption during high-price periods.
- **Automated Control:** Smart home and building automation systems, integrated with machine learning, can automatically adjust heating, cooling,

lighting, and other energy-consuming systems to align with demand response signals.

- **Incentives and Rewards:** Machine learning models can predict when demand response actions are needed, and consumers or businesses can receive incentives or rewards for participating in energy-saving activities.

Demand response systems enhance grid stability by reducing peak demand, minimizing backup power requirements, and optimizing renewable energy use. They promote a more responsive and sustainable energy ecosystem by aligning energy consumption with clean energy generation.

Edge Computing for Renewable Energy:

Edge computing is gaining prominence in renewable energy, especially in remote or distributed settings, as it reduces latency, allows real-time decision-making, and processes data closer to the source (Agrawal et al., 2024; Rahamathunnisa, Sudhakar, et al., 2023; Satav et al., 2024).

- **Data Processing at the Source:** Renewable energy systems, such as wind turbines and solar panels, generate vast amounts of data related to their performance and environmental conditions. Edge computing devices analyze this data locally, providing immediate insights.
- **Predictive Maintenance:** Edge computing devices can employ machine learning algorithms to monitor the health of renewable energy equipment in real-time. They detect anomalies, wear and tear, and impending failures, enabling timely maintenance and reducing downtime.
- **Grid Integration:** Edge devices at renewable energy installations can make local decisions about energy production and distribution, adjusting operations to match supply with demand and grid conditions without relying on central control (Kumara et al., 2023; Maheswari et al., 2023; Syamala et al., 2023).
- **Security and Privacy:** By processing data at the edge, sensitive information can be kept closer to the source, enhancing security and privacy while minimizing the need to transmit data over long distances.
- **Reduced Communication Costs:** Edge computing reduces the volume of data that needs to be transmitted to central data centers, minimizing communication costs and improving network efficiency.

Edge computing enhances the performance, reliability, and efficiency of renewable energy systems by enabling rapid response to changing conditions. It supports decentralized energy generation in remote areas, contributing to sustainable energy solutions (Hema et al., 2023). When combined with machine learning, demand response systems and edge computing enable data-driven decisions, reducing energy waste, enhancing grid stability, and promoting sustainability, ultimately contributing to the efficient utilization and integration of renewable energy sources.

SYNERGY BETWEEN CLOUD COMPUTING AND MACHINE LEARNING

The integration of cloud computing and machine learning is revolutionizing various industries, including the green power sector, by maximizing their potential (Figure 2).

- **Data Accessibility:** Cloud computing provides a vast and easily accessible repository for storing the extensive datasets required for machine learning in renewable energy applications. This enables researchers and organizations to access, share, and analyze data from various sources efficiently (Veeranjaneyulu, Boopathi, Kumari, et al., 2023; Veeranjaneyulu, Boopathi, Narasimharao, et al., 2023; Zekrifa et al., 2023).
- **Scalable Computing Resources:** Cloud platforms offer the scalability needed for machine learning tasks. As machine learning models grow in complexity, cloud resources can be readily provisioned to handle the increased computational demands, ensuring timely results.
- **Parallel Processing:** Cloud infrastructure enables parallel processing, a critical component for training large machine learning models. Parallelization accelerates the model training process, making it feasible to analyze extensive datasets quickly.
- **Data Integration:** Cloud platforms facilitate data integration by providing tools for data preprocessing and transformation. This ensures that data from diverse sources can be harmonized for machine learning applications, enhancing the accuracy of models.
- **Real-time Deployment:** Cloud services support the deployment of machine learning models in real-time or near-real-time scenarios. This is particularly important in green power applications, where real-time data analytics and decision-making are essential for optimizing energy production and distribution.
- **Cost Efficiency:** Cloud computing offers cost-efficient machine learning infrastructure, where users pay only for the resources they use. This is advantageous for organizations seeking to minimize capital expenditure while leveraging advanced machine learning capabilities.

Figure 2. Synergy between cloud computing and machine learning

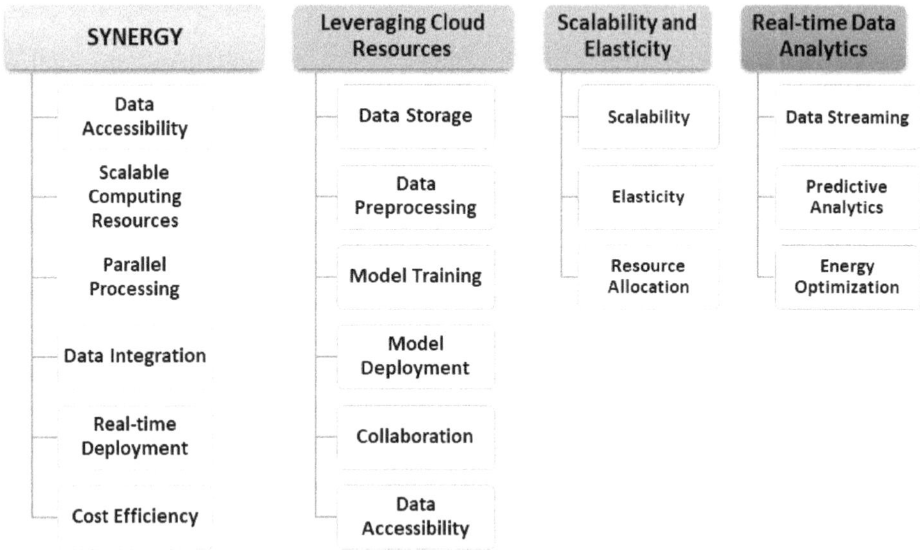

Leveraging Cloud Resources for Machine Learning:

Cloud resources significantly facilitate machine learning in the green power sector (Boopathi & Kanike, 2023; Maheswari et al., 2023; Ramudu et al., 2023; Syamala et al., 2023).

- **Data Storage:** Cloud platforms offer scalable and secure data storage solutions, ensuring that the vast amounts of data generated by renewable energy systems can be stored efficiently and accessed as needed.
- **Data Preprocessing:** Cloud-based data preprocessing tools help clean, transform, and normalize data before it is fed into machine learning algorithms, ensuring the quality and consistency of input data.
- **Model Training:** The cloud's computational power enables the training of complex machine learning models on large datasets, reducing the time and hardware costs associated with on-premises infrastructure.
- **Model Deployment:** Cloud services provide infrastructure for deploying machine learning models as web services or APIs, allowing real-time predictions and integration into energy management systems.
- **Collaboration:** Cloud-based collaboration platforms and version control systems facilitate collaboration among researchers, data scientists, and engineers working on machine learning projects in the green power sector.

Scalability and Elasticity in Data Processing

Cloud computing offers scalability and elasticity, crucial for data processing in the green power sector due to its key advantages (Dhanya et al., 2023; Pramila et al., 2023; Rahamathunnisa, Subhashini, et al., 2023).

- **Scalability:** Cloud resources can be scaled up or down based on demand. This is especially beneficial for renewable energy applications, where data processing requirements can fluctuate significantly due to changing weather conditions and energy consumption patterns.
- **Elasticity:** Cloud platforms provide the elasticity needed to handle bursts of data processing, ensuring that machine learning algorithms can adapt to varying workloads without manual intervention.
- **Resource Allocation:** Cloud services offer tools to allocate computational resources optimally, matching them to the specific needs of machine learning tasks. This minimizes wastage of resources and reduces operational costs.

Real-time Data Analytics and Insights:

Cloud computing's real-time capabilities empower machine learning models to provide timely insights in the green power sector (Chandrika et al., 2023; Domakonda et al., 2022; Gnanaprakasam et al., 2023):

- **Data Streaming:** Cloud platforms support data streaming and real-time analytics, allowing organizations to monitor renewable energy systems continuously and make instantaneous decisions based on incoming data.
- **Predictive Analytics:** Machine learning models running on cloud infrastructure can predict energy generation, consumption, and grid performance in real time, enabling proactive responses to dynamic conditions.
- **Energy Optimization:** Cloud-based machine learning algorithms can optimize energy production, storage, and distribution in real-time, minimizing waste and maximizing the use of renewable energy sources.

Cloud computing and machine learning enhance data processing efficiency, enabling the green power sector to maximize renewable energy resources while minimizing environmental impact and operational costs.

SUSTAINABILITY IN CLOUD COMPUTING

The cloud computing industry is addressing sustainability concerns due to the increasing demand for cloud services and the significant energy consumption of data centers (B et al., 2024; Boopathi, Alqahtani, et al., 2023; Boopathi & Davim, 2023; Sampath, 2021; Venkateswaran et al., 2023).

Energy-Efficient Data Centers:

- **Data Center Design:** Cloud providers are investing in energy-efficient data center designs that incorporate innovations such as hot/cold aisle containment, free cooling, and efficient cooling systems. These measures reduce the energy needed to maintain data center temperatures.
- **Server Virtualization:** Virtualization technologies enable multiple virtual machines to run on a single physical server. By consolidating workloads, cloud providers reduce the number of servers required, leading to significant energy savings.
- **Liquid Cooling:** Some data centers are exploring liquid cooling solutions, which are more efficient than traditional air cooling. Liquid-cooled data centers can operate at higher temperatures, further reducing energy consumption.
- **Energy Management Systems:** Cloud providers are implementing advanced energy management systems that optimize data center operations, dynamically adjusting power usage based on demand and environmental conditions.

Renewable Energy-Powered Cloud Services:

- **Sourcing Renewable Energy:** Many cloud providers are committed to sourcing renewable energy to power their data centers. This includes investing in wind, solar, and hydroelectric power generation facilities to offset their energy consumption.
- **Power Purchase Agreements (PPAs):** Cloud providers often enter into long-term PPAs with renewable energy providers to secure a consistent supply of clean energy. This not only reduces their carbon footprint but also supports the growth of renewable energy infrastructure.
- **Carbon Offsets:** Some cloud providers invest in carbon offset programs to neutralize the emissions associated with their data center operations. These initiatives contribute to global sustainability efforts.

Sustainable Hardware Design:

- **Energy-Efficient Servers:** Hardware manufacturers are designing energy-efficient servers and components that consume less power while maintaining high performance. This extends to processors, memory, storage devices, and networking equipment.
- **Lifecycle Management:** Sustainable hardware design also encompasses the full lifecycle of equipment, including efficient production processes, recycling, and responsible disposal of electronic waste (e-waste).
- **Modular Data Centers:** Modular data center designs allow for efficient scaling, reducing the environmental impact of expanding data center infrastructure.

Sustainability in cloud computing involves energy-efficient data center practices, renewable energy use, and sustainable hardware design principles. As the industry grows, these initiatives are crucial for reducing environmental impact and aligning with global climate change efforts.

Carbon Footprint Reduction Strategies

Carbon footprint reduction strategies are crucial for organizations, individuals, and governments to reduce greenhouse gas emissions and mitigate climate change. These strategies involve various actions and practices to decrease the release of carbon dioxide and other greenhouse gases into the atmosphere (Boopathi, 2022; Kannan et al., 2022; Sampath, 2021).

- **Transition to Renewable Energy:** Invest in solar and wind power to generate renewable energy for homes, businesses, and institutions. Consider purchasing renewable energy from utility providers or joining community solar programs. Implement energy-efficient technologies like LED lighting, appliances, and smart thermostats, and conduct energy audits to identify waste areas. Support grid integration by using energy storage systems like batteries to store excess energy during peak demand or low renewable energy production.
- **Transportation and Mobility:** Transitioning to electric or hybrid vehicles, using public transportation, carpooling, biking, or walking, and encouraging remote work can reduce emissions. Charging EVs with renewable energy further reduces their carbon footprint. Supporting public transportation infrastructure and encouraging remote work can also contribute to a lower carbon footprint.

- **Energy-Efficient Buildings:** Green Building Standards promote energy-efficient and sustainable construction, such as LEED. Insulation and weatherization improve energy efficiency, while passive design principles maximize natural lighting, ventilation, and temperature control, reducing the need for artificial heating and cooling.
- **Sustainable Practices and Lifestyle Choices:** To promote sustainability, reduce waste by reusing items and recycling materials. Adopt a sustainable diet with plant-based foods and reduce meat and dairy consumption. Minimalism is another way to reduce consumption and promote a sustainable mindset. These practices help reduce energy consumption and waste management.
- **Renewable Energy Investments:** Community solar involves collective ownership or financing of solar installations, while renewable energy certificates (RECs) are purchased to support renewable energy production and offset carbon emissions.
- **Carbon Offsetting:** Support carbon offset programs that invest in projects such as reforestation, afforestation, methane capture, and renewable energy development to compensate for your emissions.
- **Government Policies and Advocacy:** Support policies that promote renewable energy, energy efficiency, and carbon reduction at the local, regional, and national levels. Advocate for carbon pricing mechanisms like carbon taxes or cap-and-trade systems to incentivize emissions reduction.
- **Monitoring and Reporting:** Regularly assess your carbon footprint to understand your emissions sources and track progress in reducing them. Encourage transparency in organizations and governments by reporting on emissions and reduction efforts.

By implementing these strategies, individuals, businesses, and governments can make meaningful contributions to reducing their carbon footprints and combatting climate change.

ENVIRONMENTAL IMPACT AND MITIGATION

The environmental impact of cloud services, green data center practices, and sustainable data storage solutions are crucial steps in reducing the environmental footprint of cloud computing (Figure 3).

Figure 3. Environmental impact and mitigation

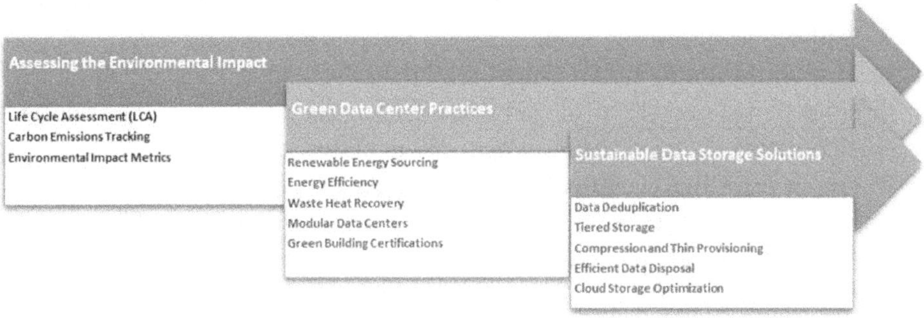

Assessing the Environmental Impact of Cloud Services:

- **Life Cycle Assessment (LCA):** Conduct LCAs to assess the environmental impact of cloud services. LCAs consider the entire life cycle of a service, from raw material extraction and manufacturing to use and disposal. This helps identify areas where improvements can be made to reduce environmental impact.
- **Carbon Emissions Tracking:** Measure and track carbon emissions associated with cloud operations, including data centers, cooling systems, and energy sources. This data can be used to set emissions reduction targets and prioritize sustainable practices.
- **Environmental Impact Metrics:** Develop and use specific environmental impact metrics to quantify the effects of cloud services on factors like energy consumption, water usage, and land use. This information informs sustainability strategies (Boopathi, 2023; Boopathi, Alqahtani, et al., 2023; Hanumanthakari et al., 2023; Maguluri et al., 2023).

Green Data Center Practices:

- **Renewable Energy Sourcing:** Power data centers with renewable energy sources, such as solar, wind, or hydropower, to reduce carbon emissions associated with electricity consumption (Boopathi, 2021; Fowziya et al., 2023).
- **Energy Efficiency:** Implement energy-efficient technologies and practices within data centers, including advanced cooling systems, optimized server layouts, and efficient power distribution systems.

- **Waste Heat Recovery:** Capture and repurpose waste heat generated by data centers for heating nearby buildings or facilities, thus reducing overall energy waste.
- **Modular Data Centers:** Adopt modular data center designs that allow for efficient scaling based on demand. This reduces energy consumption by eliminating the need to power and cool underutilized space.
- **Green Building Certifications:** Certify data center facilities to meet green building standards, such as LEED, to ensure environmentally responsible construction and operation.

Sustainable Data Storage Solutions:

- **Data Deduplication:** Implement data deduplication techniques to reduce redundant data storage, optimizing storage space and reducing the environmental impact associated with hardware requirements.
- **Tiered Storage:** Use tiered storage solutions that automatically move less frequently accessed data to lower-energy storage devices, reducing energy consumption.
- **Compression and Thin Provisioning:** Employ data compression and thin provisioning technologies to reduce storage volume, leading to fewer hardware requirements and lower energy consumption.
- **Efficient Data Disposal:** Implement proper data disposal practices, including secure data erasure and recycling of retired storage devices, to minimize electronic waste and its associated environmental impact.
- **Cloud Storage Optimization:** Optimize data storage in the cloud by archiving, tiering, or compressing data as needed, reducing costs and energy consumption.

By adopting these environmental impact assessment practices, green data center technologies, and sustainable data storage solutions, cloud service providers and organizations can significantly reduce their carbon footprint and contribute to a more sustainable and environmentally responsible cloud computing ecosystem.

CASE STUDIES AND BEST PRACTICES

Case studies and best practices offer valuable insights into successful implementation of sustainable practices in cloud computing and the green power sector.

Case Study 1: Google's Carbon-Free Energy Commitment

Background: Google is committed to operating its data centers and cloud services using 100% carbon-free energy. They have made significant investments in renewable energy projects and energy-efficient data center designs.

Best Practices:

- **Renewable Energy Investments:** Google has invested in large-scale renewable energy projects, such as wind and solar farms, to offset their energy consumption.
- **Power Purchase Agreements:** They have entered into long-term power purchase agreements (PPAs) to ensure a consistent supply of renewable energy for their operations.
- **Energy-Efficient Data Centers:** Google designs its data centers for maximum energy efficiency, using techniques like free cooling and artificial intelligence for optimization.
- **Carbon Offset Initiatives:** Google invests in carbon offset programs to neutralize emissions associated with their data centers and operations.

Case Study 2: Microsoft's Underwater Data Center

Background: Microsoft's Project Natick, an underwater data center off Scotland's coast, aimed to evaluate the energy efficiency and cooling capabilities of such facilities.

Best Practices:

- **Energy Efficiency:** The underwater data center leveraged the cold ocean water for cooling, reducing the need for energy-intensive air conditioning.
- **Rapid Deployment:** Submerging the data center in the ocean allowed for quick deployment and reduced infrastructure on land.
- **Sustainability Research:** Microsoft is studying the environmental and operational benefits of underwater data centers for potential future use.

Case Study 3: Amazon Web Services' Renewable Energy Initiatives

Background: Amazon Web Services (AWS) has committed to powering its data centers with 100% renewable energy. They have undertaken various initiatives to achieve this goal.

Best Practices:

- **Solar and Wind Investments:** AWS has invested in large-scale solar and wind farms to generate renewable energy for its data centers.
- **Renewable Energy Certificates:** They purchase renewable energy certificates to offset their energy consumption when local renewable energy generation is insufficient.
- **Energy Efficiency:** AWS focuses on energy-efficient data center designs and operations to reduce energy consumption.
- **Sustainability Reports:** AWS publishes sustainability reports to transparently communicate their progress toward renewable energy goals.

Case studies showcase organizations' implementation of sustainability in cloud computing and green power, highlighting potential for reducing environmental impact, lowering energy consumption, and advancing sustainability goals.

CHALLENGES, FUTURE TRENDS, AND EMERGING TECHNOLOGIES

The challenges, future trends and emerging technologies are illustrated in Figure 4 and explained below.

Challenges:

- **Energy Consumption:** While cloud computing has the potential to reduce energy consumption through server consolidation, the rapid growth of data centers has led to increased overall energy usage. Addressing this challenge requires continued efforts to improve data center efficiency and increase the use of renewable energy sources.
- **E-Waste Management:** The proliferation of electronic devices and cloud infrastructure contributes to electronic waste (e-waste). Proper disposal and recycling of hardware are essential to minimize the environmental impact (Hanumanthakari et al., 2023; Selvakumar, Adithe, et al., 2023; Selvakumar, Shankar, et al., 2023).
- **Data Privacy and Security:** Storing sensitive data in the cloud raises concerns about data privacy and security. Organizations must implement robust security measures and comply with regulations like GDPR and CCPA.

Figure 4. Challenges, future trends, and emerging technologies

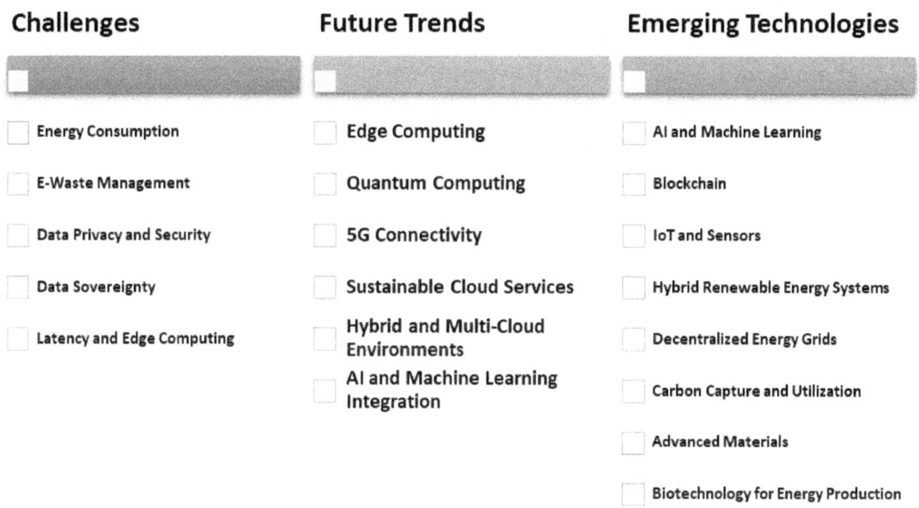

- **Data Sovereignty:** Cloud providers often store data in multiple geographic regions. This can raise concerns about data sovereignty and compliance with local data protection laws.
- **Latency and Edge Computing:** Latency issues can arise when data is processed in distant data centers. Edge computing, which processes data closer to the source, is an emerging solution to address latency concerns.

Future Trends:

- **Edge Computing:** The rise of edge computing will enable faster data processing, reducing latency and improving real-time decision-making. This is particularly relevant for applications like renewable energy management and autonomous vehicles.
- **Quantum Computing:** Quantum computing has the potential to revolutionize cloud computing by solving complex problems more efficiently. It may impact areas like cryptography and optimization.
- **5G Connectivity:** The deployment of 5G networks will enhance the capabilities of cloud services, particularly in areas requiring high bandwidth and low latency, such as augmented reality, virtual reality, and autonomous vehicles.

- **Sustainable Cloud Services:** Cloud providers will continue to invest in renewable energy and energy-efficient data center designs to reduce their carbon footprint. Sustainable cloud services will become more prevalent.
- **Hybrid and Multi-Cloud Environments:** Organizations will increasingly adopt hybrid and multi-cloud strategies to optimize resource allocation, data management, and redundancy.
- **AI and Machine Learning Integration:** Cloud providers will integrate AI and machine learning services into their platforms, making it easier for organizations to leverage these technologies for various applications, including green power sector optimization.

Emerging Technologies:

- **AI and Machine Learning:** AI and machine learning will play a significant role in optimizing energy production and consumption, enhancing renewable energy forecasting, and improving energy grid management (Karthik et al., 2023; Koshariya et al., 2023; Maguluri et al., 2023).
- **Blockchain:** Blockchain technology may be used to increase transparency and traceability in energy transactions, enable peer-to-peer energy trading, and enhance the security of data in the green power sector.
- **IoT and Sensors:** The Internet of Things (IoT) and sensor technologies will continue to be instrumental in collecting real-time data from renewable energy sources and energy infrastructure for analysis and optimization.
- **Hybrid Renewable Energy Systems:** Innovative hybrid systems that combine multiple renewable energy sources (e.g., wind, solar, and energy storage) will become more prevalent, increasing energy reliability and sustainability.
- **Decentralized Energy Grids:** Decentralized energy grids, enabled by distributed ledger technology and smart contracts, will empower local energy generation and sharing in communities.
- **Carbon Capture and Utilization (CCU):** CCU technologies will be used to capture and utilize carbon emissions from industrial processes, further reducing the carbon footprint of cloud computing and other industries.
- **Advanced Materials:** The development of advanced materials for energy storage and generation, such as more efficient batteries and next-generation solar panels, will impact the green power sector.
- **Biotechnology for Energy Production:** Emerging biotechnologies may enable the production of biofuels and other forms of sustainable energy from biological sources.

The sustainability and efficiency of cloud computing and the green power sector will be significantly enhanced by addressing challenges and embracing future trends and emerging technologies.

SUMMARY

This chapter explores the relationship between cloud computing, machine learning, and the green power sector, focusing on renewable energy. Machine learning algorithms optimize the performance of renewable energy sources like wind, solar, and hydroelectric power, enhancing renewable energy forecasting and grid integration. The chapter also explores grid optimization and demand response systems, where machine learning algorithms analyze vast datasets from energy grids to make real-time decisions that balance supply and demand while incorporating fluctuating renewable energy inputs. This enhances grid stability and maximizes the utilization of clean energy sources, a critical aspect of sustainability in the green power sector.

The integration of edge computing and machine learning enables rapid, real-time analysis of data from renewable energy sources, reducing latency and enhancing energy management systems' responsiveness. The transformational power of cloud computing and machine learning extends beyond renewable energy generation and grid management, focusing on sustainable practices within cloud computing itself. Energy-efficient data center designs and renewable energy sourcing are key roles, and strategies for reducing carbon footprints are showcased.

By presenting case studies and insights into emerging technologies, this chapter offers a panoramic view of how these innovations are driving sustainability and reshaping the green power sector, paving the way towards a future where environmentally responsible energy practices are not just a goal but a reality.

ABBREVIATIONS

ML: Machine Learning
RE: Renewable Energy
EC: Energy Consumption
AI: Artificial Intelligence
DC: Data Center
IoT: Internet of Things
DL: Deep Learning
CSR: Carbon Footprint Reduction
LCA: Life Cycle Assessment

EM: Edge Computing
AWS: Amazon Web Services
PPA: Power Purchase Agreement
E-Waste: Electronic Waste
SaaS: Software as a Service
IaaS: Infrastructure as a Service
PaaS: Platform as a Service
GDPR: General Data Protection Regulation
CCPA: California Consumer Privacy Act
5G: Fifth Generation
GD: Green Data Center
BC: Blockchain
EVS: Electric Vehicles
CPS: Carbon Offset Programs
HRE: Hybrid Renewable Energy Systems
CCU: Carbon Capture and Utilization

REFERENCES

Agrawal, A. V., Shashibhushan, G., Pradeep, S., Padhi, S. N., Sugumar, D., & Boopathi, S. (2024). Synergizing Artificial Intelligence, 5G, and Cloud Computing for Efficient Energy Conversion Using Agricultural Waste. In Practice, Progress, and Proficiency in Sustainability (pp. 475–497). IGI Global. doi:10.4018/979-8-3693-1186-8.ch026

Andronie, M., Lăzăroiu, G., Iatagan, M., Hurloiu, I., & Dijmărescu, I. (2021). Sustainable cyber-physical production systems in big data-driven smart urban economy: A systematic literature review. *Sustainability (Basel)*, *13*(2), 751. doi:10.3390/su13020751

B, M. K., K, K. K., Sasikala, P., Sampath, B., Gopi, B., & Sundaram, S. (2024). Sustainable Green Energy Generation From Waste Water. In *Practice, Progress, and Proficiency in Sustainability* (pp. 440–463). IGI Global. doi:10.4018/979-8-3693-1186-8.ch024

Boopathi, S. (2021). Improving of Green Sand-Mould Quality using Taguchi Technique. *Journal of Engineering Research*, in–Press.

Boopathi, S. (2022). An investigation on gas emission concentration and relative emission rate of the near-dry wire-cut electrical discharge machining process. *Environmental Science and Pollution Research International*, *29*(57), 86237–86246. doi:10.1007/s11356-021-17658-1 PMID:34837614

Boopathi, S. (2023). Deep Learning Techniques Applied for Automatic Sentence Generation. In Promoting Diversity, Equity, and Inclusion in Language Learning Environments (pp. 255–273). IGI Global. doi:10.4018/978-1-6684-3632-5.ch016

Boopathi, S., Alqahtani, A. S., Mubarakali, A., & Panchatcharam, P. (2023). Sustainable developments in near-dry electrical discharge machining process using sunflower oil-mist dielectric fluid. *Environmental Science and Pollution Research International*, 1–20. doi:10.1007/s11356-023-27494-0 PMID:37199846

Boopathi, S., & Davim, J. P. (2023). *Sustainable Utilization of Nanoparticles and Nanofluids in Engineering Applications*. IGI Global. doi:10.4018/978-1-6684-9135-5

Boopathi, S., & Kanike, U. K. (2023). Applications of Artificial Intelligent and Machine Learning Techniques in Image Processing. In *Handbook of Research on Thrust Technologies' Effect on Image Processing* (pp. 151–173). IGI Global. doi:10.4018/978-1-6684-8618-4.ch010

Boopathi, S., Kumar, P. K. S., Meena, R. S., Sudhakar, M., & Associates. (2023). Sustainable Developments of Modern Soil-Less Agro-Cultivation Systems: Aquaponic Culture. In Human Agro-Energy Optimization for Business and Industry (pp. 69–87). IGI Global.

Buyya, R., Ilager, S., & Arroba, P. (2023). Energy-Efficiency and Sustainability in New Generation Cloud Computing: A Vision and Directions for Integrated Management of Data Centre Resources and Workloads. *arXiv Preprint arXiv:2303.10572*.

Chandrika, V., Sivakumar, A., Krishnan, T. S., Pradeep, J., Manikandan, S., & Boopathi, S. (2023). Theoretical Study on Power Distribution Systems for Electric Vehicles. In *Intelligent Engineering Applications and Applied Sciences for Sustainability* (pp. 1–19). IGI Global. doi:10.4018/979-8-3693-0044-2.ch001

Dhanya, D., Kumar, S. S., Thilagavathy, A., Prasad, D., & Boopathi, S. (2023). Data Analytics and Artificial Intelligence in the Circular Economy: Case Studies. In Intelligent Engineering Applications and Applied Sciences for Sustainability (pp. 40–58). IGI Global.

Domakonda, V. K., Farooq, S., Chinthamreddy, S., Puviarasi, R., Sudhakar, M., & Boopathi, S. (2022). Sustainable Developments of Hybrid Floating Solar Power Plants: Photovoltaic System. In Human Agro-Energy Optimization for Business and Industry (pp. 148–167). IGI Global.

Fan, Z., Yan, Z., & Wen, S. (2023). Deep Learning and Artificial Intelligence in Sustainability: A Review of SDGs, Renewable Energy, and Environmental Health. *Sustainability (Basel)*, *15*(18), 13493. doi:10.3390/su151813493

Fowziya, S., Sivaranjani, S., Devi, N. L., Boopathi, S., Thakur, S., & Sailaja, J. M. (2023). Influences of nano-green lubricants in the friction-stir process of TiAlN coated alloys. *Materials Today: Proceedings*. Advance online publication. doi:10.1016/j.matpr.2023.06.446

Gnanaprakasam, C., Vankara, J., Sastry, A. S., Prajval, V., Gireesh, N., & Boopathi, S. (2023). Long-Range and Low-Power Automated Soil Irrigation System Using Internet of Things: An Experimental Study. In Contemporary Developments in Agricultural Cyber-Physical Systems (pp. 87–104). IGI Global.

Hanumanthakari, S., Gift, M. M., Kanimozhi, K., Bhavani, M. D., Bamane, K. D., & Boopathi, S. (2023). Biomining Method to Extract Metal Components Using Computer-Printed Circuit Board E-Waste. In *Handbook of Research on Safe Disposal Methods of Municipal Solid Wastes for a Sustainable Environment* (pp. 123–141). IGI Global. doi:10.4018/978-1-6684-8117-2.ch010

Hema, N., Krishnamoorthy, N., Chavan, S. M., Kumar, N., Sabarimuthu, M., & Boopathi, S. (2023). A Study on an Internet of Things (IoT)-Enabled Smart Solar Grid System. In *Handbook of Research on Deep Learning Techniques for Cloud-Based Industrial IoT* (pp. 290–308). IGI Global. doi:10.4018/978-1-6684-8098-4.ch017

Kannan, E., Trabelsi, Y., Boopathi, S., & Alagesan, S. (2022). Influences of cryogenically treated work material on near-dry wire-cut electrical discharge machining process. *Surface Topography : Metrology and Properties*, *10*(1), 015027. doi:10.1088/2051-672X/ac53e1

Karthik, S., Hemalatha, R., Aruna, R., Deivakani, M., Reddy, R. V. K., & Boopathi, S. (2023). Study on Healthcare Security System-Integrated Internet of Things (IoT). In Perspectives and Considerations on the Evolution of Smart Systems (pp. 342–362). IGI Global.

Koshariya, A. K., Kalaiyarasi, D., Jovith, A. A., Sivakami, T., Hasan, D. S., & Boopathi, S. (2023). AI-Enabled IoT and WSN-Integrated Smart Agriculture System. In *Artificial Intelligence Tools and Technologies for Smart Farming and Agriculture Practices* (pp. 200–218). IGI Global. doi:10.4018/978-1-6684-8516-3.ch011

Kumara, V., Mohanaprakash, T., Fairooz, S., Jamal, K., Babu, T., & Sampath, B. (2023). Experimental Study on a Reliable Smart Hydroponics System. In *Human Agro-Energy Optimization for Business and Industry* (pp. 27–45). IGI Global. doi:10.4018/978-1-6684-4118-3.ch002

Maguluri, L. P., Ananth, J., Hariram, S., Geetha, C., Bhaskar, A., & Boopathi, S. (2023). Smart Vehicle-Emissions Monitoring System Using Internet of Things (IoT). In Handbook of Research on Safe Disposal Methods of Municipal Solid Wastes for a Sustainable Environment (pp. 191–211). IGI Global.

Maheswari, B. U., Imambi, S. S., Hasan, D., Meenakshi, S., Pratheep, V., & Boopathi, S. (2023). Internet of Things and Machine Learning-Integrated Smart Robotics. In Global Perspectives on Robotics and Autonomous Systems: Development and Applications (pp. 240–258). IGI Global. doi:10.4018/978-1-6684-7791-5.ch010

Murugesan, S. (2008). Harnessing green IT: Principles and practices. *IT Professional*, *10*(1), 24–33. doi:10.1109/MITP.2008.10

Mustapha, U. F., Alhassan, A.-W., Jiang, D.-N., & Li, G.-L. (2021). Sustainable aquaculture development: A review on the roles of cloud computing, internet of things and artificial intelligence (CIA). *Reviews in Aquaculture*, *13*(4), 2076–2091. doi:10.1111/raq.12559

Nishanth, J., Deshmukh, M. A., Kushwah, R., Kushwaha, K. K., Balaji, S., & Sampath, B. (2023). Particle Swarm Optimization of Hybrid Renewable Energy Systems. In *Intelligent Engineering Applications and Applied Sciences for Sustainability* (pp. 291–308). IGI Global. doi:10.4018/979-8-3693-0044-2.ch016

Pandey, V., Sircar, A., Bist, N., Solanki, K., & Yadav, K. (2023). Accelerating the renewable energy sector through Industry 4.0: Optimization opportunities in the digital revolution. *International Journal of Innovation Studies*, *7*(2), 171–188. doi:10.1016/j.ijis.2023.03.003

Pramila, P., Amudha, S., Saravanan, T., Sankar, S. R., Poongothai, E., & Boopathi, S. (2023). Design and Development of Robots for Medical Assistance: An Architectural Approach. In Contemporary Applications of Data Fusion for Advanced Healthcare Informatics (pp. 260–282). IGI Global.

Rahamathunnisa, U., Subhashini, P., Aancy, H. M., Meenakshi, S., Boopathi, S., & ... (2023). Solutions for Software Requirement Risks Using Artificial Intelligence Techniques. In *Handbook of Research on Data Science and Cybersecurity Innovations in Industry 4.0 Technologies* (pp. 45–64). IGI Global.

Rahamathunnisa, U., Sudhakar, K., Murugan, T. K., Thivaharan, S., Rajkumar, M., & Boopathi, S. (2023). Cloud Computing Principles for Optimizing Robot Task Offloading Processes. In *AI-Enabled Social Robotics in Human Care Services* (pp. 188–211). IGI Global. doi:10.4018/978-1-6684-8171-4.ch007

Ramudu, K., Mohan, V. M., Jyothirmai, D., Prasad, D., Agrawal, R., & Boopathi, S. (2023). Machine Learning and Artificial Intelligence in Disease Prediction: Applications, Challenges, Limitations, Case Studies, and Future Directions. In Contemporary Applications of Data Fusion for Advanced Healthcare Informatics (pp. 297–318). IGI Global.

Samikannu, R., Koshariya, A. K., Poornima, E., Ramesh, S., Kumar, A., & Boopathi, S. (2022). Sustainable Development in Modern Aquaponics Cultivation Systems Using IoT Technologies. In *Human Agro-Energy Optimization for Business and Industry* (pp. 105–127). IGI Global.

Sampath, B. (2021). *Sustainable Eco-Friendly Wire-Cut Electrical Discharge Machining: Gas Emission Analysis*. Academic Press.

Satav, S. D., Lamani, D. G, H. K., Kumar, N. M. G., Manikandan, S., & Sampath, B. (2024). Energy and Battery Management in the Era of Cloud Computing. In Practice, Progress, and Proficiency in Sustainability (pp. 141–166). IGI Global. doi:10.4018/979-8-3693-1186-8.ch009

Selvakumar, S., Adithe, S., Isaac, J. S., Pradhan, R., Venkatesh, V., & Sampath, B. (2023). A Study of the Printed Circuit Board (PCB) E-Waste Recycling Process. In Sustainable Approaches and Strategies for E-Waste Management and Utilization (pp. 159–184). IGI Global.

Selvakumar, S., Shankar, R., Ranjit, P., Bhattacharya, S., Gupta, A. S. G., & Boopathi, S. (2023). E-Waste Recovery and Utilization Processes for Mobile Phone Waste. In *Handbook of Research on Safe Disposal Methods of Municipal Solid Wastes for a Sustainable Environment* (pp. 222–240). IGI Global. doi:10.4018/978-1-6684-8117-2.ch016

Shaw, R., Howley, E., & Barrett, E. (2022). Applying reinforcement learning towards automating energy efficient virtual machine consolidation in cloud data centers. *Information Systems*, *107*, 101722. doi:10.1016/j.is.2021.101722

Srinivas, B., Maguluri, L. P., Naidu, K. V., Reddy, L. C. S., Deivakani, M., & Boopathi, S. (2023). Architecture and Framework for Interfacing Cloud-Enabled Robots. In *Handbook of Research on Data Science and Cybersecurity Innovations in Industry 4.0 Technologies* (pp. 542–560). IGI Global. doi:10.4018/978-1-6684-8145-5.ch027

Syamala, M., Komala, C., Pramila, P., Dash, S., Meenakshi, S., & Boopathi, S. (2023). Machine Learning-Integrated IoT-Based Smart Home Energy Management System. In *Handbook of Research on Deep Learning Techniques for Cloud-Based Industrial IoT* (pp. 219–235). IGI Global. doi:10.4018/978-1-6684-8098-4.ch013

Vanitha, S., Radhika, K., & Boopathi, S. (2023). Artificial Intelligence Techniques in Water Purification and Utilization. In *Human Agro-Energy Optimization for Business and Industry* (pp. 202–218). IGI Global. doi:10.4018/978-1-6684-4118-3.ch010

Veeranjaneyulu, R., Boopathi, S., Kumari, R. K., Vidyarthi, A., Isaac, J. S., & Jaiganesh, V. (2023). Air Quality Improvement and Optimisation Using Machine Learning Technique. *IEEE- Explore*, 1–6.

Veeranjaneyulu, R., Boopathi, S., Narasimharao, J., Gupta, K. K., Reddy, R. V. K., & Ambika, R. (2023). Identification of Heart Diseases using Novel Machine Learning Method. *IEEE- Explore*, 1–6.

Venkateswaran, N., Vidhya, K., Ayyannan, M., Chavan, S. M., Sekar, K., & Boopathi, S. (2023). A Study on Smart Energy Management Framework Using Cloud Computing. In 5G, Artificial Intelligence, and Next Generation Internet of Things: Digital Innovation for Green and Sustainable Economies (pp. 189–212). IGI Global. doi:10.4018/978-1-6684-8634-4.ch009

Xu, M., Toosi, A. N., & Buyya, R. (2020). A self-adaptive approach for managing applications and harnessing renewable energy for sustainable cloud computing. *IEEE Transactions on Sustainable Computing*, *6*(4), 544–558. doi:10.1109/TSUSC.2020.3014943

Zekrifa, D. M. S., Kulkarni, M., Bhagyalakshmi, A., Devireddy, N., Gupta, S., & Boopathi, S. (2023). Integrating Machine Learning and AI for Improved Hydrological Modeling and Water Resource Management. In *Artificial Intelligence Applications in Water Treatment and Water Resource Management* (pp. 46–70). IGI Global. doi:10.4018/978-1-6684-6791-6.ch003

Chapter 10
Convergence of AI and Self-Sustainability:
Technology Integration in the Healthcare Ecosystem

R. Anitha
Department of Biomedical Engineering, Jerusalem College of Engineering, Pallikaranai, India

M. Rajkumar
Department of Smart Computing, School of Computer Science Engineering and Information Systems, Vellore Institute of Technology, VIT University, India

B. Jothi
Department of Computational Intelligence, SRM Institute of Science and Technology, Kattankulathur, India

H. Mickle Aancy
Department of Master of Business Administration, Panimalar Engineering College, Chennai, India

G. Sujatha
Department of Networking and Communications, School of Computing, College of Engineering and Technology, Faculty of Engineering and Technology, SRM Institute of Science and Technology, Chennai, India

B. Sam
Mahendra Engineering College, India

ABSTRACT

The integration of technology in healthcare presents both opportunities and challenges. This chapter explores the relationship between technology and healthcare, emphasizing the need for security, ethical standards, and social implications. It examines vulnerabilities in digitalizing healthcare data, highlighting the importance of robust encryption methods, access controls, and cybersecurity frameworks to protect sensitive patient information and ensure data confidentiality, integrity, and availability. The chapter discusses the ethical implications of technology integration

DOI: 10.4018/979-8-3693-1694-8.ch010

in healthcare, focusing on data privacy, informed consent, AI-driven decision-making, and responsible technology use. It proposes ethical frameworks to foster trust and transparency while addressing social implications like accessibility, equity, and the digital divide. The chapter advocates for a comprehensive approach that combines technological advancements with strict security measures, ethical guidelines, and social awareness, urging multidisciplinary collaboration to maximize benefits and mitigate risks.

INTRODUCTION

Technology integration in healthcare is revolutionizing service delivery, patient experiences, and medical practices. This convergence includes AI algorithms for diagnostics and wearable devices for real-time health data. This shift promises improved efficiencies, improved outcomes, and personalized care. The integration not only revolutionizes traditional healthcare but also democratizes access to quality services. Telemedicine, powered by digital platforms and remote monitoring tools, reaches remote or underserved populations. Health apps and wearable devices empower individuals to manage their well-being, fostering a culture of preventive healthcare and self-monitoring (Ramudu et al., 2023; Sengeni et al., 2023).

However, this technological revolution is not without its challenges, notably in the realm of security. The digitization of patient records, while enabling seamless information exchange among healthcare providers, introduces vulnerabilities to cyber threats. The safeguarding of sensitive medical data against breaches, ensuring its confidentiality and integrity, stands as a paramount concern. Moreover, ethical considerations loom large as the use of AI and machine learning algorithms raises questions about data privacy, bias mitigation, and the ethical boundaries of utilizing patient information for predictive analytics (Karthik et al., 2023; Pramila et al., 2023).

Yet, amid these challenges lies an opportunity for conscientious innovation. Striking the delicate balance between technological advancements and ethical considerations is imperative. By fostering a culture of responsibility and accountability, stakeholders can collaboratively navigate these complexities. Moreover, as technology evolves, it becomes crucial to ensure that the benefits are equitably distributed, addressing societal disparities in access to and utilization of healthcare technologies. Ultimately, the integration of technology in healthcare stands at the precipice of transformation, demanding not just technical prowess but a holistic approach that prioritizes security, ethics, and social responsibility (Reddy, Gaurav, et al., 2023; Satav, Hasan, et al., 2024).

The evolution of technology in healthcare has traversed a remarkable journey, reshaping the landscape of medical practices and patient care over the years. Initially, technology's role was confined to basic tools and equipment aiding diagnosis and treatment. However, with the advent of digitalization, the healthcare industry witnessed a monumental shift. In its early stages, technology manifested primarily through the automation of administrative tasks, streamlining record-keeping and appointment scheduling. The introduction of Electronic Health Records (EHRs) marked a pivotal moment, enabling healthcare providers to consolidate patient data, enhancing accuracy and accessibility while laying the groundwork for future innovations (Boopathi, 2023c; Reddy, Reddy, et al., 2023).

The integration of imaging technologies, such as X-rays and MRI scans, revolutionized diagnostics, allowing for non-invasive visualization of internal structures, thereby advancing medical understanding and precision in treatment. Concurrently, advancements in medical devices, from pacemakers to insulin pumps, have steadily enhanced patient care, offering personalized and targeted interventions. However, perhaps the most transformative phase of technological evolution in healthcare is epitomized by the fusion of data analytics, AI, and machine learning. These technologies have empowered healthcare professionals with predictive analytics, enabling early disease detection, personalized treatment plans, and prognostic insights based on vast datasets (Boopathi, 2023d, 2023c).

Telemedicine, a convergence of technology and healthcare delivery, has emerged as a cornerstone, particularly in the wake of global events necessitating remote access to medical services. It facilitates virtual consultations, remote monitoring, and even surgical interventions performed with robotic assistance, transcending geographical barriers and expanding access to expert care. Looking ahead, the trajectory of healthcare technology evolution points toward even more sophisticated applications. The rise of wearable health devices, implantable sensors, and the Internet of Medical Things (IoMT) promises a future where real-time health monitoring and proactive interventions become commonplace, ushering in an era of preventive and personalized medicine (Reddy, Gaurav, et al., 2023; Sengeni et al., 2023).

The advancement of technology in healthcare has shifted from basic automation to data-driven insights, AI, and telemedicine, revolutionizing care delivery and transforming global healthcare systems. These technologies not only treat illnesses but also proactively manage health, redefining patient care, medical research, and delivery systems. The profound impact of technology integration in healthcare is profound. Foremost, technology integration stands as a catalyst for efficiency and precision in healthcare operations. Streamlining administrative tasks through digital platforms and automation liberates healthcare professionals from mundane paperwork, allowing them to devote more time and focus to patient care. Electronic Health Records (EHRs) consolidate patient information, enabling seamless data access and enhancing coordination among multidisciplinary care teams, thereby reducing errors and optimizing treatment strategies (Kavitha et al., 2023; Ugandar et al., 2023; Venkateswaran et al., 2023).

Moreover, technology integration fosters a culture of patient-centered care. From wearable health devices capturing real-time data to telemedicine platforms facilitating remote consultations, patients now have greater agency and accessibility in managing their health. This empowerment not only encourages proactive health management but also engenders a deeper patient-provider relationship, fostering trust and improving health outcomes. The impact of technology integration transcends individual patient interactions to influence the broader healthcare ecosystem. Big data analytics, powered by advanced algorithms, glean insights from massive datasets, revolutionizing medical research, drug development, and epidemiological studies. Predictive analytics enable early disease detection, personalized treatment regimens, and population health management strategies, paving the way for preventive medicine and more targeted interventions (Boopathi, 2023d, 2023c).

Economically, the integration of technology holds significant promise in cost containment and resource optimization within healthcare systems. Remote monitoring, predictive modeling, and AI-driven decision support systems not only enhance clinical outcomes but also contribute to the prudent allocation of resources, reducing unnecessary procedures, hospital readmissions, and overall healthcare spending. Furthermore, technology integration drives innovation and fosters a culture of continuous improvement within healthcare. As emerging technologies like artificial intelligence, genomics, and robotics advance, they inspire novel solutions, transforming healthcare paradigms and sparking interdisciplinary collaborations that push the boundaries of what's possible in medicine (Boopathi, 2023a; Maguluri, Ananth, et al., 2023).

Technology integration in healthcare is crucial for improving clinical outcomes, operational efficiencies, and patient experiences, fostering a proactive, personalized, and accessible future that is influenced by its multifaceted impact.

SECURITY IN HEALTHCARE TECHNOLOGY

Cybersecurity Measures in Healthcare

Healthcare technology security, particularly cybersecurity measures, is crucial due to the confidential nature of patient information stored and transmitted in digital systems. These measures are multifaceted, encompassing strategies and technologies to protect patient data from unauthorized access and cyber threats. One of the foundational aspects of cybersecurity in healthcare involves robust encryption methods. Encryption techniques ensure that sensitive patient information, whether in transit or storage, is encoded in a manner that makes it unreadable to unauthorized individuals or malicious entities. Advanced encryption standards are employed to protect data integrity and confidentiality, mitigating the risk of data breaches and unauthorized access (Maguluri, Arularasan, et al., 2023).

Access controls and authentication mechanisms form another critical layer of cybersecurity measures. Role-based access control (RBAC) systems and multifactor authentication protocols restrict and authenticate users' access to sensitive healthcare data. By implementing these measures, healthcare organizations can ensure that only authorized personnel have the necessary permissions to access specific patient records or critical systems, reducing the risk of insider threats and unauthorized access. Additionally, healthcare entities deploy comprehensive threat detection and incident response protocols. Intrusion detection systems (IDS), firewalls, and continuous monitoring tools are employed to detect and preemptively respond to potential cyber threats. These systems analyze network traffic, identify anomalies, and raise alerts or take corrective actions to thwart cyberattacks, thereby bolstering the overall security posture of healthcare IT infrastructure (Ugandar et al., 2023; Venkateswaran et al., 2023).

Furthermore, adherence to regulatory frameworks such as the Health Insurance Portability and Accountability Act (HIPAA) is pivotal in shaping cybersecurity practices in healthcare. Compliance with regulations ensures that healthcare organizations implement stringent security measures, conduct regular risk assessments, and maintain data privacy standards, reinforcing the protection of patient health information. Healthcare organizations must implement a comprehensive cybersecurity strategy, including collaboration with cybersecurity experts, staff training on best practices, and regular security audits, to protect patient confidentiality and trust in the healthcare ecosystem. As cyber threats evolve, organizations must adapt and strengthen their defenses.

Encryption and Data Protection

Encryption is a crucial aspect of data protection in healthcare technology, encoding sensitive information so only authorized parties can access and decipher it. It applies to various aspects of healthcare systems (Boopathi, 2023d; Karthik et al., 2023; Reddy, Reddy, et al., 2023).

- **Data at Rest:** Encryption of data stored in databases, electronic health records (EHRs), or other repositories ensures that even if unauthorized access occurs, the data remains unreadable.
- **Data in Transit:** Encryption of data while being transmitted between systems, devices, or across networks using secure communication protocols

(such as SSL/TLS) prevents interception and eavesdropping, maintaining confidentiality.

- **End-to-End Encryption:** Ensuring that data remains encrypted from its origin to its destination, guaranteeing continuous protection against unauthorized access throughout its journey.

Access Controls and Authentication

Access controls and authentication mechanisms are crucial in regulating and validating user access to healthcare systems and patient data (Boopathi et al., 2023; Boopathi & Davim, 2023).

- **Role-Based Access Control (RBAC):** Assigning access permissions based on specific roles within the healthcare organization, allowing only authorized personnel to access certain information or perform particular actions.
- **Multi-factor Authentication (MFA):** Requiring multiple forms of verification, such as passwords, biometrics, or token-based authentication, to enhance security beyond just a username and password.
- **User Authentication Protocols:** Implementing strong authentication protocols to verify user identities, reducing the risk of unauthorized access or data breaches due to compromised credentials.

Threat Detection and Incident Response

Healthcare organizations utilize various tools and strategies to effectively detect and respond to cybersecurity threats, including (Boopathi, 2023d; Maguluri, Arularasan, et al., 2023):

- **Intrusion Detection Systems (IDS) and Intrusion Prevention Systems (IPS):** Monitoring network traffic for suspicious activities, detecting potential threats or anomalies, and taking preemptive actions to prevent cyberattacks.
- **Security Information and Event Management (SIEM) Systems:** Aggregating and analyzing security-related data from various sources to identify potential security incidents or breaches in real-time.
- **Incident Response Plans:** Developing comprehensive plans outlining steps to be taken in case of a security incident or breach, including mitigation, containment, recovery, and reporting procedures to minimize the impact on patient data and operational continuity.

The integration of encryption methods, access controls, and threat detection strategies enhances healthcare technology's security, safeguarding patient data and mitigating cyber threats.

Privacy and Confidentiality

HIPAA Compliance and Regulatory Frameworks

The Health Insurance Portability and Accountability Act (HIPAA) establishes standards and regulations for safeguarding patient information, requiring compliance with certain requirements (Boopathi, 2023d; Sharma et al., 2024).

- **Data Privacy Rules:** Ensuring that protected health information (PHI) is securely handled, accessed, and disclosed only for authorized purposes.
- **Security Rules:** Implementing safeguards to protect electronic PHI (ePHI), including encryption, access controls, and risk assessment procedures.
- **Breach Notification Requirements:** Mandating timely notification to affected individuals, regulators, and, in some cases, the media, in the event of a data breach compromising PHI.

Data Breach Prevention and Management

Proactive measures are crucial for preventing and managing data breaches, thereby ensuring the integrity of patient information.

- **Risk Assessments and Audits:** Regularly assessing vulnerabilities, conducting risk analyses, and audits to identify potential weak points in security measures and address them proactively.
- **Employee Training:** Educating staff on security best practices, emphasizing the importance of safeguarding patient data, recognizing phishing attempts, and reporting suspicious activities.
- **Encryption and Anonymization:** Employing encryption methods and anonymization techniques to render data unreadable or unidentifiable, thereby reducing the impact of breaches.

Secure Data Sharing Practices

The sharing of patient data among healthcare providers, researchers, and other entities necessitates strict protocols to ensure privacy and facilitate necessary information exchange (Boopathi, 2023d; Kumar et al., 2023).

- **Interoperability Standards:** Adopting standardized formats and protocols for data exchange, ensuring compatibility and secure transmission between disparate systems.
- **Secure Communication Channels:** Using encrypted communication channels and secure data transfer methods (e.g., VPNs, secure portals) to transmit sensitive information securely.
- **Patient Consent and Authorization:** Obtaining explicit consent or authorization from patients before sharing their information, ensuring compliance with legal and ethical standards.

Healthcare entities can ensure patient privacy and confidentiality by adhering to regulatory frameworks like HIPAA, implementing robust data breach prevention strategies, and embracing secure data sharing practices for quality care and research.

ETHICAL CONSIDERATIONS IN HEALTHCARE TECHNOLOGY

Data Ethics and Patient Privacy

In the rapidly evolving landscape of healthcare technology, the ethical implications of handling patient data loom large. Upholding data ethics and preserving patient privacy stand as foundational principles guiding the responsible use, sharing, and protection of sensitive health information. As technology advances, navigating the ethical complexities surrounding data collection, consent, and utilization becomes pivotal, necessitating a delicate balance between innovation and ensuring patient autonomy, confidentiality, and trust. This introduction outlines a comprehensive analysis of the intricate interplay between data ethics and patient privacy in the healthcare sector (Boopathi, 2023c, 2023d).

Informed Consent in Digital Healthcare

In the digital healthcare sector, it is crucial to obtain patients' informed consent for data collection, storage, and utilization (Durairaj et al., 2023; Ravisankar et al., 2023).

- **Transparency and Clarity:** Providing comprehensive information about how patient data will be collected, used, and shared, ensuring patients understand the implications before consenting.
- **Granular Consent Options:** Allowing patients to choose the level of data sharing and specifying the purposes for which their data will be utilized, empowering them to make informed decisions.

- **Continuous Consent Management:** Offering mechanisms for patients to revise or revoke consent at any time, maintaining their autonomy and control over their data.

Ethical Use of Patient Data

Ethical considerations require responsible handling and utilization of patient data to maintain trust and ensure patient welfare (Boopathi, 2023d; Karthik et al., 2023).

- **Data Anonymization and De-identification:** Safeguarding patient identities by anonymizing or de-identifying data while retaining its utility for research or analytics.
- **Purpose Limitation:** Restricting the use of patient data to specific, defined purposes and avoiding indiscriminate or unrelated utilization.
- **Mitigating Bias and Discrimination:** Ensuring algorithms and analyses applied to patient data are free from bias, discrimination, or prejudice that might disproportionately impact certain groups.

Balancing Privacy and Innovation

The ethical challenge of balancing innovation with patient privacy remains a delicate balance that requires careful consideration (Boopathi, 2023d).

- **Ethical Review and Governance:** Instituting ethical review boards or committees to evaluate the potential risks and benefits of innovative technologies or data uses.
- **Ethical Impact Assessments:** Conducting assessments to anticipate and address potential ethical implications before deploying new technologies or data-driven approaches.
- **Engagement and Collaboration:** Engaging stakeholders, including patients, healthcare providers, and technology developers, in dialogues to ensure ethical considerations are embedded in technological advancements.

Ethical considerations in digital healthcare prioritize patient autonomy, data security, and responsible innovation, navigating complexities of data ethics, informed consent, and privacy preservation.

Figure 1. Integration of artificial intelligence (AI) in ethical decision-making

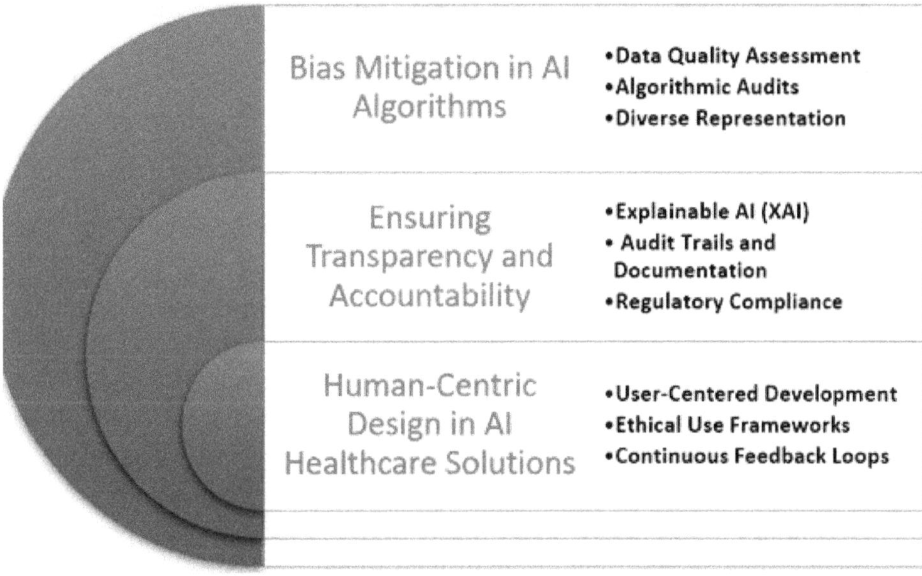

Ethical AI and Decision-Making

In the healthcare arena, the integration of Artificial Intelligence (AI) brings forth transformative potential, shaping decision-making processes and treatment paradigms. However, at the core of this evolution lies a crucial ethical landscape where the responsible use of AI in healthcare becomes paramount. Ethical considerations surrounding AI-driven decision-making encompass a myriad of concerns, including data privacy, algorithmic bias, transparency, and the human-centric approach to implementing these technologies (Boopathi, 2023d; Gunasekaran & Boopathi, 2023; Maguluri, Arularasan, et al., 2023). This explores the ethical implications of AI integration in healthcare decision-making, aiming to balance innovation with ethical integrity. The integration of Artificial Intelligence (AI) in ethical decision-making is depicted in Figure 1.

Bias Mitigation in AI Algorithms

AI algorithms can perpetuate healthcare disparities and inequalities due to bias, and addressing this can involve various strategies.

- **Data Quality Assessment:** Scrutinizing datasets to identify and rectify biases stemming from historical imbalances or inaccuracies.

- **Algorithmic Audits:** Regularly auditing AI models to detect and address biases that might affect decision-making, ensuring fairness across diverse populations.
- **Diverse Representation:** Ensuring diverse representation in data collection and model development to prevent underrepresentation or skewed perspectives.

Ensuring Transparency and Accountability

Transparency is crucial for fostering trust and accountability in AI-driven healthcare.

- **Explainable AI (XAI):** Designing AI systems that can explain their decisions in understandable terms, providing clarity on how conclusions are reached.
- **Audit Trails and Documentation:** Maintaining comprehensive records of AI processes and decisions, enabling traceability and accountability.
- **Regulatory Compliance:** Adhering to ethical guidelines and regulations, ensuring that AI applications comply with established standards and policies.

Human-Centric Design in AI Healthcare Solutions

Human-centricity is a principle that ensures AI prioritizes the best interests of patients and healthcare providers (Rahamathunnisa et al., 2023; Ramudu et al., 2023).

- **User-Centered Development:** Involving healthcare professionals and patients in the design and development phases to address real needs and concerns.
- **Ethical Use Frameworks:** Establishing frameworks that prioritize human well-being and safety, emphasizing the augmentation rather than replacement of human decision-making.
- **Continuous Feedback Loops:** Implementing mechanisms for continuous evaluation and improvement based on user feedback and evolving ethical standards.

Ethical considerations in AI-driven healthcare solutions can foster trust among stakeholders by addressing bias, promoting transparency, and prioritizing human-centric design, thereby ensuring responsible implementation and alignment with ethical principles and societal values.

SOCIAL IMPLICATIONS OF TECHNOLOGY INTEGRATION

Accessibility and Healthcare Disparities

In the vast landscape of healthcare technology integration, the profound impact on accessibility and its implications for healthcare disparities emerge as critical focal points. While technology promises innovation and efficiency, its unequal distribution and utilization across diverse populations often exacerbate existing healthcare disparities. This introductory exploration seeks to unravel the intricate interplay between technology integration and accessibility, shedding light on how advancements can bridge gaps or inadvertently widen disparities. Understanding these dynamics is crucial for creating an inclusive healthcare system that promotes equitable access and reduces disparities among diverse socio-economic and geographical groups. It highlights the digital divide, socio-economic disparities, and telemedicine's role in healthcare accessibility, advocating for interventions promoting equitable access (Boopathi, 2023c; Rahamathunnisa et al., 2023; Reddy, Reddy, et al., 2023).

Digital Divide in Healthcare Access:

- **Infrastructure Disparities:** Variances in internet connectivity and access to technological devices create disparities in accessing telehealth services, particularly in rural or underserved areas.
- **Technological Literacy:** Differences in digital literacy levels among various demographics hinder the effective utilization of healthcare technologies, creating barriers to accessing online medical resources or telemedicine platforms.
- **Economic Constraints:** Affordability issues regarding smartphones, computers, or internet access contribute to disparities, limiting individuals' ability to engage in virtual healthcare consultations or access digital health resources.
- **Geographical Isolation:** Remote or geographically isolated communities face challenges in receiving adequate healthcare due to limited access to healthcare facilities or technology-enabled care options.
- **Healthcare Provider Accessibility:** Disparities in healthcare provider availability online or through telemedicine services further deepen the digital divide, particularly in regions with a shortage of healthcare professionals.

Addressing Socio-Economic Disparities:

- **Equitable Access Programs:** Initiatives aimed at providing subsidized or free technological devices and internet access to marginalized or low-income communities to bridge the digital divide (Pramila et al., 2023; Ramudu et al., 2023; Reddy, Gaurav, et al., 2023).
- **Community Education:** Promoting digital literacy programs targeting underserved populations to enhance their proficiency in utilizing healthcare technologies effectively.
- **Policy Interventions:** Advocating for policies that incentivize investment in technology infrastructure in underserved areas to ensure equitable access to healthcare resources.
- **Collaborative Partnerships:** Forging collaborations between public and private sectors to create affordable healthcare technology solutions tailored to socio-economically disadvantaged communities.
- **Cultural Competence:** Designing healthcare technologies that consider cultural diversity and linguistic variations to cater to the needs of diverse populations, ensuring inclusivity in digital healthcare delivery.

Telemedicine and Remote Care Initiatives:

- **Enhanced Accessibility:** Telemedicine initiatives extend healthcare access to remote or rural areas, allowing patients to consult healthcare providers remotely, overcoming geographical barriers.
- **Continuity of Care:** Facilitating ongoing care management for patients with chronic conditions through remote monitoring, reducing the need for frequent in-person visits.
- **Emergency Response:** Telemedicine serves as a vital tool during emergencies, enabling timely consultations and medical guidance, especially in areas with limited emergency care facilities.
- **Cost and Time Savings:** Remote care initiatives reduce travel costs and time for patients, making healthcare more accessible and convenient, especially for those with mobility issues.
- **Scalability and Reach:** Telemedicine offers scalability, allowing healthcare providers to reach a larger population, thereby potentially improving healthcare access and outcomes on a broader scale.

Equity and Inclusivity

The evolution of healthcare technology has highlighted the importance of equity and inclusivity in promoting a progressive and just ecosystem. These principles aim to dismantle barriers, foster diversity, and ensure healthcare technologies serve all populations, regardless of socio-economic status, geographical location, or cultural background. Addressing these principles is crucial for creating a healthcare landscape that transcends disparities and embraces diversity, leading to more accessible, fair, and patient-centric care (Satav, Hasan, et al., 2024; Sundaramoorthy et al., 2023).

Cultural Competence in Healthcare Technology

- **Diversity in Design:** Creating healthcare technologies that reflect cultural diversity in user interfaces, languages, and visual representations, ensuring inclusivity for diverse populations.
- **Language Accessibility:** Incorporating multilingual interfaces and translation features within healthcare technologies to accommodate individuals with varying linguistic backgrounds.
- **Culturally Relevant Content:** Providing healthcare information, resources, and educational materials that resonate with different cultural beliefs, practices, and health perspectives.
- **Cultural Sensitivity Training:** Training healthcare professionals and technology developers to understand diverse cultural norms, beliefs, and values to design and deliver culturally competent care.
- **Customizable Care:** Offering customizable healthcare solutions that respect individual cultural preferences and values, fostering a sense of trust and comfort among diverse patient groups.

Reaching Underserved Populations

- **Targeted Outreach Programs:** Implementing outreach initiatives to raise awareness about healthcare technologies and their benefits among underserved communities.
- **Mobile Health Solutions:** Leveraging mobile technology to reach populations with limited access to traditional healthcare facilities, bringing healthcare services directly to their fingertips.
- **Partnerships and Collaborations:** Forming partnerships between healthcare providers, community organizations, and technology developers to create tailored solutions for underserved populations.

- **Telemedicine Initiatives:** Expanding telehealth services to connect remote or marginalized communities with healthcare professionals, bridging geographical gaps in access.
- **Financial Accessibility:** Introducing affordable healthcare technology options or subsidization programs to ensure cost-effective access for economically disadvantaged groups.

Community Engagement and Empowerment

- **Education and Training Programs:** Empowering communities through education on healthcare technologies, promoting digital literacy and enabling active participation in managing personal health (Das et al., 2024; Satav, Hasan, et al., 2024; Satav, Lamani, et al., 2024; Sharma et al., 2024).
- **Involving Stakeholders:** Involving community leaders, patient advocacy groups, and representatives in the design and development of healthcare technologies to ensure relevance and acceptance.
- **Empowering Self-Advocacy:** Equipping individuals with the knowledge and tools to advocate for their healthcare needs using technological solutions and resources.
- **Support Networks:** Creating online communities or support groups through technology platforms, fostering peer support and shared experiences among marginalized or isolated populations.
- **Feedback Mechanisms:** Establishing channels for community feedback and engagement in the continuous improvement and adaptation of healthcare technologies to better meet their needs.

Cultural sensitivity, targeted outreach, and community involvement are crucial for ensuring equitable access to healthcare technologies, promoting empowerment and inclusivity among diverse populations.

INTEGRATING SECURITY, ETHICS, AND SOCIAL RESPONSIBILITY

Multidisciplinary Collaboration

The integration of security, ethics, and social responsibility in healthcare technology relies on multidisciplinary collaboration across various disciplines. This approach unites experts from various fields to navigate the complex interplay between

Figure 2. Various of multidisciplinary collaboration in security, ethics, and social responsibility

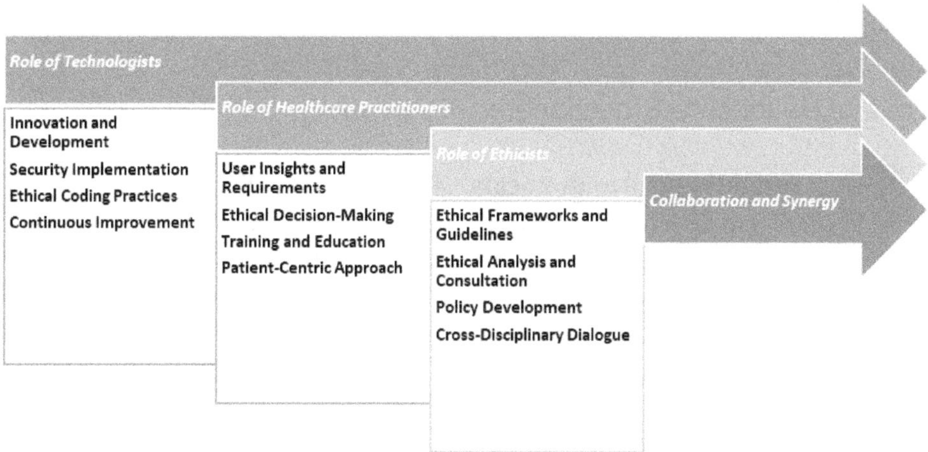

technological advancements, ethical considerations, and societal implications. The synergy between technologists, healthcare practitioners, policymakers, ethicists, and social advocates fosters a holistic approach that maximizes benefits while minimizing risks, ensures ethical integrity, and promotes inclusivity for diverse populations. Understanding the synergistic impact of multidisciplinary collaboration is crucial for shaping a healthcare landscape prioritizing security, ethical standards, and societal well-being. Figure 2 depicts various examples of multidisciplinary collaboration in areas such as security, ethics, and social responsibility (Maguluri, Ananth, et al., 2023).

Role of Technologists

- **Innovation and Development:** Technologists are at the forefront of developing and implementing technological solutions within healthcare, ensuring the design and deployment of secure, ethical, and socially responsible systems.
- **Security Implementation:** They are responsible for integrating robust security measures, encryption protocols, and access controls into healthcare technologies to safeguard patient data.
- **Ethical Coding Practices:** Technologists embed ethical considerations into the coding process, developing algorithms and systems that prioritize patient privacy, fairness, and transparency.

- **Continuous Improvement:** They play a crucial role in ongoing monitoring, maintenance, and updates to ensure that healthcare technologies evolve to address emerging ethical challenges and security threats.

Role of Healthcare Practitioners

- **User Insights and Requirements:** Healthcare practitioners provide critical insights into user needs, ensuring that technological solutions align with clinical workflows and patient care requirements.
- **Ethical Decision-Making:** They navigate ethical dilemmas, ensuring that the implementation of technology aligns with ethical guidelines, patient rights, and informed consent.
- **Training and Education:** Healthcare practitioners educate their peers and patients on the ethical use and benefits of healthcare technologies, fostering responsible adoption and utilization.
- **Patient-Centric Approach:** They advocate for patient-centric care, ensuring that technological advancements enhance patient-provider relationships and promote patient well-being.

Role of Ethicists

- **Ethical Frameworks and Guidelines:** Ethicists contribute by developing and advocating for ethical frameworks and guidelines that guide the responsible development and use of healthcare technologies.
- **Ethical Analysis and Consultation:** They offer ethical analysis and consultation, assessing the potential ethical implications of technological implementations and guiding decision-making processes.
- **Policy Development:** Ethicists collaborate with policymakers to shape regulations and policies that align with ethical principles, promoting equitable access and protecting patient rights.
- **Cross-Disciplinary Dialogue:** They facilitate discussions among technologists, healthcare practitioners, policymakers, and other stakeholders, fostering a shared understanding of ethical considerations and promoting collaboration.

Figure 3. The various policies and governance recommendations

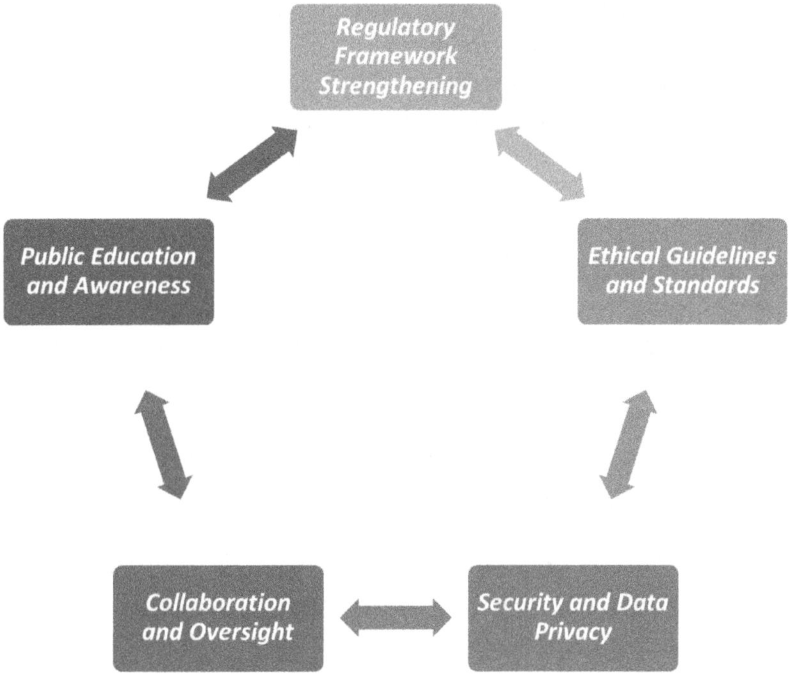

Collaboration and Synergy

Stakeholders work together to ensure healthcare technological innovations prioritize security, ethical standards, and societal implications. Their efforts lead to the development and implementation of technologies that advance medical care while upholding ethical integrity and social responsibility, benefiting all stakeholders. Figure 3 depicts various policies and governance recommendations (Das et al., 2024).

POLICY AND GOVERNANCE RECOMMENDATIONS

Regulatory Framework Strengthening

- **Comprehensive Data Protection Laws:** Develop and enforce stringent data protection laws that specifically address healthcare data, outlining clear guidelines for its collection, storage, and sharing.

- **Adaptive Regulatory Frameworks:** Establish agile and adaptive regulatory frameworks that can swiftly respond to technological advancements, ensuring ongoing relevance and protection.
- **Standardization and Interoperability:** Encourage standardized formats and interoperable systems to facilitate seamless and secure data exchange between different healthcare providers and technologies.

Ethical Guidelines and Standards

- **Ethical Impact Assessments:** Mandate thorough ethical impact assessments for new healthcare technologies before deployment, ensuring alignment with established ethical principles.
- **Guidelines for AI and Algorithm Use:** Develop guidelines for the ethical use of AI and algorithms in healthcare, emphasizing fairness, transparency, and accountability.
- **Informed Consent Standards:** Set clear standards for informed consent in digital healthcare, ensuring that patients have a comprehensive understanding of data usage and technology implications.

Security and Data Privacy

- **Cybersecurity Mandates:** Enforce cybersecurity standards specific to healthcare, requiring robust encryption, access controls, and incident response protocols to protect patient data (Agrawal, Magulur, et al., 2023; Kumar Reddy R. et al., 2023; Srinivas et al., 2023).
- **Data Breach Reporting Requirements:** Implement mandatory reporting of data breaches within specified timeframes, fostering transparency and enabling timely responses to breaches.
- **Vendor Accountability:** Establish guidelines holding technology vendors accountable for security measures in healthcare solutions, ensuring they comply with industry standards.

Collaboration and Oversight

- **Multi-Stakeholder Collaboration:** Foster collaboration among government bodies, healthcare providers, technologists, ethicists, and patient advocacy groups to develop comprehensive policies.

- **Ethics Review Boards:** Form independent ethics review boards to evaluate and approve healthcare technology implementations, ensuring alignment with ethical guidelines.
- **Ongoing Monitoring and Evaluation:** Institute mechanisms for continuous monitoring and evaluation of policy effectiveness, adapting regulations based on evolving technology and ethical landscapes.

Public Education and Awareness

- **Public Awareness Campaigns:** Launch educational campaigns to inform patients and healthcare professionals about their rights, responsibilities, and risks associated with healthcare technology.
- **Training Programs:** Develop training programs for healthcare staff to ensure their understanding of policy guidelines and their implications in daily practice.

Healthcare systems can address ethical concerns, reinforce security measures, and promote responsible technology integration through robust policy frameworks and governance structures, ensuring patient privacy, ethical integrity, and equitable access to healthcare technologies.

FUTURE OUTLOOK AND RECOMMENDATIONS

The current phase of healthcare technology presents a crucial opportunity to shape its trajectory, ensuring it aligns with ethical standards, security measures, and inclusivity. This exploration aims to guide the evolution towards a future characterized by equitable access, ethical integrity, and technological innovation. Strategic recommendations are needed to prioritize patient well-being, embrace technological advancements, and maintain ethical principles and societal responsibilities in a healthcare ecosystem. Figure 4 depicts the impact of emerging technologies on healthcare (Agrawal, Magulur, et al., 2023; Maguluri, Arularasan, et al., 2023; Sankar et al., 2023; Satav, Lamani, et al., 2024; Sharma et al., 2024; Venkateswaran et al., 2023).

Figure 4. Emerging technologies and impact on healthcare

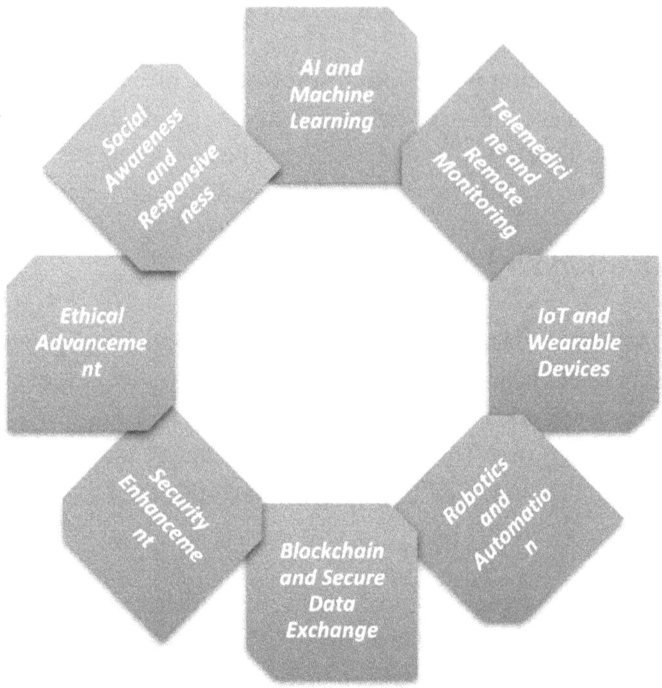

Emerging Technologies and Impact on Healthcare

AI and Machine Learning

- **Diagnostic Precision:** AI-powered algorithms can analyze vast datasets and imaging results, aiding in early and accurate disease detection.
- **Personalized Treatment:** Machine learning models can predict treatment responses based on individual patient data, enabling personalized therapy plans.
- **Operational Efficiency:** AI streamlines administrative tasks, optimizing workflows, and resource allocation, enhancing healthcare operational efficiency.

Telemedicine and Remote Monitoring

- **Remote Consultations:** Telemedicine expands access to healthcare, allowing patients to consult professionals regardless of geographical barriers (Boopathi, 2023c; Kumar B et al., 2024; Rahamathunnisa et al., 2023).
- **Chronic Disease Management:** Remote monitoring devices enable real-time data collection, aiding in the continuous management of chronic conditions.
- **Emergency Care Support:** Telemedicine facilitates immediate consultations during emergencies, guiding first responders or aiding remote healthcare delivery.

IoT and Wearable Devices

- **Continuous Health Tracking:** Wearable devices capture real-time health data, empowering individuals to monitor and manage their well-being proactively (Kumar B et al., 2024; Pachiappan et al., 2023; Rahamathunnisa et al., 2023; Sundaramoorthy et al., 2023).
- **Preventive Healthcare:** IoT devices aid in preventive measures by detecting early warning signs and promoting healthier lifestyles.
- **Enhanced Patient-Provider Connectivity:** These devices facilitate seamless communication between patients and healthcare providers, enabling more comprehensive care.

Robotics and Automation

- **Surgical Precision:** Robotic-assisted surgeries offer greater precision, reducing invasiveness and improving surgical outcomes (Koshariya et al., 2023; Mohanty et al., 2023; Pramila et al., 2023; Senthil et al., 2023; Srinivas et al., 2023).
- **Rehabilitation Support:** Robotics aids in rehabilitation therapies, providing precise assistance and monitoring during recovery.
- **Workflow Optimization:** Automation in administrative tasks and medication management streamlines healthcare operations, reducing errors and improving efficiency.

Blockchain and Secure Data Exchange

- **Secure Health Records:** Blockchain ensures the integrity and security of patient data, reducing the risk of data breaches (Boopathi, 2023d; Kumar et al., 2023; Sundaramoorthy et al., 2023).
- **Interoperability:** Blockchain enables secure sharing of patient records across different healthcare providers, ensuring data accuracy and accessibility.
- **Supply Chain Management:** Blockchain enhances transparency and traceability in drug supply chains, reducing counterfeit medications and ensuring quality.

Emerging technologies are transforming healthcare delivery by focusing on personalized care, accessibility, and efficiency, while requiring ethical considerations and safeguarding patient data and privacy.

Security Enhancement

- **Adaptive Cybersecurity Measures:** Regularly update and evolve cybersecurity protocols to stay ahead of emerging threats, incorporating the latest encryption standards and threat detection technologies (Kavitha et al., 2023; Pachiappan et al., 2023; Ravisankar et al., 2023).
- **Vigilant Monitoring and Response:** Implement real-time monitoring systems to swiftly detect and respond to security breaches or vulnerabilities, ensuring proactive mitigation.
- **User Education:** Provide ongoing training to healthcare staff on cybersecurity best practices, fostering a culture of security awareness and preparedness.

Ethical Advancement

- **Ethics Committees and Reviews:** Establish regular ethics review boards to assess new technologies, ensuring alignment with ethical principles and patient rights.
- **Ethical Guidelines Updates:** Continuously update and refine ethical guidelines to adapt to evolving technology and societal values, addressing emerging ethical dilemmas.
- **Inclusive Decision-Making:** Involve diverse stakeholders in ethical discussions and decision-making processes, fostering a comprehensive understanding of different perspectives.

Social Awareness and Responsiveness

- **Community Engagement:** Engage with communities to understand their needs and concerns regarding healthcare technology, fostering trust and addressing specific challenges.
- **Education and Empowerment:** Promote public education on the benefits and risks of healthcare technology, empowering individuals to make informed decisions about their health (Agrawal, Pitchai, et al., 2023; Boopathi, 2023b; Das et al., 2024; Durairaj et al., 2023; Sharma et al., 2024).
- **Advocacy for Inclusivity:** Advocate for policies and practices that prioritize inclusivity, aiming to bridge the digital divide and ensure equitable access to healthcare technologies for all.

To ensure ethical, secure, and inclusive healthcare technology, a proactive approach involving collaboration, adaptation to new challenges, and prioritizing ethical and societal implications is crucial. This involves refining security measures, upholding ethical standards, and promoting social responsibility.

CONCLUSION

The chapter discusses the potential transformative change in healthcare due to the integration of technology, highlighting the need to navigate the complex interplay of security, ethics, and societal implications in this evolving landscape. This exploration reveals that:

- Ethical considerations must underpin every technological advancement, guiding the responsible development and implementation of innovations to ensure patient rights, data privacy, and fairness.
- Robust security measures are non-negotiable, safeguarding sensitive patient data against cyber threats and ensuring the trust and integrity of healthcare technology.
- The pursuit of technological integration should be coupled with efforts to bridge the digital divide, ensuring equitable access to healthcare technologies for all populations.
- A commitment to continuous improvement in security, ethics, and social awareness is crucial, demanding ongoing collaboration, adaptability, and responsiveness to evolving challenges.

The future of healthcare technology integration requires synergistic collaboration among stakeholders across disciplines, prioritizing ethical integrity, security measures, inclusivity, and social responsibility. This will lead to groundbreaking, beneficial, accessible, and ethically sound innovation for all individuals and communities.

REFERENCES

Agrawal, A. V., Magulur, L. P., Priya, S. G., Kaur, A., Singh, G., & Boopathi, S. (2023). Smart Precision Agriculture Using IoT and WSN. In Advances in Information Security, Privacy, and Ethics (pp. 524–541). IGI Global. doi:10.4018/978-1-6684-8145-5.ch026

Agrawal, A. V., Pitchai, R., Senthamaraikannan, C., Alangudi Balaji, N., Sajithra, S., & Boopathi, S. (2023). Digital Education System During the COVID-19 Pandemic. In J. Bell & T. Gifford (Eds.), Advances in Educational Technologies and Instructional Design (pp. 104–126). IGI Global. doi:10.4018/978-1-6684-6424-3.ch005

Boopathi, S. (2023a). An Investigation on Friction Stir Processing of Aluminum Alloy-Boron Carbide Surface Composite. In R. V. Vignesh, R. Padmanaban, & M. Govindaraju (Eds.), *Advances in Processing of Lightweight Metal Alloys and Composites* (pp. 249–257). Springer Nature Singapore., doi:10.1007/978-981-19-7146-4_14

Boopathi, S. (2023b). Deep Learning Techniques Applied for Automatic Sentence Generation. In K. Becerra-Murillo & J. F. Gámez (Eds.), Advances in Educational Technologies and Instructional Design. IGI Global. doi:10.4018/978-1-6684-3632-5.ch016

Boopathi, S. (2023c). Internet of Things-Integrated Remote Patient Monitoring System: Healthcare Application. In A. Suresh Kumar, U. Kose, S. Sharma, & S. Jerald Nirmal Kumar (Eds.), Advances in Healthcare Information Systems and Administration. IGI Global. doi:10.4018/978-1-6684-6894-4.ch008

Boopathi, S. (2023d). Securing Healthcare Systems Integrated With IoT: Fundamentals, Applications, and Future Trends. In A. Suresh Kumar, U. Kose, S. Sharma, & S. Jerald Nirmal Kumar (Eds.), Advances in Healthcare Information Systems and Administration. IGI Global. doi:10.4018/978-1-6684-6894-4.ch010

Boopathi, S., & Davim, J. P. (2023). Applications of Nanoparticles in Various Manufacturing Processes. In S. Boopathi & J. P. Davim (Eds.), Advances in Chemical and Materials Engineering. IGI Global. doi:10.4018/978-1-6684-9135-5.ch001

Boopathi, S., Umareddy, M., & Elangovan, M. (2023). Applications of Nano-Cutting Fluids in Advanced Machining Processes. In S. Boopathi & J. P. Davim (Eds.), Advances in Chemical and Materials Engineering. IGI Global. doi:10.4018/978-1-6684-9135-5.ch009

Das, S., Lekhya, G., Shreya, K., Lydia Shekinah, K., Babu, K. K., & Boopathi, S. (2024). Fostering Sustainability Education Through Cross-Disciplinary Collaborations and Research Partnerships: Interdisciplinary Synergy. In P. Yu, J. Mulli, Z. A. S. Syed, & L. Umme (Eds.), Advances in Higher Education and Professional Development. IGI Global. doi:10.4018/979-8-3693-0487-7.ch003

Durairaj, M., Jayakumar, S. Monika, Karpagavalli, V. S., Maheswari, B. U., & Boopathi, S. (2023). Utilization of Digital Tools in the Indian Higher Education System During Health Crises. In C. S. V. Negrão, I. G. P. Maia, & J. A. F. Brito (Eds.), Advances in Logistics, Operations, and Management Science (pp. 1–21). IGI Global. doi:10.4018/978-1-7998-9213-7.ch001

Gunasekaran, K., & Boopathi, S. (2023). Artificial Intelligence in Water Treatments and Water Resource Assessments. In V. Shikuku (Ed.), Advances in Environmental Engineering and Green Technologies. IGI Global. doi:10.4018/978-1-6684-6791-6.ch004

Karthik, S. A., Hemalatha, R., Aruna, R., Deivakani, M., Reddy, R. V. K., & Boopathi, S. (2023). Study on Healthcare Security System-Integrated Internet of Things (IoT). In M. K. Habib (Ed.), Advances in Systems Analysis, Software Engineering, and High Performance Computing. IGI Global. doi:10.4018/978-1-6684-7684-0.ch013

Kavitha, C. R., Varalatchoumy, M., Mithuna, H. R., Bharathi, K., Geethalakshmi, N. M., & Boopathi, S. (2023). Energy Monitoring and Control in the Smart Grid: Integrated Intelligent IoT and ANFIS. In M. Arshad (Ed.), Advances in Bioinformatics and Biomedical Engineering. IGI Global. doi:10.4018/978-1-6684-6577-6.ch014

Koshariya, A. K., Khatoon, S., Marathe, A. M., Suba, G. M., Baral, D., & Boopathi, S. (2023). Agricultural Waste Management Systems Using Artificial Intelligence Techniques. In S. Kautish, N. K. Chaubey, S. B. Goyal, & P. Whig (Eds.), Advances in Computational Intelligence and Robotics. IGI Global. doi:10.4018/978-1-6684-8171-4.ch009

Kumar, B. M., Kumar, K. K., Sasikala, P., Sampath, B., Gopi, B., & Sundaram, S. (2024). Sustainable Green Energy Generation From Waste Water: IoT and ML Integration. In B. K. Mishra (Ed.), Practice, Progress, and Proficiency in Sustainability. IGI Global. doi:10.4018/979-8-3693-1186-8.ch024

Kumar, P. R., Meenakshi, S., Shalini, S., Devi, S. R., & Boopathi, S. (2023). Soil Quality Prediction in Context Learning Approaches Using Deep Learning and Blockchain for Smart Agriculture. In R. Kumar, A. B. Abdul Hamid, & N. I. Binti Ya'akub (Eds.), Advances in Computational Intelligence and Robotics. IGI Global. doi:10.4018/978-1-6684-9151-5.ch001

Kumar Reddy, R. V., Rahamathunnisa, U., Subhashini, P., Aancy, H. M., Meenakshi, S., & Boopathi, S. (2023). Solutions for Software Requirement Risks Using Artificial Intelligence Techniques. In T. Murugan & N. E. (Eds.), Advances in Information Security, Privacy, and Ethics (pp. 45–64). IGI Global. doi:10.4018/978-1-6684-8145-5.ch003

Maguluri, L. P., Ananth, J., Hariram, S., Geetha, C., Bhaskar, A., & Boopathi, S. (2023). Smart Vehicle-Emissions Monitoring System Using Internet of Things (IoT). In P. Srivastava, D. Ramteke, A. K. Bedyal, M. Gupta, & J. K. Sandhu (Eds.), Practice, Progress, and Proficiency in Sustainability. IGI Global., doi:10.4018/978-1-6684-8117-2.ch014

Maguluri, L. P., Arularasan, A. N., & Boopathi, S. (2023). Assessing Security Concerns for AI-Based Drones in Smart Cities. In R. Kumar, A. B. Abdul Hamid, & N. I. Binti Ya'akub (Eds.), Advances in Computational Intelligence and Robotics. IGI Global. doi:10.4018/978-1-6684-9151-5.ch002

Mohanty, A., Jothi, B., Jeyasudha, J., Ranjit, P. S., Isaac, J. S., & Boopathi, S. (2023). Additive Manufacturing Using Robotic Programming. In S. Kautish, N. K. Chaubey, S. B. Goyal, & P. Whig (Eds.), Advances in Computational Intelligence and Robotics. IGI Global. doi:10.4018/978-1-6684-8171-4.ch010

Pachiappan, K., Anitha, K., Pitchai, R., Sangeetha, S., Satyanarayana, T. V. V., & Boopathi, S. (2023). Intelligent Machines, IoT, and AI in Revolutionizing Agriculture for Water Processing. In B. B. Gupta & F. Colace (Eds.), Advances in Computational Intelligence and Robotics. IGI Global. doi:10.4018/978-1-6684-9999-3.ch015

Pramila, P. V., Amudha, S., Saravanan, T. R., Sankar, S. R., Poongothai, E., & Boopathi, S. (2023). Design and Development of Robots for Medical Assistance: An Architectural Approach. In G. S. Karthick & S. Karupusamy (Eds.), Advances in Healthcare Information Systems and Administration. IGI Global. doi:10.4018/978-1-6684-8913-0.ch011

Rahamathunnisa, U., Sudhakar, K., Padhi, S. N., Bhattacharya, S., Shashibhushan, G., & Boopathi, S. (2023). Sustainable Energy Generation From Waste Water: IoT Integrated Technologies. In A. S. Etim (Ed.), Advances in Human and Social Aspects of Technology. IGI Global. doi:10.4018/978-1-6684-5347-6.ch010

Ramudu, K., Mohan, V. M., Jyothirmai, D., Prasad, D. V. S. S. S. V., Agrawal, R., & Boopathi, S. (2023). Machine Learning and Artificial Intelligence in Disease Prediction: Applications, Challenges, Limitations, Case Studies, and Future Directions. In G. S. Karthick & S. Karupusamy (Eds.), Advances in Healthcare Information Systems and Administration. IGI Global. doi:10.4018/978-1-6684-8913-0.ch013

Ravisankar, A., Sampath, B., & Asif, M. M. (2023). Economic Studies on Automobile Management: Working Capital and Investment Analysis. In C. S. V. Negrão, I. G. P. Maia, & J. A. F. Brito (Eds.), Advances in Logistics, Operations, and Management Science. IGI Global. doi:10.4018/978-1-7998-9213-7.ch009

Reddy, M. A., Gaurav, A., Ushasukhanya, S., Rao, V. C. S., Bhattacharya, S., & Boopathi, S. (2023). Bio-Medical Wastes Handling Strategies During the COVID-19 Pandemic. In C. S. V. Negrão, I. G. P. Maia, & J. A. F. Brito (Eds.), Advances in Logistics, Operations, and Management Science. IGI Global. doi:10.4018/978-1-7998-9213-7.ch006

Reddy, M. A., Reddy, B. M., Mukund, C. S., Venneti, K., Preethi, D. M. D., & Boopathi, S. (2023). Social Health Protection During the COVID-Pandemic Using IoT. In F. P. C. Endong (Ed.), Advances in Electronic Government, Digital Divide, and Regional Development. IGI Global. doi:10.4018/978-1-7998-8394-4.ch009

Sankar, K. M., Booba, B., & Boopathi, S. (2023). Smart Agriculture Irrigation Monitoring System Using Internet of Things. In G. S. Karthick (Ed.), Advances in Environmental Engineering and Green Technologies. IGI Global. doi:10.4018/978-1-6684-7879-0.ch006

Satav, S. D., Hasan, D. S., Pitchai, R., Mohanaprakash, T. A., Sultanuddin, S. J., & Boopathi, S. (2024). Next Generation of Internet of Things (NGIoT) in Healthcare Systems. In B. K. Mishra (Ed.), Practice, Progress, and Proficiency in Sustainability. IGI Global. doi:10.4018/979-8-3693-1186-8.ch017

Satav, S. D., Lamani, D. K. G., H., Kumar, N. M. G., Manikandan, S., & Sampath, B. (2024). Energy and Battery Management in the Era of Cloud Computing: Sustainable Wireless Systems and Networks. In B. K. Mishra (Ed.), Practice, Progress, and Proficiency in Sustainability (pp. 141–166). IGI Global. doi:10.4018/979-8-3693-1186-8.ch009

Sengeni, D., Padmapriya, G., Imambi, S. S., Suganthi, D., Suri, A., & Boopathi, S. (2023). Biomedical Waste Handling Method Using Artificial Intelligence Techniques. In P. Srivastava, D. Ramteke, A. K. Bedyal, M. Gupta, & J. K. Sandhu (Eds.), Practice, Progress, and Proficiency in Sustainability. IGI Global. doi:10.4018/978-1-6684-8117-2.ch022

Senthil, T. S., Ohmsakthi Vel, R., Puviyarasan, M., Babu, S. R., Surakasi, R., & Sampath, B. (2023). Industrial Robot-Integrated Fused Deposition Modelling for the 3D Printing Process. In R. Keshavamurthy, V. Tambrallimath, & J. P. Davim (Eds.), Advances in Chemical and Materials Engineering. IGI Global. doi:10.4018/978-1-6684-6009-2.ch011

Sharma, D. M., Venkata Ramana, K., Jothilakshmi, R., Verma, R., Uma Maheswari, B., & Boopathi, S. (2024). Integrating Generative AI Into K-12 Curriculums and Pedagogies in India: Opportunities and Challenges. In P. Yu, J. Mulli, Z. A. S. Syed, & L. Umme (Eds.), Advances in Higher Education and Professional Development. IGI Global. doi:10.4018/979-8-3693-0487-7.ch006

Srinivas, B., Maguluri, L. P., Naidu, K. V., Reddy, L. C. S., Deivakani, M., & Boopathi, S. (2023). Architecture and Framework for Interfacing Cloud-Enabled Robots: In T. Murugan & N. E. (Eds.), Advances in Information Security, Privacy, and Ethics (pp. 542–560). IGI Global. doi:10.4018/978-1-6684-8145-5.ch027

Sundaramoorthy, K., Singh, A., Sumathy, G., Maheshwari, A., Arunarani, A. R., & Boopathi, S. (2023). A Study on AI and Blockchain-Powered Smart Parking Models for Urban Mobility. In B. B. Gupta & F. Colace (Eds.), Advances in Computational Intelligence and Robotics. IGI Global. doi:10.4018/978-1-6684-9999-3.ch010

Ugandar, R. E., Rahamathunnisa, U., Sajithra, S., Christiana, M. B. V., Palai, B. K., & Boopathi, S. (2023). Hospital Waste Management Using Internet of Things and Deep Learning: Enhanced Efficiency and Sustainability. In M. Arshad (Ed.), Advances in Bioinformatics and Biomedical Engineering. IGI Global. doi:10.4018/978-1-6684-6577-6.ch015

Venkateswaran, N., Kumar, S. S., Diwakar, G., Gnanasangeetha, D., & Boopathi, S. (2023). Synthetic Biology for Waste Water to Energy Conversion: IoT and AI Approaches. In M. Arshad (Ed.), Advances in Bioinformatics and Biomedical Engineering. IGI Global. doi:10.4018/978-1-6684-6577-6.ch017

Chapter 11
Image Enhancement Using Holistic Transformer Super Resolution

S. Meganathan
https://orcid.org/0000-0003-4570-8259
SASTRA University, India

S. SanthoshKumar
https://orcid.org/0000-0001-7271-721X
Alagappa University, India

Thasil Mohamed
Compunnel, USA

ABSTRACT

Higher resolution images are integral across diverse applications due to several compelling reasons. Firstly, they offer superior detail and clarity, making them indispensable in fields such as medical imaging, satellite observations, and scientific research where capturing intricate details is paramount. In medical imaging, high resolution is pivotal. Despite the advantages of high-resolution images, they are not always accessible due to the costly setup required for high-resolution imaging. Feasibility may be constrained by essential limitations in sensor optics manufacturing technology. To overcome these challenges, cost-effective deep learning methods can be employed. In this context, the proposed holistic transformer super-resolution technique aims to enhance the resolution of an image beyond its original level.

DOI: 10.4018/979-8-3693-1694-8.ch011

1. INTRODUCTION

Deep learning models play a crucial role in image enhancement (Singh & Mittal, 2014), aiming to enhance visual quality and clarity in images. The process typically begins with extensive data preparation, involving pairs of input images and their corresponding enhanced versions for training. The selection of an appropriate deep learning model depends on the specific image enhancement task at hand, with common choices including convolutional neural networks (CNNs), auto encoders, and Generative Adversarial Networks (GANs) (Dong et al., 2015; Li et al., 2021). An advanced-resolution image frequently describes visual information. Higher-resolution photos with clean and egregious object borders or expansive visual descriptions are needed to better understand the semantics of real-world images. Obtaining HR film land using colorful tackle-grounded technologies, on the other hand, is time-consuming and costly. As a result, using algorithmic approaches to pursue HR images from LR source images is preferable. Super-resolution (SR) (Chen et al., 2022) is a fashion for creating an advanced-resolution image from a lower-resolution image (Yamashita & Markov, 2020). The significance of high resolution is particularly pronounced in medical imaging. However, obtaining high-resolution images is not always feasible. The setup for high-resolution imaging is often costly, and practical constraints, such as those imposed by sensor optics manufacturing technology, may hinder its implementation. Deep learning methods present a cost-effective solution to overcome these challenges (Wang et al., 2020). HTSR, in particular, provides a versatile approach to enhance image quality. The model architecture is carefully designed to meet the requirements of the enhancement task, incorporating layers that capture and process relevant features. A loss function, such as mean squared error (MSE) or adversarial loss, is selected to quantify the difference between predicted enhanced images and ground truth during training. The training process involves iterative adjustments to the model's internal parameters to minimize the chosen loss function. Post-training, the model is validated on a separate dataset, and fine-tuning may be performed to improve performance. During inference, the trained model is applied to new, unseen images to produce enhanced versions. Optional post-processing steps, such as histogram equalization or contrast adjustment, may be applied to further refine the output. Finally, the deployed model can be integrated into various applications, such as image editing software, mobile apps, or embedded systems, enabling real-time image enhancement for diverse purposes. The success of deep learning models in tasks like super-resolution, de-noising, de-blurring, and color correction lies in their capacity to learn complex mappings and reproduce intricate details, resulting in visually appealing and high-quality enhanced images.

Image Processing With Deep Learning

Step 1 - Sensor: After receiving the image, the system converts it into signal data. Only signal data is discussed here. It also solves problems related to resolution, bandwidth and other factors.
Step 2 - Segmentation: In the next step, the process of segmentation begins. In this step, the machine removes all unnecessary objects, such as the background and related objects.
Step 3 - Feature Extraction: It detects image attributes and labels them according to classification.
Step 4 - Classification: Once the image is classified, it is assigned to a specific category.
Step 5 - Post-processing: This is where the machine makes the decision.

Single-Image Super-Resolution (SISR): Is a method aimed at restoring a single high-resolution image from a low-resolution counterpart. The challenge lies in the complexity of retrieving high-frequency details from a low-resolution image. This task proves difficult because a low-resolution image lacks inherent high-frequency information, imposing limitations on the quality of the resultant high-resolution image. Furthermore, SISR poses a misrepresentation problem, as a single low-resolution image may correspond to multiple high-resolution images.

Multi Frame Super Resolution: Is when many photographs of the same scene are obtained from somewhat different positions, sometimes at various times, the combined information is more than any single image. MFSR (Bhat et al., 2021) combines various low-res inputs to create a composite high-res image that can reveal some of the original detail that isn't visible in any one low-res image. Applications of Super- Resolution Image Enhancement: Photoshop and Photoshop Lightroom have been receiving machine-learning and AI-powered capabilities from Adobe. Adobe's AI technology, Adobe Sensei, is used in Super-Resolution to quadruple an image's horizontal and vertical resolution. It quadruples the number of pixels, effectively transforming a 12-megapixel photo into a 48-megapixel one. Super Resolution makes the file large, and Enhance Details ensures that it appears well if you're working with RAW data.

Surveillance & Forensics: Super-resolution techniques are used in surveillance and digital forensics to detect, identify, and perform facial recognition on low-resolution images received from security cameras.

Satellite Imaging: Enhance satellite imagery beyond its native resolution to detect objects accurately.

Medical Imaging: Acquiring high-resolution MRI images can be challenging due to scan time (SNR), geographic coverage, and signal-to-noise ratio. Super-resolution helps solve this problem by creating high-resolution MRI images from otherwise low-quality MRI images.

Increasing Gaming Performance: In the modern environment, industry giants such as Intel, Nvidia and AMD have incorporated super-resolution capabilities in their graphics processing units (GPUs). This allows imaging of ultra-high resolution images at a lower resolution imaging performance level. Machine learning is critical to this feature, as it produces images that resemble the quality of the original ultra-high-resolution imaging. This is accomplished by reconstructing details from surrounding pixels and sub-pixels based on motion-compensated previous frames. The reconstruction process, coupled with neural network training, is designed to deliver high performance and exceptional image quality.

- INTEL: XeSS (Xe Super Sampling): AI-enhanced upscaling
- NVIDIA DLSS is a deep-learning neural network that increases frame rates and produces sharp frames that approach or exceed native rendering
- AMD FidelityFX SR (FSR): delivers super optimized super resolution and the spatial upscaling algorithm super high quality edges and detail

Interpolation Techniques: In the realm of image processing, interpolation emerged as one of the initial solutions to address the challenge of low-resolution images. This technique entails enlarging a low-resolution image by a factor of 2x or 4x through the application of different interpolation methods (Fadnavis, 2014; Garnero & Godone, 2014), including nearest neighbor, bilinear, or bicubic interpolation. Essentially, interpolation leverages existing information to estimate values at points that are not explicitly known. This process works both ways for images and tries to form the best approximation of the intensity of a pixel region based on the values of the surrounding pixels. However, when low-resolution images are enhanced using upscaling techniques like resampling and interpolation, they often only result in larger pixels instead of providing finer details in the zoomed-in region (Li et al., 2022). This means that the image becomes pixelated and lacks the sharpness and clarity that would be ideal.

2. RELATED WORK

Interpolation techniques such as bicubic – interpolation (Xiang et al., 2022; Zhu et al., 2022), bilinear or nearest - neighbor methods simply scales the individual pixels based on the pixel intensity of the surrounding pixels, thereby resulting in a bigger image with very large pixels, but does not provide finer details when zoomed into

Figure 1. Drawbacks of interpolation method

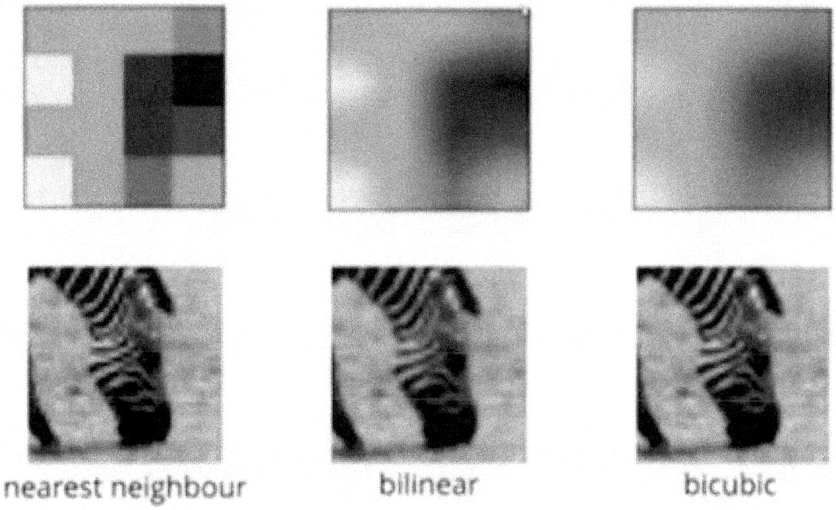

a particular region of interest. Figure 1 represents the SR image zoomed into ROI is pixelated.

- Drawbacks: SRCNN uses bicubic interpolation, where larger the image higher the complexity of upsampling.
- FSRCNN uses a smaller kernel size and suffers from vanishing gradient issues.
- SRGAN & ESRGAN uses perpetual loss, playing an adversarial game to produce photo-realistic images. It is Unable to reconstruct real-world low-resolution images due to sparse features and weak supervision.Interpolation techniques such as bicubic-interpolation, bilinear, or nearest-neighborhoods simply scale the individual pixels based on the pixel intensity of the surrounding pixels, thereby resulting in a bigger image with very large pixels, but do not provide finer details when zoomed into a particular region of interest.

3. PROPOSED SYSTEM

This study introduces a robust baseline model, HTSR, for single-image super-resolution. HTSR combines the advantages of CNN, which is effective for processing

Figure 2. Proposed model

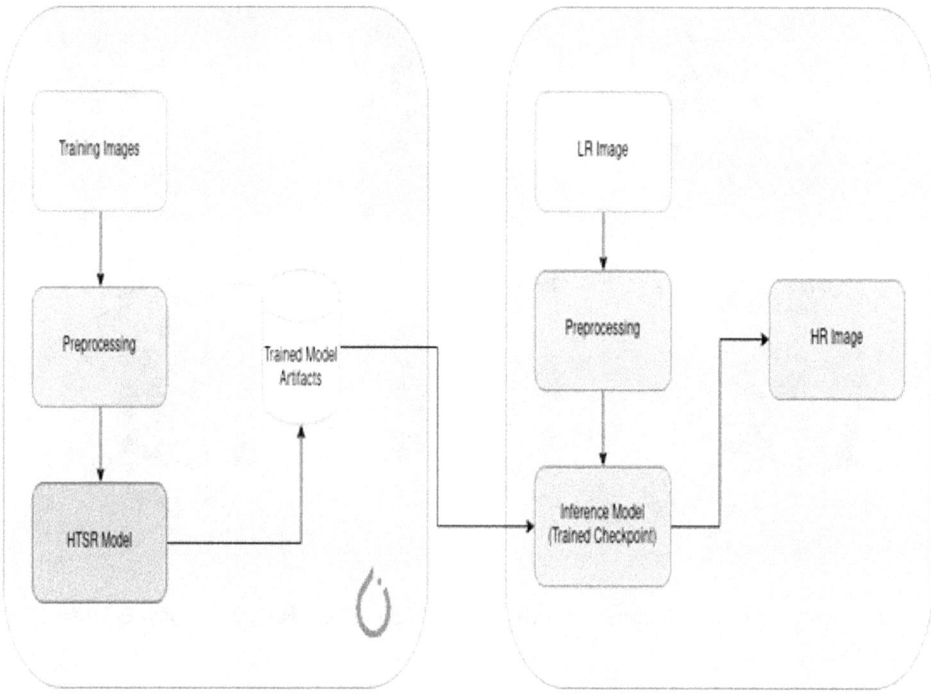

large-sized images due to its local attention mechanism, and transformers, which excel in modeling long-range dependencies through the shifted window scheme.

HTSR consists of three parts:

- Shallow Feature extraction
- Deep Feature extraction
- High quality image super-resolution

By including a convolution layer at the end of the feature extraction stage, an inductive change of the convolution process can be achieved in a transformer-based network. This creates a more stable foundation for the accumulation of shallow and deep features. The convolutional layer demonstrates superior performance in initial visual processing, contributing to more seamless optimization and improved outcomes. Additionally, it facilitates the mapping of the input image space to a higher-dimensional feature space.

To extract deep features, a residual transform block (RST) and a 3 x 3 convolutional layer were applied to the previously extracted shallow object layer. This process enhances the representation of features in the network.

The incorporation of a convolution layer at the conclusion of the feature extraction stage introduces an inductive change to the convolution process within a transformer-based network. This modification establishes a more robust foundation for accumulating both shallow and deep features.

The production of a high-quality image involves the combination of shallow and deep features. Shallow features primarily encompass low-frequencies, whereas deep features concentrate on the recovery of lost high-frequencies. By incorporating long skip connections, residual blocks facilitate the transmission of low-frequency information to the enhancement function.

This aids the deep feature extraction process in focusing on high-frequency information and contributes to training stability. In implementing enhancement functions, sub-pixel convolution layers are utilized to upsample the features. Rather than directly using the high-quality image, we employ a residual learning approach to reconstruct the residual between the low-quality (LQ) and high-quality (HQ) images.

HTSR System Architecture

To store low-frequency information, the low-frequency feature extractor uses a convolutional layer to extract low-frequency features, which are then sent directly to the reconstruction module. The deep Feature Extractor consists of CNN layers and Residual Transform Blocks (RTB). Each RTB contains multi-head attention for local attention and inter-window interactions, as well as multiple transformer layers with encoder and decoder stacks. The remaining link is added to create a shortcut to combine functions, and a convolution layer is added to the end of the block to add functions. Finally, a high-quality image super-resolution module combines shallow and deep functions.

Training Phase: Initially the LR, HR images i.e dataset is collected for our approach we are using DIV2K (800 images) + Flickr 2K (2560 images) + FFHQ (2000 images). The images are preprocessed and transformed appropriately. The preprocessed images are fed to the HTSR model to be trained for many epochs. Finally the trained model weights (artifacts) are stored for later reuse during the inference phase. Training the network iteratively for many epochs requires high performance hardware such as GPUs or TPU. So this process is performed on a remote machine.

Inference Phase: During the Inference phase any passed LR image is super sampled into the HR image. First the LR image is transformed using image transformations and passed to the Inference model which as the previously trained model artifacts loaded in. So the model performs a forward pass and yields the HR reconstruction of the LR image as output. Since inference is relatively inexpensive when compared to the training process, once a network is trained on remote machines, it can be deployed on local machines for inference purpose. Figure 3 shows Layer wise model of HTSR.

Figure 3. Layer-Wise model of HTSR

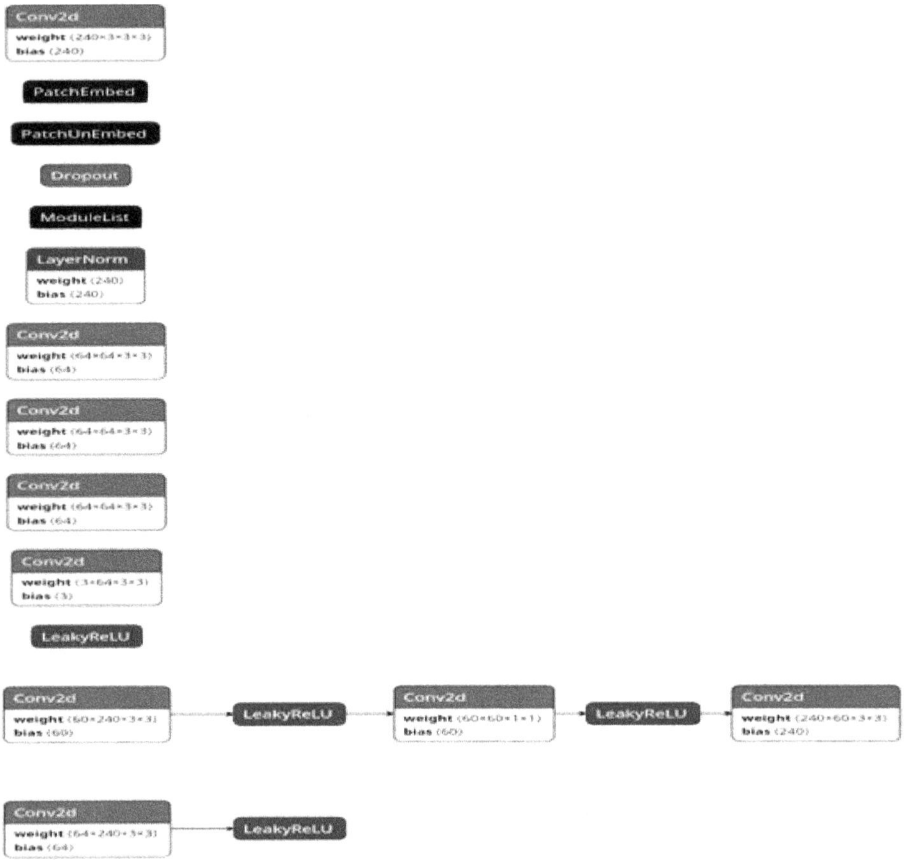

4. EXPERIMENTAL DETAILS

Input Validation:

Input validation is employed to verify that the input received by the application adheres to the standards established within the application. It can range from simple tasks such as enforcing specific parameter types to more intricate processes like validating images based on predetermined constraints, including specified extensions and sizes.

The input image validation is done at UI level using streamlit's file_uploader api's type parameter which is constrained to accept only images of type:png, .jpg, .jpeg, .bmp.

Uploaded image size is restricted to be within 200 MB to provide QOS during inference. Our model expects the input image to be a torch.Tensor with dimensions (batch_size, channels, height, width).

Model also assumes that image tensor is pinned in appropriate device memory i.e GPU or CPU based on torch.device both during training & inference phase.

Image Preprocessing:

- To produce remarkably realistic results, to tweak the input image using various transformations and preprocessing.
- Pixel normalization is used to scale pixel values to the range 0-1 from 0-1.
- Pixel centering is used to scale pixel values to have a zero mean.
- Pixel standardization scales pixel values to have a zero mean and unit variance (standard Gaussian).
- torchvision.transforms.Resize(224, 224) is used to resize the input image to 224 x224 which is expected by our HTSR model.
- torchvision.transforms.Normalize(mean=0.5, std=[R,G,B]) is used to normalize the tensor image with mean of 0.5 and std as RGB intensity of image
- torchvision.transforms.to_grayscale is used to convert PIL image of RGB/ BGR/LAB to grayscale version of image.
- torchvision.transforms.ToTensor() is used to convert PIL image to torch. Tensor which is expected by our model.

HTSR Model Optimization

- Quantization involves employing methods to carry out computations and store tensors at bit widths lower than floating-point precision.
- In PyTorch, INT8 quantization is supported as opposed to the more common FP32 models, resulting in a fourfold reduction in the model size and a corresponding reduction in memory bandwidth requirements.
- For the quantization process, we utilize fbgemm as the quantization configuration, deploy the CPU as the backend, and adopt Eager mode for post-training static quantization.
- Static quantization entails the quantization of both weights and activations in the model. It also consolidates activations into preceding layers wherever feasible.
- This process specifically targets the quantization of nn.Linear, nn.Conv2D, nn.LSTM, and nn.Embeddings layers in the HTSR model.
- The outcome is a reduction in the CPU model size from 140 MB to 64 MB post quantization, as traced using torchScript.

HTSR Model Inference

- Inference application is deployed using streamlit, which allows us to upload images to web interface, enhance image & visually compare it with raw image.
- For inference we provide two options i.e GPU model & CPU model.
- GPU model uses NCCL & CUDA to perform inference, while CPU model uses intel AVX, SSE, torch_CCL to perform inference on much slower general purpose CPU cores.
- Using multithreading we perform loading of models into device memory based on user selection in the UI. Use OpenCV intrinsics to open the uploaded image, preprocess & transform it to required format as expected by our inference model.
- Uploading the image forks another background thread to perform required preprocessing & transforms and save it locally, in order to speed up the inference process.
- Using a callback function named predict in streamlit button API, we enhanced the preprocessed image & rendered it on the web interface.

Comparison of HTSR Results With RCAN

To train the proposed HTSR model combining DIV2K, Flickr 2K, FFHQ for real-world image super resolution (x4) and test it on Berkeley Segmentation Data (BSD100). In direct comparison with RCAN, HTSR exhibits notable advantages in performance and efficiency. This distinctive approach results in improved outcomes, demonstrating better performance with fewer parameters. Notably, when examining the impact of training samples, HTSR showcases a rapid performance increase with

Table 1. Training patch size and PSNR convergence

Training Patches	PSNR (db)	
	HTSR	RCAN
32	39.398	39.332
40	39.432	39.395
48	39.516	39.415
56	39.574	39.422
64	39.6	39.449
72	39.632	39.500
80	39.668	39.522

Figure 4. Training patch size and PSNR convergence

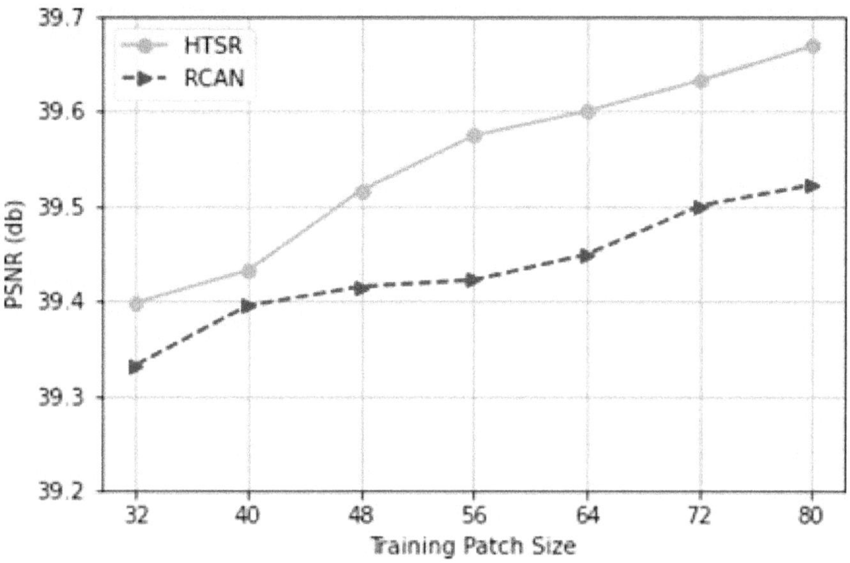

an augmented number of images, underscoring its resilience and efficacy. In contrast to RCAN and other existing methods, HTSR consistently produces visually appealing images with well-defined and sharp edges in real-world situations, minimizing the occurrence of undesirable artifacts. This comparative analysis underscores HTSR's superiority over RCAN, particularly in achieving superior results while utilizing the same training data, showcasing its potential as an advanced and efficient model in image processing tasks. Table 1 and Figure 4 show the PSNR produced for respective training patch sizes by both HTSR & RCAN models.

Table 2. Sample size used and PSNR convergence

Number of Images Used	Percentage of Used Images (%)	PSNR (db)	
		HTSR	RCAN
108	2	39.176	38.853
268	5	39.395	39.180
536	10	39.546	39.450
1072	20	39.729	39.498
1608	30	39.853	39.680
2144	40	39.897	39.693
2680	50	39.900	39.720

Figure 5. Impact of sample size and PSNR convergence

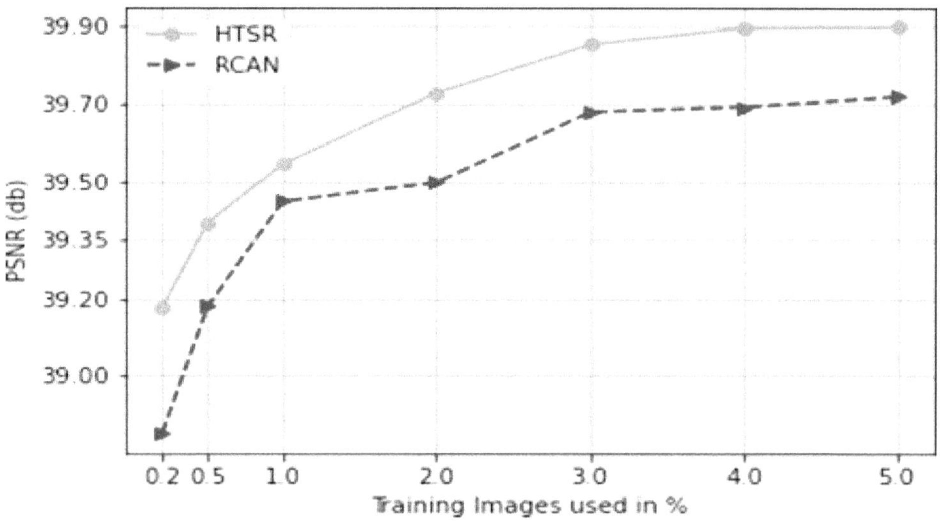

Figure 6. Impact of training epochs and PSNR convergence

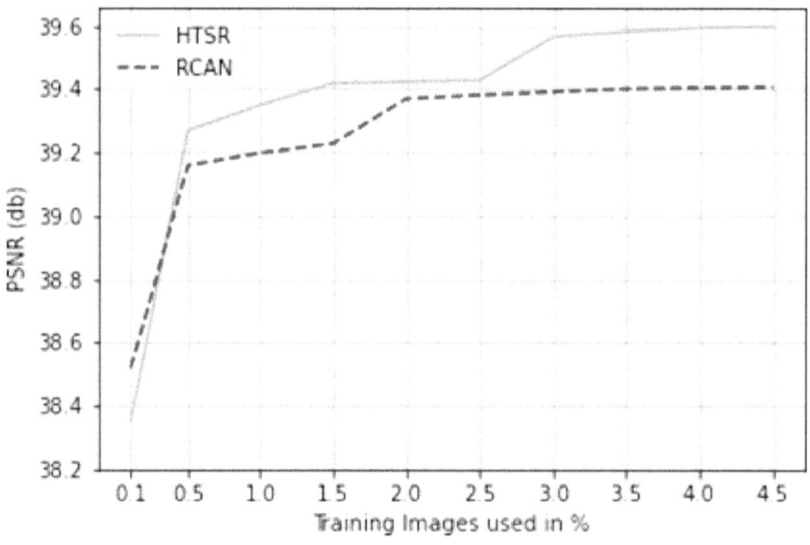

Table 2 and Figure 5 show the effect of the training samples used. In other words, the performance of HTSR increases dramatically with the number of photos used. This shows that while transformer-based models inherently rely on a huge amount of training data, HTSR outperforms CNN-based models with the same training data.

Figure 7. Human face super resolution using HTSR

While transformer-based models heavily depend on extensive training data, HTSR outperforms CNN-based models even when trained on the same dataset. Figure 6 shows HTSR exhibits faster convergence and a quicker stabilization of PSNR compared to RCAN, leading to enhanced accuracy and reduced training times when contrasted with conventional CNN-based models like RCAN. Figure 7 shows the performance of HTSR for the given input image.

5. CONCLUSION

HTSR allows for the interaction of visual content and content-based attention weights. The HTSR (High-Resolution Image Super-Resolution) model has consistently demonstrated superior performance by yielding higher accuracy compared to other models in various tasks. The HTSR model capturing intricate details, preserving image quality, and outperforming alternative methods, making it a reliable choice for tasks demanding elevated accuracy in image processing and super-resolution. It is a spatially varying convolution, and the shifted window allows efficient modeling of long-range relationships. It improves performance at lower settings and can create visually appealing images with sharp and sharp edges in real-world conditions. However, other state-of-the-art approaches need help with unwanted artifacts. The future scope of this work is implementing a custom JPEG compression technique using Variational AutoEncoders (VAE) to compress the input images during training phase into a compressed latent space, so it has less overhead on pinned device memory & accelerates both our training and inference process.

REFERENCES

Bhat, G., Danelljan, M., Yu, F., Van Gool, L., & Timofte, R. (2021). Deep reparametrization of multi-frame super-resolution and denoising. In *Proceedings of the IEEE/CVF International Conference on Computer Vision* (pp. 2460-2470). IEEE.

Chen, H., He, X., Qing, L., Wu, Y., Ren, C., Sheriff, R. E., & Zhu, C. (2022). Real-world single image super-resolution: A brief review. *Information Fusion*, *79*, 124–145.

Dong, C., Loy, C. C., He, K., & Tang, X. (2015). Image super-resolution using deep convolutional networks. *IEEE Transactions on Pattern Analysis and Machine Intelligence*, *38*(2), 295–307.

Fadnavis, S. (2014). Image interpolation techniques in digital image processing: An overview. *International Journal of Engineering Research and Applications*, *4*(10), 70–73.

Garnero, G., & Godone, D. (2014). Comparisons between different interpolation techniques. *The International Archives of the Photogrammetry, Remote Sensing and Spatial Information Sciences*, *40*, 139–144.

Li, G., Yang, Y., Qu, X., Cao, D., & Li, K. (2021). A deep learning based image enhancement approach for autonomous driving at night. *Knowledge-Based Systems*, *213*, 106617.

Li, W., Hu, X., Wu, J., Fan, K., Chen, B., & Wu, P. (2022). Dual-color terahertz spatial light modulator for single-pixel imaging. *Light, Science & Applications*, *11*(1), 191.

Singh, G., & Mittal, A. (2014). Various image enhancement techniques-a critical review. *International Journal of Innovation and Scientific Research*, *10*(2), 267–274.

Wang, Z., Chen, J., & Hoi, S. C. (2020). Deep learning for image super-resolution: A survey. *IEEE Transactions on Pattern Analysis and Machine Intelligence*, *43*(10), 3365–3387.

Xiang, R., Yang, H., Yan, Z., Mohamed Taha, A. M., Xu, X., & Wu, T. (2022). Super-resolution reconstruction of GOSAT CO2 products using bicubic interpolation. *Geocarto International*, *37*(27), 15187–15211.

Yamashita, K., & Markov, K. (2020). Medical image enhancement using super resolution methods. *Computational Science–ICCS 2020: 20th International Conference, Amsterdam, The Netherlands, June 3–5, 2020 Proceedings*, *20*(Part V), 496–508.

Zhu, Y., Dai, Y., Han, K., Wang, J., & Hu, J. (2022). An efficient bicubic interpolation implementation for real-time image processing using hybrid computing. *Journal of Real-Time Image Processing*, *19*(6), 1211–1223.

Chapter 12
Cloud-Based Offensive Code Mixed Text Classification Using Hierarchical Attention Network

Durga Karthik
https://orcid.org/0000-0003-3199-8814
SASTRA University, India

Rajeswari Natarajan
SASTRA University, India

R. Bhavani
SASTRA University, India

D. Rajalakshmi
SASTRA University

ABSTRACT

The use of mixed language in social media has increased and the need of the hour is to detect abusive and offensive content. Hierarchical attention network (HAN) is employed for classifying offensive content both at word and sentence level. Data from Thinkspeak cloud tweets containing annotated Tamil and English text is used as a training set for the HAN model. The attention mechanism captures the significance from both word and sentence levels. Cross-entropy loss function and backpropagation algorithm in the model classify offensive code-mixed text with an accuracy of 0.58. The above model can be employed for classifying other mixed language text too.

DOI: 10.4018/979-8-3693-1694-8.ch012

INTRODUCTION

Classifying offensive code in social media content is difficult because of the mixed language use. Social media text are difficult for analysis as they do not follow grammar, are non-vocabulary, presence of slang usage and with native contents in English. Sentiment analysis on codemixed data involves categorizing it as positive or negative. LSTM based model for the above task has yielded a good f1 score and rank (Chaturanga & Ranathunga, 2021). Preprocessing of code mixed text includes splitting, stopword removal and stemming. Machine learning techniques can be employed for classification and XLM classifier outperforms BERT for YouTube content containing English and Malayalam text (Kazhuparambil & Kaushik, 2020).

Ensemble methods on various ML algorithms can be employed for code mixed sentiment analysis. An ensemble voting classifier on Dravidian languages with English code for message level polarity yielded nearly 0.6 accuracy (Hidayatullah et al., 2023). Embedded models Capsule with BIGRU outperforms BERT for English language and XLM_R for Sinhala code mixed with English. The above recurrent model for baselining followed by improvements such as regularization,integration and extraction on the text. As a final step a capsule network was formed to classify Sinhalese text and obtained an accuracy of 0.82 (Kalaivani & Thenmozhi, 2020). Tamil language code mixed with English is very common and sentiment analysis using Deep learning for predicting tags and for character embedding had a better f1 score than other machine learning algorithms on the same data set (Kazhuparambil & Kaushik, 2020).

Indonesian code mixed with English and Japanese tweets were tuned with BERT for word level identification of the language and is a reliable model even for sub word level identification with a good precision and recall (Kumar Mahata et al., 2021). Sentiment analysis and identification of offensive content on Dravidian languages using Adaptive BERT has yielded 0.79 accuracy (Mariyam et al., 2023). Malayalam with English code mixed data classification for both sentiment and offensive content using Deep learning models has yielded an accuracy of 0.76 (Rashmi et al., n.d.). HAN has an accuracy of 0.96 in classifying long document in both sentence and word level (Shanmugavadivel et al., 2022). HAN helps in optimal feature selection for text classification using Invasive weed tunicate method (Singh et al., 2023) and has lead to Improved Invasive weed optimization technique for text classification (Singh et al., 2022).

HIERARCHICAL TECHNIQUES

Text classification on large scale data has inherent problem of misclassification and blocking. The above problems can be resolved using top down based hierarchical methods. News text classification as technical, sport, economic, world using SVM, KNN, Naïve Bayes classifiers has yielded better accuracy (Cao & Duan, 2011). Named entities as features has helped in classifying News documents into two predefined models as Boolean and vector model. SVM is used in the above models to train the News articles with improved performance (Gui et al., 2012).

Hierarchical Attention networks are recently popular as it uses hierarchical based mechanism to reveal the hierarchy in the documents followed by two levels of attention mechanism such as word level and sentence levels. The above method can differentiate between important and less important contents and outperforms qualitatively in classifying documents when compared to existing techniques. HAN can capture syntax and semantics from text documents. HAN is better in text classification on comparison with traditional ML methods such as SVM, Random forest, Naïve Bayes etc., Cancer pathology reports were analyzed to extract information like primary site and grade classification as G1-G4 obtained good accuracy (Gao et al., 2018). HAN can also be used for multilingual news document classification. Shared attention encoders for multi languages using aligned semantic space with multiple task learning were used as input. Disjoint labels on multi lingual news documents in various languages were used on both low resource and full resource settings. The above model achieved better computational accuracy with fewer parameters (Pappas & Popescu-Belis, 2017).

Label Attentive HAN helps in text classification by avoiding semantic loss in text and label information. Label information in both word and sentence levels are utilized to reveal a better classification model.Finally the classification layers predicts the class using full text label representation (Li et al., 2020). Due to improvement in IoT produces a larger and distributed data from power grid. The grid data classification is important for power grid efficiency. It has classified the grid text into five categories to decide on maintenance scheduling and other operation. Comparing the results with traditional model has better accuracy for HAN (Zhang & Rao, 2020). HAN method has been implemented for analyzing student sentiment analysis and behavior from MOOC discussion forum. Sentiment labels were used from the discussion data post. Higher classification accuracy is obtained and also helps in evolving an automated tool for sentiment analysis (Chanaa & El Faddouli, 2021).

Cyber bullying has caused illness to both physical and mental health of people on internet. Semantic features from local environment are extracted using BHF model that uses BERT pre trained model for global semantic extraction. Words, short sentences followed by full text were the features used for classifying text with improved accuracy (Feng et al., 2022). Social media news spread across at a great speed and the generated news does not have positive impact always. Fake news and true news are classified using HAN with Hyper graph based methods. Fast checking of fake news using bottom up hierarchical attention network using weights assigned to different parts of the news (Borse & Kharate, 2022). Twitter based mental health status detection using HAN and Metaphor concept mapping can track depression in individuals. The model uses two HAN layers for encoding and has resulted in better accuracy, precision and recall for classifying a tweet data using metaphors (Han et al., 2022). Keywords is an important feature in article classification. HAN based method helps in better interpretation and analysis of keywords using label based HAN (Xia, 2022). Opinion mining is challenging in market basket analysis. Reviews from users were extracted and contextual meaning from the words were generated and fed into HAN. User reviews were classified into positive or negative or neutral based on the above model with a very good accuracy and precision (Ratmele & Thakur, 2022). Content based classification is an age old method for classification that can be also be applied for document classification. Meta data like key words and Title from research articles were analyzed based on novel method that uses multi labels from the documents for classification (Sajid, 2023).

CLOUD AND QUANTUM ANALYSIS

Cloud provides various models like software as service, Infrastructure and Platform as service with data secured using encryption methods. Customers opinions,emotions and their feedbacks are analyzed for sentiment analysis using Tweeter data. Also other cloud providers such as Google cloud, AWS and AZURE Cloud data are compared for sentiment analysis. Polarity features are extracted and classified for negative and positive tweets (Karamitsos et al., 2019). Cloud traffic has increased rapidly and traffic classification requires novel techniques to provide a cost effective and rapid methods. Pruning based CNN can extract features and helps to classify the following chats,emails,file transfers and streaming (Han, 2021).

Arabic language documents classification was compared using Quantum and ML based approaches. Sentiment analysis on tweet data obtained good precision and recall when compared with ML based techniques. With quantum computing it completed the classification tasks with time lesser than other ML methods (Omar & Abd El-Hafeez, 2023). Quantum computing has made quantum text classifier using classical data with quantum processing. Quantum ML algorithms requires following steps such as data encoding, feature mapping, quantum modelling with error mitigation, optimization and post processing. Quantum based support vector machine, variational quantum classifiers, quantum neural network based classifiers were compared with classical classifiers algorithms (Santi et al., 2023). Speed up achieved in quantum based ML algorithms is better than other models hence can also be used for classifying tweet messages into offensive and non offensive category.

METHODOLOGY

HAN, a neural network design shown in Figure 1, has shown positive outcomes in text classification activities. Documents are made out of sentences, in turn sentences are evolved from words. As all words are not very important an attention model is derived that derives a sentence vector that has more attention than others. Attention models has Bi directional Recurrent Neural Network [rnn] and also Attention network.

While RNN learns the meaning in the consecutive words and delivers vector for it. The attention mechanism assigns a weight for each of the words in the vector. It finally sums the weighted sum of words from all the vector to form words. Similarly for sentences RNN identifies the meaning and derives a vector for it. The attention layer assigns a weight for the sentences in the vector. The aggregate of the sum of sentence vector derives the whole document. As two levels are applied in the attention mechanism, it is popularly known as HAN.

The attention mechanisms of HAN are divided into two levels: word-level and sentence-level. The attention mechanism at the word level captures each word's significance in a sentence, whereas the attention mechanism at the sentence level captures each sentence's significance in a document.HAN-based model takes as input a code-mixed text and outputs a label showing whether or not the text is offensive.

Dataset is stored in Thing Speak cloud. Thing speak cloud is a platform in which data can be stored, processed, analyzed, or transformed. It helps to visualize the data by means of customizable graphs, and charts. Mostly, it is used for Internet of Things based applications. The model can be trained on a dataset of annotated code-mixed texts, where each text is labeled as offensive or not.

The steps for classifying code mixed text as offensive or not consists of initially aattention layer that encodes the sentences. The next layer consists of word attention that encodes words.

Detailed steps for classification is given below:

First, the input text tokenized into words and sentences. Then, pre-trained word embeddings are used to embed it into a high-dimensional vector space. The embedded words undergo a word-level attention mechanism, resulting in a weighted representation of the input text. The sentence-level attention mechanism is then applied to the weighted word representations to get a final representation of the input text. The final representation is input to a fully connected layer, which outputs

Figure 1. Structure of hierarchical neural network

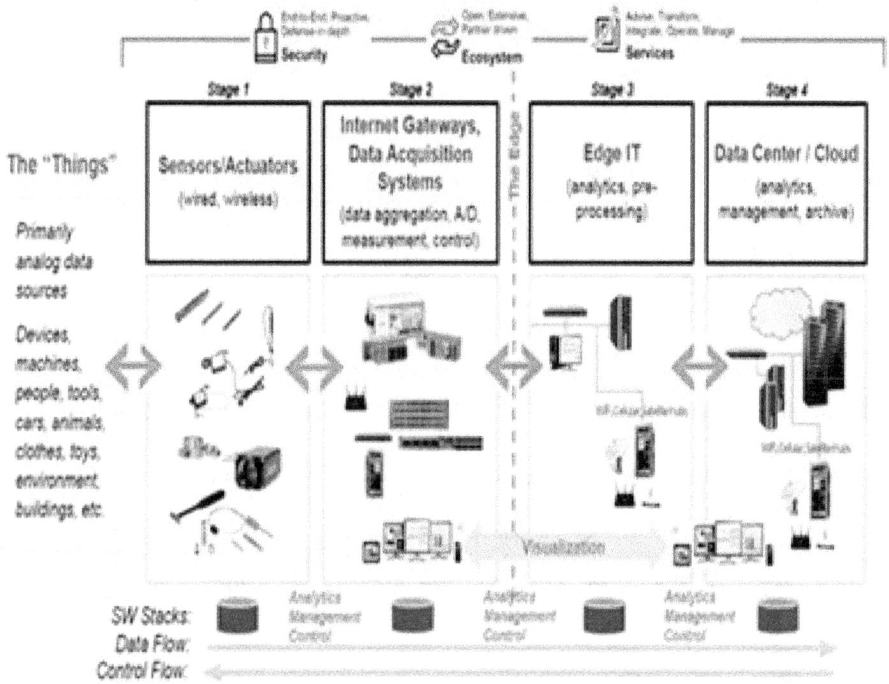

a probability distribution over the two classes (offensive and non-offensive). The cross-entropy loss function is used and the model is optimized using backpropagation.

RESULTS AND DISCUSSION

Social media has evolved as a source of corpus data. We have collected around 940 comments from social media. The data is labeled as either offensive or non-offensive. Data is converted into a suitable form. Natural language tool kit is used for data cleaning. We removed the emoji's, punctuations, and symbols. The text has been converted to its lower case. The training dataset is converted to a 3-dimensional array. The first dimension, second dimension and the third dimension represents the total number of documents, sentences in a document, and words in a sentence respectively.

The training data has 419 documents, 6000 sentences, and 55 words. We tested the model with 83 documents. Keras Embedding layer is used for word to vector conversion. We use TimeDistributed method to apply a Dense layer to each of the

Table 1. Hierarchical attention network model for offensive text classification

Layer (Type)	Output Shape	Parameters #
Input	[(None, 6000, 55)]	0
Time Distributed	(None, 6000, 400)	372580
BiDirectional	(None, 6000, 400)	722400
Hierarchical Attention Network	(None, 400)	80400
Total parameters: 1,176,182 Trainable parameters: 1,176,182 Non-trainable parameters: 0		

Table 2. Accuracy (in %) obtained by various state-of-the art methods for offensive code-mixed text classification task

Machine Learning-Based Approach	Accuracy (in %)
K Nearest Neighbors	82.97
Decision Tree	83.82
Random Forest	88.93
Logistic Regression	89.36
SGD Classifier	85.95
Naive Bayes	88.51
SVM Linear	86.38

time-steps independently. To reduce overfitting, we use L2 regularizes and drop out methods. Table 1 shows the model parameters of the hierarchical attention network.

The above table shown the number of parameters that was used for HAN. On executing the HAN with the above dataset, it classified the content into offensive and non offensive. An accuracy of 58% is obtained using Hierarchical Attention Network. We also evaluated the dataset using the state-of-art methods. The data are converted to on-hot-encoder representation. These act the text features to the algorithms. The results are presented in Table 2. We also tested the ensemble of classifiers. For any given test data, the class label is assigned based on the maximum voting strategy. Table 3 shows the result of using the ensemble of classifiers.

The above table reveals that logistic regression based classifier for code mixed data has maximum accuracy percentage of 89.36%. K nearest neighbor method has the least accuracy of 82.97% though KNN is a classical and a simpler method it cannot give better performance that involves identifying the semantics in the sentences. Random forest approach for offensive text classification is 88.9% which is near to

Figure 2. Accuracy of algorithms for code mixed classification

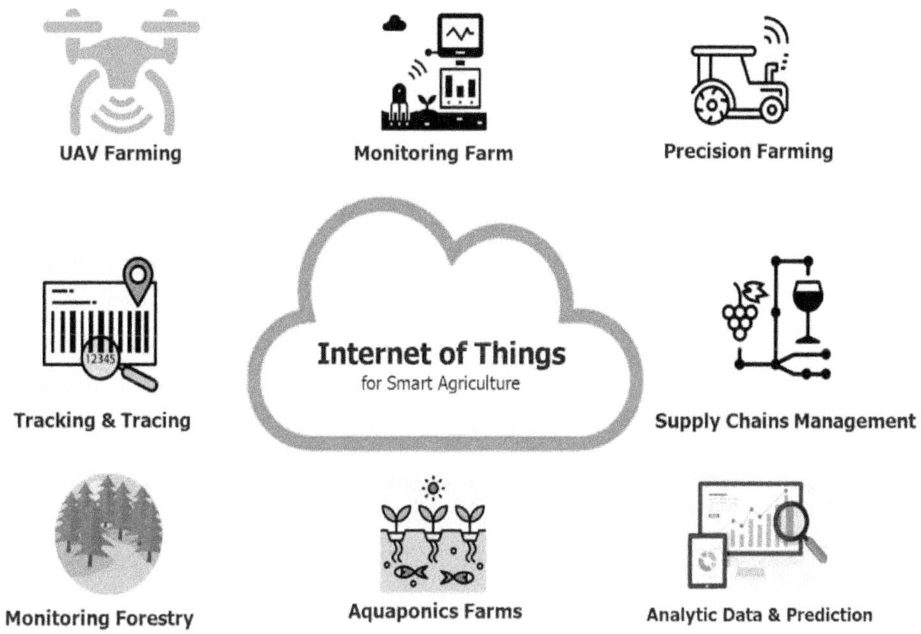

Table 3. Evaluation metric scores obtained by an ensemble of classifiers for offensive code-mixed text classification task

	Precision	Recall	F1-Score	Support
Non-Offensive	0.84	0.94	0.89	115
Offensive	0.93	0.82	0.88	120
Accuracy			0.88	235
Macro Average	0.89	0.88	0.88	235
Weighted Average	0.89	0.88	0.88	235

logistic regression method. Similarly 88.5% for Naïve Bayes algorithm, so it can also be used for code mixed classification of text. SGD Classifier and SVM Linear methods did not yield higher accuracy and has produced only 85% and 86% only.

Figure 2 shows the accuracy of classical algorithms for code mixed data classification from tweet data.

Figure 3. Performance evaluation of classification of documents

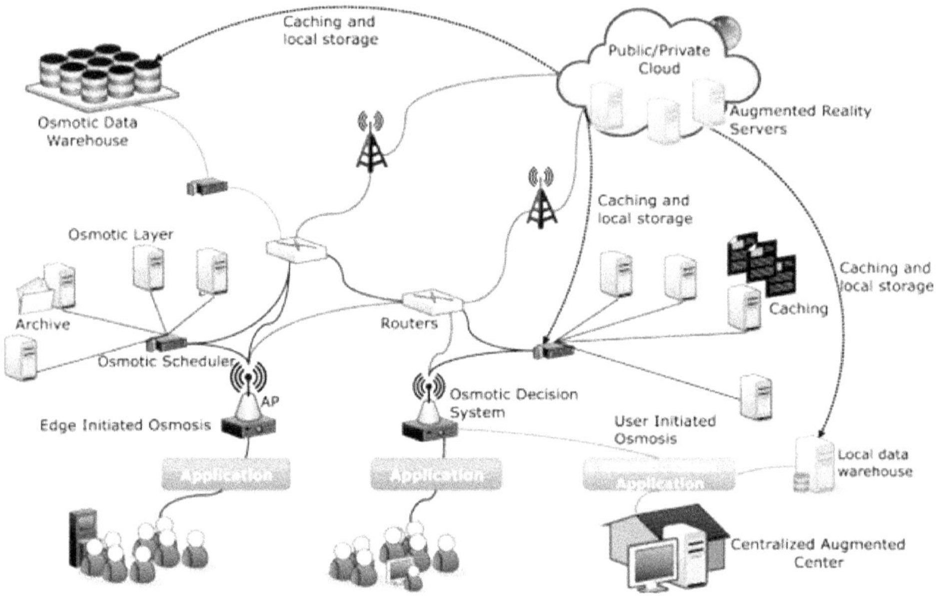

Table 4. Confusion matrix obtained by an ensemble of classifiers for offensive code-mixed text classification task

		Predicted	
		Offensive	**Non-Offensive**
Actual	**Offensive**	108	7
	Non Offensive	21	99

Various other evaluation parameters such as precision, recall, f1 score and support for the model is also required for validating the model. The Table. 3 given below reveals the other parameters obtained for the classification model.

The classification model has 93% precision for offensive contents and 84% for non offensive contents. The recall for non offensive is 94% but for offensive it has yielded 88%. F1 score for non offensive is 89% and 88% for offensive content as it is near to 1 the model can be accepted. The average, macro average and weighted average is approximately 88%.

Figure 4 shows the accuracy in classifying offensive and non offensive contents on code mixed tweet data.

Figure 5 shows the chart with predicted values of offensive and non offensive contents on code mixed tweet data. It shows 108 contents were predicted offensive

Figure 4. Comparison of predicted and actual classification of tweets

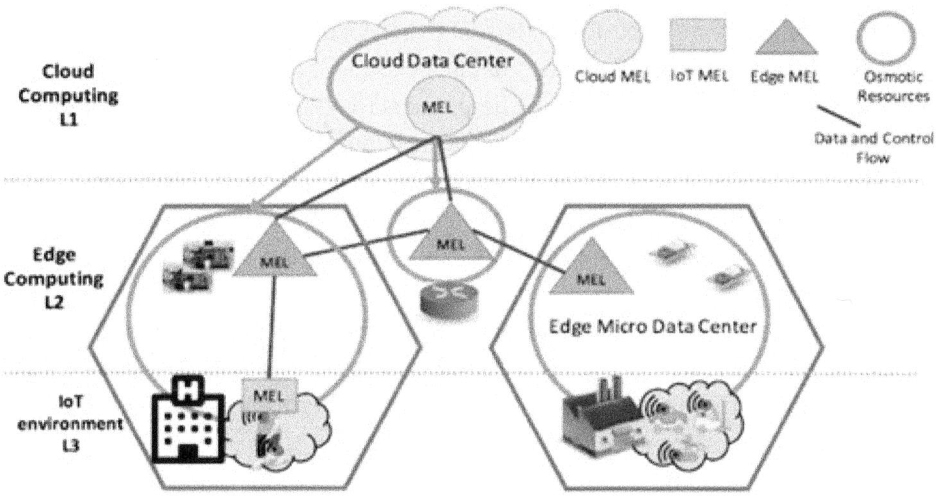

and the actual content was also the same. Similarly 21 contents were predicted non offensive and actual content was also the same. 99 Non offensive were actual and in predicted same.

An accuracy of 88% is obtained by an ensemble the classifiers. From the confusion matrix in Table 4, it is observed that 21 non-offensive texts are classified as offensive texts. This could be possible due to the meaning conveyed by the word i.e., 'Hair' could be treated as both offensive and non-offensive. Hence, it is important to build the language models by considering the semantics of the sentences also. It is also found that the state of the art methods perform better than Hierarchical Attention Network model. The reason for this is due to the limited use of training data. When enough training data is used, HAN based approach is expected to outperform the state-of-the methods.

CONCLUSION

An HAN-based model can classify offensive code-mixed text by leveraging the attention mechanisms to use the important features in the text at the both word and sentence levels. Accuracy of 0.58 on code mixed data reveals that it can help to improve classification accuracy, mainly in the presence of mixed languages. The HAN based approach shall also be used for representation of a text. This can further be used as an input to a machine learning classifier which can give good results

FUTURE WORK

The model took more time for classifying the document as offensive and non-offensive. So quantum based algorithms can be used for document classification for the above cloud data. IBM Q account helps users to utilize the quantum framework for their programs. Quantum execution of programs require Jupiter environment and Qiskit for result visualization. Essential steps for executing a program in IBM Q are to convert the problem into quantum format followed by optimization of the operators and circuits. Next step is to execute the quantum function and finally to analyze the output obtained.

Quantum based SVM, Hierarchical Attention Network and Random forest can be implemented for the tweet datasets as offensive and non-offensive contents. Time taken to execute in non-quantum techniques are higher usually than the quantum execution.

REFERENCES

Borse, A., & Kharate, D. G. (2022). Fake News Prediction using Hierarchical Attention Network and Hypergraph. SSRN *Electron. J.*, 1–11. doi:10.2139/ssrn.4043857

Cao, Y., & Duan, R. Y. (2011). Novel top-down methods for hierarchical text classification. *Procedia Engineering*, *24*, 329–334. doi:10.1016/j.proeng.2011.11.2651

Chanaa, A., & El Faddouli, N. (2021). E-learning Text Sentiment Classification Using Hierarchical Attention Network (HAN). *International Journal of Emerging Technologies in Learning*, *16*(no. 13), 157–167. doi:10.3991/ijet.v16i13.22579

Chaturanga, S., & Ranathunga, S. (2021). Classification of Code-Mixed Text Using Capsule Networks. *International Conference Recent Advances in Natural Language Processing, RANLP*, 256–263. 10.26615/978-954-452-072-4_030

Feng, Z., Su, J., & Cao, J. (2022). BHF: BERT-based Hierarchical Attention Fusion Network for Cyberbullying Remarks Detection. *ACM Int. Conf. Proceeding Ser.*, 1–7. 10.1145/3578741.3578742

Gao, S., Young, M. T., Qiu, J. X., Yoon, H.-J., Christian, J. B., Fearn, P. A., Tourassi, G. D., & Ramanthan, A. (2018). Hierarchical attention networks for information extraction from cancer pathology reports. *Journal of the American Medical Informatics Association : JAMIA*, *25*(3), 321–330. doi:10.1093/jamia/ocx131 PMID:29155996

Gui, Y., Gao, Z., Li, R., & Yang, X. (2012). Hierarchical text classification for news articles based-on named entities. Lect. Notes Comput. Sci. (including Subser. Lect. Notes Artif. Intell. Lect. Notes Bioinformatics), 7713, 318–329. doi:10.1007/978-3-642-35527-1_27

Han, S., Mao, R., & Cambria, E. (2022). Hierarchical Attention Network for Explainable Depression Detection on Twitter Aided by Metaphor Concept Mappings. *Proc. - Int. Conf. Comput. Linguist. COLING*, *29*(1), 94–104.

Han, Z. (2021). An Effective Encrypted Traffic Classification Method Based on Pruning Convolutional Neural Networks for Cloud Platform. *Proc. - 2021 2nd Int. Conf. Electron. Commun. Inf. Technol. CECIT 2021*, 206–211. 10.1109/CECIT53797.2021.00043

Hidayatullah, A. F., Apong, R. A., Lai, D. T. C., & Qazi, A. (2023). Corpus creation and language identification for code-mixed Indonesian-Javanese-English Tweets. *PeerJ. Computer Science*, *9*, e1312. Advance online publication. doi:10.7717/peerj-cs.1312 PMID:37409088

Kalaivani, A., & Thenmozhi, D. (2020). *SSN_NLP_MLRG@Dravidian-CodeMix-FIRE2020: Sentiment Code-Mixed Text Classification in Tamil and Malayalam using ULMFiT*. Available: http://ceur-ws.org

Karamitsos, I., Albarhami, S., & Apostolopoulos, C. (2019). Tweet Sentiment Analysis (TSA) for Cloud Providers Using Classification Algorithms and Latent Semantic Analysis. *J. Data Anal. Inf. Process.*, *07*(04), 276–294. doi:10.4236/jdaip.2019.74016

KazhuparambilS.KaushikA. (2020). Cooking Is All About People: Comment Classification On Cookery Channels Using BERT and Classification Models (Malayalam-English Mix-Code). doi:10.20944/preprints202006.0223.v1

Kumar Mahata, S., Das, D., & Bandyopadhyay, S. (2021). Sentiment Classification of Code-Mixed Tweets using Bi-Directional RNN and Language Tags. *Proceedings of the First Workshop on Speech and Language Technologies for Dravidian Languages*, 28-35. Available: https://scikit-learn.org/stable/

Li, X., Song, J., & Liu, W. (2020). Label-Attentive Hierarchical Attention Network for Text Classification. *ACM Int. Conf. Proceeding Ser.*, 90–96. 10.1145/3404687.3404706

Mariyam, M. A., Althaf, S. K., Basha, H., & Raju, S. V. (2023). Long Document Classification using Hierarchical Attention Networks. *International Journal of Intelligent Systems and Applications in Engineering, 2,* 343–353. Available: www.ijisae.org

Omar, A., & Abd El-Hafeez, T. (2023). Quantum computing and machine learning for Arabic language sentiment classification in social media. *Scientific Reports, 13*(1), 1–18. doi:10.1038/s41598-023-44113-7 PMID:37828056

PappasN.Popescu-BelisA. (2017). Multilingual Hierarchical Attention Networks for Document Classification. Available: http://arxiv.org/abs/1707.00896

Rashmi, Guruprasad, & Shambhavi. (n.d.). *Sentiment Classification on Bilingual Code-Mixed Texts for Dravidian Languages using Machine Learning Methods.* Academic Press.

Ratmele, A., & Thakur, R. (2022). OpExHAN: Opinion extraction using hierarchical attention network from unstructured reviews. *Social Network Analysis and Mining, 12*(1), 1–16. doi:10.1007/s13278-022-00971-z PMID:36217360

Sajid, N. A. (2023). A Novel Metadata Based Multi-Label Document Classification Technique. *Computer Systems Science and Engineering, 46*(2), 2195–2214. doi:10.32604/csse.2023.033844

SantiD. P.MishraK.MohantyS. (2023). Quantum Text Classifier — A Synchronistic Approach Towards Classical and Quantum Machine Learning. Available: http://arxiv.org/abs/2305.12783

Shanmugavadivel, K., Sathishkumar, V. E., Raja, S., Lingaiah, T. B., Neelakandan, S., & Subramanian, M. (2022, December). Deep learning based sentiment analysis and offensive language identification on multilingual code-mixed data. *Scientific Reports, 12*(1), 21557. Advance online publication. doi:10.1038/s41598-022-26092-3 PMID:36513786

Singh, G., Nagpal, A., & Singh, V. (2022). Text Classification using Improved IWO-HAN. In *Procedia Computer Science* (pp. 1184–1195). Elsevier B.V. doi:10.1016/j.procs.2023.01.097

Singh, G., Nagpal, A., & Singh, V. (2023). Optimal feature selection and invasive weed tunicate swarm algorithm-based hierarchical attention network for text classification. *Connection Science, 35*(1), 2231171. Advance online publication. doi:10.1080/09540091.2023.2231171

Xia, F. (2022). Label Oriented Hierarchical Attention Neural Network for Short Text Classification. *Acad. J. Eng. Technol. Sci.*, *5*(1), 53–62. doi:10.25236/AJETS.2022.050111

Zhang, Y., & Rao, Z. (2020). Hierarchical attention networks for grid text classification. *Proc. 2020 IEEE Int. Conf. Inf. Technol. Big Data Artif. Intell. ICIBA 2020*, 491–494. 10.1109/ICIBA50161.2020.9277489

Chapter 13
Diabetes Prediction Model Using Stochastic Gradient Descent Logistic Regression Approach

A. Sumathi
https://orcid.org/0000-0003-4700-5573
Department of CSE, SASTRA University, India

S. Meganathan
https://orcid.org/0000-0003-4570-8259
SASTRA University, India

ABSTRACT

Diabetes is a chronic disorder caused by either inadequate insulin production by the pancreas or inadequate insulin absorption by the body. Many machine learning approaches handle a wide range of chronic conditions and keep track of patient health data. The analysis of medical data from various angles and the creation of knowledge from it can be accomplished using a variety of machine learning techniques. Creating new features by combining two or more features can provide more insights for health-related data. It aids in revealing a data set's hidden relationships. This work implements LR, RFECV-LR, and RFECV-SGDLR for comparison purposes and comes with the best suitable classification model. Further, this work suggests an IoT-based diabetes model that can also record information about their location, body temperature, and blood glucose levels and can help patients live healthier lifestyles by tracking their activities and diets.

DOI: 10.4018/979-8-3693-1694-8.ch013

1. INTRODUCTION

Diabetes poses a serious threat to life. Every second person in the world dies as a result of diabetes complications (Joshi & Chawan, 2018; Yuvaraj & SriPreethaa, 2017). Diabetes mellitus develops when the body's insulin synthesis is inadequate, resulting in a high blood sugar level. There are various distinct kinds of chronic diabetes mellitus. The tendency for prolonged hyperglycemia is a typical concern among diabetes individuals. Weight loss, increased appetite, increased urination, and dehydration is all symptoms of diabetes. Furthermore, too much sugar in the circulation can lead to the likelihood of heart attacks and strokes rising. This occurs when diabetes is not recognized early. Despite the fact that diabetes is a dangerous condition, it can be managed with accurate therapy and medication. Insulin injections and proper exercise or nutrition are used to manage diabetes. Medical professionals, on the other hand, believe that early detection can go a long way toward assisting patients in living healthy life. Many machine learning approaches are used to handle a wide range of chronic conditions and to keep track of patient health data (Shankaracharya, 2017; Swapna et al., 2018; Zou et al., 2018). For classification, this study examined a variety of diabetic datasets (PIMA Indian Diabetes Dataset, Frankfurt Dataset, Diabetes Screening provided by Dr. Plum). Creating features is the process of creating new variables from already existing variables. It helps to unleash the hidden relationship of a dataset. New input or target feature is constructed from the original diabetes dataset. These characteristics are derived from diagnostic analyses. This work proposed a Stochastic Gradient Descent-based logistic regression approach that provides a better classification and this work suggests IoT-based approach to assist in the management of diabetes.

2. LITERATURE SURVEY

Minyechil Alehegn and Rahul Joshi 2017, Proposed Predictive algorithms such as KNN, Nave Bayes, Random Forest, and J48. Using PIDD data, an ensemble hybrid model was constructed by integrating any approaches and procedures into one which gives better performance (Alehegn, 2019). Deepti Sisodia, Dilip Singh Sisodia 2018 In this experiment, three ML classification algorithms, Decision Tree, SVM, and Naive Bayes are used to identify diabetic conditions. (PIDD) is utilized in experiments. The performance of matrices is just a handful to evaluate how well the three algorithms perform. Their results show that, when compared to other algorithms, Naive Bayes performs the best (Sisodia, 2018). KM Jyoti Rani 2020 proposed a diabetic prediction model that makes use of KNN, LR,Random Forest, SVM, and Decision Tree. Their experimental findings determine the suitability of the suggested system, with greater accuracy, reached utilizing the Decision Tree method (Jyothi Rani, n.d.). Ram D. Joshi and Chandra K. Dhakal 2021 recommended using a decision tree and logistic regression model to treat type 2 with the help of PIDD. According to their findings, the five most important predictors of type 2 diabetes are age, BMI, pregnancy, the function of the diabetic lineage, and glucose. The ten-node tree identifies significant predictors, while the six fold classification tree identifies key elements (Joshi & Dhakal, 2021). However, Prediction might be challenging for doctors to forecast diabetes. If machine learning is utilized, the patterns can be quickly found so that diabetes can be diagnosed early.

3. RELATED WORK

In the realm of diabetes management, the integration of data mining, machine learning, and the Internet of Things (IoT) has ushered in transformative advancements. Data mining (Rastogi & Bansal, 2023), a technique focused on extracting meaningful patterns from extensive datasets, plays a crucial role in unraveling hidden insights within the complex landscape of diabetes-related information. Machine learning (Rajendra, 2021; Tuppad & Patil, 2022), a subset of artificial intelligence, leverages sophisticated algorithms to predict, analyze, and optimize various aspects of diabetes care. From risk assessment to treatment personalization, machine learning empowers healthcare professionals with powerful tools for more effective decision-making. Concurrently, the Internet of Things introduces a new dimension by enabling continuous and real-time monitoring through interconnected devices. Wearable sensors and smart glucose monitoring devices, integrated into IoT frameworks, offer a wealth of data, including glucose levels and physical activity, contributing to a more comprehensive understanding of individual health (Farooq, 2023). The synergy of these technologies not only enhances early detection of diabetes and its complications but also fosters personalized and proactive approaches to treatment, marking a paradigm shift in the landscape of diabetes care.

3.1. Proposed Methodology

The proposed work involves the following steps:

- Feature creation
- Feature Selection

Recursive Feature Elimination with Cross-Validation

- Logistic Regression
- Stochastic Gradient Descent Based Logistic Regression

New features are created from the existing features to unleash the hidden relationship of the datasets. Feature selection is carried out using recursive feature elimination with cross-validation (RFECV) for selecting the best features. Develop a Stochastic Gradient Descent-based Logistic Regression diabetic classification model for diabetes with greater accuracy.

3.1.1 Feature Creation

To generate features, it is essential to create new variables that will contribute most effectively to our model. In this scenario, features may be introduced or removed. Feature creation involves the generation of new variables derived from existing ones, facilitating the unveiling of hidden relationships within a dataset. Identifying crucial factors represents the initial phase in feature development, constituting a subjective process that demands a creative approach. Feature engineering, a fundamental aspect of data mining, holds immense significance in optimizing the performance of machine learning models. By crafting new features, also known as feature engineering, data scientists can substantially enhance the capabilities of their models. This process is essential for improving model performance by providing additional discriminative information and effectively representing complex relationships within the data. Furthermore, feature engineering aids in reducing noise and improving model robustness, as well as in capturing non-linear patterns that may exist in real-world datasets. Importantly, the creation of meaningful features enhances the interpretability of model results, making them more accessible to stakeholders and facilitating a deeper understanding of predictions. Feature engineering also plays a crucial role in handling missing data, converting categorical variables, and integrating domain-specific knowledge, aligning the models with the expertise of domain experts. In essence, the process of creating new features is integral to unleashing the full potential of machine learning models and extracting meaningful insights from complex datasets in the realm of data mining.

3.1.2 Feature Selection

Feature selection reduces the complexity of a model. Each process depends on feature engineering, mainly consisting of feature extraction and feature selection. Recursive Feature Elimination with Cross-Validation (RFECV) provides an important ranking for the features that are significant. Cross-validation and RFE identify the best features by removing the less significant or redundant features in stages.

Figure 1. Proposed model

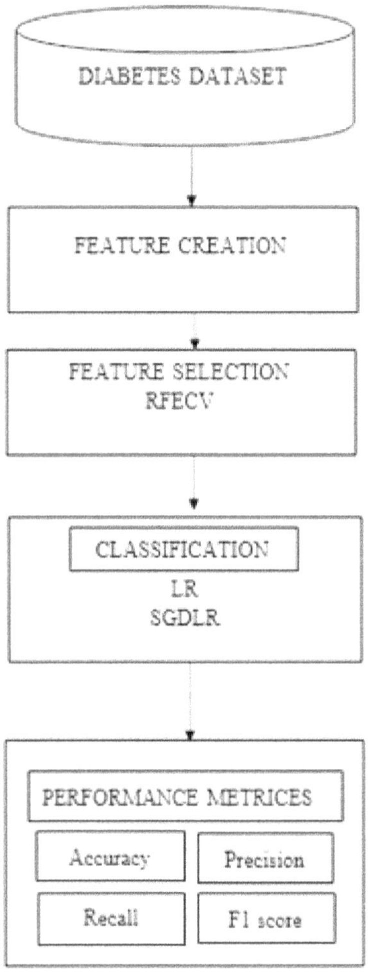

3.1.3 Stochastic Gradient Descent-Based Logistic Regression (SGDLR)

When using logistic regression, the binary response variable is modeled as linear combinations of one or more independent factors. Stochastic Gradient Descent is a variant of the gradient descent algorithm that allows our model to learn much faster. Stochastic Gradient Descent-based Logistic Regression combines logistic regression principles with stochastic gradient descent optimization. This approach is valuable for scenarios involving extensive datasets or real-time data sets, providing

Figure 2. Dataset description

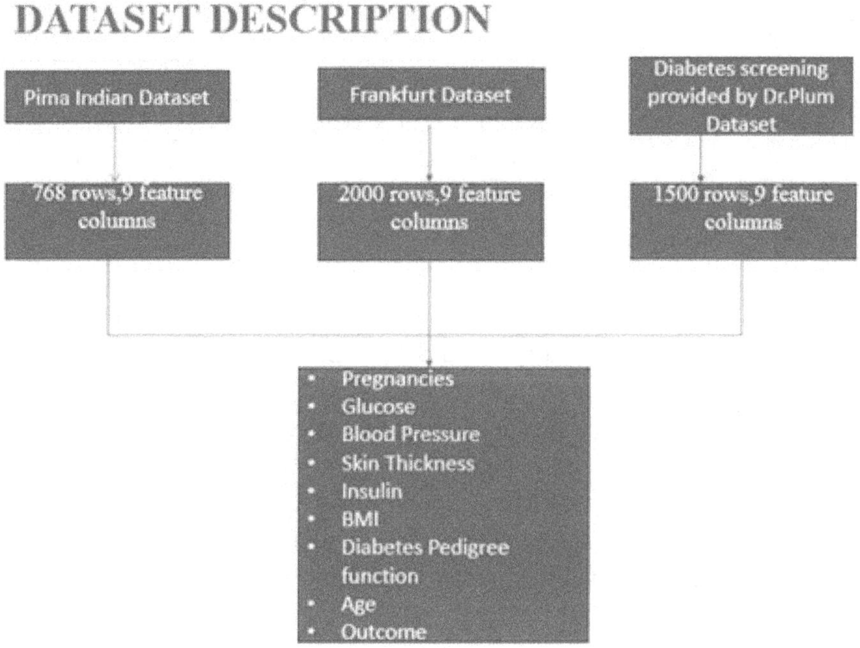

an efficient solution for training logistic regression models in dynamic and large-scale environments.

4. EXPERIMENTAL RESULTS

Creating new features: From the already-existing features, six additional features are produced and added to the original Diabetic datasets. These characteristics were produced through research into specialized diagnostic measures suitable for diabetes persons.**NF1, NF2, NF3, NF4, NF5, and NF6** refer the new features.

- **NF1**-The fact that people over 30 are frequently much less susceptible to this diabetic condition led to the first element NF1, being chosen. Under 140 mg/dL of blood sugar is also regarded as a normal situation.
- **NF2**-NF2 for people who are more likely to develop diabetes and have a BMI of more than 30 kg/m2.
- **NF3**-According to NF3, women who have more than three pregnancies are more likely to get diabetes than those aged 30.

Table 1.

NEW FEATURES	VALUES
NF1	IF ((AND (AGE<=30, GLUCOSE<=140)), "0", "1")
NF2	IF(BMI<=30,"0","1")
NF3	IF ((AND (AGE<=30, PREGNANCIES<=3)),"0", "1")
NF4	IF ((AND (GLUCOSE<=140, BLOODPRESSURE<=80)), "0", "1")
NF5	IF ((AND (GLUCOSE<=140, BMI<=45)), "0", "1")
NF6	IF(BMI>=30,"0","1")

- **NF4**-The primary criteria taken into account for feature NF4 is the normal DBP, which is less than or equal to 80.
- **NF5**-A normal glucose reading combined with a higher BMI reading results in NF5.
- **NF6**-The final aspect a BMI of 30 or higher is considered obese. Obesity increases the risk of nearly every pregnancy issue, including hypertension, gestational diabetes mellitus, and a higher prevalence of abnormalities than in women with a normal BMI.

4.1.1 Selecting the Best Features Using Recursive Feature Elimination With Cross-Validation (RFECV)

PIMA INDIAN DIABETES DATASET

Original dataset:(8+1=9 feature columns): Pregnancies, Glucose, Blood pressure, Skin Thickness, Insulin, BMI, Diabetes Pedigree function, Age, Outcome

Adding New Features:(14+1=15 feature columns): Pregnancies, Glucose, Blood Pressure, Skin Thickness, Insulin, BMI, Diabetes Pedigree function, Age, NF1, NF2, NF3, NF4, NF5, NF6, Outcome

After Appling RFECV the Selected Features are:(10+1=11 feature columns)

Pregnancies, Glucose, Blood Pressure, Diabetes Pedigree function, NF1, NF2, NF3, NF4, NF5, NF6, Outcome.

Figure 3,4,5 shows performance of the proposed methodology on pima dataset.

FRANKFURT-DATASET OF DIABETES

Original dataset:(8+1=9 feature columns): Pregnancies, Glucose, Blood pressure, Skin Thickness, Insulin, BMI, Diabetes Pedigree function, Age, Outcome

Figure 3. Cross-validation scores of PIDD dataset features

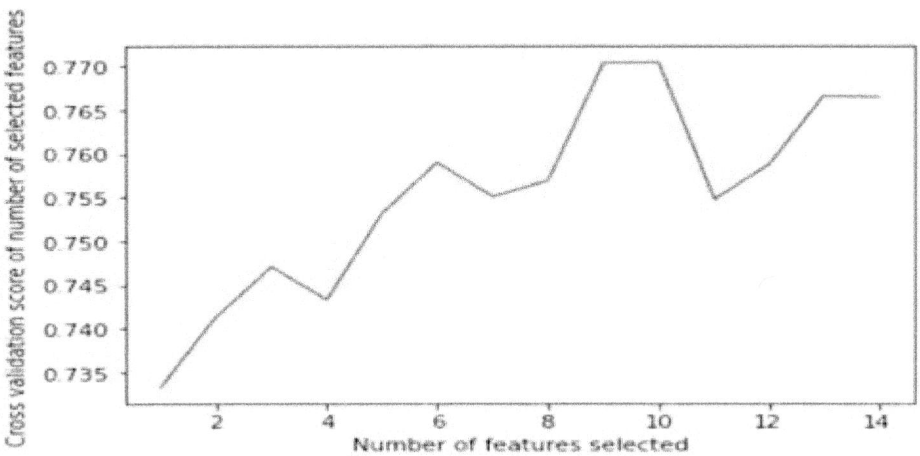

Figure 4. Performance measures: PIMA dataset

PIMA DATASET RESULTS

LOGISTIC REGRESSION

	precision	recall	f1-score	support
0.0	0.78	0.90	0.84	164
1.0	0.75	0.54	0.63	90
accuracy			0.78	254
macro avg	0.77	0.72	0.74	254
weighted avg	0.77	0.78	0.77	254

LOGISTIC REGRESSION WITH RFECV

	precision	recall	f1-score	support
0.0	0.81	0.90	0.85	164
1.0	0.77	0.61	0.68	90
accuracy			0.80	254
macro avg	0.79	0.76	0.77	254
weighted avg	0.80	0.80	0.79	254

STOCHASTIC GRADIENT DESCENT BASED LOGISTIC REGRESSION

Accuracy: 96.732%
Precision: 96.149%
Recall: 95.505%
F1 score: 95.781%

Adding New Features:(14+1=15 feature columns): Pregnancies, Glucose, Blood Pressure, Skin Thickness, Insulin, BMI, Diabetes Pedigree function, Age, NF1, NF2, NF3, NF4, NF5, NF6, Outcome

After Appling RFECV the Selected Features are:(13+1=11 feature columns)

Pregnancies, Glucose, Blood pressure, Skin Thickness, BMI, DiabetesPedigreeFunction, Age, NF1, NF2, NF3, NF4, NF5, NF6, Outcome.

Figure 5. Comparison of classification accuracies: PIMA dataset

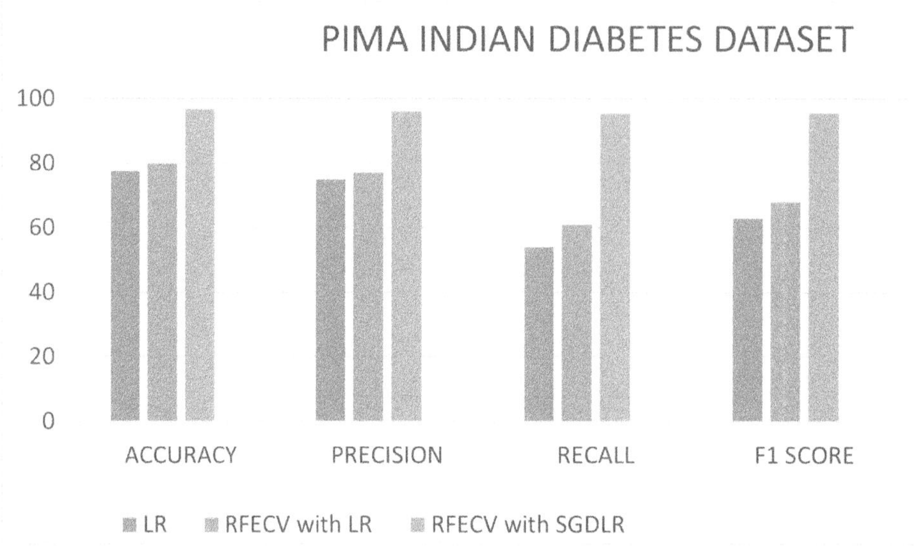

Figure 6. Cross-validation scores of Frankfurt dataset features

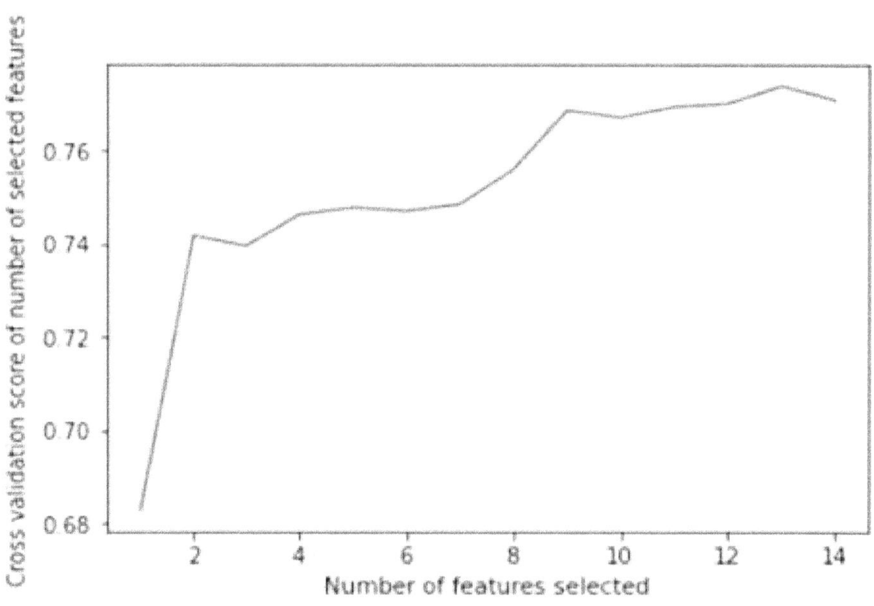

Figure 6, 7 and 8 shows performance of the proposed methodology on Frankfurt hospital dataset.

Figure 7. Performance measures: Frankfurt dataset

FRANKFURT DATASET RESULTS

LOGISTIC REGRESSION

	precision	recall	f1-score	support
0.0	0.81	0.89	0.85	436
1.0	0.74	0.58	0.65	224
accuracy			0.79	660
macro avg	0.77	0.74	0.75	660
weighted avg	0.78	0.79	0.78	660

LOGISTIC REGRESSION WITH RFECV

	precision	recall	f1-score	support
0.0	0.82	0.88	0.85	436
1.0	0.73	0.61	0.67	224
accuracy			0.79	660
macro avg	0.77	0.75	0.76	660
weighted avg	0.79	0.79	0.79	660

STOCHASTIC GRADIENT DESCENT BASED LOGISTIC REGRESSION

Accuracy: 98.450%
Precision: 97.198%
Recall: 98.829%
F1 score: 97.994%

Figure 8. Comparison of classification accuracies: Frankfurt Hospital dataset

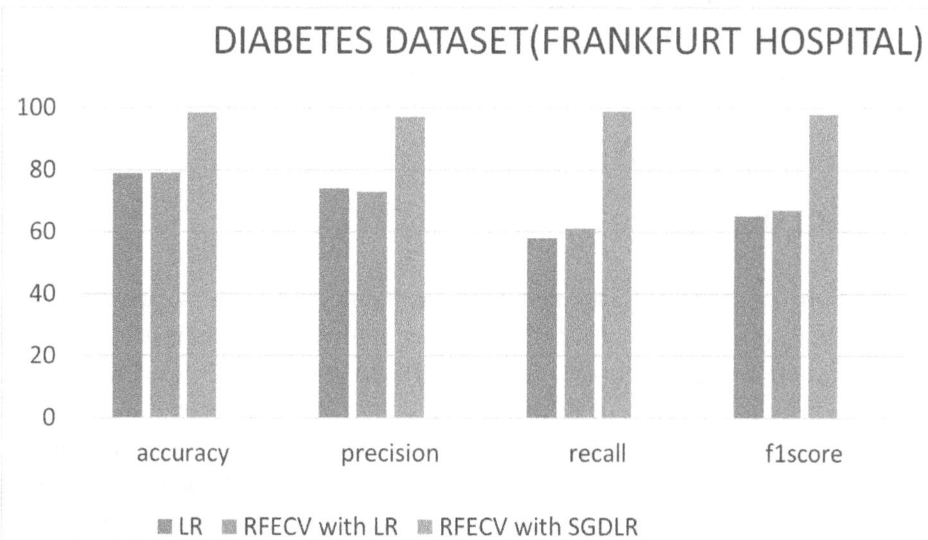

Figure 9. Cross-validation scores of plum dataset features

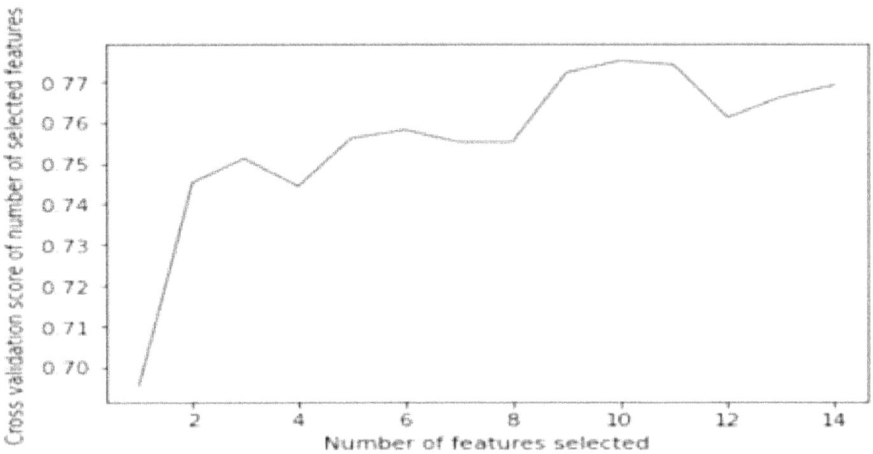

DIABETES SCREENING DATASET

Original dataset:(8+1=9 feature columns):Pregnancies, Glucose, Blood pressure, Skin Thickness, Insulin, BMI, Diabetes Pedigree function, Age, Outcome

Adding New Features:(14+1=15 feature columns): Pregnancies, Glucose, Blood Pressure, Skin Thickness, Insulin, BMI, Diabetes Pedigree function, Age, NF1, NF2, NF3, NF4, NF5, NF6, Outcome

After Appling RFECV the Selected Features are:(10+1=11 feature columns)

Pregnancies, Glucose, DiabetesPedigreeFunction, Age, NF1, NF2, NF3, NF4, NF5, NF6, Out come.

Figure 9, 10 and 11 shows performance of the proposed methodology on Frankfurt hospital dataset. The proposed method achieved higher accuracy.

5. CONCLUSION

Diabetes, being an ailment lacking a permanent cure, necessitates early detection. To efficiently classify diabetic conditions, data mining and machine learning (ML) algorithms are employed. In this study, the PIMA Indian Diabetes (PID) dataset from the National Institute of Diabetes and Kidney Diseases center, the Diabetes screening dataset, and the diabetes dataset from Frankfurt hospital were utilized. Each dataset comprises eight medical predictor variables and one target variable. In the pursuit of constructing an intelligent model for diabetic classification, feature creation is implemented to unveil the concealed relationships among the features. The stochastic gradient descent optimization technique improves the accuracy of

Figure 10. Performance measures: Diabetic screening dataset

DIABETIC SCREENING DATASET

LOGISTIC REGRESSION

	precision	recall	f1-score	support
0.0	0.78	0.89	0.84	318
1.0	0.74	0.56	0.64	177
accuracy			0.77	495
macro avg	0.76	0.73	0.74	495
weighted avg	0.77	0.77	0.77	495

LOGISTIC REGRESSION WITH RFECV

	precision	recall	f1-score	support
0.0	0.81	0.87	0.84	314
1.0	0.73	0.64	0.68	181
accuracy			0.78	495
macro avg	0.77	0.75	0.76	495
weighted avg	0.78	0.78	0.78	495

STOCHASTIC GRADIENT DESCENT BASED LOGISTIC REGRESSION

Accuracy: 97.933%
Precision: 97.080%
Recall: 97.573%
F1 score: 97.321%

Figure 11. Comparison of classification accuracies: Diabetes screening dataset

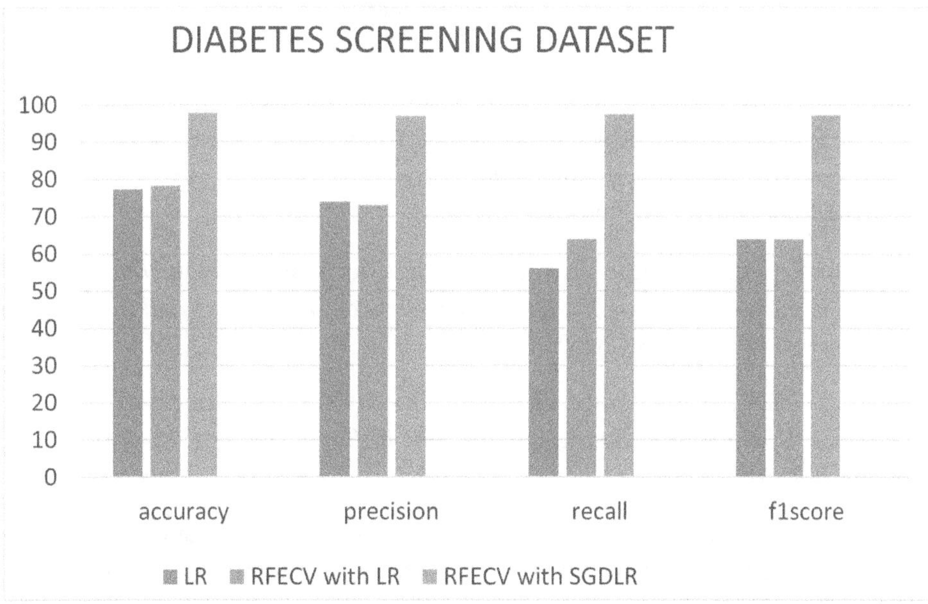

the model. IoT demonstrates significant potential in critical areas of Environment, Health, and Safety (EHS), particularly where human lives are at risk. Applications leveraging IoT offer solutions that prioritize safety, reliability, and efficiency. Additionally, IoT-based monitoring systems for the well-being of the elderly, ensuring remote integrity assistance, allow them to maintain their comfort and stay at home. Utilizing IoT sensors, patient data is gathered, and sophisticated methodologies, including data mining and machine learning, are applied to analyze this information for predicting the probability of severe conditions such as diabetes. The real-time data is then incorporated into the proposed methodology, resulting in an accurate classification of chronic diseases, particularly the presence of diabetes, in patients.

REFERENCES

Alehegn. (2019). Diabetes Analysis and Prediction Using Random Forest, KNN, Naïve Bayes, And J48: An Ensemble Approach. *International Journal of Scientific & Technology Research, 8*(9).

Farooq. (2023). Role of Internet of things in diabetes healthcare: Network infrastructure, taxonomy, challenges, and security model. *Digit Health, 9.* . doi:10.1177/20552076231179056

Joshi & Chawan. (2018). Logistic regression and SVM based diabetes prediction system. *Int. J. Technol. Res. Eng., 11*(5).

Joshi, R. D., & Dhakal, C. K. (2021). Predicting Type 2 Diabetes Using Logistic Regression and Machine Learning Approaches. *International Journal of Environmental Research and Public Health*, *18*(14), 7346. doi:10.3390/ijerph18147346 PMID:34299797

Jyothi Rani. (n.d.). Diabetes Prediction using Machine Learning. *International Journal of Scientific Research in Computer Science, Engineering and Information Technology*. doi:10.32628/CSEIT206463

Rajendra. (2021). Prediction of diabetes using logistic regression and ensemble techniques. *Computer Methods and Programs in Biomedicine, 1.* . doi:10.1016/j.cmpbup.2021.100032

Rastogi, R., & Bansal, M. (2023). Diabetes prediction model using data mining techniques Measurement. *Measurement. Sensors*, *25*(February). doi:10.1016/j.measen.2022.100605

Shankaracharya, S. (2017). *Diabetes risk prediction using machine learning: prospect and challenges*. Bioinform., Proteom. Imaging Anal.

Sisodia. (2018). Prediction of Diabetes using Classification Algorithms. *Procedia Computer Science, 132*, 1578-1585. doi:10.1016/j.procs.2018.05.122

Swapna, G., Soman, K. P., & Vinayakumar, R. (2018). Automated detection of diabetes using CNN and CNN-LSTM network and heart rate signals. *Procedia Computer Science*, *132*, 1253–1262. doi:10.1016/j.procs.2018.05.041

Tuppad, A., & Patil, S. D. (2022). Machine learning for diabetes clinical decision support: A review. *Advances in Computational Intelligence*, *2*(2), 22. doi:10.1007/s43674-022-00034-y PMID:35434723

Yuvaraj, N., & SriPreethaa, K. R. (2017). Diabetes prediction in healthcare systems using machine learning algorithms on Hadoop cluster. *Cluster Computing*, *22*(S1), 1–9. doi:10.1007/s10586-017-1532-x

Zou, Qu, Luo, Yin, Ju, Tang. (2018). *Predicting diabetes mellitus with machine learning techniques*. Academic Press.

Chapter 14
IoT's Role in Smart Manufacturing Transformation for Enhanced Household Product Quality

Md Nasir Ali
Department of Mechanical Engineering, Faculty of Engineering and Technology, Khaja Bandanawaz University, India

Dler Salih Hasan
https://orcid.org/0009-0008-3212-5509
Department of Computer Science and Information Tech, College of Science, University of Salahaddin-Erbil, Iraq

T. S. Senthil
Department of Marine Engineering, Noorul Islam Centre for Higher Education, India

N. Bala Sundara Ganapathy
Department of Information Technology, Panimalar Engineering College, India

T. Ilakkiya
Department of Management Studies, Sri Sairam Institute of Technology, India

Sampath Boopathi
https://orcid.org/0000-0002-2065-6539
Mechanical Engineering, Muthayammal Engineering College, India

ABSTRACT

The convergence of the internet of things (IoT) and smart manufacturing technologies has revolutionized the way household products are designed, manufactured, and maintained. This chapter explores the pivotal role of IoT in the transformation of smart manufacturing processes to enhance household product quality. It delves into the various facets of this transformative journey, including data-driven insights, predictive maintenance, product customization, and sustainability. By harnessing the power of IoT, manufacturers can streamline operations, reduce costs, and ultimately deliver higher-quality household products that meet the evolving demands of consumers.

DOI: 10.4018/979-8-3693-1694-8.ch014

INTRODUCTION

In an era characterized by relentless technological innovation, the convergence of the Internet of Things (IoT) and smart manufacturing has ushered in a paradigm shift in the way household products are conceived, created, and consumed. The marriage of these two powerful forces has transcended the boundaries of traditional manufacturing, paving the way for a new era of efficiency, customization, and sustainability in the production of household goods. Household products have long been an integral part of our daily lives, from appliances that simplify our chores to electronics that keep us connected (Yang et al., 2019). For consumers, the bar for product quality, convenience, and environmental responsibility has never been higher. Consequently, manufacturers are under constant pressure to meet these escalating demands while navigating the intricacies of an ever-evolving global market. This book chapter embarks on a journey into the heart of this transformation, exploring the pivotal role that IoT plays in reshaping the landscape of smart manufacturing, with a keen focus on enhancing household product quality. We delve deep into the multifaceted dimensions of this remarkable journey, unraveling the threads of data-driven insights, predictive maintenance, product customization, and sustainability, all woven together by the transformative power of IoT (Qu et al., 2019).

As we embark on this exploration, it becomes evident that IoT is not merely a technological trend but a catalyst for revolutionizing the way manufacturers operate and interact with consumers. By harnessing the capabilities of IoT, manufacturers can harness real-time data to make informed decisions, predict maintenance needs before failures occur, offer tailored products that resonate with individual preferences, and embrace sustainability practices that align with the environmental consciousness of today's consumers (Zhang et al., 2019). The chapters that follow will dissect each of these critical facets, shedding light on the ways in which IoT empowers manufacturers to not only survive but thrive in an era defined by rapid change and heightened consumer expectations. Through real-world case studies, practical insights, and future projections, we aim to equip industry professionals, researchers, and enthusiasts with the knowledge and inspiration needed to navigate this transformative landscape effectively (Abuhasel & Khan, 2020).

Join us on this exciting journey as we uncover how IoT is not just a technological tool but a cornerstone of smart manufacturing's evolution, driving the creation of household products that are not only of the highest quality but also aligned with the values and aspirations of modern consumers. The age of smarter, more responsive, and sustainable household products has dawned, and IoT is the beacon guiding us toward this promising future.

BACKGROUND AND SIGNIFICANCE

The Changing Landscape of Manufacturing

Manufacturing, a cornerstone of modern society, has undergone profound changes over the years. The transition from craft production to mass manufacturing in the early 20th century marked a pivotal moment in human history, transforming the scale and efficiency of production. However, as we entered the digital age, manufacturing faced new challenges and opportunities (Saqlain et al., 2019; Yang et al., 2019). Traditional manufacturing methods, which were rigid and linear, led to high costs and limited flexibility. This was insufficient in a world where consumers demanded personalized products, higher quality, and environmental sustainability, causing manufacturers to adapt or risk obsolescence.

The Rise of Smart Manufacturing

Smart manufacturing is a response to challenges in manufacturing, integrating technologies like IoT, AI, data analytics, and automation to create a more agile, efficient, and responsive production ecosystem. The IoT network of interconnected devices and sensors collects and transmits real-time data.The IoT has empowered manufacturers with unprecedented insights into their operations, enabling them to optimize production, reduce downtime, and enhance product quality (Abuhasel & Khan, 2020; Mourtzis et al., 2021).

Household Products and Consumer Expectations

Household products have been at the forefront of this manufacturing revolution. These products, ranging from kitchen appliances to electronics, are integral to daily life. Consumers demand household products that not only perform flawlessly but also align with their preferences, values, and environmental concerns. The era of generic, mass-produced goods is giving way to one of personalized, sustainable, and high-quality items.

The Significance of IoT in Household Product Manufacturing

The chapter highlights the significant role of IoT in transforming household product manufacturing by providing real-time data collection from products, machines, and supply chains, thereby enabling a data-driven approach.

- **Data-Driven Insights:** Manufacturers can gain valuable insights into product performance, user behavior, and supply chain efficiencies. This information informs decision-making and quality improvement.
- **Predictive Maintenance:** IoT-driven predictive maintenance minimizes downtime by identifying and addressing equipment issues before they cause failures. This enhances product reliability and reduces costs.
- **Product Customization:** IoT facilitates the customization of household products, tailoring them to individual preferences and needs. This personalization enhances user satisfaction.
- **Sustainability:** IoT supports sustainable manufacturing practices by optimizing resource usage, reducing waste, and ensuring eco-friendly product design.

Objectives

- To elucidate the core concepts and technologies behind the Internet of Things (IoT) and its relevance to the manufacturing industry, particularly in the context of household products.
- To emphasize the significance of smart manufacturing as a response to the evolving demands of consumers and the need for greater efficiency, customization, and sustainability in production.
- To explore how IoT facilitates the collection and analysis of real-time data, enabling manufacturers to make informed decisions that enhance product quality and operational efficiency.
- To delve into the role of IoT in predictive maintenance, showcasing how it minimizes downtime, reduces costs, and ensures the reliability of household products.
- To illustrate how IoT technologies enable product customization and personalization, meeting the diverse needs and preferences of consumers while maintaining product quality.
- To analyze how IoT supports sustainable manufacturing practices by optimizing resource utilization, reducing waste, and fostering eco-friendly product design.
- To identify and examine the challenges and risks associated with implementing IoT in manufacturing, including security, integration, and workforce issues.
- To provide insights into emerging IoT technologies and trends, as well as the integration of artificial intelligence and machine learning in smart manufacturing.

- To offer real-world case studies and examples that demonstrate successful implementations of IoT in household product manufacturing, along with lessons learned from these experiences.

FOUNDATIONS OF IOT IN MANUFACTURING

Introduction to IoT

The Internet of Things (IoT) is a network of interconnected physical objects, devices, and sensors that collect and exchange data with minimal human intervention. It can range from simple sensors in household products to complex industrial machinery. Integrating IoT in manufacturing offers greater efficiency, reduced costs, and enhanced product quality.

The Evolution of IoT

Understanding the evolution of IoT is crucial to grasp its significance in manufacturing. The concept of IoT has evolved through several stages:

- **M2M Communication:** The early stages of IoT were characterized by machine-to-machine (M2M) communication, where devices could communicate with one another without human intervention. This laid the foundation for more complex IoT ecosystems.
- **Connected Devices:** As technology advanced, devices became increasingly connected to the internet, enabling remote monitoring and control. This connectivity extended to everyday objects, giving rise to the idea of "smart" devices.
- **Data-Driven Insights:** With the proliferation of connected devices, vast amounts of data became available. IoT shifted from simply connecting devices to leveraging data analytics to gain actionable insights. Manufacturers began to harness this data for process optimization.
- **Integration with AI and Automation:** The integration of artificial intelligence (AI) and automation into IoT systems has further enhanced their capabilities. AI algorithms can analyze data in real time, making IoT systems smarter and more responsive.

Figure 1. IoT roles in the smart manufacturing

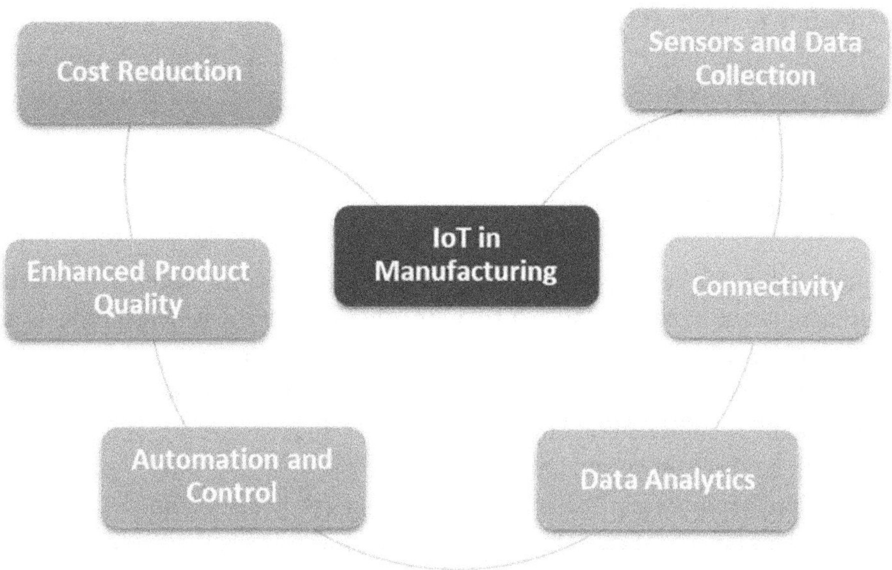

IoT in Manufacturing

In manufacturing, IoT plays a pivotal role in transforming traditional processes into smart, data-driven operations (Boopathi, Lewise, Sarojwal, et al., 2022; Jeevanantham et al., 2022; Samikannu et al., 2022). Key aspects of IoT in manufacturing included (Figure 1):

- **Sensors and Data Collection:** IoT relies on sensors and data collection devices to gather information from machines, products, and the environment. These sensors can monitor variables like temperature, pressure, humidity, and more.
- **Connectivity:** IoT devices use various communication protocols (e.g., Wi-Fi, Bluetooth, Zigbee) to transmit data to centralized systems or cloud platforms. This connectivity enables real-time monitoring and control.
- **Data Analytics:** Data collected by IoT devices is processed and analyzed using data analytics tools. This analysis provides insights into production efficiency, product quality, and predictive maintenance.
- **Automation and Control:** IoT can enable automation and control of manufacturing processes based on data-driven decisions. For example, machines can adjust their operations in response to real-time data.

- **Enhanced Product Quality:** By continuously monitoring production processes and product performance, IoT helps identify defects and deviations, leading to improved product quality.
- **Cost Reduction:** Predictive maintenance and process optimization through IoT can result in cost savings by reducing downtime and resource waste (Boopathi & Davim, 2023b).

IoT's Impact on Manufacturing

The integration of the Internet of Things (IoT) into the manufacturing industry has brought about a profound transformation, revolutionizing the way products are made, monitored, and maintained (Syamala et al., 2023; Koshariya, Kalaiyarasi, et al., 2023; Hema et al., 2023; Boopathi, 2023c). IoT's impact on manufacturing can be understood through several key dimensions:

Operational Efficiency and Optimization:

Real-time Monitoring: IoT sensors and devices provide continuous, real-time data on various aspects of manufacturing processes. This data allows manufacturers to monitor equipment performance, resource utilization, and product quality in real time.

Predictive Maintenance: IoT enables predictive maintenance by analyzing equipment data. Manufacturers can proactively address maintenance needs, reducing unplanned downtime and optimizing maintenance schedules.

Quality Assurance:

Data-Driven Insights: IoT-generated data offers insights into product quality and process consistency. Manufacturers can identify defects or deviations early in the production process, ensuring higher-quality products.

Statistical Process Control: IoT facilitates the implementation of statistical process control (SPC) techniques, which help maintain consistent product quality and reduce defects.

Supply Chain Visibility:

End-to-End Visibility: IoT extends visibility across the entire supply chain. Manufacturers can track the movement and condition of raw materials, components, and finished products in real time, improving inventory management and reducing delays.

Demand Forecasting: IoT data can be leveraged for demand forecasting, allowing manufacturers to adjust production volumes and schedules to meet consumer demand accurately.

Customization and Personalization:

Product Customization: IoT enables the customization of products to meet individual consumer preferences. Manufacturers can adjust product features, designs, or configurations in response to customer requests.

Mass Personalization: IoT supports the concept of mass personalization, where products can be tailored on a large scale without incurring the costs associated with traditional customization.

Energy Efficiency and Sustainability:

Resource Optimization: IoT helps optimize resource usage, including energy, water, and raw materials, reducing waste and environmental impact.

Eco-Friendly Design: IoT can aid in designing more eco-friendly products by providing data on the environmental footprint of materials and manufacturing processes.

Quality Data for Continuous Improvement:

Historical Data Analysis: IoT-generated historical data can be analyzed to identify trends, patterns, and areas for improvement. Manufacturers can continuously refine their processes based on this data.

Enhanced Decision-Making:

Data-Driven Decision-Making: IoT empowers manufacturing decision-makers with data-driven insights. Managers can make informed choices about production, maintenance, and resource allocation.

Risk Mitigation: IoT can help identify potential risks or disruptions in the manufacturing process, allowing for proactive risk mitigation strategies.

Competitive Advantage: IoT enables manufacturers to swiftly adapt to market changes and consumer demands, providing a competitive edge. It also encourages innovation in product design, manufacturing techniques, and business models.

Concepts and Technologies

IoT in manufacturing relies on a combination of key concepts and technologies that enable the seamless integration of physical devices, data collection, and intelligent decision-making (Figure 2). Here are some of the fundamental concepts and technologies underpinning IoT in manufacturing (Boopathi, 2023c; Jeevanantham et al., 2022; Reddy et al., 2023; Samikannu et al., 2022):

Sensors and Actuators:

Sensors: These devices are the backbone of IoT, collecting data from the physical world. In manufacturing, sensors measure parameters such as temperature, humidity, pressure, vibration, and more (Anitha et al., 2023; Gunasekaran & Boopathi, 2023; Koshariya, Kalaiyarasi, et al., 2023; Zekrifa et al., 2023).

Actuators: These devices enable IoT systems to interact with the physical environment by controlling machinery, valves, switches, and other components.

Figure 2. IoT technologies for manufacturing processes

Connectivity:

Wireless Protocols: Various wireless communication protocols, such as Wi-Fi, Bluetooth, Zigbee, and cellular networks, enable devices to transmit data to centralized systems or other devices.

Wired Connections: Ethernet and other wired connections are used in situations where stable, high-speed communication is required.

Data Collection and Aggregation:

Edge Computing: In IoT, data can be processed at the "edge" (near the data source) using edge computing devices. This reduces latency and conserves bandwidth (Boopathi, 2023a; Hema et al., 2023; Syamala et al., 2023; Venkateswaran, Vidhya, Naik, et al., 2023).

Cloud Computing: IoT data is often sent to cloud platforms for storage, analysis, and processing. Cloud computing provides scalability and accessibility (Agrawal et al., 2024; Satav et al., 2024; Srinivas et al., 2023; Venkateswaran, Vidhya, Ayyannan, et al., 2023).

Data Analytics:

Big Data Analytics: IoT generates large volumes of data. Big data analytics tools and techniques are used to extract meaningful insights from this data, including machine learning and data mining.

Real-time Analytics: In manufacturing, real-time analytics provide immediate insights into ongoing processes, enabling rapid decision-making.

Artificial Intelligence (AI):

Machine Learning: Machine learning algorithms are employed to identify patterns, anomalies, and trends in IoT data. They enable predictive maintenance and process optimization (Boopathi & Kanike, 2023; Ingle et al., 2023; Maheswari et al., 2023; Syamala et al., 2023; Venkateswaran, Kumar, et al., 2023).

Natural Language Processing (NLP): NLP can be used for analyzing unstructured data, such as maintenance reports or customer feedback.

Security:

Cybersecurity: IoT devices are susceptible to cyber threats. Security measures, including encryption, authentication, and access control, are crucial to protect data and devices.

Blockchain: In some cases, blockchain technology is used to enhance the security and transparency of IoT data transactions.

Interoperability:

Standardization: Industry-specific standards and protocols ensure that IoT devices and systems from different manufacturers can seamlessly communicate and work together.

APIs: Application Programming Interfaces (APIs) enable integration between different IoT components and software applications.

Human-Machine Interaction:

Human-Machine Interfaces (HMIs): These interfaces allow operators to monitor and control manufacturing processes, often through graphical user interfaces (GUIs) or touchscreens (Koshariya, Khatoon, et al., 2023; Vanitha et al., 2023; Vennila et al., 2022).

Voice and Gesture Recognition: Some IoT systems incorporate voice or gesture recognition for hands-free control and monitoring.

Digital Twins:

Digital Twin Technology: Digital twins are virtual replicas of physical assets or processes. They are used for simulation, monitoring, and optimization, providing a virtual mirror of real-world operations.

Edge Devices:

IoT Gateways: These devices aggregate data from sensors and preprocess it before sending it to the cloud or other systems.

Fog Computing: Similar to edge computing, fog computing distributes data processing across the network, reducing latency and improving response times.

Figure 3. Smart manufacturing in Industry 4.0

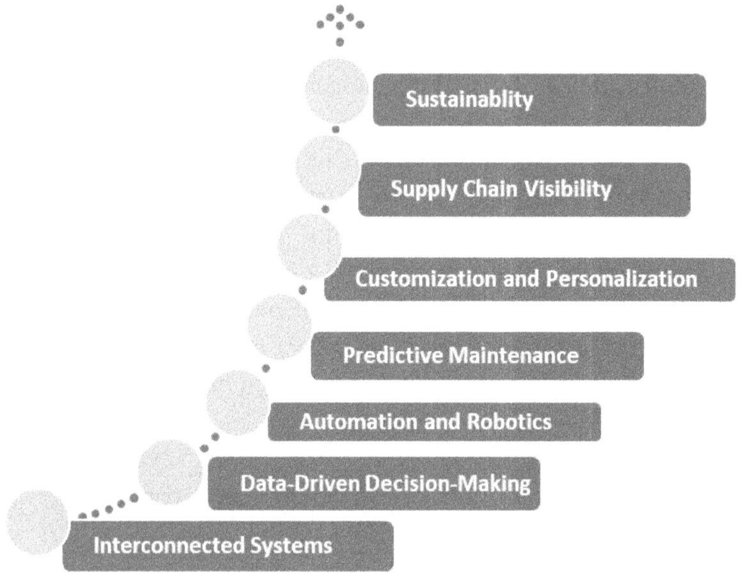

SMART MANUFACTURING IN THE HOUSEHOLD PRODUCT INDUSTRY

Smart manufacturing represents a transformative approach to production that leverages advanced technologies and data-driven processes to optimize efficiency, quality, and sustainability. In the context of the household product industry, smart manufacturing plays a pivotal role in reshaping the way household goods are designed, produced, and delivered to consumers (Boopathi, Khare, et al., 2023; Boopathi & Davim, 2023a; Mohanty et al., 2023). Let's delve into the concept of smart manufacturing and its applications within the household product sector:

Smart Manufacturing in Industry 4.0

Smart manufacturing, often referred to as Industry 4.0 or the Fourth Industrial Revolution, is characterized by the integration of digital technologies into every aspect of manufacturing operation (Figure 3). It represents a departure from traditional, linear manufacturing processes and embraces a holistic, data-centric approach (Karthik et al., 2023; Maguluri et al., 2023; Syamala et al., 2023).

- **Interconnected Systems**: Smart manufacturing relies on a network of interconnected devices, sensors, machines, and systems that communicate and collaborate seamlessly. This interconnectedness enables real-time data exchange and coordination.

- **Data-Driven Decision-Making**: Data is at the core of smart manufacturing. Advanced data analytics, machine learning, and artificial intelligence are used to collect, analyze, and derive actionable insights from vast amounts of data generated throughout the production process.
- **Automation and Robotics**: Automation and robotics play a significant role in smart manufacturing, automating repetitive tasks and enhancing precision. In the household product industry, robots may be involved in assembly, quality control, or even packaging.
- **Predictive Maintenance**: Through IoT sensors and data analysis, smart manufacturing systems can predict when equipment or machinery is likely to fail, enabling proactive maintenance to reduce downtime.
- **Customization and Personalization**: Smart manufacturing facilitates the customization and personalization of household products. Manufacturers can adjust product features, colors, or designs to meet individual consumer preferences.
- **Supply Chain Visibility**: Smart manufacturing extends visibility into the supply chain, allowing manufacturers to track the movement of raw materials and finished products in real time. This visibility improves inventory management and responsiveness to market demands.
- **Sustainability**: Sustainability is a key aspect of smart manufacturing. It encourages eco-friendly practices by optimizing resource usage, minimizing waste, and designing products with reduced environmental impact.

Applications in the Household Product Industry

In the household product industry, smart manufacturing has far-reaching implications (Hema et al., 2023; Koshariya, Kalaiyarasi, et al., 2023; Kumara et al., 2023):

- **Quality Enhancement**: Smart manufacturing enables real-time monitoring of production processes and product quality. Manufacturers can identify defects or deviations early, ensuring that household products meet stringent quality standards.
- **Customized Products**: Consumers increasingly seek products tailored to their specific needs and preferences. Smart manufacturing allows manufacturers to customize household products efficiently and cost-effectively.
- **Energy Efficiency**: Household product manufacturers can optimize energy usage by implementing smart systems that control energy consumption based on real-time data and demand.

- **Inventory Management**: Smart manufacturing systems provide real-time visibility into inventory levels, helping manufacturers manage stock more efficiently and reduce carrying costs.
- **Sustainability Initiatives**: The household product industry can leverage smart manufacturing to embrace sustainable practices. IoT sensors and analytics can track the environmental impact of materials and processes, facilitating eco-friendly product design.
- **Market Responsiveness**: Smart manufacturing enables manufacturers to respond quickly to changing market conditions and consumer preferences. This agility is crucial in a rapidly evolving industry.

Data-Driven Insights for Quality Improvement

In the realm of smart manufacturing for household products, data-driven insights are central to enhancing product quality and operational efficiency. This involves the collection, analysis, and real-time monitoring of data throughout the production process (Boopathi, 2021a; Veeranjaneyulu, Boopathi, Kumari, et al., 2023). Let's explore how data-driven insights are harnessed for quality improvement, focusing on data collection and analysis, as well as real-time monitoring and reporting:

Data Collection and Analysis

- **Sensor Technology**: In smart manufacturing, a multitude of sensors are strategically placed throughout the production line and on machinery. These sensors collect a wide array of data, including temperature, pressure, humidity, vibration, and more. For instance, sensors in an oven used in appliance manufacturing can measure temperature and ensure consistent heating.
- **IoT Devices**: The Internet of Things (IoT) plays a crucial role in data collection. IoT devices and connected sensors transmit data to centralized systems, ensuring that information flows seamlessly. For example, an IoT-enabled washing machine can transmit data on water temperature and detergent levels.
- **Data Aggregation**: Data from sensors and devices are aggregated and stored in databases or cloud platforms. This data can be structured, semi-structured, or unstructured, depending on the information source. Manufacturers utilize data lakes and data warehouses to store and organize this information.
- **Data Pre-processing**: Raw data may contain noise or anomalies. Data pre-processing techniques, including cleaning, normalization, and outlier detection, are employed to ensure data quality and accuracy.

- **Analytics Tools**: Advanced data analytics tools and algorithms are applied to extract meaningful insights from the collected data. Machine learning algorithms can uncover patterns, anomalies, and correlations in the data.

Real-time Monitoring and Reporting

- **Continuous Monitoring**: IoT and sensor data are used for real-time monitoring of manufacturing processes. This continuous monitoring ensures that operations remain within specified tolerances and that product quality is consistent (Boopathi, 2021b, 2023b; Maguluri et al., 2023; Sankar et al., 2023).
- **Alert Systems**: Real-time data is integrated into alert systems that notify operators and engineers of any deviations or anomalies. For example, if a sensor detects a sudden temperature spike in a baking process, an alert is generated.
- **Dashboard Interfaces**: User-friendly dashboard interfaces provide a visual representation of real-time data. Operators can track various parameters and performance metrics at a glance. Dashboards can also highlight any production bottlenecks or quality issues.
- **Predictive Analytics**: Predictive analytics models are employed to forecast potential quality issues or equipment failures based on historical data trends. This enables proactive intervention to prevent defects or downtime.
- **Reporting and Documentation**: Real-time data is logged and documented for regulatory compliance and quality assurance purposes. Manufacturers can generate reports that detail process parameters, quality metrics, and any deviations from standards.

Quality Improvement Through Data-Driven Insights

- **Early Defect Detection**: Data-driven insights enable early detection of defects or variations in the production process. This allows for immediate corrective actions, reducing waste and rework (Boopathi & Sivakumar, 2016; Ramudu et al., 2023; Sampath et al., 2022).
- **Process Optimization**: Data analysis identifies areas where processes can be optimized for efficiency and quality. Manufacturers can make data-informed adjustments to improve production parameters (Boopathi, Kumar, et al., 2023; Domakonda et al., 2022; Kumara et al., 2023; Nishanth et al., 2023; Saravanan et al., 2022).

- **Consistent Product Quality**: Real-time monitoring ensures that each product adheres to quality standards, resulting in consistent quality across the entire product line.
- **Cost Reduction**: By minimizing defects and downtime, manufacturers can reduce production costs, improve resource utilization, and enhance profitability.
- **Customer Satisfaction**: Consistently high-quality products lead to increased customer satisfaction and brand loyalty, benefiting the bottom line.

PREDICTIVE MAINTENANCE WITH IOT

Predictive maintenance is a critical aspect of smart manufacturing that harnesses the power of the Internet of Things (IoT) to optimize maintenance processes and reduce downtime. In the context of household product manufacturing, predictive maintenance ensures that equipment and machinery operate at their peak efficiency, ultimately leading to enhanced product quality and production cost savings (Ayvaz & Alpay, 2021).

Sensor Integration: Predictive maintenance starts with the integration of sensors and IoT devices on manufacturing equipment, such as machines used in appliance manufacturing or assembly lines for household products. These sensors continuously collect data on various parameters, including temperature, vibration, pressure, and operating conditions (Compare et al., 2019).

Data Collection and Analysis: The IoT sensors collect data in real time and transmit it to a centralized data repository or cloud platform. Data analytics tools and algorithms process this data to identify patterns and anomalies. Machine learning models are often applied to historical data to train algorithms for predictive analysis. These models can predict when equipment is likely to fail or require maintenance based on past performance and deviations from normal operation (Cheng et al., 2020).

Condition Monitoring: Predictive maintenance systems continuously monitor the condition of machinery and equipment. This involves comparing real-time data from sensors with established baselines and predefined thresholds. Anomalies or deviations from expected conditions trigger alerts or notifications to maintenance teams or engineers, indicating the need for further investigation (Teoh et al., 2021).

Predictive Algorithms: Advanced predictive algorithms consider multiple factors, including sensor data, historical maintenance records, and environmental conditions. These algorithms can predict equipment failures or performance degradation with a high degree of accuracy. Predictive algorithms may also estimate the remaining useful life of a component or piece of equipment, allowing for precise planning of maintenance activities (Shamayleh et al., 2020).

Proactive Maintenance: Predictive maintenance allows for proactive intervention by scheduling maintenance activities during planned downtimes or shifts, ranging from simple tasks like lubrication or cleaning to complex repairs or component replacements, with minimal impact on production.

Cost Savings and Efficiency: Predictive maintenance reduces unscheduled downtime, preventing costly production interruptions. This results in cost savings by avoiding emergency repairs and minimizing the need for spare parts inventory. Equipment efficiency is optimized as maintenance is performed precisely when needed, ensuring that machinery operates at peak performance levels (Calabrese et al., 2020).

Improved Product Quality: Predictive maintenance ensures consistent and reliable manufacturing processes, improving product quality and reducing defects by preventing equipment failures.

Data-Driven Decision-Making: Predictive maintenance systems offer crucial data for manufacturers to optimize maintenance schedules, equipment lifecycles, and resource allocation, providing valuable insights for decision-making.

Safety Benefits: Predictive maintenance with IoT is a proactive approach that helps household product manufacturers minimize downtime, reduce maintenance costs, enhance equipment reliability, and improve product quality. By using real-time data and predictive analytics, manufacturers can ensure smooth production processes, meeting consumer demands for high-quality household products, and reduce maintenance costs.

IoT Sensors and Predictive Analytics: Preventing Product Failures

IoT sensors and predictive analytics are instrumental in preventing product failures in manufacturing, especially in the context of household product production. These technologies enable manufacturers to detect issues before they result in defective products, reducing waste, improving quality, and enhancing customer satisfaction (Liu et al., 2021). Here's how IoT sensors and predictive analytics work together to prevent product failures:

IoT Sensors for Data Collection:

- **Diverse Sensor Types**: IoT sensors are strategically deployed throughout the manufacturing process and on critical machinery. These sensors can measure various parameters such as temperature, humidity, pressure, vibration, and more, depending on the specific needs of the production process (Anitha et al., 2023; Boopathi, 2023c; Karthik et al., 2023).

- **Real-time Data Collection**: IoT sensors continuously collect data in real time. This data includes information about the operating conditions, performance, and health of equipment and the products being manufactured.
- **Wireless Connectivity**: IoT sensors are often wireless, allowing them to transmit data seamlessly to a centralized data repository or cloud platform for analysis.

Data Aggregation and Storage:

- **Data Aggregation**: The data collected by IoT sensors is aggregated and stored in databases or data lakes. This aggregated data forms the foundation for predictive analytics.
- **Data Preprocessing**: Raw sensor data may require preprocessing, including data cleaning, normalization, and outlier detection, to ensure data quality and accuracy.

Predictive Analytics:

- **Machine Learning Algorithms**: Predictive analytics involves the application of machine learning algorithms to historical and real-time data. These algorithms can identify patterns, anomalies, and correlations in the data (Maheswari et al., 2023; Ramudu et al., 2023; Syamala et al., 2023; Veeranjaneyulu, Boopathi, Narasimharao, et al., 2023; Zekrifa et al., 2023).
- **Predictive Models**: Predictive models are trained using historical data to forecast potential issues or failures. These models consider various factors, including sensor data, equipment health, and environmental conditions.

Early Detection of Anomalies:

- **Threshold-Based Alerts**: Predictive analytics models establish thresholds for normal operation. When sensor data deviates from these thresholds, alerts or notifications are triggered. For example, if a sensor detects a sudden spike in temperature or vibration in a production machine, it may signal an anomaly.
- **Statistical Analysis**: Predictive analytics can perform statistical analysis on sensor data to detect subtle deviations from expected patterns. These deviations can indicate early signs of equipment degradation or product quality issues.

Proactive Maintenance and Intervention:

- **Maintenance Alerts**: Predictive analytics can predict when equipment is likely to fail or degrade significantly. Maintenance alerts are generated, allowing maintenance teams to plan and execute maintenance activities during scheduled downtimes or when it is most cost-effective.
- **Component Replacement**: Predictive analytics can also estimate the remaining useful life of components or parts. Manufacturers can replace or refurbish these components before they fail, avoiding production interruptions (Zonta et al., 2020).

Improved Product Quality:

- **Consistent Production**: Early detection and prevention of equipment issues ensure consistent and reliable production processes, reducing the likelihood of defects and product failures.

Cost Savings and Efficiency:

- **Downtime Reduction**: Preventing product failures through predictive analytics minimizes unscheduled downtime, saving costs associated with emergency repairs and loss of production.
- **Resource Optimization**: Maintenance activities are optimized, as they are performed precisely when needed. This reduces maintenance costs and ensures that equipment operates at peak performance levels.

By continuously monitoring equipment and product parameters, analyzing data, and providing early warnings and maintenance recommendations, manufacturers can maintain high-quality production processes and meet customer expectations for reliable household products (Zonta et al., 2020).

PRODUCT CUSTOMIZATION AND PERSONALIZATION IN SMART MANUFACTURING

Product customization and personalization are pivotal aspects of smart manufacturing, and they play a significant role in meeting consumer demands for unique and tailored household products (Figure 4). Here's how product customization and personalization are achieved within the context of smart manufacturing (Lu et al., 2020):

Data-Driven Insights

- **Consumer Data**: Smart manufacturing systems collect and analyze consumer data to gain insights into individual preferences, purchase histories, and usage patterns. This data provides valuable information for product customization.
- **Market Trends**: Data analytics also help manufacturers identify emerging market trends and consumer preferences. This information guides decisions about product features, designs, and variations.

Design Flexibility

- **Parametric Design**: Manufacturers use parametric design tools that allow them to create products with customizable parameters. These parameters may include size, color, materials, and features (Ghobakhloo, 2020).
- **3D Printing**: Additive manufacturing techniques like 3D printing enable the creation of highly customizable components and products. Consumers can request specific designs or alterations to existing designs (Boopathi, Khare, et al., 2023; Mohanty et al., 2023; Palaniappan et al., 2023; Senthil et al., 2023).

Configurable Product Lines

- **Modular Design**: Products are designed with modularity in mind, allowing consumers to mix and match components to create their desired configurations. For instance, modular kitchen appliances can be customized by combining various modules like ovens, cooktops, and refrigerators.

Digital Twins

- **Virtual Prototypes**: Digital twins, which are virtual replicas of physical products, allow consumers to visualize and interact with customized product configurations before making a purchase. This reduces the risk of dissatisfaction with the final product.

IoT and Connectivity

- **Connected Products**: IoT-enabled household products can be personalized through software updates. Manufacturers can provide new features or functionalities through over-the-air updates, enhancing the user experience.

Figure 4. Product customization and personalization

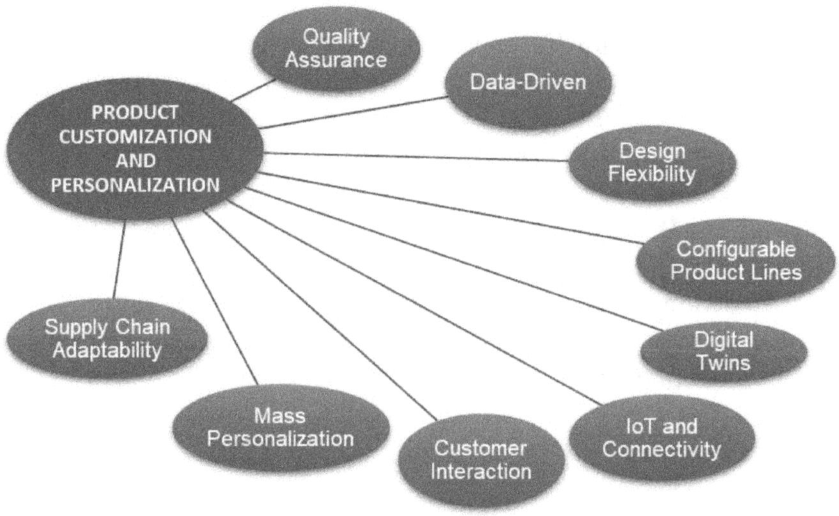

Customer Interaction

- **Online Customization Tools**: Manufacturers offer online tools or configurators that allow consumers to design and customize products according to their preferences. These tools guide consumers through the customization process.
- **Direct Customer Feedback**: Manufacturers actively engage with customers to gather feedback on product preferences and customization options. This feedback loop helps refine and expand customization offerings.

Mass Personalization

- **Scalability**: Smart manufacturing technologies enable mass personalization, where products can be tailored to individual preferences on a large scale without the cost and complexity of traditional customization methods.

Supply Chain Adaptability

- **Flexible Supply Chains**: Manufacturers implement flexible supply chain models that can accommodate customization. This includes agile production processes, just-in-time inventory, and component sourcing flexibility.

Quality Assurance:

- **Testing and Verification**: Customized products undergo rigorous testing and verification to ensure they meet quality standards. Manufacturers implement quality control processes that account for product variations (Boopathi, 2021a; Boopathi, 2022; Kumar et al., 2023).

Data Security and Privacy

- **Data Protection**: Manufacturers prioritize data security and customer privacy when collecting and storing customization preferences. Compliance with data protection regulations, such as GDPR, is essential.

Sustainable Customization

- **Eco-Friendly Materials**: Smart manufacturing allows for eco-friendly material choices and sustainable customization options. Manufacturers can offer environmentally conscious choices to eco-minded consumers (Boopathi, 2022; Boopathi & Sivakumar, 2012; Dass james & Boopathi, 2016; Sampath et al., 2021).

These customization options are made possible through data-driven insights, flexible design approaches, IoT connectivity, and responsive supply chains (Boopathi, 2022d; Gowri et al., 2023; Janardhana et al., 2023; Sampath, 2021). As consumer preferences continue to evolve, manufacturers must embrace customization as a central tenet of smart manufacturing to remain competitive and deliver household products that resonate with individual tastes and needs.

Mass Customization vs. Personalization:

Mass Customization: Mass customization is the practice of offering a variety of standardized product options and configurations that consumers can choose from to create a product that aligns with their preferences.

- **Standardized Options**: Manufacturers provide a predefined set of options, features, or modules from which consumers can choose.
- **Scalability**: Mass customization is scalable, allowing manufacturers to offer a wide range of product variations efficiently.
- **Efficiency**: It combines the advantages of mass production (efficiency) and customization (meeting individual preferences).

Examples:

- A car manufacturer offers various models with optional features like leather seats, sunroofs, and navigation systems.
- A furniture company offers modular sofa sets with customizable configurations and upholstery choices.

Personalization:

Definition: Personalization takes customization to a more individualized level. It involves tailoring products to meet the specific needs, preferences, and requirements of each individual consumer (Kusiak, 2019).

Implementing Customization Through IoT

IoT-Enabled Data Collection: IoT sensors collect data on consumer behavior, preferences, and usage patterns. For example, a smart kitchen appliance can gather data on cooking habits (Phuyal et al., 2020).

Data Analytics and Machine Learning: Advanced data analytics and machine learning algorithms process the data collected by IoT sensors. These algorithms identify patterns and generate insights into consumer preferences.

Real-time Feedback and Customization: Manufacturers use real-time data and insights to adapt products or services to consumer needs. For instance, a connected fitness device can adjust workout routines based on user progress.

Personalized Recommendations: IoT can deliver personalized recommendations to consumers based on their historical data and preferences. This is common in e-commerce platforms, where product recommendations are tailored to individual users.

Dynamic Product Configurations: Smart manufacturing processes can dynamically adjust product configurations based on consumer preferences. For example, a car's infotainment system can be customized based on user preferences stored in the cloud.

SUSTAINABILITY AND IOT IN MANUFACTURING

Sustainability has become a paramount consideration in modern manufacturing, and the integration of the Internet of Things (IoT) has played a significant role in advancing sustainable manufacturing practices (Figure 5). Here, we'll explore how IoT is used to promote sustainability in manufacturing, including sustainable manufacturing practices and eco-friendly product design (Grabowska, 2020; Phuyal et al., 2020; Wang et al., 2021):

Figure 5. Sustainability and IoT in manufacturing

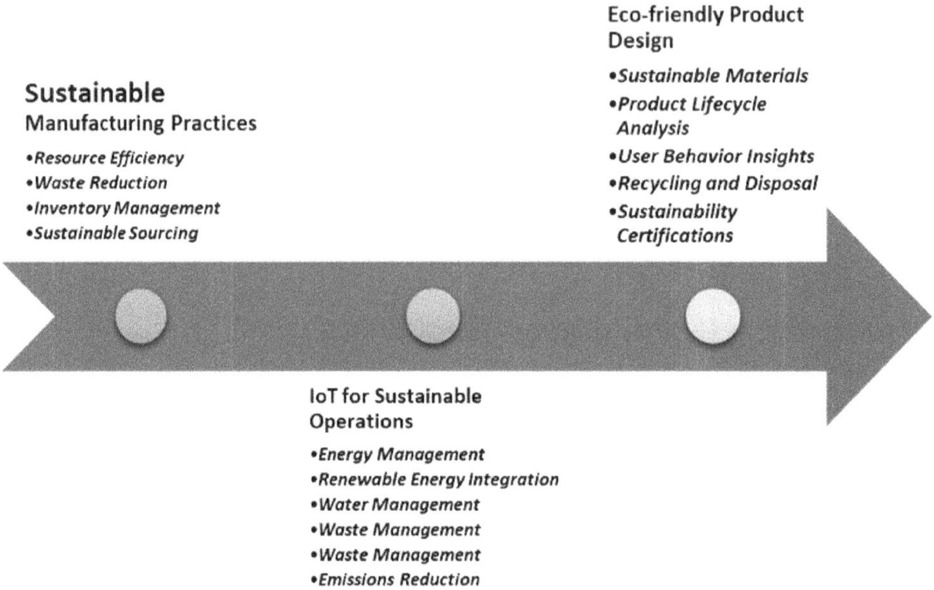

Sustainable Manufacturing Practices

Resource Efficiency: IoT sensors monitor resource consumption in real time, allowing manufacturers to optimize energy, water, and raw material usage. For example, sensors can track equipment energy consumption and trigger alerts for abnormalities or inefficiencies.

Waste Reduction: IoT-enabled predictive maintenance minimizes unexpected equipment failures, reducing the need for emergency repairs and the disposal of damaged components.

Production Process Monitoring

IoT sensors monitor production processes for anomalies, ensuring that products meet quality standards and reducing the production of defective items (Boopathi, 2021b, 2023b; Maguluri et al., 2023; Sankar et al., 2023).

Inventory Management: IoT provides real-time visibility into the supply chain, allowing manufacturers to optimize inventory levels and reduce excess inventory waste.

Sustainable Sourcing: IoT can trace the origin and environmental impact of raw materials. Manufacturers can choose suppliers with sustainable and eco-friendly practices.

IoT for Sustainable Operations

Energy Management: IoT-controlled lighting and heating, ventilation, and air conditioning (HVAC) systems adjust based on occupancy and environmental conditions, reducing energy consumption.

Renewable Energy Integration: IoT devices monitor renewable energy systems like solar panels and wind turbines, optimizing their performance and integration into manufacturing operations.

Water Management: IoT sensors measure water quality parameters, helping manufacturers identify issues and improve water usage efficiency (Boopathi, 2021b; Boopathi, Lewise, Subbiah, et al., 2022; Boopathi, Thillaivanan, et al., 2022; Boopathi & Sivakumar, 2014).

Waste Management: IoT devices monitor waste levels in bins and containers, optimizing waste collection routes and reducing unnecessary pickups.

Emissions Reduction: IoT can monitor emissions from manufacturing processes and provide data for compliance with environmental regulations (Boopathi, 2022b; Maguluri et al., 2023; Sampath, 2021).

Eco-friendly Product Design:

Sustainable Materials: IoT can track the environmental impact of materials used in product manufacturing, promoting the use of sustainable and recycled materials (Ayvaz & Alpay, 2021; Compare et al., 2019; Lu et al., 2020).

Product Lifecycle Analysis: IoT sensors in products allow manufacturers to gather data on product usage and performance throughout its lifecycle. This data informs design improvements and extends product lifespans.

User Behavior Insights: IoT-enabled products collect data on user behavior and preferences. This information guides the design of products that align with eco-friendly practices, such as energy-efficient appliances.

Recycling and Disposal: IoT data can inform manufacturers about the end-of-life stage of products, enabling responsible disposal and recycling planning (Hanumanthakari et al., 2023; Harikaran et al., 2023; Janardhana et al., 2023; Selvakumar, Adithe, et al., 2023; Selvakumar, Shankar, et al., 2023).

Sustainability Certifications: IoT can help manufacturers track compliance with sustainability certifications and standards, such as ISO 14001 for environmental management.

Benefits of IoT-Driven Sustainability:

- **Cost Reduction**: IoT-driven sustainability practices can result in reduced energy, water, and material costs, leading to higher profitability.
- **Environmental Impact Reduction**: Sustainable manufacturing practices decrease the environmental footprint of manufacturing operations, reducing greenhouse gas emissions and resource depletion.
- **Compliance and Reputation**: IoT ensures compliance with environmental regulations and certification standards, enhancing a company's reputation and appeal to eco-conscious consumers.
- **Competitive Advantage**: Manufacturers that embrace IoT-driven sustainability can gain a competitive edge by aligning with consumer preferences for eco-friendly products and practices.

Challenges and Risks

While the adoption of IoT in manufacturing offers numerous benefits, it also presents challenges and risks that manufacturer must address to ensure successful implementation. Here are some of the key challenges and risks associated with IoT in manufacturing (Phuyal et al., 2020; Wang et al., 2021; Leng et al., 2021; Yang et al., 2019; Qu et al., 2019):

Security and Privacy Concerns:

- **Data Security**: IoT devices collect and transmit sensitive data. Ensuring the security of this data from cyberattacks, breaches, and unauthorized access is a critical concern. Manufacturers must implement robust security measures, including encryption, authentication, and intrusion detection systems.
- **Device Vulnerabilities**: IoT devices can be susceptible to security vulnerabilities if not properly maintained and updated. Manufacturers need strategies for regular patching and firmware updates to address potential security flaws.
- **Privacy**: Collecting data from IoT devices, especially in consumer-oriented manufacturing, raises privacy concerns. Manufacturers must have clear privacy policies and comply with relevant data protection regulations, such as GDPR.

Integration Challenges

Legacy Systems: Many manufacturing facilities rely on legacy systems and equipment that may not be IoT-compatible. Integrating IoT with these legacy systems can be complex and costly.

Interoperability: Ensuring that IoT devices and systems from different manufacturers can seamlessly communicate and work together is a significant challenge. Standardization efforts and the use of open APIs can help address this issue.

Data Integration: Managing and integrating vast amounts of data from various IoT devices and sensors into existing data systems and analytics platforms can be daunting. Data silos should be avoided through proper data integration strategies.

Skillset and Workforce Issues: The implementation and maintenance of IoT systems require specialized skills in areas such as data analytics, cybersecurity, and IoT device management. Manufacturers may face challenges in finding and retaining talent with these skills. Existing employees may require training to adapt to the new IoT-driven manufacturing environment. Upskilling programs are essential to ensure a proficient workforce.

Scalability and Cost: The deployment of IoT infrastructure, including sensors, connectivity, and data analytics platforms, can require a significant initial investment. Manufacturers need to assess the cost-benefit ratio. As manufacturing operations grow or change, scaling IoT infrastructure to accommodate evolving needs can be complex and expensive.

Reliability and Downtime: IoT devices can fail or experience technical issues, potentially leading to production downtime. Manufacturers must implement robust maintenance and support processes. Manufacturers need contingency plans and redundancy measures to minimize the impact of IoT-related failures on production.

Regulatory Compliance: Manufacturers must navigate complex regulatory landscapes that govern data privacy, environmental standards, and safety requirements. Compliance with various regulations, such as ISO standards and industry-specific regulations, is crucial.

Data Overload: IoT generates vast amounts of data. Manufacturers must have the capacity to manage, store, analyze, and derive actionable insights from this data. Data analytics tools and techniques are essential for handling this data effectively.

Vendor and Supply Chain Risks: Manufacturers rely on IoT device vendors and suppliers for critical components. Vendor-related risks, such as supply chain disruptions or the financial stability of vendors, can impact IoT implementations.

Intellectual Property Protection: Clarifying ownership and usage rights of data generated by IoT devices is crucial. Manufacturers must protect their intellectual property and data assets.

FUTURE TRENDS AND INNOVATIONS

The future of IoT in manufacturing holds exciting possibilities, with emerging technologies and trends shaping the landscape. Here are some key areas of development and innovation (Grabowska, 2020; Leng et al., 2021; Mourtzis et al., 2021):

Edge Computing: Edge computing, which processes data closer to the source (at the edge of the network), will become more prevalent. This allows for real-time data analysis and decision-making, reducing latency and dependence on cloud resources.

5G Connectivity The rollout of 5G networks will enable faster, more reliable IoT connectivity. This is particularly beneficial for applications that require low latency and high bandwidth, such as remote control of machinery and augmented reality (AR) for maintenance (Venkateswaran, Vidhya, Ayyannan, et al., 2023).

Digital Twins: Digital twin technology will evolve, providing more accurate and detailed virtual representations of physical manufacturing processes and products. This will enhance simulation, optimization, and predictive maintenance capabilities (Agrawal et al., 2023; Reddy et al., 2023; Venkateswaran, Vidhya, Naik, et al., 2023).

AI and Machine Learning: AI and machine learning will play an even more significant role in manufacturing automation. Smart factories will leverage AI for predictive maintenance, quality control, and demand forecasting (Dhanya et al., 2023; Gunasekaran & Boopathi, 2023).

Sustainability and Green Manufacturing

IoT for Sustainability: IoT will continue to support sustainability efforts by optimizing resource usage, monitoring emissions, and enabling eco-friendly product design (Boopathi, 2022c, 2022a; Domakonda et al., 2022; Sampath, 2021). Blockchain technology will enhance transparency and traceability in supply chains, reducing the risk of counterfeiting and ensuring product authenticity.

Augmented Reality (AR) will aid in real-time maintenance, reducing downtime and enhancing workforce training. Quantum computing could revolutionize optimization problems like supply chain logistics and material design, enhancing efficiency. Human-machine interfaces will facilitate interaction with IoT devices, enhancing collaboration. As IoT adoption increases, cybersecurity will become a top priority, necessitating robust security solutions to protect manufacturing systems from cyber threats. IoT-driven customization and personalization will become even more sophisticated, enabling highly individualized products and experiences for consumers. Autonomous vehicles and drones will be used for material transport within smart factories, reducing the need for manual transportation (Babu et al., 2022; Boopathi et al., 2021; Maguluri et al., 2023).

CONCLUSION

In conclusion, the integration of the Internet of Things (IoT) into manufacturing is revolutionizing the industry, ushering in an era of smart manufacturing and industrial transformation. This transformation extends to various sectors, including the household product industry, where IoT is enhancing product quality, customization, sustainability, and efficiency.

- IoT-driven data collection, analysis, and real-time monitoring enable manufacturers to maintain consistent product quality, reduce defects, and enhance consumer satisfaction.
- IoT-based predictive maintenance practices minimize downtime, optimize equipment performance, and contribute to cost savings while ensuring the uninterrupted production of high-quality household products.
- IoT empowers manufacturers to tailor products to individual consumer preferences, offering a range of customization options and personalized experiences.
- IoT-driven sustainability initiatives focus on resource efficiency, waste reduction, eco-friendly product design, and compliance with environmental regulations, aligning manufacturing practices with eco-conscious consumer demands.

ABBREVIATIONS

IoT: Internet of Things
AI: Artificial Intelligence
GDPR: General Data Protection Regulation
AR: Augmented Reality
VR: Virtual Reality

REFERENCES

Abuhasel, K. A., & Khan, M. A. (2020). A secure industrial internet of things (IIoT) framework for resource management in smart manufacturing. *IEEE Access : Practical Innovations, Open Solutions*, *8*, 117354–117364. doi:10.1109/ACCESS.2020.3004711

Agrawal, A. V., Pitchai, R., Senthamaraikannan, C., Balaji, N. A., Sajithra, S., & Boopathi, S. (2023). Digital Education System During the COVID-19 Pandemic. In Using Assistive Technology for Inclusive Learning in K-12 Classrooms (pp. 104–126). IGI Global. doi:10.4018/978-1-6684-6424-3.ch005

Agrawal, A. V., Shashibhushan, G., Pradeep, S., Padhi, S. N., Sugumar, D., & Boopathi, S. (2024). Synergizing Artificial Intelligence, 5G, and Cloud Computing for Efficient Energy Conversion Using Agricultural Waste. In Practice, Progress, and Proficiency in Sustainability (pp. 475–497). IGI Global. doi:10.4018/979-8-3693-1186-8.ch026

Anitha, C., Komala, C., Vivekanand, C. V., Lalitha, S., & Boopathi, S. (2023). Artificial Intelligence driven security model for Internet of Medical Things (IoMT). *IEEE Explore*, 1–7.

Ayvaz, S., & Alpay, K. (2021). Predictive maintenance system for production lines in manufacturing: A machine learning approach using IoT data in real-time. *Expert Systems with Applications*, *173*, 114598. doi:10.1016/j.eswa.2021.114598

Babu, B. S., Kamalakannan, J., Meenatchi, N., Karthik, S., & Boopathi, S. (2022). Economic impacts and reliability evaluation of battery by adopting Electric Vehicle. *IEEE Explore*, 1–6.

Boopathi, S. (2022). Effects of Cryogenically-treated Stainless Steel on Eco-friendly Wire Electrical Discharge Machining Process. Springer.

Boopathi, S. (2021a). Improving of Green Sand-Mould Quality using Taguchi Technique. *Journal of Engineering Research*.

Boopathi, S. (2021b). *Pollution monitoring and notification: Water pollution monitoring and notification using intelligent RC boat*. Academic Press.

Boopathi, S. (2022a). An extensive review on sustainable developments of dry and near-dry electrical discharge machining processes. *ASME: Journal of Manufacturing Science and Engineering*, *144*(5), 050801–1.

Boopathi, S. (2022b). An investigation on gas emission concentration and relative emission rate of the near-dry wire-cut electrical discharge machining process. *Environmental Science and Pollution Research International*, *29*(57), 86237–86246. doi:10.1007/s11356-021-17658-1 PMID:34837614

Boopathi, S. (2022c). Cryogenically treated and untreated stainless steel grade 317 in sustainable wire electrical discharge machining process: A comparative study. *Environmental Science and Pollution Research*, 1–10.

Boopathi, S. (2022d). Performance Improvement of Eco-Friendly Near-Dry wire-Cut Electrical Discharge Machining Process Using Coconut Oil-Mist Dielectric Fluid. *Journal of Advanced Manufacturing Systems.*

Boopathi, S. (2023a). Deep Learning Techniques Applied for Automatic Sentence Generation. In Promoting Diversity, Equity, and Inclusion in Language Learning Environments (pp. 255–273). IGI Global. doi:10.4018/978-1-6684-3632-5.ch016

Boopathi, S. (2023b). Internet of Things-Integrated Remote Patient Monitoring System: Healthcare Application. In *Dynamics of Swarm Intelligence Health Analysis for the Next Generation* (pp. 137–161). IGI Global. doi:10.4018/978-1-6684-6894-4.ch008

Boopathi, S. (2023c). Securing Healthcare Systems Integrated With IoT: Fundamentals, Applications, and Future Trends. In Dynamics of Swarm Intelligence Health Analysis for the Next Generation (pp. 186–209). IGI Global.

Boopathi, S., & Davim, J. P. (2023a). Applications of Nanoparticles in Various Manufacturing Processes. In *Sustainable Utilization of Nanoparticles and Nanofluids in Engineering Applications* (pp. 1–31). IGI Global. doi:10.4018/978-1-6684-9135-5.ch001

Boopathi, S., & Davim, J. P. (2023b). *Sustainable Utilization of Nanoparticles and Nanofluids in Engineering Applications*. IGI Global. doi:10.4018/978-1-6684-9135-5

Boopathi, S., Gavaskar, T., Dogga, A. D., Mahendran, R. K., Kumar, A., Kathiresan, G., N., V., Ganesan, M., Ishwarya, K. R., & Ramana, G. V. (2021). *Emergency medicine delivery transportation using unmanned aerial vehicle (Patent Grant).* Academic Press.

Boopathi, S., & Kanike, U. K. (2023). Applications of Artificial Intelligent and Machine Learning Techniques in Image Processing. In *Handbook of Research on Thrust Technologies' Effect on Image Processing* (pp. 151–173). IGI Global. doi:10.4018/978-1-6684-8618-4.ch010

Boopathi, S., & Khare, R. (2023). Additive Manufacturing Developments in the Medical Engineering Field. In Development, Properties, and Industrial Applications of 3D Printed Polymer Composites (pp. 86–106). IGI Global.

Boopathi, S., Kumar, P. K. S., Meena, R. S., & Sudhakar, M. (2023). Sustainable Developments of Modern Soil-Less Agro-Cultivation Systems: Aquaponic Culture. In Human Agro-Energy Optimization for Business and Industry (pp. 69–87). IGI Global.

Boopathi, S., Lewise, K. A. S., Sarojwal, A., Arulvendhan, K., Sandeepkumar, S., & Subbiah, R. (2022). *An improved aqueous lithium-ion battery with IoT connectivity*. Academic Press.

Boopathi, S., Lewise, K. A. S., Subbiah, R., & Sivaraman, G. (2022). Near-dry wire-cut electrical discharge machining process using water–air-mist dielectric fluid: An experimental study. *Materials Today: Proceedings*, *50*(5), 1885–1890. doi:10.1016/j.matpr.2021.08.077

Boopathi, S., & Sivakumar, K. (2012). Experimental Analysis of Eco-friendly Near-dry Wire Electrical Discharge Machining Process. *Archives des Sciences*, *65*(10), 334–346.

Boopathi, S., & Sivakumar, K. (2014). Study of water assisted dry wire-cut electrical discharge machining. *Indian Journal of Engineering and Materials Sciences*, *21*, 75–82.

Boopathi, S., & Sivakumar, K. (2016). Optimal parameter prediction of oxygen-mist near-dry wire-cut EDM. *Inderscience: International Journal of Manufacturing Technology and Management*, *30*(3–4), 164–178. doi:10.1504/IJMTM.2016.077812

Boopathi, S., Thillaivanan, A., Mohammed, A. A., Shanmugam, P., & VR, P. (2022). Experimental investigation on Abrasive Water Jet Machining of Neem Wood Plastic Composite. *IOP: Functional Composites and Structures*, *4*, 025001.

Calabrese, M., Cimmino, M., Fiume, F., Manfrin, M., Romeo, L., Ceccacci, S., Paolanti, M., Toscano, G., Ciandrini, G., Carrotta, A., Mengoni, M., Frontoni, E., & Kapetis, D. (2020). SOPHIA: An event-based IoT and machine learning architecture for predictive maintenance in industry 4.0. *Information (Basel)*, *11*(4), 202. doi:10.3390/info11040202

Cheng, J. C., Chen, W., Chen, K., & Wang, Q. (2020). Data-driven predictive maintenance planning framework for MEP components based on BIM and IoT using machine learning algorithms. *Automation in Construction*, *112*, 103087. doi:10.1016/j.autcon.2020.103087

Compare, M., Baraldi, P., & Zio, E. (2019). Challenges to IoT-enabled predictive maintenance for industry 4.0. *IEEE Internet of Things Journal*, *7*(5), 4585–4597. doi:10.1109/JIOT.2019.2957029

Dass james, A., & Boopathi, S. (2016). Experimental Study of Eco-friendly Wire-Cut Electrical Discharge Machining Processes. *International Journal of Innovative Research in Science, Engineering and Technology, 5*.

Dhanya, D., Kumar, S. S., Thilagavathy, A., Prasad, D., & Boopathi, S. (2023). Data Analytics and Artificial Intelligence in the Circular Economy: Case Studies. In Intelligent Engineering Applications and Applied Sciences for Sustainability (pp. 40–58). IGI Global.

Domakonda, V. K., Farooq, S., Chinthamreddy, S., Puviarasi, R., Sudhakar, M., & Boopathi, S. (2022). Sustainable Developments of Hybrid Floating Solar Power Plants: Photovoltaic System. In Human Agro-Energy Optimization for Business and Industry (pp. 148–167). IGI Global.

Ghobakhloo, M. (2020). Determinants of information and digital technology implementation for smart manufacturing. *International Journal of Production Research, 58*(8), 2384–2405. doi:10.1080/00207543.2019.1630775

Gowri, N. V., Dwivedi, J. N., Krishnaveni, K., Boopathi, S., Palaniappan, M., & Medikondu, N. R. (2023). Experimental investigation and multi-objective optimization of eco-friendly near-dry electrical discharge machining of shape memory alloy using Cu/SiC/Gr composite electrode. *Environmental Science and Pollution Research International, 30*(49), 1–19. doi:10.1007/s11356-023-26983-6 PMID:37126160

Grabowska, S. (2020). Smart factories in the age of Industry 4.0. *Management Systems in Production Engineering, 2*(28), 90–96.

Gunasekaran, K., & Boopathi, S. (2023). Artificial Intelligence in Water Treatments and Water Resource Assessments. In *Artificial Intelligence Applications in Water Treatment and Water Resource Management* (pp. 71–98). IGI Global. doi:10.4018/978-1-6684-6791-6.ch004

Hanumanthakari, S., Gift, M. M., Kanimozhi, K., Bhavani, M. D., Bamane, K. D., & Boopathi, S. (2023). Biomining Method to Extract Metal Components Using Computer-Printed Circuit Board E-Waste. In *Handbook of Research on Safe Disposal Methods of Municipal Solid Wastes for a Sustainable Environment* (pp. 123–141). IGI Global. doi:10.4018/978-1-6684-8117-2.ch010

Harikaran, M., Boopathi, S., Gokulakannan, S., & Poonguzhali, M. (2023). Study on the Source of E-Waste Management and Disposal Methods. In *Sustainable Approaches and Strategies for E-Waste Management and Utilization* (pp. 39–60). IGI Global. doi:10.4018/978-1-6684-7573-7.ch003

Hema, N., Krishnamoorthy, N., Chavan, S. M., Kumar, N., Sabarimuthu, M., & Boopathi, S. (2023). A Study on an Internet of Things (IoT)-Enabled Smart Solar Grid System. In *Handbook of Research on Deep Learning Techniques for Cloud-Based Industrial IoT* (pp. 290–308). IGI Global. doi:10.4018/978-1-6684-8098-4.ch017

Ingle, R. B., Senthil, T. S., Swathi, S., Muralidharan, N., Mahendran, G., & Boopathi, S. (2023). Sustainability and Optimization of Green and Lean Manufacturing Processes Using Machine Learning Techniques. IGI Global. doi:10.4018/978-1-6684-8238-4.ch012

Janardhana, K., Singh, V., Singh, S. N., Babu, T. R., Bano, S., & Boopathi, S. (2023). Utilization Process for Electronic Waste in Eco-Friendly Concrete: Experimental Study. In Sustainable Approaches and Strategies for E-Waste Management and Utilization (pp. 204–223). IGI Global.

Jeevanantham, Y. A., Saravanan, A., Vanitha, V., Boopathi, S., & Kumar, D. P. (2022). Implementation of Internet-of Things (IoT) in Soil Irrigation System. *IEEE Explore*, 1–5.

Karthik, S., Hemalatha, R., Aruna, R., Deivakani, M., Reddy, R. V. K., & Boopathi, S. (2023). Study on Healthcare Security System-Integrated Internet of Things (IoT). In Perspectives and Considerations on the Evolution of Smart Systems (pp. 342–362). IGI Global.

Koshariya, A. K., Kalaiyarasi, D., Jovith, A. A., Sivakami, T., Hasan, D. S., & Boopathi, S. (2023). AI-Enabled IoT and WSN-Integrated Smart Agriculture System. In *Artificial Intelligence Tools and Technologies for Smart Farming and Agriculture Practices* (pp. 200–218). IGI Global. doi:10.4018/978-1-6684-8516-3.ch011

Koshariya, A. K., Khatoon, S., Marathe, A. M., Suba, G. M., Baral, D., & Boopathi, S. (2023). Agricultural Waste Management Systems Using Artificial Intelligence Techniques. In *AI-Enabled Social Robotics in Human Care Services* (pp. 236–258). IGI Global. doi:10.4018/978-1-6684-8171-4.ch009

Kumar, P., Sampath, B., Kumar, S., Babu, B. H., & Ahalya, N. (2023). Hydroponics, Aeroponics, and Aquaponics Technologies in Modern Agricultural Cultivation. In Trends, Paradigms, and Advances in Mechatronics Engineering (pp. 223–241). IGI Global.

Kumara, V., Mohanaprakash, T., Fairooz, S., Jamal, K., Babu, T., & Sampath, B. (2023). Experimental Study on a Reliable Smart Hydroponics System. In *Human Agro-Energy Optimization for Business and Industry* (pp. 27–45). IGI Global. doi:10.4018/978-1-6684-4118-3.ch002

Kusiak, A. (2019). Fundamentals of smart manufacturing: A multi-thread perspective. *Annual Reviews in Control*, *47*, 214–220. doi:10.1016/j.arcontrol.2019.02.001

Leng, J., Wang, D., Shen, W., Li, X., Liu, Q., & Chen, X. (2021). Digital twins-based smart manufacturing system design in Industry 4.0: A review. *Journal of Manufacturing Systems, 60*, 119–137. doi:10.1016/j.jmsy.2021.05.011

Liu, Y., Yu, W., Dillon, T., Rahayu, W., & Li, M. (2021). Empowering IoT predictive maintenance solutions with AI: A distributed system for manufacturing plant-wide monitoring. *IEEE Transactions on Industrial Informatics, 18*(2), 1345–1354. doi:10.1109/TII.2021.3091774

Lu, Y., Xu, X., & Wang, L. (2020). Smart manufacturing process and system automation–a critical review of the standards and envisioned scenarios. *Journal of Manufacturing Systems, 56*, 312–325. doi:10.1016/j.jmsy.2020.06.010

Maguluri, L. P., Ananth, J., Hariram, S., Geetha, C., Bhaskar, A., & Boopathi, S. (2023). Smart Vehicle-Emissions Monitoring System Using Internet of Things (IoT). In Handbook of Research on Safe Disposal Methods of Municipal Solid Wastes for a Sustainable Environment (pp. 191–211). IGI Global.

Maheswari, B. U., Imambi, S. S., Hasan, D., Meenakshi, S., Pratheep, V., & Boopathi, S. (2023). Internet of Things and Machine Learning-Integrated Smart Robotics. In Global Perspectives on Robotics and Autonomous Systems: Development and Applications (pp. 240–258). IGI Global. doi:10.4018/978-1-6684-7791-5.ch010

Mohanty, A., Jothi, B., Jeyasudha, J., Ranjit, P., Isaac, J. S., & Boopathi, S. (2023). Additive Manufacturing Using Robotic Programming. In *AI-Enabled Social Robotics in Human Care Services* (pp. 259–282). IGI Global. doi:10.4018/978-1-6684-8171-4.ch010

Mourtzis, D., Angelopoulos, J., & Panopoulos, N. (2021). Smart manufacturing and tactile internet based on 5G in industry 4.0: Challenges, applications and new trends. *Electronics (Basel), 10*(24), 3175. doi:10.3390/electronics10243175

Nishanth, J., Deshmukh, M. A., Kushwah, R., Kushwaha, K. K., Balaji, S., & Sampath, B. (2023). Particle Swarm Optimization of Hybrid Renewable Energy Systems. In *Intelligent Engineering Applications and Applied Sciences for Sustainability* (pp. 291–308). IGI Global. doi:10.4018/979-8-3693-0044-2.ch016

Palaniappan, M., Tirlangi, S., Mohamed, M. J. S., Moorthy, R. S., Valeti, S. V., & Boopathi, S. (2023). Fused Deposition Modelling of Polylactic Acid (PLA)-Based Polymer Composites: A Case Study. In Development, Properties, and Industrial Applications of 3D Printed Polymer Composites (pp. 66–85). IGI Global.

Phuyal, S., Bista, D., & Bista, R. (2020). Challenges, opportunities and future directions of smart manufacturing: A state of art review. *Sustainable Futures : An Applied Journal of Technology, Environment and Society*, *2*, 100023. doi:10.1016/j.sftr.2020.100023

Qu, Y., Ming, X., Liu, Z., Zhang, X., & Hou, Z. (2019). Smart manufacturing systems: State of the art and future trends. *International Journal of Advanced Manufacturing Technology*, *103*(9-12), 3751–3768. doi:10.1007/s00170-019-03754-7

Ramudu, K., Mohan, V. M., Jyothirmai, D., Prasad, D., Agrawal, R., & Boopathi, S. (2023). Machine Learning and Artificial Intelligence in Disease Prediction: Applications, Challenges, Limitations, Case Studies, and Future Directions. In Contemporary Applications of Data Fusion for Advanced Healthcare Informatics (pp. 297–318). IGI Global.

Reddy, M. A., Reddy, B. M., Mukund, C., Venneti, K., Preethi, D., & Boopathi, S. (2023). Social Health Protection During the COVID-Pandemic Using IoT. In *The COVID-19 Pandemic and the Digitalization of Diplomacy* (pp. 204–235). IGI Global. doi:10.4018/978-1-7998-8394-4.ch009

Samikannu, R., Koshariya, A. K., Poornima, E., Ramesh, S., Kumar, A., & Boopathi, S. (2022). Sustainable Development in Modern Aquaponics Cultivation Systems Using IoT Technologies. In *Human Agro-Energy Optimization for Business and Industry* (pp. 105–127). IGI Global.

Sampath, B. (2021). *Sustainable Eco-Friendly Wire-Cut Electrical Discharge Machining: Gas Emission Analysis*. Academic Press.

Sampath, B., Pandian, M., Deepa, D., & Subbiah, R. (2022). Operating parameters prediction of liquefied petroleum gas refrigerator using simulated annealing algorithm. *AIP Conference Proceedings*, *2460*(1), 070003. doi:10.1063/5.0095601

Sampath, B., Sureshkumar, T., Yuvaraj, M., & Velmurugan, D. (2021). Experimental Investigations on Eco-Friendly Helium-Mist Near-Dry Wire-Cut EDM of M2-HSS Material. *Materials Research Proceedings*, *19*, 175–180.

Sankar, K. M., Booba, B., & Boopathi, S. (2023). Smart Agriculture Irrigation Monitoring System Using Internet of Things. In *Contemporary Developments in Agricultural Cyber-Physical Systems* (pp. 105–121). IGI Global. doi:10.4018/978-1-6684-7879-0.ch006

Saqlain, M., Piao, M., Shim, Y., & Lee, J. Y. (2019). Framework of an IoT-based industrial data management for smart manufacturing. *Journal of Sensor and Actuator Networks*, *8*(2), 25. doi:10.3390/jsan8020025

Saravanan, M., Vasanth, M., Boopathi, S., Sureshkumar, M., & Haribalaji, V. (2022). Optimization of Quench Polish Quench (QPQ) Coating Process Using Taguchi Method. *Key Engineering Materials, 935*, 83–91. doi:10.4028/p-z569vy

Satav, S. D., & Lamani, D. (2024). Energy and Battery Management in the Era of Cloud Computing. In Practice, Progress, and Proficiency in Sustainability (pp. 141–166). IGI Global. doi:10.4018/979-8-3693-1186-8.ch009

Selvakumar, S., Adithe, S., Isaac, J. S., Pradhan, R., Venkatesh, V., & Sampath, B. (2023). A Study of the Printed Circuit Board (PCB) E-Waste Recycling Process. In Sustainable Approaches and Strategies for E-Waste Management and Utilization (pp. 159–184). IGI Global.

Selvakumar, S., Shankar, R., Ranjit, P., Bhattacharya, S., Gupta, A. S. G., & Boopathi, S. (2023). E-Waste Recovery and Utilization Processes for Mobile Phone Waste. In *Handbook of Research on Safe Disposal Methods of Municipal Solid Wastes for a Sustainable Environment* (pp. 222–240). IGI Global. doi:10.4018/978-1-6684-8117-2.ch016

Senthil, T., Puviyarasan, M., Babu, S. R., Surakasi, R., Sampath, B., & Associates. (2023). Industrial Robot-Integrated Fused Deposition Modelling for the 3D Printing Process. In Development, Properties, and Industrial Applications of 3D Printed Polymer Composites (pp. 188–210). IGI Global.

Shamayleh, A., Awad, M., & Farhat, J. (2020). IoT based predictive maintenance management of medical equipment. *Journal of Medical Systems, 44*(4), 1–12. doi:10.1007/s10916-020-1534-8 PMID:32078712

Srinivas, B., Maguluri, L. P., Naidu, K. V., Reddy, L. C. S., Deivakani, M., & Boopathi, S. (2023). Architecture and Framework for Interfacing Cloud-Enabled Robots. In *Handbook of Research on Data Science and Cybersecurity Innovations in Industry 4.0 Technologies* (pp. 542–560). IGI Global. doi:10.4018/978-1-6684-8145-5.ch027

Syamala, M., Komala, C., Pramila, P., Dash, S., Meenakshi, S., & Boopathi, S. (2023). Machine Learning-Integrated IoT-Based Smart Home Energy Management System. In *Handbook of Research on Deep Learning Techniques for Cloud-Based Industrial IoT* (pp. 219–235). IGI Global. doi:10.4018/978-1-6684-8098-4.ch013

Teoh, Y. K., Gill, S. S., & Parlikad, A. K. (2021). IoT and fog computing based predictive maintenance model for effective asset management in industry 4.0 using machine learning. *IEEE Internet of Things Journal.*

Vanitha, S., Radhika, K., & Boopathi, S. (2023). Artificial Intelligence Techniques in Water Purification and Utilization. In *Human Agro-Energy Optimization for Business and Industry* (pp. 202–218). IGI Global. doi:10.4018/978-1-6684-4118-3.ch010

Veeranjaneyulu, R., Boopathi, S., Kumari, R. K., Vidyarthi, A., Isaac, J. S., & Jaiganesh, V. (2023). Air Quality Improvement and Optimisation Using Machine Learning Technique. *IEEE Explore*, 1–6.

Veeranjaneyulu, R., Boopathi, S., Narasimharao, J., Gupta, K. K., Reddy, R. V. K., & Ambika, R. (2023). Identification of Heart Diseases using Novel Machine Learning Method. *IEEE Explore*, 1–6.

Venkateswaran, N., Kumar, S. S., Diwakar, G., Gnanasangeetha, D., & Boopathi, S. (2023). Synthetic Biology for Waste Water to Energy Conversion: IoT and AI Approaches. In M. Arshad (Ed.), Advances in Bioinformatics and Biomedical Engineering (pp. 360–384). IGI Global. doi:10.4018/978-1-6684-6577-6.ch017

Venkateswaran, N., Vidhya, K., Ayyannan, M., Chavan, S. M., Sekar, K., & Boopathi, S. (2023). A Study on Smart Energy Management Framework Using Cloud Computing. In 5G, Artificial Intelligence, and Next Generation Internet of Things: Digital Innovation for Green and Sustainable Economies (pp. 189–212). IGI Global. doi:10.4018/978-1-6684-8634-4.ch009

Venkateswaran, N., Vidhya, R., Naik, D. A., Raj, T. M., Munjal, N., & Boopathi, S. (2023). Study on Sentence and Question Formation Using Deep Learning Techniques. In *Digital Natives as a Disruptive Force in Asian Businesses and Societies* (pp. 252–273). IGI Global. doi:10.4018/978-1-6684-6782-4.ch015

Vennila, T., Karuna, M., Srivastava, B. K., Venugopal, J., Surakasi, R., & Sampath, B. (2022). New Strategies in Treatment and Enzymatic Processes: Ethanol Production From Sugarcane Bagasse. In Human Agro-Energy Optimization for Business and Industry (pp. 219–240). IGI Global.

Wang, B., Tao, F., Fang, X., Liu, C., Liu, Y., & Freiheit, T. (2021). Smart manufacturing and intelligent manufacturing: A comparative review. *Engineering (Beijing)*, *7*(6), 738–757. doi:10.1016/j.eng.2020.07.017

Yang, H., Kumara, S., Bukkapatnam, S. T., & Tsung, F. (2019). The internet of things for smart manufacturing: A review. *IISE Transactions*, *51*(11), 1190–1216. doi:10.1080/24725854.2018.1555383

Zekrifa, D. M. S., Kulkarni, M., Bhagyalakshmi, A., Devireddy, N., Gupta, S., & Boopathi, S. (2023). Integrating Machine Learning and AI for Improved Hydrological Modeling and Water Resource Management. In *Artificial Intelligence Applications in Water Treatment and Water Resource Management* (pp. 46–70). IGI Global. doi:10.4018/978-1-6684-6791-6.ch003

Zhang, Y., Xu, X., Liu, A., Lu, Q., Xu, L., & Tao, F. (2019). Blockchain-based trust mechanism for IoT-based smart manufacturing system. *IEEE Transactions on Computational Social Systems*, *6*(6), 1386–1394. doi:10.1109/TCSS.2019.2918467

Zonta, T., Da Costa, C. A., da Rosa Righi, R., de Lima, M. J., da Trindade, E. S., & Li, G. P. (2020). Predictive maintenance in the Industry 4.0: A systematic literature review. *Computers & Industrial Engineering*, *150*, 106889. doi:10.1016/j.cie.2020.106889

Chapter 15
Visual Speech Recognition by Lip Reading Using Deep Learning

V. Prakash
SASTRA University, India

R. Bhavani
SASTRA University, India

Durga Karthik
https://orcid.org/0000-0003-3199-8814
SASTRA University, India

D. Rajalakshmi
SASTRA University, India

N. Rajeswari
SASTRA University, India

M. Martinaa
SASTRA University, India

ABSTRACT

By using image processing techniques, visual voice recognition (VSR) is able to extract voice or textual data from facial features. Similar to speech recognition systems, lip reading (LR) systems encounter issues because of variations in facial characteristics, speaking rates, skin tones, and pronunciations. An audio speech recognition system can be synchronised with the LR systems. The lip movement data, also known as lip characteristics or visemes, were obtained from the input video clip that was saved in the cloud. It takes each frame's lip features and stores them. Furthermore, training using a varied number of frames prevents a training dataset from yielding suitable text matches. Two parts make up the system: a feature extraction approach that turns lip characteristics into a visual feature cube and a Conv3D algorithm that matches words to their associated visemes. Precision is found in around 89% of the words. As a result, the 3D-CNN for the MIRACL-VC1 dataset performs better and offers increased classification accuracy when compared to the prior system.

DOI: 10.4018/979-8-3693-1694-8.ch015

INTRODUCTION

The goal of visual speech recognition is to translate lip motions into legible text. Numerous techniques have been developed for automatic speech recognition systems that identify words based on auditory characteristics. Recent advances in society have been greatly influenced by machine learning techniques, which have accelerated the advancement of artificial intelligence and provided solutions to a wide range of real-world issues. One of the key elements of virtual reality (VR) and human–computer interaction (HCI) technology is automatic lip-reading (Thanda & Venkatesan, 2016).

It is necessary for human verbal communication as well as visual perception (Wang et al., 2016). Visual signals can enhance speech recognition in noisy environments and virtual reality settings. They can also reduce redundant data, raise the multipurpose input size of immersive communication, shorten the time and effort needed for humans to acquire lip motion and lip words, and enhance automatic recognition of speech.

It makes the virtual reality experience more lifelike. Meanwhile, assisted driving systems, virtual reality, security of information, and voice recognition may all make extensive use of automatic lip-reading technologies. Numerous academic disciplines, including recognising patterns, artificial intelligence, natural language comprehension, and image processing, are involved in the study of automatic lip reading. The study's contents include the most recent advancements in a number of academic fields. Still, research on lip mobility.

Because of deep learning, computer vision (picture depiction, human behaviour recognition, objective identification, and media recognition) has significantly progressed in the modern era. As a result, research will inevitably shift the subject of automatic speaking technology from the end-to-end deep learning framework to the conventional manual feature extraction categorization approach. Academics have lately used convolutional neural networks (CNNs) to focus on certain regions of interest using attention processes. This has tremendously aided target identification and image classification. A sequence of successive frames can be used to depict visual content, as lip movement is an ongoing process that conveys temporal information (Petajan, Bischoff, Bodoff, & Brooke, 1988).

The goal of the novel paradigm known as "osmotic computing" is to make it easier for Internet of Things (IoT) services and applications to function efficiently at the network edge. Due to lower server latency, cloud and edge computing are used in most smart city applications. Cloud computing leverages centralised computer capacity to provide significant advantages. The processing power offered by cloud computing is enormous, but the access latencies are longer. When deep learning applications focus on edge or cloud computing, they become less scalable because they are unable to manage one of these constraints (Villari et al., 2016).

Due to the availability of different and huge datasets, deep learning technology, which has been effectively applied in computer vision and language modelling in the past, is now finding application in new disciplines. To reach this objective, numerous paradigms, like Osmotic Computing, have been developed, which encourage the dispersion of data analysis workloads between Cloud and Edge computing platforms (Morshed et al., 2017). However, conventional paradigms are unable to provide an accurate depiction of how technologies such as deep learning might be coordinated to take full use of the cloud, edge, and mobile edge settings.

SECTION II

Existing Work

A computer capable of lipreading would have been considered inconceivable just a few decades ago. But in recent years, machine learning has grown at an exponential rate, to the point that a machine can now comprehend human speech only by looking at images. Several studies suggest that lip reading alone, or visual data comprehension, accounts for a relatively small portion of the English language (Mudaliar et al., 2020). Word-level classification has been achieved with this visual voice recognition method by utilising the deep learning idea. 3D convolution layers are utilised as the encoder, and Gated Recurrent Units (GRU) are employed as the decoder in the ResNet architecture. This method used the entire video sequence as an input. The suggested method produces good outcomes. With the BBC data set, it achieves 90% accuracy, and with the bespoke video data set, 88% accuracy. The suggested method is just word-level and is readily expandable to encompass brief phrases or sentences.

This work aims to develop the first transceiver (PHY layer) prototype for cloud-based audio-visual (AV) speech enhancement (SE) and to satisfy the high data rate and low latency requirements of future multimodal hearing assistive technology. Several challenging criteria, including up/downlink communications, transmission delay and signal processing, and real-time AV SE model processing, must be met by the innovative design. The transceiver's features include frame detection, device detection, channel estimation, and frequency offset estimation (Bishnu, 2022). It creates both uplink frame structures (hearing aid to the cloud) and downlink frame structures (cloud to hearing aid) based on the necessary data rate and delay. Due of the changeable nature of uplink information (audio and lipreading), the uplink channel allows numerous data rate frame structures. In contrast, the downstream channel has a fixed data rate frame structure. One drawback of this study is that software-defined radio (such as Universal Software Radio Peripheral) can be used to apply it to real-time demonstration settings.

The Multi-head Visual-audio Memory (MVM) is proposed as a solution to the two lip reading challenges. First, by modelling the relationships between paired audio-visual representations, MVM learns to remember audio representations through training on audio-visual datasets (Kim et al., n.d.). By analysing the acquired inter-relationships, visual input alone at the inference stage is able to retrieve the saved audio representation from memory. Furthermore, multi-head key memories are used in MVM to store visual features, and one value memory is used to store audio knowledge that is intended to differentiate homophones. MVM is used at multiple temporal levels to distinguish homophenes and take the context into account when retrieving memory.

SECTION III

Proposed Work

Similar to speech recognition systems, lip reading (LR) systems encounter issues because of variations in facial characteristics, speaking rates, skin tones, and pronunciations. A lipreading system used on its own could not be particularly effective. This efficiency is limited by a number of criteria, including skin tone, accents, and utterance duration. By combining the benefits of both models, the LR systems and an ASR system may be synchronised to increase the classification certainty. Rather than including all possible sentences, some systems limit the datasets to a limited selection of specific phrases and words in order to simplify this difficulty.

There are two types of speech recognition systems: speaker-independent and speaker-independent. Speaker-independent systems (SIs) find uses in voice-controlled apps and word extraction since they can generalise through training on data from many speakers. In this work, a speaker-independent system was trained using lip movement data, sometimes referred to as lip properties or visemes, that was obtained from a source video clip that was saved in the cloud.

The proposed technique concatenates a predefined quantity of frames to identify an order of the visemes straight to words instead of phonetics. There are two parts to it: a feature extraction method that creates a visual feature cube from lip characteristics, and a convolutional neural network that matches words to their associated visemes after being trained on a large dataset. Furthermore, training with a varied number of frames prevents a training dataset from yielding exact text matches.

Figure 1. High level architecture of the proposed work

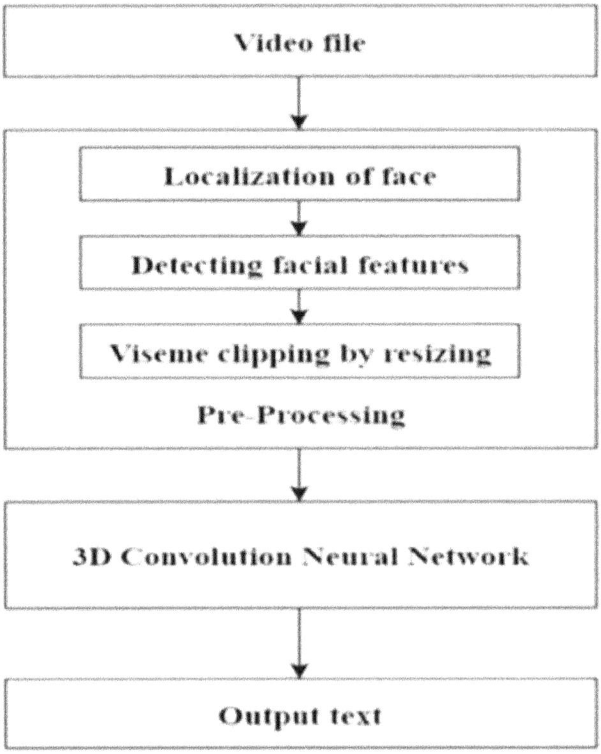

The proposed system's high-level architecture is depicted in Figure 1. Initially, the lip area is taken out of the cloud video. A 3D CNN with the ability to classify visemes to their corresponding text is further equipped with the features. The CNN unit and the pre-processing unit are two distinct modules that contain two different processes. Before the input video clip is sent to CNN for text categorization of the visemes, lip features are extracted from the face features.

The six modules that make up the suggested system depicted in Figure 2 have the primary goal of utilising 3D-CNN to create a visual speech recognition model. These are the stages involved in creating a speaker-independent system. The following are the modules.

Module 1: Make Videos

Create a video sequence for every word by combining all of the coloured images from the cloud.

Module 2: Extract Features

68 facial landmarks are used to track the facial region and identify the important features. The system uses the shape predictor and frontal face detector modules from the dlib package to do this.

Module 3: Detect Viseme Region

The sizes of the face photos could vary. To help CNN process the faces it finds more efficiently, the faces are scaled and clipped to the same size (30x48). To do this, locate the border lines of the lip section and crop the needed area of the image.

Module 4: Training Model

The 8 neurons, 16 neurons, and 32 neurons in the 3D CNN layers learn from the pattern of each word, or the sequence of visemes. A three-tiered structure is employed to acquire progressively more complex characteristics, such the patterns and motions of lips, and more basic aspects, like the viseme's boundaries and lines..

Module 5: Testing Model

Test data, comprising 15% of the total, is used in this module to evaluate the CNN model.

Module 6: Result Analysis

The model in this module will assess the system's accuracy along with metrics such as precision, recall, F-measure metrics, and confusion matrix.

Convolutional Neural Networks (CNN)

CNN is a neural network that learns from input data by using feed-forwarding techniques. To enable the model to behave in accordance with the training data, a set of weights or filter values was defined as part of the learning process. There will be a difference between the initial output that the system provided and the output

Figure 2. The proposed modules

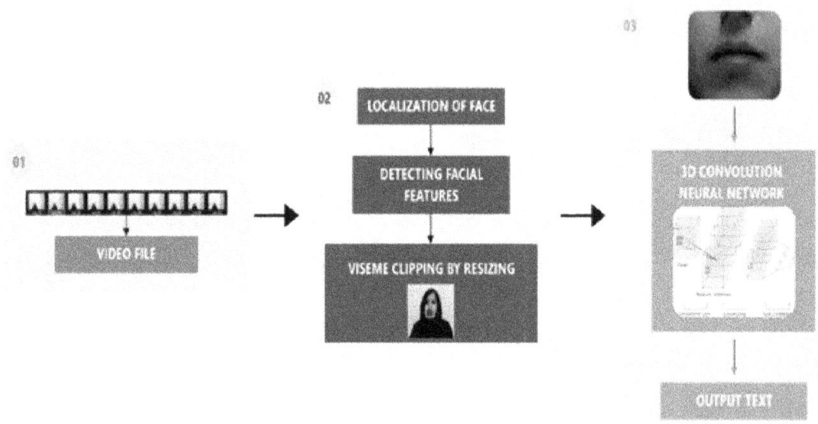

that CNN produced. Additionally, the variation in weights will be backpropagated through the CNN layers to modify the neuronal weights, thereby lowering error and enabling the production of output that is comparable to the intended one.

CNN is quite good at identifying hierarchical and spatial information in images. It employs filters that translate specific areas of an input image with a given window size into an output. Subsequently, it advances the window to a preset distance to encompass the complete image in other regions. Thus, in a sequence of succeeding layers, each convolution filter layer hierarchically records the attributes of the input image, first capturing details like lines and subsequently shapes and entire objects. When feeding images from a dataset and categorising them into different classes, CNN can be a good fit.

The most popular use case for convolutional neural networks is image processing. Figure 3 displays the CNN architecture that was utilised. A series of visemes with dimensions of 15x30x48x1 are fed into the model. Three Conv3D layers—each with eight, sixteen, and thirty-two neurons—process the input (Torfi, Iranmanesh, Nasrabadi, & Dawson, 2017). Both lower-level information, like the borders and lines of the viseme, and progressively higher-level information, like lip movements and their logical patterns, are learned using a three-layer framework. The layers that come after each of these are activation and batch normalisation. The traits from the layers as mentioned above are obtained by a max-pooling layer, which uses the information to sample down and vectorize the features using the flatten layer.

After activation layers and batch normalisation, the 32 neurons in a fully linked layer using L2 regularisation receive the learnt characteristics as input. The SoftMax

Figure 3. Architecture of CNN used

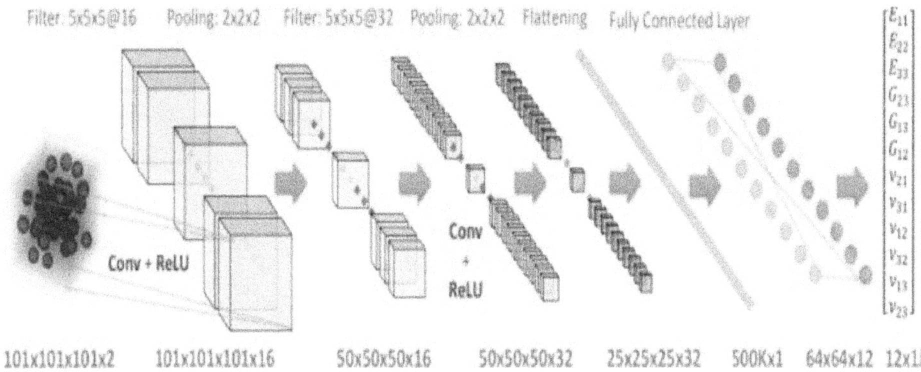

method, consisting of 10 neurons equal to the quantity of output classes, receives the characteristics after that (Torfi, Iranmanesh, Nasrabadi, & Dawson, 2017).

DLIB

The position of 68 coordinates (x, y) that indicate the facial points on a person's face is found using pre-trained models and the facial detector of a landmark.The face detector makes use of a sliding window detection approach, an image pyramid, a linear classifier, and the well-known Histogram of Oriented Gradients (HOG) feature. The landmark points, ranging from 48 to 68, are considered to represent the lip part. Therefore, while cropping, certain landmarks are taken into account as edge points.

Methodology applied:

While the second module makes use of CNN and the cloud-stored MIRACLVC1 dataset, the DLIB module functions are used to do the viseme extraction utilising a pre-trained dataset.

Shape Predictor:

Dlib matches visemes using a trained dataset known as shape estimator 68 landmarks of the face, or MIRACL-VC1. It provides a method for lining up facial characteristics. The interface is provided by the dlib package's detector and predictor classes. The face detector is made using a sliding window detection method, a picture structure, a classifier based on linearity, and the traditional Histogram of Oriented Gradients (HOG) feature (Alothmany, Boston, Li, Shaiman, & Durrant, 2010). It is considered that the lip part is roughly represented by the landmark points in Figure 4 from 48 to 68. Therefore, while cropping, certain landmarks are taken into account as edge points.

Figure 4. 68-point facial feature image

MIRACL-VC1

A lipreading database called MIRACL-VC1 has features for both colour and depth images. It makes a number of research fields easier, including biometrics, facial identification, and speech recognition. As indicated in Table 1, sited in front of a Microsoft Kinect sensor, fifteen speakers—ten women and five men—repeat a series of ten phrases and ten sentences ten times.

Every sample in the collection is a synced 640x480 colour picture with depth. Figure 5 displays the sample colour and depth pictures. Three thousand instances total—15 × 10 x 10 = 1500 photographs—colour and depth photos separately—are included in the dataset. The method exclusively makes use of coloured text images.

Pre-Processing

Every frame has to have its visemes removed. The video is initially divided into separate frames for this. Videos need to be equalised in order to have the same frame rate (30 frames per second), as frame rates vary amongst them (Sengupta, 2008). The face tracking module receives the processed frames.

Figure 5. Sample colour image and depth image frame

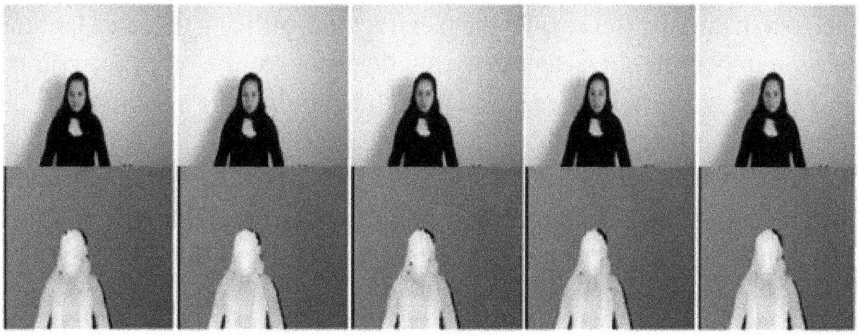

Table 1. Terms and expressions included in the Miracl-Vc1 dataset

ID	Word	ID	Phrase
01	Begin	01	Stop navigation
02	Choose	02	Excuse me
03	Connection	03	I am sorry
04	Navigation	04	Thank you
05	Next	05	Good bye
06	Previous	06	I love this game
07	Start	07	Nice to meet you
08	Stop	08	You are welcome
09	Hello	09	How are you
10	Web	10	Have a good time

Face Tracking

Facial tracking is used to gather information about still images as well as video sequences by automatically recognising aspects of the face. There are specific facial landmarks that have been mapped, like 48 and 68 face landmarks. There are two steps involved: Face localization and important facial structure detection (Hour et al., 2020).

The system initially tracks only the facial region, utilising 68 facial landmarks to identify the important characteristics, as it does not require all of the points in the frame. To do this, the system makes use of the dlib package's frontal face detector and form predictor components.

1) **Face localization is accomplished using a pre-trained Histogram of Oriented Gradients (HOG).** Deep learning-based methods or the Linear SVM Object Detector can be used to locate the face. Using these techniques, the goal is to get the face's (x, y) coordinates (formed as a bounding box) (Sengupta, 2008).
2) **Identification of Important Facial Structures:** The right and left eyebrows, eyes, mouth, jaw, nose and right and left eyes are just a few of the face regions that several facial characteristic detectors on the market aim to locate and identify precisely. The One Millisecond Face Alignment using an Ensemble of Regression trees face detector developed by Kazemi and Sullivan is used by the dlib package. The following describes how the process works:

Figure 6. Lip region bordered input

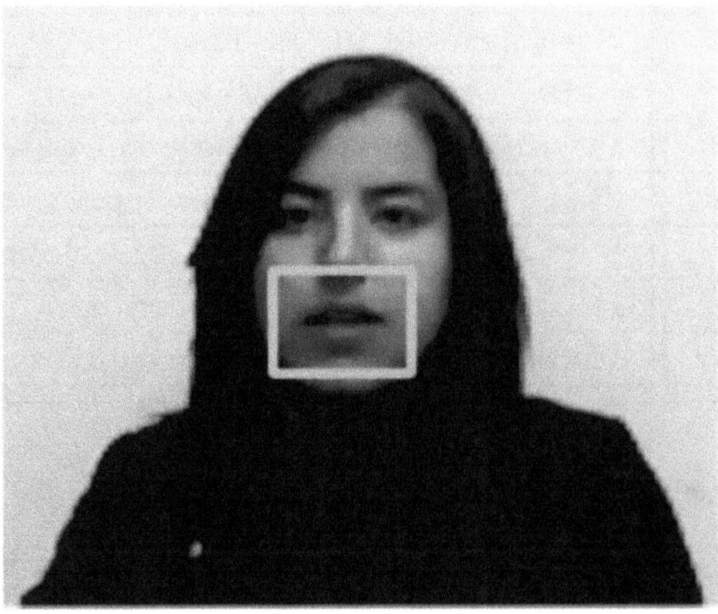

1) To extract features, the picture is expected into a normalised synchronize system. Until convergence, this method is repeated (Saeed & Dugelay, 2010).
2) Past probabilities based on the separation of input pixel pairs, which improve the algorithm's performance across a wide range of pertinent information.

The approach uses the training data to create an ensemble of regression trees to predict the positions of face landmarks by determining the pixel intensities that correlate with the landmarks (Alothmany, Boston, Li, Shaiman, & Durrant, 2010). When used with OpenCV, In Figure 6, the lip viseme zone that borders the input video is the sign that this module can provide to collect the necessary points.

Resizing

The tracked facial photographs can be taken from any viewpoint. As they spoke, the speaker could have glanced elsewhere or straight into the camera. This makes it more difficult to distinguish certain facial features because they may be hidden. This may limit the speakers' range of view, or they may need them to crop and adjust the image size so that only the lip area is visible. The sizes of the face photos could vary. To facilitate CNN's effective processing of the detected faces, the faces are cropped and scaled to the same size (30x48) (Almajai, Cox, Harvey, & Lan, 2016). To achieve this, locate the edge points of the lip region and crop the relevant area of the picture. Figure 7 displays the resized photos.

The images will be scaled before being fed into the 3D-CNN model and cycled through each layer. Once the viseme sequence has been identified, multiple metrics

Figure 7. Resized lip photos

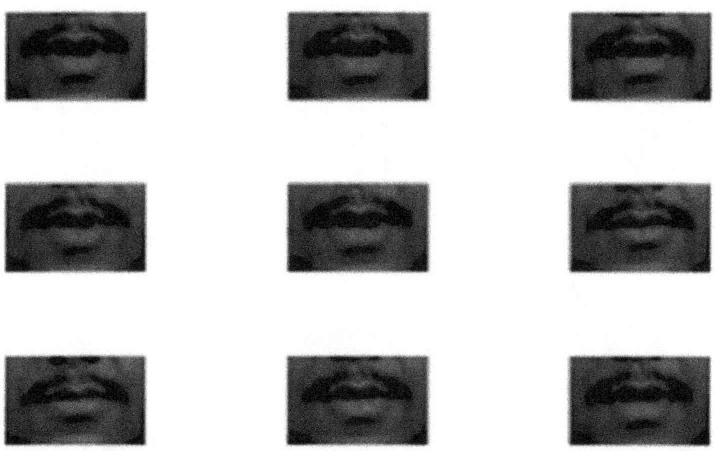

including accuracy, precision, recall, and F-measure score will be used to compare the outcome.

3D CNN Layer

Many architecture configurations were tested, including time-distributed convolution layers, max pooling, flattening, dropout, density, and other features utilised in different combinations. Neural Network layers were arranged in series (Borde et al., 2015). A detailed list of the top performers is provided. To see which layers and parameters were utilised to build them, refer to model 1 in Figure 9 listings. The accompanying architecture, Figure 8, displays a high-level view of the layers utilised to construct the models.

The most popular use case for convolutional neural networks is image processing. Figure 8 displays the CNN architecture that was utilised. A series of visemes with dimensions of 15x30x48x1 are fed into the model. The input is processed by three Conv3D layers, each with 8, 16, and 32 neurons. Three Conv3D layers—each having eight, sixteen, and thirty- two neurons—process the input. This three-layer building aids in the progressive learning of low-level aspects like the viseme's boundaries and lines as well as upper-level details like lip motions and their logical patterns (Almajai, Cox, Harvey, & Lan, 2016). Following each of these stages are the activation and batch normalisation layers.

A max-pooling layer samples down the properties that are learnt from these layers, and a flatten layer vectorizes the results (Sengupta, 2008). After batch

Figure 8. 3D CNN architecture

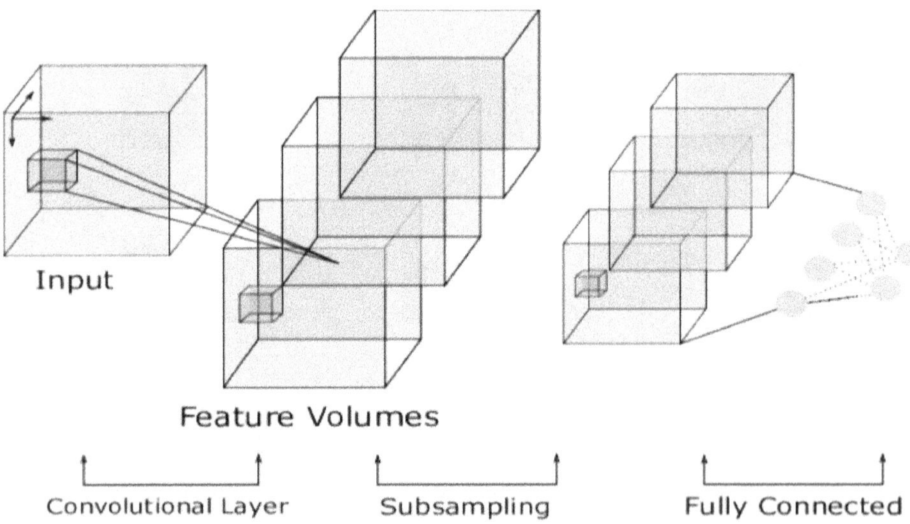

Figure 9. 3D CNN layer

```
---3D CNN for Visual Speech Recognition---
Model: "sequential"
_________________________________________________________________
Layer (type)                 Output Shape              Param #
=================================================================
conv1 (Conv3D)               (None, 13, 28, 46, 8)     224
_________________________________________________________________
batch_normalization (BatchNo (None, 13, 28, 46, 8)     32
_________________________________________________________________
activation (Activation)      (None, 13, 28, 46, 8)     0
_________________________________________________________________
conv2 (Conv3D)               (None, 11, 26, 44, 16)    3472
_________________________________________________________________
batch_normalization_1 (Batch (None, 11, 26, 44, 16)    64
_________________________________________________________________
activation_1 (Activation)    (None, 11, 26, 44, 16)    0
_________________________________________________________________
conv3 (Conv3D)               (None, 9, 24, 42, 32)     13856
_________________________________________________________________
batch_normalization_2 (Batch (None, 9, 24, 42, 32)     128
_________________________________________________________________
activation_2 (Activation)    (None, 9, 24, 42, 32)     0
_________________________________________________________________
pool1 (MaxPooling3D)         (None, 9, 11, 20, 32)     0
_________________________________________________________________
flatten (Flatten)            (None, 63360)             0
_________________________________________________________________
fc1 (Dense)                  (None, 32)                2027552
_________________________________________________________________
batch_normalization_3 (Batch (None, 32)                128
_________________________________________________________________
activation_3 (Activation)    (None, 32)                0
_________________________________________________________________
dropout (Dropout)            (None, 32)                0
_________________________________________________________________
fc2 (Dense)                  (None, 10)                330
_________________________________________________________________
softmax (Activation)         (None, 10)                0
=================================================================
Total params: 2,045,786
Trainable params: 2,045,610
Non-trainable params: 176
_________________________________________________________________
None
```

normalisation and activation layers, the learnt parameters are fed into a fully linked layer of thirty- two neurons using L2 regularisation. The features are then sent to the SoftMax classifier method, which consists of ten neurons equal to the number of output classes. The ratio of the parameter's exponential to the total of its exponential parameters is the SoftMax function's output. At a high level, θ is the total score of

Figure 10. Preprocess images for the word 'Choose'

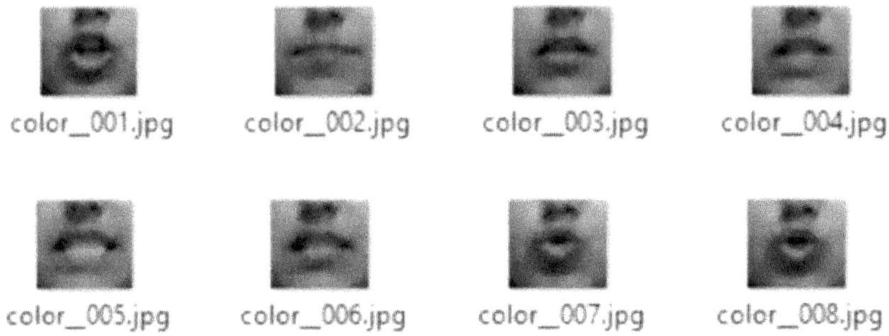

Table 2. Hyperparameters for the CNN model

Parameter	Value
Kernel size	3x3x3
Stride	1x1x1
Pool size	1x3x3
Activation	ReLU
Optimizer	SGD
Learning rate	1e-2
Regularization factor	1e-2
Dropout factor	20%
Batch size	32

all elements that occur in the vector. A generalised version of this expression might be: θ = weight w * feature x, where weight w is the weight matrix.

Table 2 lists the hyper-parameters that were employed in the 3D-CNN, including the kernel size, pooling size, learning rate, regularisation factor, batch size, and so forth.

Figure 10 displays the final preprocessed pictures for the viseme sequence of the dataset's second word, "Choose."

All of the architectures that were previously discussed showed the following outcomes. The proposed system employed performance indicators specified in equation 1 such F-Measure, Accuracy, Precision, and Recall to compare them. Over each training run epoch, "Loss" is the evaluation parameter taken into consideration.

"val_loss," or the average loss following an epoch, is provided by Keras to calculate value loss across each epoch.

Recall, often referred to as sensitivity, quantifies the portion of relevant instances that were recovered. In contrast, precision in pattern recognition refers to the proportion of relevant examples within the retrieved instances. Another name for accuracy in categorization and information retrieval is positive predictive value. The ratio of true positives to false negatives, or tp / (tp + fn), is known as the recall. Essentially, recall refers to the classifier's capacity to identify every positive sample. Value 1 is optimal, whereas value 0 is the worst. An F-score, or F1-score, is a measure of a model's accuracy on a dataset. The F-score is widely used in the assessment of many kinds of machine learning models and information retrieval systems, such as search engines.

The recommended technique creates a training example by concatenating the frames for every word. The algorithm fixed the amount of frames at 15 and padded the arrangement with less than 15 frames using a viseme for a locked mouth because the amount of frames varies for every word owing to sound length variation. The closed-mouth posture of non-speaking people is mimicked by the method of padding, which makes processing more human-like. Following training, a graph representing the train validation loss will be computed and shown. Below is a graph of the data. Accuracy in train tests will also be computed. Figure 11 displays the graph plotting

Figure 11. Loss

Figure 12. Accuracy

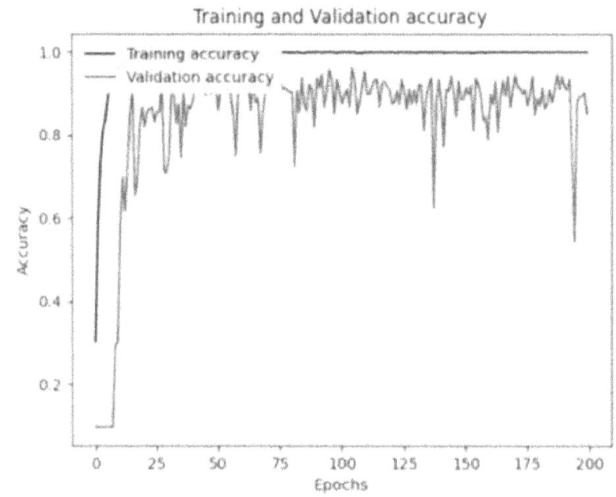

the validation loss and training, and Figure 12 displays the graph charting the validation accuracy and training.

The confusion matrix created for the suggested model is shown in Figure 13. The model's classification performance of the viseme sequence to the target text is displayed in this matrix. The model's F-measure further demonstrates the classifier's greater generalisation and lack of bias towards any particular class.

The confusion matrix indicates the degree to which the model correctly identifies each word, as well as whether or not the actual and predicted words are same. In the confusion matrix, the expected words are displayed on the y axis, while the actual words are displayed on the x axis.

The overall class-wise metrics for each word are given in Fig. 14, where all the parameters, including accuracy, recall, f1-score, and precision, are shown for each word.

The accuracy of the suggested method is around 86.22% after 200 epochs, with a weighted average score of approximately 86.32%.

Figure 13. Confusion matrix

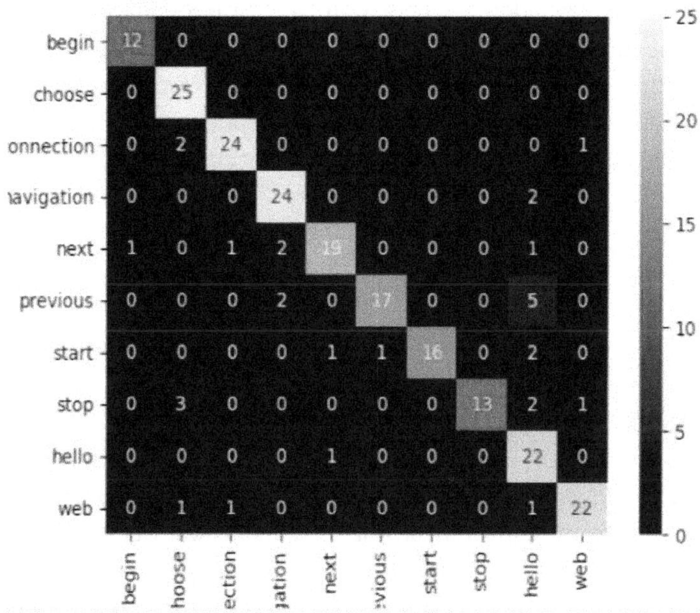

SECTION IV

Conclusion

Around 89% of the words have precision, while 86.2% of the words have total recall. The F1-Score as a whole is approximately 86.32%. Consequently, compared to the previous system, this 3D-CNN for the MIRACL-VC1 Dataset performs better and provides improved classification accuracy.

In order to achieve speaker-independent visual speech identification, the suggested study offers a unified method for visemes concatenation and 3D convolutional neural networks. The technique to localise the facial traits in each frame made use of the dlib face detection module. After that, the lip region was extracted using 68 face traits. The retrieved visemes are cropped and resized to improve the performance of the classifier by preventing them from being at various angles. To create an input feature, the suggested method concatenated these word frames. The number of frames is fixed at 15 in order to account for the fluctuation in the number of frames caused by the length of each word's utterance. Each word's pattern, or the sequence of visemes, is what the 3D CNN learns from. The hidden CNN layers provide the relevant knowledge for both low-level and high-level features. The suggested system demonstrates how this strategy overcomes the most advanced models by increasing classification accuracy.

Consequently, a speaker-independent Visual Speech Recognition system was constructed utilising the novel combination of 3D convolution neural networks and visemes concatenation. where the lip region and face features are extracted using the Dlibs Face Detection Module. By analysing the word patterns and the input video frame sequence, the 3D CNN improves classification accuracy.

SECTION V

Future Work

Utilising a parallel network of network layers to monitor particular behaviour on different branches can greatly enhance the proposed work's performance. There might be CNN layers in one branch, RNN layers in the other, and a thick layer combining the output from both branches at the conclusion. Such problems are addressed by RESNET (Deep Residual networks) (Borde et al., 2015), a modular learning system. Though shallower than RESNETs, modern deep neural networks, or "plain" equivalents, nevertheless require the same number of parameters, or weights. An excellent method for solving such issues is to apply Reinforcement Learning techniques to ascertain the viseme sequence of each word or phrase. Several lip-reading researches are in progress by merging many algorithms like RESNET, WideRESNET, ViT (Arakane & Saitoh, 2023). A decoder can be used to visualize the information for text prediction (Xue et al., 2023).

REFERENCES

Almajai, I., Cox, S., Harvey, R., & Lan, Y. (2016). Improved speaker independent lip reading using speaker adaptive training and deep neural networks. In *2016 IEEE International Conference on Acoustics, Speech and Signal Processing (ICASSP)*. IEEE. 10.1109/ICASSP.2016.7472172

Alothmany, N., Boston, R., Li, C., Shaiman, S., & Durrant, J. (2010). Classification of visemes using visual cues. In *Proceedings ELMAR-2010*. IEEE.

Arakane, T., & Saitoh, T. (2023). Efficient DNN Model for Word Lip-Reading. *Algorithms*, *16*(6), 269. doi:10.3390/a16060269

Bishnu, A. (2022). A Novel Frame Structure for Cloud-Based Audio-Visual Speech Enhancement in Multimodal Hearing-aids. *2022 IEEE International Conference on E-health Networking, Application & Services (HealthCom)*, 75-80. 10.1109/HealthCom54947.2022.9982772

Borde, P., Varpe, A., Manza, R., & Yannawar, P. (2015, June). Recognition of isolated words using zernike and mfcc features for audio visual speech recognition. *International Journal of Speech Technology*, *18*(2), 167–175. doi:10.1007/s10772-014-9257-1

Hour, Chen, Guo, & Xiao. (2020). Lip Reading Sentences Using Deep Learning With Only Visual Cues. *IEEE Access*.

Kim, M., Yeo, J. H., & Ro, Y. M. (n.d.). Distinguishing homophenes using multi-head visual-audio memory for lip reading. *Proceedings of the AAAI Conference on Artificial Intelligence, 36*(1), 1174-1182. 10.1609/aaai.v36i1.20003

Morshed, A., Jayaraman, P. P., Sellis, T., Georgakopoulos, D., Villari, M., & Ranjan, R. (2017). Deep Osmosis: Holistic Distributed Deep Learning in Osmotic Computing. IEEE Cloud Computing, 4(6), 22-32. doi:10.1109/MCC.2018.1081070

Mudaliar, N. K., Hegde, K., Ramesh, A., & Patil, V. (2020). Visual Speech Recognition: A Deep Learning Approach. *2020 5th International Conference on Communication and Electronics Systems (ICCES)*, 1218-1221. 10.1109/ICCES48766.2020.9137926

Petajan, E., Bischoff, B., Bodoff, D., & Brooke, N. M. (1988). An improved automatic lipreading system to enhance speech recognition. *Proceedings of the SIGCHI conference on Human factors in computing systems*, 19–25. 10.1145/57167.57170

Saeed, U., & Dugelay, J.-L. (2010). Combining edge detection and region segmentation for lip contour extraction. In *International Conference on Articulated Motion and Deformable Objects*. Springer. 10.1007/978-3-642-14061-7_2

Sengupta, T. N. (2008). S.: Lip localization and viseme recognition from video sequences. *Fourteenth National Conference on Communications.*

Thanda, A., & Venkatesan, S. M. (2016). *Audio visual speech recognition using deep recurrent neural networks. In IAPR workshop on multimodal pattern recognition of social signals in human-computer interaction.* Springer.

Torfi, Iranmanesh, Nasrabadi, & Dawson. (2017). 3d convolutional neural networks for cross audio-visual matching recognition. *IEEE Access, 5*(22), 81-91.

Villari, M., Fazio, M., Dustdar, S., Rana, O., & Ranjan, R. (2016). Osmotic Computing: A New Paradigm for Edge/Cloud Integration. IEEE Cloud Computing, 3(6), 76-83. doi:10.1109/MCC.2016.124

Wang, J., Zhang, J., Honda, K., Wei, J., & Dang, J. (2016). Audio-visual speech recognition integrating 3D lip information obtained from the Kinect. *Multimedia Systems*, *22*(3), 315–323. Advance online publication. doi:10.1007/s00530-015-0499-9

Xue, J., Huang, S., Song, H., & Shi, L. (2023). Fine-grained sequence-to-sequence lip reading based on self-attention and self-distillation. *Frontiers of Computer Science*, *17*(6), 176344. doi:10.1007/s11704-023-2230-x

Chapter 16
An Enhanced Real-Time Automatic Speech Recognition System for Tamil Language Using Wav2Vec2 Model

J. Sangeetha
SASTRA University, India

M. Priyanka
SASTRA University, India

D. Rekha
SASTRA University, India

M. Dhivya
SASTRA University, India

ABSTRACT

Automatic speech recognition (ASR) is a vital technology that transforms spoken language into written text, facilitating effective accessibility and communication. Despite the ongoing development of deep learning approaches, speech recognition remains a formidable task, especially for languages with limited data resources, such as Tamil. This work presents the development of an ASR system by utilizing the real-time spontaneous Tamil speech data collected from various types of people's communications in public places. The corpus is trained by fine-tuning the pre-trained wav2vec2 XLSR model. This model captures the diverse acoustic features and patterns and even applied to multiple dialects, making it adaptable to real-world speech. The implemented model is evaluated on various noisy environments like markets, hospitals, shops, etc. In terms of various evaluation metrics such as word error rate (WER) and character error rate (CER), the designed model exhibits an optimal performance by achieving a lower error rate when compared to the baseline ASR models.

DOI: 10.4018/979-8-3693-1694-8.ch016

1. INTRODUCTION

Automatic speech recognition is one of the most important and popular developments and stands as a cornerstone for facilitating human-computer interaction across various devices such as computers and smart phones, which simplifies and enhances user engagement. Speech Recognition (SR) technology enables computers to recognize spoken words via a microphone and transcribe them into textual form (Thilak et al., 2004). SR systems are adaptable by responding to various speech characteristics, vocabularies, and speakers. The selection of these categories is contingent upon the specific application needs of users (Radha, 2012a). In contemporary times, ASR applications are increasingly prevalent and valuable, owing to the widespread design and production of modern technologies with a user-friendly approach to cater to the convenience of the general users (Kiran et al., 2017).

Machine-oriented interfaces have limited computer usage in the existing Indian context to a mere fraction of the population—those who are adept in both computer literacy and written English. Since human communication depends predominantly on spoken language, which prompts a natural expectation for audio interfaces that can articulate and comprehend native languages. It would allow a normal person to seamlessly access and leverage the myriad advantages provided by information technology. India is a multilingual country with 18 constitutional languages written in ten different scripts. Therefore, it is essential to develop the ASR system in the native language to meet specific needs (Radha, 2012b) and (Al-Qatab et al., 2010).

ASR operates on various domains, including military, telephony, medical, commercial, and education. Beyond these applications, one of its significant contributions is to improve accessibility for differently-abled persons by allowing them to use speech technology to access internet and the computers. SR systems can be categorized into various types based on the type of utterance, vocabulary size, speaker model etc. Because of this heterogeneity, the development of speech recognition systems is becoming increasingly complex and a challenging task (Vimala et al., 2015) and (Saksamudre et al., 2015).

Based on these types, the ASR models are implemented for both high-resource and low-resource languages. Despite being well-developed for high-resource languages, ASR technology faces challenges when applied to low-resource languages. It is primarily owing to the limited availability of data resources, particularly for Tamil. Tamil is one of the ancient Dravidian languages, which encompasses various dialects where each has its own linguistic and lexicon characteristics. To address challenges such as contextual ambiguity, noisy environments, phonemic complexity, and pronunciation variability, the development of an advanced ASR system is required for Tamil speakers (Khan et al., 2001) and (Akhilesh et al., 2022).

In recent years, several deep learning-based network models have been employed for low-resource languages to overcome the challenges by enhancing their performance and adaptability. Aiming to discern speech intent in both Sinhala and Tamil languages, an Automatic Speech Recognition system based on English phonemes (Karunanayake et al., 2019) was developed. The integration of 1D and 2D Convolutional Neural Networks (CNNs) played a pivotal role in this effort. The proposed model has been achieved the WER as 20%.A technique for speech recognition was proposed (Dalmiya et al., 2013) on the other hand that involves signal pre-processing approach followed by feature extraction using Mel-Frequency Cepstral Coefficients (MFCC). The MFCCs were used to describe the short-term power spectrum of sound using a linear cosine transform of a log power spectrum on a nonlinear Mel frequency scale. The process of feature matching was carried out using Dynamic Time Warping (DTW), a template matching method implemented in Matlab that provides an overview of the major technological perspective and fundamental progress in speech recognition.

Furthermore, for an Indian regional language, the Acoustic Model was designed using a Convolutional Neural Network (CNN) (Girirajan et al., 2022a). It effectively identified phones in the given speech signal, incorporating first and second-order derivations of MFSC and GFCC for feature extraction. The designed model achieved a training accuracy of 90.63% and a testing accuracy of 81.25% using an open-sourced multi-speaker dataset, with isolated Tamil words. To address the challenge of sense distinctions in various dialects, an ensemble of clustering techniques have been employed (Rajendran et al., 2021) for the automatic segregation of sentence senses. The proposed model facilitated the mapping of characters to word senses, incorporating weights from Senticnet determined through tuning and trial-and-error methods. With an accuracy of 72.78% for regional dialects, word senses were distinguished through the utilization of stop words.

Consecutively, for developing a speech recognition model with minimal resources using the Mozilla DeepSpeech architecture have been implemented (Changrampadi et al., 2022). For training, freely available online computational resources were utilized which allows similar approaches to be carried out for research in financially constrained environments and low-resourced languages. The proposed ASR model achieved the best result of a 24.7% Word Error Rate (WER), compared to a 55% WER by Google speech-to-text. In integrated frontend feature extraction, a mixture of Gammatone Cepstral Coefficients (GTCC) and Constant Q Cepstral Coefficients (CQCC) has been employed (Akanksha, 2022). A hybrid acoustic model was used, which combined a two-dimensional convolutional neural network (Conv2D) with a backend model based on bidirectional gated recurrent units (BiGRU). Along with the acoustic model, the ASR system was built with a Connectionist Temporal Classification (CTC) loss function, CTC, and a prefix-based greedy decoder.The

Word Error Rate (WER) has been improved by 9–16% when compared to the isolated delta-delta features within the integrated model.

To enhance ASR accuracy in noisy environments, a hybrid feature extraction technique integrating perceptual linear predictive (PLP) and mel frequency cepstral coefficient (MFCC) has been implemented (Girirajan et al., 2022b). Phoneme modelling was improved by utilizing voice activity and detection (VAD)-based frame dropping which eliminating pauses and distorted elements in the given speech signal. Compared to the state-of-the-art methodology, the hybrid model with VAD demonstrated a 12% increase in recognition rate. For further enhancement, the efforts were directed towards addressing low-resource Indian languages through a TDNN-based speech recognition system (Fathima et al., 2018). The utilization of GMM-HMM, DNN-HMM, and TDNN models reflected an endeavor to improve acoustic modelling. The observed WER of 16.07% showed potential for developing SR systems in low-resource languages.

Widely used feature extractors such as GPT-x, BERT, and ResNet are typically pre-trained on vast amounts of unlabeled data across multiple domains using self-supervision. The training in this study (Yi et al., 2020) specifically utilized the Librispeech corpus for the wav2vec2 model. Although the model had been trained on a large dataset, its performance had not been tested in real-world scenarios or languages other than English. When applied to low-resource speech recognition tasks in various languages, the pre-trained models demonstrated significant improvements, with over 20% relative gains observed in six languages compared to previous work. Notably, a remarkable gain of 52.4% was achieved for English.

The popularity of Automatic Speech Recognition (ASR) and its applications, coupled with reasonable inference results, has led to the adoption of significantly large-scale models in recent state-of-the-art approaches. However, there has been a tendency to overlook detailed performance analysis, particularly in the context of low-resource language applications. The goal of this work (Mishra et al., 2023) was to revisit ASR within the domain of Connected Number Recognition (CNR). A new dataset, HCNR, was introduced specifically to understand various errors of ASR models in the context of CNR. The study involved establishing a preliminary benchmark and baseline model for CNR, exploring the effects of error mitigation strategies, and making comparisons with end-to-end large-scale ASR models for reference. The findings demonstrate the effectiveness of these models in the context of Connected Number Recognition.

In the evaluation of end-to-end speech recognition for several Indian languages (Anoop et al., 2023), a notable observation was made. Despite the fact that most Indian languages are spoken in syllable units, prevailing trends in existing speech recognition systems involve the use of characters or phonemes as modeling units. The study aimed to assess the performance of syllable-based modeling units, employing three different text representations: native script, Sanskrit library phonetics (SLP1) encoding, and syllables. Tokenization was carried out using sub-word units such as characters, byte-pair encoding (BPE), and unigram language modeling (ULM). The study compared their performances in both monolingual training and cross-lingual transfer learning scenarios. Notably, promising results were achieved with syllable-based BPE/ULM subword units in the monolingual setup, particularly when the dataset adequately represented the syllable distribution in the language.

In public places, speech recognition systems tailored for Tamil language were designed to convert spoken language into written text, specifically addressing the needs of seniors and transgender individuals. Seniors required assistance due to a lack of awareness of available facilities, while speech served as a means for transgender people, who face social stigma and often lack primary education, to meet their needs. The development of the system involved the use of pretrained models, including the IIT Madras transformer ASR model and the akashsivanandan/wav2vec2-large-xls-r-300m-tamil model, utilizing spontaneous speech data. The Word Error Rates for test speech utterances were 37.7144% and 40.55%, respectively (Saranya et al., 2023).

The task involved creating an automatic speech recognition system for Tamil by utilizing data collected from elderly Tamil speakers. The proposed ASR system was built around a pre-trained model (Suhasini et al., 2023) fine-tuned using the Tamil common voice dataset. The test data provided by the task was processed by the proposed system, resulting in the generation of transcriptions for the test samples. Subsequently, these transcriptions were submitted for evaluation, with the Word Error Rate (WER) serving as the evaluation metric. The designed system achieved a WER of 39.8091%, as indicated by the submitted results.

Constructed with minimal resources using Nvidia's NeMo Toolkit, this study (Ghadekar et al., 2023) focused on developing a speech recognition model, specifically tailored for the Tamil dataset. Training utilized openly available and freely accessible NeMo resources, emphasizing the approach's potential applicability to researching low-resource languages. The primary goal of the paper was to reduce the Word Error Rate (WER) metric when transcribing audio files, such as WAV files. Impressively, the proposed model achieved a remarkable 17% WER, outperforming Google's speech-to-text with a 55% WER and Mozilla DeepSpeech architecture with a 24.7% WER.

The aim of this research is to develop an advanced Automatic Speech Recognition (ASR) model specifically designed for the Tamil language. This study adopts the XLSR-Wav2Vec2.0 model as an approach for continuous speech recognition in Tamil. A key contribution of this paper lies in acquiring raw speech representations from different speakers in Tamil audio. It is primarily intended for speaker-independent continuous speech utterance, by utilizing audio samples recorded from different people in various environments.

The paper is structured as follows: In Section 2, we explore various types of speech recognition. Section 3 delves into the dataset and provides details about the XLSR Wav2Vec2.0 model. Moving to Section 4, we discuss the performance evaluation and experimentation of the ASR model using different metrics. Finally, Section 5 concludes the work and outlines future scope.

2. TYPES OF SPEECH RECOGNITION

Speech recognition is systematically classified into distinct types (Vimala et al., 2015) and (Saksamudre et al., 2015), as illustrated in **Fig. 1**. The subsequent sections provide detailed elucidation on each of these categorized types.

2.1. Based on Utterance

2.1.1 Isolated Speech Recognition (ISR)

Isolated speech recognition serves as a foundational pillar in the expansive landscape of speech technology. This type of recognition is characterized by its ability to decipher and understand individual words or short phrases uttered by a speaker. The precision and accuracy associated with isolated speech recognition make it particularly well-suited for applications where discrete and specific commands are required. The mechanism underlying isolated speech recognition involves breaking down an audio signal into distinct units, typically individual words. These units are then matched against a predefined set of words or commands, enabling the system to accurately identify and respond to the user's spoken input.

Isolated speech recognition has a wide range of applications. Users of voice-activated devices, such as smartphones and smart speakers, frequently interact with isolated commands such as "Call Mom" or "Set a timer for 10 minutes." The efficiency of ISR lies in its ability to precisely interpret user instructions without the need for extensive context analysis. The limitation of isolated speech recognition becomes apparent, however, in scenarios where context is critical for accurate interpretation. While it is excellent for discrete commands, it may fall short when it comes to understanding the nuances of more complex language structures found in natural conversation.

2.1.2 Connected Speech Recognition (CSR)

Connected speech recognition marks a progression beyond isolated recognition, aiming to comprehend not only individual words but also the context in which they are spoken. In CSR, the system analyzes entire phrases or sentences, allowing for a more comprehensive understanding of the user's intent. The difficulty in CSR lies in deciphering the transitions between words and identifying the boundaries of phrases within an ongoing stream of speech. This requires advanced algorithms capable of contextual analysis and linguistic comprehension. Virtual assistants, such as Apple's Siri or Amazon's Alexa, rely heavily on connected speech recognition to understand user queries and provide appropriate responses.

It is important to understand not only the literal meaning of words, but also the nuances of language, such as intonation, emphasis, and context. This capability improves the user experience by allowing for more natural and conversational interactions with voice-activated systems. Voice-controlled interfaces in various domains are among the applications of connected speech recognition. In dictation software, for example, connected speech recognition allows users to dictate entire sentences or paragraphs, promoting a smooth transition between spoken and written text.

2.1.3 Continuous Speech Recognition

It is a technological advancement that addresses the challenge of processing natural, uninterrupted speech. Continuous speech recognition systems must decode speech signals without breaks, unlike isolated or connected recognition, where pauses between words aid in segmentation. Because people typically speak in a continuous and fluid manner, this presents a more realistic and challenging scenario. The significance of continuous speech recognition becomes evident in applications where users engage in extended conversations or dictate lengthy pieces of text. Transcription services, for example, convert spoken words into written text accurately. This application is crucial in various fields, including journalism, legal documentation, and content creation, where the ability to efficiently transcribe spoken words is invaluable.

The technology behind continuous speech recognition involves advanced signal processing algorithms and machine learning models. These models are trained to recognize human speech nuances such as variations in pitch, rhythm, and pronunciation. Additionally, language models play a crucial role in predicting the likelihood of word sequences, which aids in the accurate transcription of continuous speech.

2.1.4 Spontaneous Speech Recognition

Within the spectrum of speech technology, it represents a distinct and challenging category. In contrast to scripted or rehearsed speech, spontaneous speech is informal and unstructured. It includes the dynamic and unpredictable aspects of everyday communication in which people express themselves freely without following a script. The challenges in spontaneous speech recognition arise from the variability in language use, pronunciation, and pacing. People can use colloquial expressions, pause or hesitate while speaking, and exhibit a wide range of speaking styles. As a result, to provide accurate and meaningful interpretations, spontaneous speech recognition systems must be robust enough to handle these variations.

Spontaneous speech recognition has a wide range of applications, from analyzing customer service interactions to developing voice-activated systems for casual and natural conversations. For example, in call centres, spontaneous speech recognition can be used to extract insights from customer-agent interactions, allowing businesses to improve service quality and customer satisfaction. It is powered by sophisticated machine learning algorithms and natural language processing (NLP) techniques. These algorithms are trained on massive datasets of spontaneous speech examples, allowing them to adapt to the nuances of real-world communication.

2.2. Based on Speaker

2.2.1 Speaker Dependent Recognition

Speaker-dependent speech recognition systems are those in which the accuracy of the recognition process is intricately linked to the voice characteristics of a specific user. Before they can accurately interpret spoken words, these systems must be trained with a specific individual's voice. During this phase, the system captures and analyzes the unique vocal patterns, intonations, and nuances specific to that use. The benefit of speaker-dependent recognition is its high accuracy potential. Through training, the system learns to recognize subtle variations in the user's voice and accurately transcribe spoken words. This precision is especially useful in applications where personalized voice commands or authentication are required.

Voice-activated security systems are one common application of speaker-dependent recognition. By training the system with the authorized user's voice, the technology ensures that only the designated individual can access or control secured devices. This adds an additional layer of security and personalization to voice-controlled systems. However, one limitation of speaker-dependent systems is that they are less effective when confronted with unfamiliar voices. The lack of adaptability to new speakers restricts their utility in scenarios where multiple users may interact with the system.

2.2.2 Speaker Independent Recognition

Conversely, speaker-independent speech recognition systems are designed to comprehend a broad range of voices without the need for individualized training. During the training phase, these systems are exposed to a wide range of vocal characteristics, accents, and speech patterns. The goal is to develop models that generalize well across different languages. Speaker-independent recognition is a more versatile approach that is appropriate for applications with a large and distinct user base. Because they must cater to a wide audience with diverse linguistic backgrounds and speaking styles.

The adaptability of speaker-independent systems comes at the expense of slightly lower accuracy when compared to speaker-dependent models. However, advancements in machine learning techniques, such as deep learning and neural networks, have significantly improved the performance of speaker-independent recognition systems, making them increasingly prevalent in real-world applications.

2.2.3 Speaker Adaptive Models

Adaptive speech recognition is a dynamic approach that incorporates elements from both speaker-dependent and speaker-independent systems. Even after the initial training phase, an adaptive model continues to learn and refine its understanding of a user's speech patterns over time. This adaptability is critical in situations where the user's voice may change due to factors such as age, health, or environmental influences. The adaptive nature of these systems allows them to provide a personalized experience while still being able to handle variations in the user's voice. For example, a voice assistant that adapts to changes in a user's speech due to a cold or other temporary conditions can offer a more seamless and user-friendly experience.

The underlying technology involves a continuous learning process that is often aided by recurrent neural networks (RNNs) or other deep learning architectures. These models can dynamically adjust their parameters based on new data, ensuring that the system remains tuned to the user's evolving speech patterns.

2.3. Based on Environment

2.3.1 Noiseless Environment

In an ideal soundscape devoid of extraneous noise, speech recognition systems operate under optimal conditions. A noiseless environment provides a controlled setting where the system can focus solely on the nuances of the spoken words without interference. This controlled environment is akin to a laboratory setting, facilitating accurate training and calibration of speech recognition algorithms. Noiseless environments are essential in applications requiring precision, such as studio recordings or controlled experiments. Medical transcription, for instance, requires the utmost accuracy in converting spoken medical terms into text. In such noiseless settings, speech recognition systems can perform at their peak, ensuring precise and error-free transcriptions.

2.3.2 Noisy Environment

Contrastingly, the real world rarely mirrors the tranquility of a noiseless environment. Noisy settings introduce a myriad of challenges for speech recognition systems. Background noise, ambient chatter, and environmental sounds pose obstacles, leading to decreased accuracy and potential misinterpretation of spoken words. Noisy environments are ubiquitous, ranging from busy city streets to crowded cafes and public transportation. In these scenarios, speech recognition systems encounter difficulties in isolating the user's voice from the cacophony of sounds. The challenge is particularly pronounced in hands-free applications within vehicles or in public spaces, where users expect seamless interactions despite the ambient noise.

2.4. Based on Vocabulary

2.4.1 Small Vocabulary

Small vocabulary speech recognition systems come to the fore when precision takes precedence over diversity. This category is distinguished by a limited set of predefined words or commands. Small vocabulary systems excel in applications where the scope is well-defined, and users interact with a specific set of commands. Smart home devices exemplify the efficacy of small vocabulary recognition. Commands such as "Turn off the lights" or "Set the thermostat to 72 degrees" represent a concise and specific lexicon. In such contexts, a small vocabulary not only ensures accuracy but also streamlines the user experience, eliminating ambiguity and potential misinterpretations.

2.4.2 Medium Vocabulary

As the complexity of applications grows, the need for a more expansive vocabulary becomes apparent. Medium vocabulary speech recognition systems strike a balance between specificity and versatility. These systems cater to a broader range of tasks, accommodating different user inputs while maintaining a manageable lexicon. Voice-operated software for productivity applications often relies on medium vocabulary recognition. Tasks such as composing emails, creating documents, or executing software commands necessitate a lexicon that extends beyond the confines of a small set of commands. The challenge lies in achieving a delicate equilibrium—providing users with flexibility while avoiding information overload.

2.4.3 Large Vocabulary

The need for a more expansive vocabulary becomes apparent as the complexity of applications increases. These systems possess an extensive lexicon, allowing them to understand and transcribe a wide range of words and phrases. The applications of large vocabulary recognition span transcription services, voice assistants, and dictation software. Transcription services, for instance, require the ability to transcribe spoken words accurately across various domains—medical, legal, and general discourse. Large vocabulary recognition empowers these systems to navigate the intricacies of specialized terminology, ensuring precise and contextually relevant transcriptions.

2.4.4 Very Large Vocabulary

At the zenith of vocabulary recognition, very large vocabulary systems push the envelope by dealing with large and diverse language databases. These advanced systems play a pivotal role in natural language processing (NLP), where a vast vocabulary is essential for nuanced understanding and interpretation. In the realm of virtual assistants and conversational AI, very large vocabulary recognition becomes indispensable. Users expect these systems to comprehend natural language, understand context, and respond coherently. The expansive vocabulary allows these systems to handle a myriad of queries, engage in contextual conversations, and adapt to the diverse linguistic styles of users.

Figure 1. Different types of speech recognition

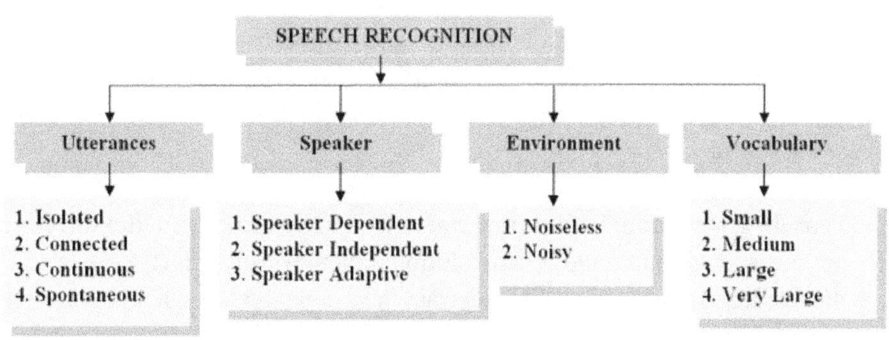

3. MATERIALS AND METHODS

3.1 Dataset Description

The real-time dataset is utilized for our study and it was collected from Coda Lab (https://codalab.lisn.upsaclay.fr/), primarily focusing on individuals whose mother tongue is Tamil. The audio recordings in the dataset are characterized by the absence of interruptions or overlaps of other individuals' voices, ensuring that only the speaker's audio is present. The dataset comprises a total audio length of 7 hours and 30 minutes and is provided in .wav format. This dataset is valuable for research and development in Tamil speech recognition, particularly for building and training models tailored to the unique characteristics of the Tamil language. Table 1 depicts the information about the dataset.

Table 1. CodaLab Dataset Description

Gender	Literates	Illiterates	Total
Male	4	9	13
Female	7	24	31
Transgenders	3	4	7
Total	**14**	**37**	**51**

3.2 XLSR-WAV2VEC2.0

Wav2Vec 2.0 is a speech recognition model developed by Facebook AI Research (FAIR). It is designed for tasks related to speech processing, such as automatic speech recognition and speech understanding (Yi et al., 2020). The components that implicitly engage with Wav2Vec 2.0 are described below and it work flow is depicted in Fig. 2:

1. **Feature Extraction**: In the initial stage of Wav2Vec 2.0, raw audio waveforms are utilized as input, and a Convolutional Neural Network (CNN) serves as the feature extractor. This CNN extract the crucial acoustic features from the

acoustic signals and transforming it into a sequence of feature vectors that encapsulate the essential characteristics of the audio signal.

2. **Context Window Creation**: Following the extraction technique, the obtained features are structured into context windows. These windows, consisting of consecutive feature vectors, plays a crucial role in capturing temporal dependencies and contextual information within the audio signal. By organizing the features into windows, the model gains a nuanced understanding of the sequential nature of the audio data, which is fundamental for discerning speech patterns.
3. **Self-Supervised Pre-training (Masked Contrastive Objective):** In the pre-training phase, Wav2Vec 2.0 adopts a self-supervised learning approach using context windows. During this phase, the model is trained to predict masked portions within these windows, where random segments are concealed. The model learns to predict the original values of the masked portions, autonomously capturing meaningful representations without relying on external labels. This enhances its ability to understand the nuances of the data.
4. **Vector Quantization (VQ):** The continuous representations obtained from the pre-trained model undergo quantization, a process that maps them to discrete codes using Vector Quantization. This step reduces the dimensionality of the representations, making them more compact and efficient. Each continuous value is paired with its nearest codebook entry, enhancing the model's capability to represent audio features in a condensed form.
5. **Transformer model:** Quantized codes from the preceding phase are input to the Transformer model, where the encoder phase processes these codes to capture essential contextual information for effective representation. Transformer models are particularly well-suited for speech-related tasks due to their effectiveness in processing the sequential input and capturing long-term dependencies which ensures the model's competency in grasping complicated speech patterns.
6. **Connectionist Temporal Classification (CTC) Loss:** The output from the encoder is utilized to predict phoneme-level representations. The model is then trained using the Connectionist Temporal Classification loss, enabling alignment of predictions with ground truth phonemes, even when lengths don't precisely match. This feature is crucial for training the model to accurately recognize and transcribe spoken words, contributing to the robustness of the model in various speech-related applications.

Figure 2. Architecture of XLSR Wav2Vec2.0

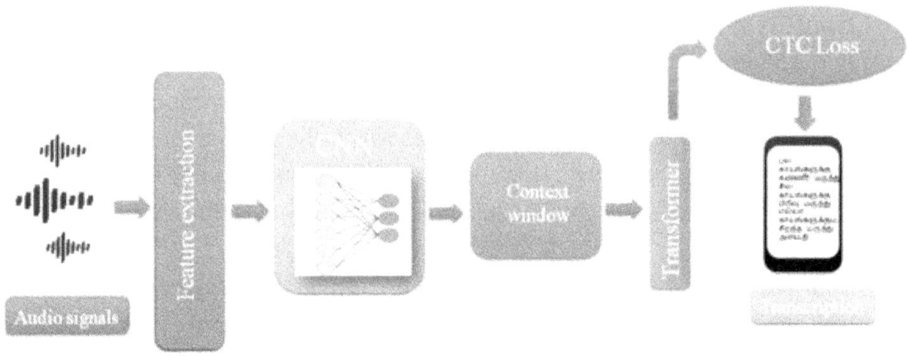

4. EXPERIMENTAL ANALYSIS

This study addresses a research gap in Tamil speech recognition, particularly given its widespread prevalence in India. We utilize a real-time dataset capturing a broad vocabulary from individuals across three separate speaker categories (male, female, and transgender) between the ages of 30 and 60 to build a speaker-independent continuous voice recognition system. The dataset comprises 908 samples sampled at 16,000 Hz, and the tests are conducted in the Jupyter Notebook environment with Python. To evaluate the performance of the Automatic Speech Recognition (ASR) system, the Word Error Rate (WER) is computed as in Eqn. 1:

$$word\ error\ rate = \frac{I + S + D}{N} \tag{1}$$

where, I→Insertion
S→Substitution
D→Deletion
N→Total Number of words

In the evaluation of speech transcription accuracy, Table 2 presents the Word Error Rate (WER) and Character Error Rate (CER) for three distinct speakers: Speaker 1 yielded a WER of 19.35% and CER of 7.95%, Speaker 2 with a WER of 15.79% and CER of 5.49%, and Speaker 3 exhibiting a WER of 12.50% and CER of 2.90%. This assessment encompasses both actual and predicted transcriptions, serving as a comprehensive measure of transcription error rates. The 'Average' category consolidates an overall average of WER and CER at 15.88% and 5.45%,

Table 2. Computing WER and CER for Independent Speakers

SPEAKER	TRANSCRIPTIONS	WER	CER
(SPEAKER 1)	**ACTUAL:**காந்திமதிஎன்னுடையவயதுஅம்பத்திஒம்போதுஇந்தஆய்வுக்குநான்முழுஒத்துழைப்புத்தரரேன்இதான்என்னோடஉறுதிமொழிமேம்எனக்குஉடல்நிலைசரில்லஅதனாலவந்துஇந்தஹாஸ்பிடல்லவந்துஅட்மிட்ஆளாம்னுநெனைச்சிருக்கேன். இதுஹார்ட்ஒருபக்கம்வந்துஎனக்கு **PREDICTION:**காந்திமதிஎன்னுடையவயதுஅம்பத்திஒம்போதுஇந்தஆய்வுக்குநான்முழுவத்துலைப்புததரரேன்இதான்என்னோடவரியமழிமேம்எனக்குஉடல்நிலைசரில்லஅதனாலவந்துஇந்தஹாஸ்பிடல்லவந்துஅட்மிட்ஆளாம்ுநெனைச்சிருக்கேன்இதுஹாத்துஒருபக்கமவந்துஎனக்கு	19.35%	7.95%
(SPEAKER 2)	**ACTUAL:**கோயிலுக்குவந்தாச்சுஅர்ச்சனபண்ணனும்அர்ச்சனசீட்டுஎங்கவாங்குறதுஅர்ச்சனபண்ணுவாங்களாபிரசாதம்எங்கக்கொடுப்பாங்கஅப்புறம்வந்துஇதுஅன்னதானம்உண்டாபோடுவாங்களா **PREDICTION:**கோயிலுக்குவந்தாச்சுஅர்ச்சனபண்ணனும்அர்ச்சனசீட்டுஎங்கவாங்குறதுஅர்ச்சனபண்ணுவாங்களாஆஹ்பிரசாதம்எங்ககொடுப்பாங்கஅப்புறம்வந்துஇதுஅண்னதானாஉண்டாபோடுவாங்களா	15.79%	5.49%
(SPEAKER 3)	**ACTUAL:**தடுப்பூசிஎங்கபோடுறாங்ககாசுகொடுப்பாங்ககேக்கணுமாகாசுகொடுக்கனுமாகேரட்என்னவிலபீன்ஸ்என்னவிலகத்திரிக்காய்என்னவிலதக்காளிஎன்னவில **PREDICTION:**தடுப்பூசிஎங்கபோடுறாங்ககாசுகொடுப்பாங்ககேக்கணுமாகாசுகொடுக்கணுமாகேரட்டுஎன்னவிலபீன்ஷஎன்னவிலகத்திரிக்காய்என்னவிலதக்காளிஎன்னவில	12.50%	2.90%
	AVERAGE	**15.88%**	**5.45%**

respectively. This analysis provides valuable insights into how well the predefined wav2vec2.0 model works for different speakers with real-time data.

Based on the comparison of accuracy, as shown in Fig. 3, the wav2vec2.0 model delivers highly accurate results in real-time data analysis, showcasing outstanding performance across different speakers. Speaker 3 takes the lead with an impressive 96.32% accuracy, demonstrating the model's precise communication understanding,

Figure 3. Accuracy comparison for independent speakers

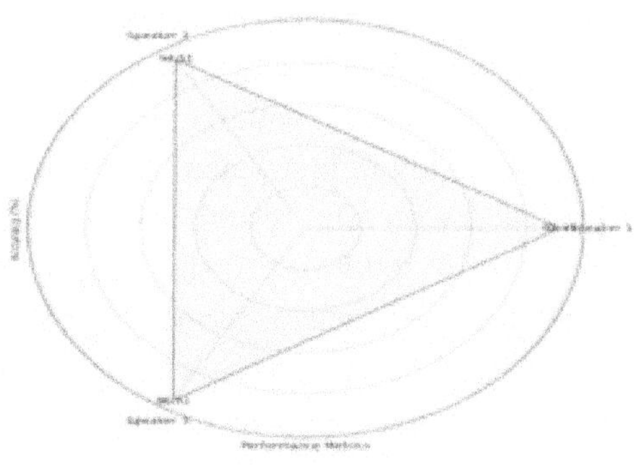

Figure 4. WER comparison between the existing model and designed model

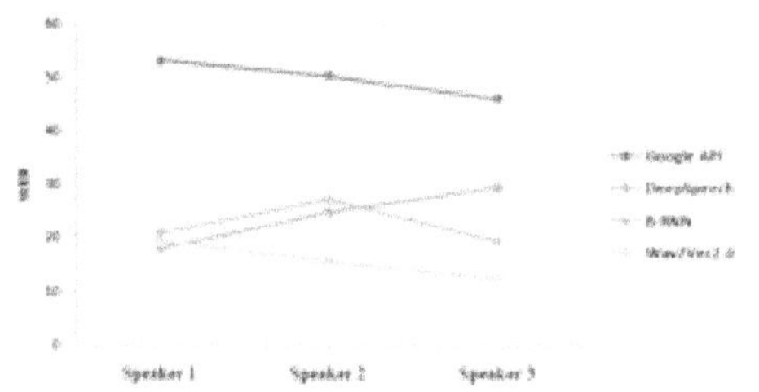

followed by Speaker 2 with 94.51% accuracy and Speaker 1 with 92.47% accuracy. These results emphasize the wav2vec2.0 model's dominance, offering a clear overview of performance distinctions among the speakers and emphasizing its notable proficiency compared to other models.

In Fig. 4, a comparison of Word Error Rates (WER) is computed for four distinct predefined speech recognition models—Google API, DeepSpeech, B-RNN, and the designed Wav2Vec2.0, revealing insightful findings. Wav2Vec2.0 consistently outperforms the other models, demonstrating the lowest WER across all speakers. Specifically, for Speaker 1, Wav2Vec2.0 achieves a WER of 19.35, surpassing Google API (53.33), DeepSpeech (18.04), and B-RNN (21.09). Similarly, for Speaker 2, Wav2Vec2.0 excels with a WER of 15.79, outshining Google API (50.47), DeepSpeech (25.07), and B-RNN (27.33). Notably, Speaker 3 consistently exhibits the lowest WER across all models, with Wav2Vec2.0 recording an impressive 12.5 WER, compared to Google API (46.14), DeepSpeech (29.71), and B-RNN (19.58). This robust performance of Wav2Vec2.0 underscores its proficiency in accurately transcribing spoken content, minimizing word recognition errors. In contrast, the Google API, DeepSpeech, and B-RNN exhibit comparatively higher error rates. This detailed analysis provides a comprehensive view of the overall model performance, with Wav2Vec2.0 standing out as a superior choice for accurate speech recognition.

Fig. 5 illustrates the computational result of the designed model, comparing the ground truth label of one test sample with the predicted value. However, in the predicted text, a slight discrepancy in interpretation is observed. Specifically, the term 'prasadham' is preceded with 'ah,' resulting in a discrepancy in contextual interpretation. The Word Error Rate (WER) for the prediction, calculated by comparing the actual and predicted texts, is found to be 15.79%. This indicates a moderate level of variance between the expected and generated content, implying that there is scope for improvement in capturing the nuances of the original message.

Figure 5. Simulation result of the designed model

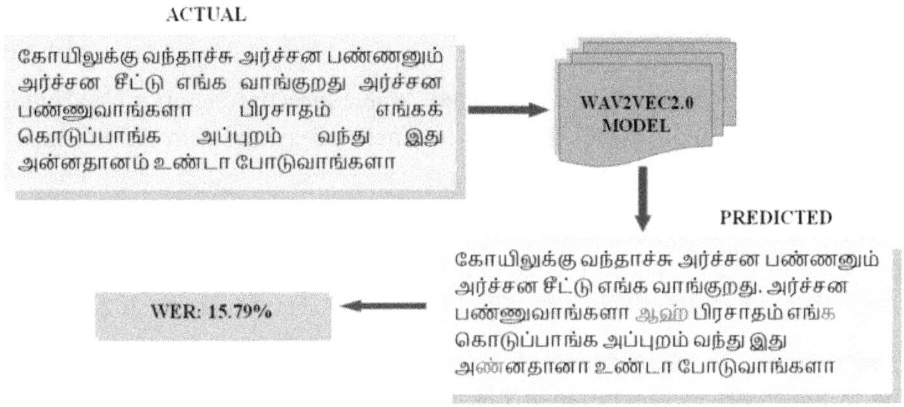

5. CONCLUSION

In this study, we developed an Automatic Speech Recognition (ASR) system by fine-tuning the pre-trained XLSR Wav2Vec2.0 model to transcribe real-time acoustic data, focusing on speaker-independent continuous utterances in the Tamil language. Our primary objective was to create an ASR system capable of accurately transcribing spoken Tamil across various speakers, accounting for factors such as pronunciation, accents, and different intonations. The system's performance was assessed using metrics like Word Error Rate (WER) and Character Error Rate (CER), resulting in an average WER of 15.88% and a CER of 5.45%, demonstrating the efficacy of the ASR system. Future work will focus on enhancing the ASR system's reliability in challenging acoustic conditions, including background noise, non-standard pronunciation, and low-quality audio. Advanced noise reduction and signal processing techniques will be utilized to ensure the system's robustness in real-world scenarios.

REFERENCES

Akanksha, A. (2022, September). Tamil Language Automatic Speech Recognition Based on Integrated Feature Extraction and Hybrid Deep Learning Model. In *International Conference on Internet of Things and Connected Technologies* (pp. 283-292). Singapore: Springer Nature Singapore.

Akhilesh, A., Brinda, P., Keerthana, S., Gupta, D., & Vekkot, S. (2022, October). Tamil Speech Recognition Using XLSR Wav2Vec2. 0 & CTC Algorithm. In *2022 13th International Conference on Computing Communication and Networking Technologies (ICCCNT)* (pp. 1-6). IEEE.

Al-Qatab, B. A., & Ainon, R. N. (2010, June). Arabic speech recognition using hidden Markov model toolkit (HTK). In 2010 international symposium on information technology (Vol. 2, pp. 557-562). IEEE.

Anoop, C. S., & Ramakrishnan, A. G. (2023). Suitability of syllable-based modeling units for end-to-end speech recognition in Sanskrit and other Indian languages. *Expert Systems with Applications*, *220*, 119722. doi:10.1016/j.eswa.2023.119722

Changrampadi, M. H., Shahina, A., Narayanan, M. B., & Khan, A. N. (2022). End-to-End Speech Recognition of Tamil Language. *Intelligent Automation & Soft Computing*, *32*(2).

Dalmiya, C. P., Dharun, V. S., & Rajesh, K. P. (2013, April). An efficient method for Tamil speech recognition using MFCC and DTW for mobile applications. In *2013 IEEE Conference on Information & Communication Technologies* (pp. 1263-1268). IEEE. 10.1109/CICT.2013.6558295

Fathima, N., Patel, T., Mahima, C., & Iyengar, A. (2018, September). TDNN-based Multilingual Speech Recognition System for Low Resource Indian Languages. In INTERSPEECH (pp. 3197-3201). doi:10.21437/Interspeech.2018-2117

Ghadekar, P., Jhanwar, K., Sivanandan, A., Shetty, T., Karpe, A., & Khushalani, P. (2023, November). ASR for Indian regional language using Nvidia's NeMo toolkit. In AIP Conference Proceedings (Vol. 2851, No. 1). AIP Publishing. doi:10.1063/5.0178629

Girirajan, S., & Pandian, A. (2022a). Convolutional Neural Network Based Automatic Speech Recognition for Tamil Language. In *Applications of Artificial Intelligence and Machine Learning: Select Proceedings of ICAAAIML 2021* (pp. 91-103). Singapore: Springer Nature Singapore. 10.1007/978-981-19-4831-2_8

Girirajan, S., & Pandian, A. (2022b). Hybrid Feature Extraction Technique for Tamil Automatic Speech Recognition System in Noisy Environment. *Recent Trends in Communication and Intelligent Systems Proceedings of ICRTCIS*, *2021*, 1–11.

Karunanayake, Y., Thayasivam, U., & Ranathunga, S. (2019, November). Sinhala and tamil speech intent identification from english phoneme based asr. In *2019 International Conference on Asian Language Processing (IALP)* (pp. 234-239). IEEE. 10.1109/IALP48816.2019.9037702

Khan, A. N., & Yegnanarayana, B. (2001). Development of speech recognition system for Tamil for small restricted task. In *Proceedings of national conference on communication* (No. 3). Academic Press.

Kiran, R., Nivedha, K., & Subha, T. (2017, February). Voice and speech recognition in Tamil language. In *2017 2nd International Conference on Computing and Communications Technologies (ICCCT)* (pp. 288-292). IEEE.

Mishra, R., Boopathy, S. R. G., Ravikiran, M., Kulkarni, S., Mukherjee, M., Ganesh, A., & Banerjee, K. (2023, September). Revisiting Automatic Speech Recognition for Tamil and Hindi Connected Number Recognition. In *Proceedings of the Third Workshop on Speech and Language Technologies for Dravidian Languages* (pp. 116-123). Academic Press.

Radha, V. (2012a). Speaker independent isolated speech recognition system for Tamil language using HMM. *Procedia Engineering*, *30*, 1097–1102. doi:10.1016/j.proeng.2012.01.968

Radha, V., & Vimala, C. (2012b). A review on speech recognition challenges and approaches. *doaj.org*, *2*(1), 1-7.

Rajendran, S., Mathivanan, S. K., Jayagopal, P., Venkatasen, M., Pandi, T., Sorakaya Somanathan, M., Thangaval, M., & Mani, P. (2021). Language dialect based speech emotion recognition through deep learning techniques. *International Journal of Speech Technology*, *24*(3), 625–635. doi:10.1007/s10772-021-09838-8

Saksamudre, S. K., Shrishrimal, P. P., & Deshmukh, R. R. (2015). A review on different approaches for speech recognition system. *International Journal of Computer Applications*, *115*(22). Advance online publication. doi:10.5120/20284-2839

Saranya, S., & Bharathi, B. (2023, September). SANBAR@ LT-EDI-2023: Automatic Speech Recognition: vulnerable old-aged and transgender people in Tamil. In *Proceedings of the Third Workshop on Language Technology for Equality, Diversity and Inclusion* (pp. 155-160). Academic Press.

Suhasini, S., & Bharathi, B. (2023, September). ASR_SSN_CSE@ LTEDI-2023: Pretrained Transformer based Automatic Speech Recognition system for Elderly People. In *Proceedings of the Third Workshop on Language Technology for Equality, Diversity and Inclusion* (pp. 161-165). Academic Press.

Thilak, R. A., & Madharaci, R. (2004). *Speech recognizer for Tamil language.* Tamil Internet.

Vimala, C., & Radha, V. (2015). Isolated speech recognition system for Tamil language using statistical pattern matching and machine learning techniques. *Journal of Engineering Science and Technology, 10*(5), 617–632.

Yi, C., Wang, J., Cheng, N., Zhou, S., & Xu, B. (2020). Applying wav2vec2.0 to speech recognition in various low-resource languages. *arXiv preprint arXiv:2012.12121.*

Compilation of References

Abdulkareem, K. H., Mohammed, M. A., Gunasekaran, S. S., Al-Mhiqani, M. N., Mutlag, A. A., Mostafa, S. A., Ali, N. S., & Ibrahim, D. A. (2019). A review of fog computing and machine learning: Concepts, applications, challenges, and open issues. *IEEE Access : Practical Innovations, Open Solutions*, *7*, 153123–153140. doi:10.1109/ACCESS.2019.2947542

Abuhasel, K. A., & Khan, M. A. (2020). A secure industrial internet of things (IIoT) framework for resource management in smart manufacturing. *IEEE Access : Practical Innovations, Open Solutions*, *8*, 117354–117364. doi:10.1109/ACCESS.2020.3004711

Agrawal, A. V., Magulur, L. P., Priya, S. G., Kaur, A., Singh, G., & Boopathi, S. (2023). Smart Precision Agriculture Using IoT and WSN. In Advances in Information Security, Privacy, and Ethics (pp. 524–541). IGI Global. doi:10.4018/978-1-6684-8145-5.ch026

Agrawal, A. V., Shashibhushan, G., Pradeep, S., Padhi, S. N., Sugumar, D., & Boopathi, S. (2024). Synergizing Artificial Intelligence, 5G, and Cloud Computing for Efficient Energy Conversion Using Agricultural Waste. In Practice, Progress, and Proficiency in Sustainability (pp. 475–497). IGI Global. doi:10.4018/979-8-3693-1186-8.ch026

Agrawal, A. V., Pitchai, R., Senthamaraikannan, C., Alangudi Balaji, N., Sajithra, S., & Boopathi, S. (2023). Digital Education System During the COVID-19 Pandemic. In J. Bell & T. Gifford (Eds.), Advances in Educational Technologies and Instructional Design (pp. 104–126). IGI Global. doi:10.4018/978-1-6684-6424-3.ch005

Ahammad, I., Khan, A. R., & Salehin, Z. U. (2021). A review on cloud, fog, roof, and dew computing: IoT perspective. *International Journal of Cloud Applications and Computing*, *11*(4), 14–41. doi:10.4018/IJCAC.2021100102

Ahuja, K., Gour, S., & Vaishnav, K. (2021). Developing Smart Cities Using Internet of Things. *International Journal of Engineering Trends and Applications*, *8*(4), 15–19.

Akanksha, A. (2022, September). Tamil Language Automatic Speech Recognition Based on Integrated Feature Extraction and Hybrid Deep Learning Model. In *International Conference on Internet of Things and Connected Technologies* (pp. 283-292). Singapore: Springer Nature Singapore.

Akhand, M. A. H., Roy, S., Siddique, N., Kamal, M. A. S., & Shimamura, T. (2021). Facial emotion recognition using transfer learning in the deep CNN. *Electronics (Basel)*, *10*(9), 1036. doi:10.3390/electronics10091036

Akhilesh, A., Brinda, P., Keerthana, S., Gupta, D., & Vekkot, S. (2022, October). Tamil Speech Recognition Using XLSR Wav2Vec2. 0 & CTC Algorithm. In *2022 13th International Conference on Computing Communication and Networking Technologies (ICCCNT)* (pp. 1-6). IEEE.

Al Bassam, N., Hussain, S. A., Al Qaraghuli, A., Khan, J., Sumesh, E. P., & Lavanya, V. (2021). IoT based wearable device to monitor the signs of quarantined remote patients of COVID-19. *Informatics in Medicine Unlocked*, *24*, 100588. doi:10.1016/j.imu.2021.100588 PMID:33997262

Alawida, M., Samsudin, A., Sen, J., & Alkhawaldeh, R. S. (2019). A new hybrid digital chaotic system with applications in image encryption. *Signal Processing*, *160*, 45–58. doi:10.1016/j.sigpro.2019.02.016

Alehegn. (2019). Diabetes Analysis and Prediction Using Random Forest, KNN, Naïve Bayes, And J48: An Ensemble Approach. *International Journal of Scientific & Technology Research, 8*(9).

Ali, M., Ahn, C. W., & Pant, M. (2014). A robust image watermarking technique using SVD and differential evolution in DCT domain. *Optik (Stuttgart)*, *125*(1), 428–434. doi:10.1016/j.ijleo.2013.06.082

Almaiah, M. A., & Alkdour, T. (2023). Securing Fog Computing Through Consortium Blockchain Integration: The Proof of Enhanced Concept (PoEC) Approach. In Recent Advancements in Multimedia Data Processing and Security: Issues, Challenges, and Techniques (pp. 107-140). IGI Global.

Almajai, I., Cox, S., Harvey, R., & Lan, Y. (2016). Improved speaker independent lip reading using speaker adaptive training and deep neural networks. In *2016 IEEE International Conference on Acoustics, Speech and Signal Processing (ICASSP)*. IEEE. 10.1109/ICASSP.2016.7472172

Almazroi, A. A., Aldhahri, E. A., Al-Shareeda, M. A., & Manickam, S. (2023). ECA-VFog: An efficient certificateless authentication scheme for 5G-assisted vehicular fog computing. *PLoS One*, *18*(6), e0287291. doi:10.1371/journal.pone.0287291 PMID:37352258

Alothmany, N., Boston, R., Li, C., Shaiman, S., & Durrant, J. (2010). Classification of visemes using visual cues. In *Proceedings ELMAR-2010*. IEEE.

Al-Qatab, B. A., & Ainon, R. N. (2010, June). Arabic speech recognition using hidden Markov model toolkit (HTK). In 2010 international symposium on information technology (Vol. 2, pp. 557-562). IEEE.

Alshammari, H. H. (2023). The internet of things healthcare monitoring system based on MQTT protocol. *Alexandria Engineering Journal*, *69*, 275–287. doi:10.1016/j.aej.2023.01.065

Alshoura, W. H., Zainol, Z., Teh, J. S., & Alawida, M. (2020). A New Chaotic Image Watermarking Scheme Based on SVD and IWT. *IEEE Access, 8*, 43391–43406. doi:10.1109/ACCESS.2020.2978186

Alshoura, W. H., Zainol, Z., Teh, J. S., Alawida, M. & Alabdulatif, A. (2021). Hybrid SVD-Based Image Watermarking Schemes: A Review. *IEEE Access, 9*, 32931–32968. doi:10.1109/ACCESS.2021.3060861

Alwasel, K., Jha, D. N., Habeeb, F., Demirbaga, U., Rana, O., Baker, T., Dustdar, S., Villari, M., James, P., Solaiman, E., & Ranjan, R. (2021). IoTSim-Osmosis: A framework for modeling and simulating IoT applications over an edge-cloud continuum. *Journal of Systems Architecture, 116*, 101956. doi:10.1016/j.sysarc.2020.101956

Anagnostopoulos, C.-N., Iliou, T., & Giannakos, I. (2015). Features and classifiers for emotion recognition from speech: A survey from 2000 to 2011. *Artificial Intelligence Review, 43*(2), 155–177.

Analytics Vidhya. (2017). https://www.analyticsvidhya.com/blog/2017/09/understaing-support-vector-machine-example-code

Anand, A., & Singh, A. K. (2020). An improved DWT-SVD domain watermarking for medical information security. *Computer Communications, 152*(January), 72–80. doi:10.1016/j.comcom.2020.01.038

Andronie, M., Lăzăroiu, G., Iatagan, M., Hurloiu, I., & Dijmărescu, I. (2021). Sustainable cyber-physical production systems in big data-driven smart urban economy: A systematic literature review. *Sustainability (Basel), 13*(2), 751. doi:10.3390/su13020751

Anitha, C., Komala, C., Vivekanand, C. V., Lalitha, S., & Boopathi, S. (2023). Artificial Intelligence driven security model for Internet of Medical Things (IoMT). *IEEE Explore*, 1–7.

Anoop, C. S., & Ramakrishnan, A. G. (2023). Suitability of syllable-based modeling units for end-to-end speech recognition in Sanskrit and other Indian languages. *Expert Systems with Applications, 220*, 119722. doi:10.1016/j.eswa.2023.119722

Arakane, T., & Saitoh, T. (2023). Efficient DNN Model for Word Lip-Reading. *Algorithms, 16*(6), 269. doi:10.3390/a16060269

Arif, A. M., Hamad, A. M., & Mansour, M. M. (2023). Internet of (Healthcare) Things Based Monitoring for COVID-19+ Quarantine/Isolation Subjects Using Biomedical Sensors, A Lesson from the Recent Pandemic, and an Approach to the Future. *Journal of Electronics, Electromedical Engineering, and Medical Informatics, 5*(1), 1–12. doi:10.35882/jeeemi.v5i1.267

Ayvaz, S., & Alpay, K. (2021). Predictive maintenance system for production lines in manufacturing: A machine learning approach using IoT data in real-time. *Expert Systems with Applications, 173*, 114598. doi:10.1016/j.eswa.2021.114598

B, M. K., K, K. K., Sasikala, P., Sampath, B., Gopi, B., & Sundaram, S. (2024). Sustainable Green Energy Generation From Waste Water. In *Practice, Progress, and Proficiency in Sustainability* (pp. 440–463). IGI Global. doi:10.4018/979-8-3693-1186-8.ch024

Babu, B. S., Kamalakannan, J., Meenatchi, N., Karthik, S., & Boopathi, S. (2022). Economic impacts and reliability evaluation of battery by adopting Electric Vehicle. *IEEE Explore*, 1–6.

Baek, J. (2023). Smart predictive analytics care monitoring model based on multi sensor IoT system: Management of diaper and attitude for the bedridden elderly. *Sensors International*, *4*, 100213. doi:10.1016/j.sintl.2022.100213

Bahreini, K., Nadolski, R., & Westera, W. (2014). Towards Multimodal Emotion Recognition in E-learning Environment. *Interactive Learning Environments*, *24*(6), 1375–1391.

Balomenos, T., Raouzaiou, A., Ioannou, S., Drosopoulos, A., Karpouzis, K., & Kollias, S. (2001). Emotion analysis in man-machine interaction systems. In *International Workshop on Machine Learning for Multimodal Interaction*. Springer.

Bandela, S. R., & Kumar, T. K. (2017). Stressed speech emotion recognition using feature fusion of teager energy operator and MFCC. *2017 8th International Conference on Computing, Communication and Networking Technologies (ICCCNT),* 1-5.

Batliner, A., Schuller, B., Seppi, D., Steidl, S., Devillers, L., Vidrascu, L., Vogt, T., Aharonson, V., & Amir, N. (2011). *The automatic recognition of emotions in speech. In Emotion-Oriented Systems*. Springer.

Benkerzaz, Elmir, & Dennai. (2019). *A Study on Automatic Speech Recognition*. Academic Press.

Bharathi, M., Geetha, K., & Mani, P. K. (2022). AI and IoT-based Electric Vehicle Monitoring System. Academic Press.

Bhat, G., Danelljan, M., Yu, F., Van Gool, L., & Timofte, R. (2021). Deep reparametrization of multi-frame super-resolution and denoising. In *Proceedings of the IEEE/CVF International Conference on Computer Vision* (pp. 2460-2470). IEEE.

Bishnu, A. (2022). A Novel Frame Structure for Cloud-Based Audio-Visual Speech Enhancement in Multimodal Hearing-aids. *2022 IEEE International Conference on E-health Networking, Application & Services (HealthCom)*, 75-80. 10.1109/HealthCom54947.2022.9982772

Boopathi, S. (2021). Improving of Green Sand-Mould Quality using Taguchi Technique. *Journal of Engineering Research*, in–Press.

Boopathi, S. (2021a). Improving of Green Sand-Mould Quality using Taguchi Technique. *Journal of Engineering Research.*

Boopathi, S. (2021b). *Pollution monitoring and notification: Water pollution monitoring and notification using intelligent RC boat*. Academic Press.

Boopathi, S. (2022). Effects of Cryogenically-treated Stainless Steel on Eco-friendly Wire Electrical Discharge Machining Process. Springer.

Boopathi, S. (2022c). Cryogenically treated and untreated stainless steel grade 317 in sustainable wire electrical discharge machining process: A comparative study. *Environmental Science and Pollution Research*, 1–10.

Boopathi, S. (2022d). Performance Improvement of Eco-Friendly Near-Dry wire-Cut Electrical Discharge Machining Process Using Coconut Oil-Mist Dielectric Fluid. *Journal of Advanced Manufacturing Systems*.

Boopathi, S. (2023). Deep Learning Techniques Applied for Automatic Sentence Generation. In Promoting Diversity, Equity, and Inclusion in Language Learning Environments (pp. 255–273). IGI Global. doi:10.4018/978-1-6684-3632-5.ch016

Boopathi, S. (2023c). Securing Healthcare Systems Integrated With IoT: Fundamentals, Applications, and Future Trends. In Dynamics of Swarm Intelligence Health Analysis for the Next Generation (pp. 186–209). IGI Global.

Boopathi, S., & Khare, R. (2023). Additive Manufacturing Developments in the Medical Engineering Field. In Development, Properties, and Industrial Applications of 3D Printed Polymer Composites (pp. 86–106). IGI Global.

Boopathi, S., Gavaskar, T., Dogga, A. D., Mahendran, R. K., Kumar, A., Kathiresan, G., N., V., Ganesan, M., Ishwarya, K. R., & Ramana, G. V. (2021). *Emergency medicine delivery transportation using unmanned aerial vehicle (Patent Grant)*. Academic Press.

Boopathi, S., Kumar, P. K. S., Meena, R. S., & Sudhakar, M. (2023). Sustainable Developments of Modern Soil-Less Agro-Cultivation Systems: Aquaponic Culture. In Human Agro-Energy Optimization for Business and Industry (pp. 69–87). IGI Global.

Boopathi, S., Kumar, P. K. S., Meena, R. S., Sudhakar, M., & Associates. (2023). Sustainable Developments of Modern Soil-Less Agro-Cultivation Systems: Aquaponic Culture. In Human Agro-Energy Optimization for Business and Industry (pp. 69–87). IGI Global.

Boopathi, S., Lewise, K. A. S., Sarojwal, A., Arulvendhan, K., Sandeepkumar, S., & Subbiah, R. (2022). *An improved aqueous lithium-ion battery with IoT connectivity*. Academic Press.

Boopathi, S., Thillaivanan, A., Mohammed, A. A., Shanmugam, P., & VR, P. (2022). Experimental investigation on Abrasive Water Jet Machining of Neem Wood Plastic Composite. *IOP: Functional Composites and Structures, 4*, 025001.

Boopathi, S. (2022). An investigation on gas emission concentration and relative emission rate of the near-dry wire-cut electrical discharge machining process. *Environmental Science and Pollution Research International, 29*(57), 86237–86246. doi:10.1007/s11356-021-17658-1 PMID:34837614

Boopathi, S. (2022a). An extensive review on sustainable developments of dry and near-dry electrical discharge machining processes. *ASME: Journal of Manufacturing Science and Engineering, 144*(5), 050801–1.

Boopathi, S. (2023a). An Investigation on Friction Stir Processing of Aluminum Alloy-Boron Carbide Surface Composite. In R. V. Vignesh, R. Padmanaban, & M. Govindaraju (Eds.), *Advances in Processing of Lightweight Metal Alloys and Composites* (pp. 249–257). Springer Nature Singapore., doi:10.1007/978-981-19-7146-4_14

Boopathi, S. (2023c). Internet of Things-Integrated Remote Patient Monitoring System: Healthcare Application. In A. Suresh Kumar, U. Kose, S. Sharma, & S. Jerald Nirmal Kumar (Eds.), Advances in Healthcare Information Systems and Administration. IGI Global. doi:10.4018/978-1-6684-6894-4.ch008

Boopathi, S. (2023d). Securing Healthcare Systems Integrated With IoT: Fundamentals, Applications, and Future Trends. In A. Suresh Kumar, U. Kose, S. Sharma, & S. Jerald Nirmal Kumar (Eds.), Advances in Healthcare Information Systems and Administration. IGI Global. doi:10.4018/978-1-6684-6894-4.ch010

Boopathi, S., Alqahtani, A. S., Mubarakali, A., & Panchatcharam, P. (2023). Sustainable developments in near-dry electrical discharge machining process using sunflower oil-mist dielectric fluid. *Environmental Science and Pollution Research International*, 1–20. doi:10.1007/s11356-023-27494-0 PMID:37199846

Boopathi, S., & Davim, J. P. (2023). Applications of Nanoparticles in Various Manufacturing Processes. In S. Boopathi & J. P. Davim (Eds.), Advances in Chemical and Materials Engineering. IGI Global. doi:10.4018/978-1-6684-9135-5.ch001

Boopathi, S., & Davim, J. P. (2023). *Sustainable Utilization of Nanoparticles and Nanofluids in Engineering Applications.* IGI Global. doi:10.4018/978-1-6684-9135-5

Boopathi, S., & Kanike, U. K. (2023). Applications of Artificial Intelligent and Machine Learning Techniques in Image Processing. In *Handbook of Research on Thrust Technologies' Effect on Image Processing* (pp. 151–173). IGI Global. doi:10.4018/978-1-6684-8618-4.ch010

Boopathi, S., Lewise, K. A. S., Subbiah, R., & Sivaraman, G. (2022). Near-dry wire-cut electrical discharge machining process using water–air-mist dielectric fluid: An experimental study. *Materials Today: Proceedings*, *50*(5), 1885–1890. doi:10.1016/j.matpr.2021.08.077

Boopathi, S., & Sivakumar, K. (2012). Experimental Analysis of Eco-friendly Near-dry Wire Electrical Discharge Machining Process. *Archives des Sciences*, *65*(10), 334–346.

Boopathi, S., & Sivakumar, K. (2014). Study of water assisted dry wire-cut electrical discharge machining. *Indian Journal of Engineering and Materials Sciences*, *21*, 75–82.

Boopathi, S., & Sivakumar, K. (2016). Optimal parameter prediction of oxygen-mist near-dry wire-cut EDM. *Inderscience: International Journal of Manufacturing Technology and Management*, *30*(3–4), 164–178. doi:10.1504/IJMTM.2016.077812

Boopathi, S., Umareddy, M., & Elangovan, M. (2023). Applications of Nano-Cutting Fluids in Advanced Machining Processes. In S. Boopathi & J. P. Davim (Eds.), Advances in Chemical and Materials Engineering. IGI Global. doi:10.4018/978-1-6684-9135-5.ch009

Borde, P., Varpe, A., Manza, R., & Yannawar, P. (2015, June). Recognition of isolated words using zernike and mfcc features for audio visual speech recognition. *International Journal of Speech Technology*, *18*(2), 167–175. doi:10.1007/s10772-014-9257-1

Borse, A., & Kharate, D. G. (2022). Fake News Prediction using Hierarchical Attention Network and Hypergraph. SSRN *Electron. J.*, 1–11. doi:10.2139/ssrn.4043857

Boumiza, S., & Bekiarski, A. (2017). Development of Model for Automatic Tutor in E-learning Environment based on Student Reactions Extraction using Facial Recognition. In *IEEE 15-th International Conference on Electrical Machines, Drives and Power Systems (ELMA)*. IEEE.

Bulla, C., & Birje, M. N. (2022). Anomaly detection in industrial IoT applications using deep learning approach. *Artificial Intelligence in Industrial Applications: Approaches to Solve the Intrinsic Industrial Optimization Problems*, 127-147.

Buyya, R., Ilager, S., & Arroba, P. (2023). Energy-Efficiency and Sustainability in New Generation Cloud Computing: A Vision and Directions for Integrated Management of Data Centre Resources and Workloads. *arXiv Preprint arXiv:2303.10572*.

Calabrese, M., Cimmino, M., Fiume, F., Manfrin, M., Romeo, L., Ceccacci, S., Paolanti, M., Toscano, G., Ciandrini, G., Carrotta, A., Mengoni, M., Frontoni, E., & Kapetis, D. (2020). SOPHIA: An event-based IoT and machine learning architecture for predictive maintenance in industry 4.0. *Information (Basel)*, *11*(4), 202. doi:10.3390/info11040202

Cao, Y., & Duan, R. Y. (2011). Novel top-down methods for hierarchical text classification. *Procedia Engineering*, *24*, 329–334. doi:10.1016/j.proeng.2011.11.2651

Carnevale, L., Celesti, A., Galletta, A., Dustdar, S., & Villari, M. (2019). Osmotic computing as a distributed multi-agent system: The body area network scenario. *Internet of Things : Engineering Cyber Physical Human Systems*, *5*, 130–139. doi:10.1016/j.iot.2019.01.001

Chanaa, A., & El Faddouli, N. (2021). E-learning Text Sentiment Classification Using Hierarchical Attention Network (HAN). *International Journal of Emerging Technologies in Learning*, *16*(no. 13), 157–167. doi:10.3991/ijet.v16i13.22579

Chandrika, V., Sivakumar, A., Krishnan, T. S., Pradeep, J., Manikandan, S., & Boopathi, S. (2023). Theoretical Study on Power Distribution Systems for Electric Vehicles. In *Intelligent Engineering Applications and Applied Sciences for Sustainability* (pp. 1–19). IGI Global. doi:10.4018/979-8-3693-0044-2.ch001

Changrampadi, M. H., Shahina, A., Narayanan, M. B., & Khan, A. N. (2022). End-to-End Speech Recognition of Tamil Language. *Intelligent Automation & Soft Computing*, *32*(2).

Chaturanga, S., & Ranathunga, S. (2021). Classification of Code-Mixed Text Using Capsule Networks. *International Conference Recent Advances in Natural Language Processing, RANLP*, 256–263. 10.26615/978-954-452-072-4_030

Cheng, J. C., Chen, W., Chen, K., & Wang, Q. (2020). Data-driven predictive maintenance planning framework for MEP components based on BIM and IoT using machine learning algorithms. *Automation in Construction*, *112*, 103087. doi:10.1016/j.autcon.2020.103087

Chen, H., He, X., Qing, L., Wu, Y., Ren, C., Sheriff, R. E., & Zhu, C. (2022). Real-world single image super-resolution: A brief review. *Information Fusion*, *79*, 124–145.

Chen, M., Zhou, P., & Fortino, G. (2016). Emotion communication system. *IEEE Access : Practical Innovations, Open Solutions*, *5*, 326–337.

Compare, M., Baraldi, P., & Zio, E. (2019). Challenges to IoT-enabled predictive maintenance for industry 4.0. *IEEE Internet of Things Journal*, *7*(5), 4585–4597. doi:10.1109/JIOT.2019.2957029

Cowie, R., Douglas-Cowie, E., Tsapatsoulis, N., Votsis, G., Kollias, S., Fellenz, W., & Taylor, J. G. (n.d.). Emotion recognition in human-computer interaction. *IEEE Signal Processing Magazine*, *18*(1), 32–80.

Cross, E. S., Williams, L. R., Lewis, D. K., Magoon, G. R., Onasch, T. B., Kaminsky, M. L., Worsnop, D. R., & Jayne, J. T. (2017). Use of electrochemical sensors for measurement of air pollution: Correcting interference response and validating measurements. *Atmospheric Measurement Techniques*, *10*(9), 3575–3588. doi:10.5194/amt-10-3575-2017

Dalal, N., & Triggs, B. (2005). Histogram of Oriented Gradients for Human Detection. In *Proceedings of the 2005 IEEE Computer Society Conference on Computer Vision and Pattern Recognition (CVPR)* (pp. 63-69). IEEE. 10.1109/CVPR.2005.177

Dalmiya, C. P., Dharun, V. S., & Rajesh, K. P. (2013, April). An efficient method for Tamil speech recognition using MFCC and DTW for mobile applications. In *2013 IEEE Conference on Information & Communication Technologies* (pp. 1263-1268). IEEE. 10.1109/CICT.2013.6558295

Dass james, A., & Boopathi, S. (2016). Experimental Study of Eco-friendly Wire-Cut Electrical Discharge Machining Processes. *International Journal of Innovative Research in Science, Engineering and Technology, 5*.

Das, S., Lekhya, G., Shreya, K., Lydia Shekinah, K., Babu, K. K., & Boopathi, S. (2024). Fostering Sustainability Education Through Cross-Disciplinary Collaborations and Research Partnerships: Interdisciplinary Synergy. In P. Yu, J. Mulli, Z. A. S. Syed, & L. Umme (Eds.), Advances in Higher Education and Professional Development. IGI Global. doi:10.4018/979-8-3693-0487-7.ch003

Demircan, S., & Kahramanlı, H. (2014). Feature extraction from speech data for emotion recognition. *J. Adv. Comput. Netw.*, *2*(1), 28–30.

Devasena, Ramya, Dharshan, Vivek, & Darshan. (2019). IoT based water distribution system. *International Journal of Engineering and Advanced Technology, 8*(6), 132-135.

Dhanya, D., Kumar, S. S., Thilagavathy, A., Prasad, D., & Boopathi, S. (2023). Data Analytics and Artificial Intelligence in the Circular Economy: Case Studies. In Intelligent Engineering Applications and Applied Sciences for Sustainability (pp. 40–58). IGI Global.

Dimmita, N., & Siddaiah, P. (2019, September). Speech Recognition Using Convolutional. *Neural Networks.*

Domakonda, V. K., Farooq, S., Chinthamreddy, S., Puviarasi, R., Sudhakar, M., & Boopathi, S. (2022). Sustainable Developments of Hybrid Floating Solar Power Plants: Photovoltaic System. In Human Agro-Energy Optimization for Business and Industry (pp. 148–167). IGI Global.

Dong, C., Loy, C. C., He, K., & Tang, X. (2015). Image super-resolution using deep convolutional networks. *IEEE Transactions on Pattern Analysis and Machine Intelligence, 38*(2), 295–307.

Durairaj, M., Jayakumar, S. Monika, Karpagavalli, V. S., Maheswari, B. U., & Boopathi, S. (2023). Utilization of Digital Tools in the Indian Higher Education System During Health Crises. In C. S. V. Negrão, I. G. P. Maia, & J. A. F. Brito (Eds.), Advances in Logistics, Operations, and Management Science (pp. 1–21). IGI Global. doi:10.4018/978-1-7998-9213-7.ch001

Ebneyousef, S., & Shirmarz, A. (2023). A taxonomy of load balancing algorithms and approaches in fog computing: A survey. *Cluster Computing, 26*(5), 1–22. doi:10.1007/s10586-023-03982-3

Ehsani. (2005). *Hybrid Electric and Fuel Cell Vehicles: Fundamentals, Theory and Design.* Academic Press.

Eltouny & Liang. (2022). Large-scale Structural Health Monitoring using Composite Recurrent neural networks and grid environments. Academic Press.

Ettiyan, R., & Geetha, V. (2023). A hybrid logistic DNA-based encryption system for securing the Internet of Things patient monitoring systems. *Healthcare Analytics, 3*, 100149. doi:10.1016/j.health.2023.100149

Fadnavis, S. (2014). Image interpolation techniques in digital image processing: An overview. *International Journal of Engineering Research and Applications, 4*(10), 70–73.

Famá, F., Faria, J. N., & Portugal, D. (2022). An IoT-based interoperable architecture for wireless biomonitoring of patients with sensor patches. *Internet of Things : Engineering Cyber Physical Human Systems, 19*, 100547. doi:10.1016/j.iot.2022.100547

Fan, Z., Yan, Z., & Wen, S. (2023). Deep Learning and Artificial Intelligence in Sustainability: A Review of SDGs, Renewable Energy, and Environmental Health. *Sustainability (Basel), 15*(18), 13493. doi:10.3390/su151813493

Fares, K., Amine, K., & Salah, E. (2020). A robust blind color image watermarking based on Fourier transform domain. *Optik (Stuttgart), 208*(February), 164562. doi:10.1016/j.ijleo.2020.164562

Farooq. (2023). Role of Internet of things in diabetes healthcare: Network infrastructure, taxonomy, challenges, and security model. *Digit Health, 9.* . doi:10.1177/20552076231179056

Fathima, N., Patel, T., Mahima, C., & Iyengar, A. (2018, September). TDNN-based Multilingual Speech Recognition System for Low Resource Indian Languages. In INTERSPEECH (pp. 3197-3201). doi:10.21437/Interspeech.2018-2117

Fazli, S., & Moeini, M. (2016). A robust image watermarking method based on DWT, DCT, and SVD using a new technique for correction of main geometric attacks. *Optik (Stuttgart), 127*(2), 964–972. doi:10.1016/j.ijleo.2015.09.205

Feng, Z., Su, J., & Cao, J. (2022). BHF: BERT-based Hierarchical Attention Fusion Network for Cyberbullying Remarks Detection. *ACM Int. Conf. Proceeding Ser.*, 1–7. 10.1145/3578741.3578742

Fernández, C. M., Rodríguez, M. D., & Muñoz, B. R. (2018, May). An edge computing architecture in the Internet of Things. In *2018 IEEE 21st international symposium on real-time distributed computing (ISORC)* (pp. 99-102). IEEE.

Feroz, B., Mehmood, A., Maryam, H., Zeadally, S., Maple, C., & Shah, M. A. (2021). Vehicle-life interaction in fog-enabled smart connected and autonomous vehicles. *IEEE Access : Practical Innovations, Open Solutions*, *9*, 7402–7420. doi:10.1109/ACCESS.2020.3049110

Ferrer-Cid, P., Barcelo-Ordinas, J. M., Garcia-Vidal, J., Ripoll, A., & Viana, M. (2020). Multi sensor data fusion calibration in IoT air pollution platforms. *IEEE Internet of Things Journal*, *7*(4), 3124–3132. doi:10.1109/JIOT.2020.2965283

Fowziya, S., Sivaranjani, S., Devi, N. L., Boopathi, S., Thakur, S., & Sailaja, J. M. (2023). Influences of nano-green lubricants in the friction-stir process of TiAlN coated alloys. *Materials Today: Proceedings*. Advance online publication. doi:10.1016/j.matpr.2023.06.446

Gaba, P., & Raw, R. S. (2020). Vehicular cloud and fog computing architecture, applications, services, and challenges. In *IoT and cloud computing advancements in vehicular ad-hoc networks* (pp. 268–296). IGI Global. doi:10.4018/978-1-7998-2570-8.ch014

Gao, S., Young, M. T., Qiu, J. X., Yoon, H.-J., Christian, J. B., Fearn, P. A., Tourassi, G. D., & Ramanthan, A. (2018). Hierarchical attention networks for information extraction from cancer pathology reports. *Journal of the American Medical Informatics Association : JAMIA*, *25*(3), 321–330. doi:10.1093/jamia/ocx131 PMID:29155996

Garnero, G., & Godone, D. (2014). Comparisons between different interpolation techniques. *The International Archives of the Photogrammetry, Remote Sensing and Spatial Information Sciences*, *40*, 139–144.

Ghadekar, P., Jhanwar, K., Sivanandan, A., Shetty, T., Karpe, A., & Khushalani, P. (2023, November). ASR for Indian regional language using Nvidia's NeMo toolkit. In AIP Conference Proceedings (Vol. 2851, No. 1). AIP Publishing. doi:10.1063/5.0178629

Ghobaei-Arani, M., & Shahidinejad, A. (2022). A cost-efficient IoT service placement approach using whale optimization algorithm in fog computing environment. *Expert Systems with Applications*, *200*, 117012. doi:10.1016/j.eswa.2022.117012

Ghobakhloo, M. (2020). Determinants of information and digital technology implementation for smart manufacturing. *International Journal of Production Research*, *58*(8), 2384–2405. doi:10.1080/00207543.2019.1630775

Gilke, Kachare, Kothalikar, Rodrigues, & Pednekar. (2012). MFCC-based Vocal Emotion Recognition Using ANN. *International Conference on Electronics Engineering and Informatics, 49.*

Girirajan, S., & Pandian, A. (2022a). Convolutional Neural Network Based Automatic Speech Recognition for Tamil Language. In *Applications of Artificial Intelligence and Machine Learning: Select Proceedings of ICAAAIML 2021* (pp. 91-103). Singapore: Springer Nature Singapore. 10.1007/978-981-19-4831-2_8

Girirajan, S., & Pandian, A. (2022b). Hybrid Feature Extraction Technique for Tamil Automatic Speech Recognition System in Noisy Environment. *Recent Trends in Communication and Intelligent Systems Proceedings of ICRTCIS, 2021*, 1–11.

Giurgiutiu. (2014). Challenges and opportunities for structural health monitoring for PVP applications. *Proceedings of the ASME 2014 Pressure vessels and piping conference, vol. 6A: Materials and Fabrication.*

Gnanaprakasam, C., Vankara, J., Sastry, A. S., Prajval, V., Gireesh, N., & Boopathi, S. (2023). Long-Range and Low-Power Automated Soil Irrigation System Using Internet of Things: An Experimental Study. In Contemporary Developments in Agricultural Cyber-Physical Systems (pp. 87–104). IGI Global.

Goudarzi, M., Palaniswami, M., & Buyya, R. (2022). Scheduling IoT applications in edge and fog computing environments: A taxonomy and future directions. *ACM Computing Surveys*, *55*(7), 1–41. doi:10.1145/3544836

Gowri, N. V., Dwivedi, J. N., Krishnaveni, K., Boopathi, S., Palaniappan, M., & Medikondu, N. R. (2023). Experimental investigation and multi-objective optimization of eco-friendly near-dry electrical discharge machining of shape memory alloy using Cu/SiC/Gr composite electrode. *Environmental Science and Pollution Research International*, *30*(49), 1–19. doi:10.1007/s11356-023-26983-6 PMID:37126160

Grabowska, S. (2020). Smart factories in the age of Industry 4.0. *Management Systems in Production Engineering, 2*(28), 90–96.

Gui, Y., Gao, Z., Li, R., & Yang, X. (2012). Hierarchical text classification for news articles based-on named entities. Lect. Notes Comput. Sci. (including Subser. Lect. Notes Artif. Intell. Lect. Notes Bioinformatics), 7713, 318–329. doi:10.1007/978-3-642-35527-1_27

Gunasekaran, K., & Boopathi, S. (2023). Artificial Intelligence in Water Treatments and Water Resource Assessments. In V. Shikuku (Ed.), Advances in Environmental Engineering and Green Technologies. IGI Global. doi:10.4018/978-1-6684-6791-6.ch004

Guo, J. M., & Prasetyo, H. (2014). False-positive-free SVD-based image watermarking. *Journal of Visual Communication and Image Representation*, *25*(5), 1149–1163. doi:10.1016/j.jvcir.2014.03.012

Gupta, Fahad, & Deepak. (2020). Pitch-synchronous single frequency filtering spectrogram for speech emotion recognition. *International Journal of Multimedia Tools and Applications.* doi:10.1007/s11042-020-09068-1

Han, S., Mao, R., & Cambria, E. (2022). Hierarchical Attention Network for Explainable Depression Detection on Twitter Aided by Metaphor Concept Mappings. *Proc. - Int. Conf. Comput. Linguist. COLING*, *29*(1), 94–104.

Han, Z. (2021). An Effective Encrypted Traffic Classification Method Based on Pruning Convolutional Neural Networks for Cloud Platform. *Proc. - 2021 2nd Int. Conf. Electron. Commun. Inf. Technol. CECIT 2021*, 206–211. 10.1109/CECIT53797.2021.00043

Hanumanthakari, S., Gift, M. M., Kanimozhi, K., Bhavani, M. D., Bamane, K. D., & Boopathi, S. (2023). Biomining Method to Extract Metal Components Using Computer-Printed Circuit Board E-Waste. In *Handbook of Research on Safe Disposal Methods of Municipal Solid Wastes for a Sustainable Environment* (pp. 123–141). IGI Global. doi:10.4018/978-1-6684-8117-2.ch010

Happy, S. L. (2013). Automated Alertness and Emotion Detection for Empathic Feedback During E-Learning. IEEE.

Harikaran, M., Boopathi, S., Gokulakannan, S., & Poonguzhali, M. (2023). Study on the Source of E-Waste Management and Disposal Methods. In *Sustainable Approaches and Strategies for E-Waste Management and Utilization* (pp. 39–60). IGI Global. doi:10.4018/978-1-6684-7573-7.ch003

Hashim, Zarifie, Abd Aziz, Zoinol, Salleh, & Najmiah. (n.d.). Agriculture monitoring system: A study. *Journal Technologies, 77*. doi:10.11113/jt.v77.4099

Hema, N., Krishnamoorthy, N., Chavan, S. M., Kumar, N., Sabarimuthu, M., & Boopathi, S. (2023). A Study on an Internet of Things (IoT)-Enabled Smart Solar Grid System. In *Handbook of Research on Deep Learning Techniques for Cloud-Based Industrial IoT* (pp. 290–308). IGI Global. doi:10.4018/978-1-6684-8098-4.ch017

Hidayatullah, A. F., Apong, R. A., Lai, D. T. C., & Qazi, A. (2023). Corpus creation and language identification for code-mixed Indonesian-Javanese-English Tweets. *PeerJ. Computer Science*, *9*, e1312. Advance online publication. doi:10.7717/peerj-cs.1312 PMID:37409088

Hossain, M. S., & Muhammad, G. (2019). Emotion recognition using deep Learning approach from audio-visual emotional big data. *Information Fusion*, *49*, 69-78.

Hour, Chen, Guo, & Xiao. (2020). Lip Reading Sentences Using Deep Learning With Only Visual Cues. *IEEE Access*.

Hu. (2008). *Evaluation of Objective Quality Measures for Speech Enhancement*. Academic Press.

Hyysalo, J., Dasanayake, S., Hannu, J., Schuss, C., Rajanen, M., Leppänen, T., Doermann, D., & Sauvola, J. (2022). Smart mask–Wearable IoT solution for improved protection and personal health. *Internet of Things : Engineering Cyber Physical Human Systems*, *18*, 100511. doi:10.1016/j.iot.2022.100511 PMID:37521492

Ilyas, A., Alatawi, M. N., Hamid, Y., Mahfooz, S., Zada, I., Gohar, N., & Shah, M. A. (2022). Software architecture for pervasive critical health monitoring system using fog computing. *Journal of Cloud Computing (Heidelberg, Germany)*, *11*(1), 84. doi:10.1186/s13677-022-00371-w PMID:36465318

Indhumathi, R., & Geetha, A. (2019). Emotional Interfaces for Effective E-Reading using Machine Learning Techniques. *International Journal of Recent Technology and Engineering, 8*(4), 4443–4449.

Ingle, R. B., Senthil, T. S., Swathi, S., Muralidharan, N., Mahendran, G., & Boopathi, S. (2023). Sustainability and Optimization of Green and Lean Manufacturing Processes Using Machine Learning Techniques. IGI Global. doi:10.4018/978-1-6684-8238-4.ch012

Ismail, Dawoud, Ismail, Marsh, & Alshami. (2022). IoT-Based Water Management Systems: Survey and Future Research Direction. *IEEE Access, 10*, 35942 – 35952.

Ismail, R., Fattah, A., Saqr, H. M., & Nasr, M. E. (2022). An efficient medical image encryption scheme for (WBAN) based on adaptive DNA and modern multi chaotic map. *Multimedia Tools and Applications*. Advance online publication. doi:10.1007/s11042-022-13343-8

Jadhav, A. R. (2017, July). Drive Cycle Analysis for Electric Vehicle using MATLAB. *International Journal of Engineering Science.*

Janardhana, K., Singh, V., Singh, S. N., Babu, T. R., Bano, S., & Boopathi, S. (2023). Utilization Process for Electronic Waste in Eco-Friendly Concrete: Experimental Study. In Sustainable Approaches and Strategies for E-Waste Management and Utilization (pp. 204–223). IGI Global.

Javaid, M., & Khan, I. H. (2021). Internet of Things (IoT) enabled healthcare helps to take the challenges of COVID-19 Pandemic. *Journal of Oral Biology and Craniofacial Research, 11*(2), 209–214. doi:10.1016/j.jobcr.2021.01.015 PMID:33665069

Jeevanantham, Y. A., Saravanan, A., Vanitha, V., Boopathi, S., & Kumar, D. P. (2022). Implementation of Internet-of Things (IoT) in Soil Irrigation System. *IEEE Explore*, 1–5.

Jeon, Y. J., Park, S. H., & Kang, S. J. (2023). Self-x based closed loop wearable IoT for real-time detection and resolution of sleep apnea. *Internet of Things : Engineering Cyber Physical Human Systems, 22*, 100767. doi:10.1016/j.iot.2023.100767

Joshi & Chawan. (2018). Logistic regression and SVM based diabetes prediction system. *Int. J. Technol. Res. Eng., 11*(5).

Joshi, R. D., & Dhakal, C. K. (2021). Predicting Type 2 Diabetes Using Logistic Regression and Machine Learning Approaches. *International Journal of Environmental Research and Public Health, 18*(14), 7346. doi:10.3390/ijerph18147346 PMID:34299797

Jyothi Rani. (n.d.). Diabetes Prediction using Machine Learning. *International Journal of Scientific Research in Computer Science, Engineering and Information Technology*. doi:10.32628/CSEIT206463

Kalaivani, A., & Thenmozhi, D. (2020). *SSN_NLP_MLRG@Dravidian-CodeMix-FIRE2020: Sentiment Code-Mixed Text Classification in Tamil and Malayalam using ULMFiT*. Available: http://ceur-ws.org

Kalajdjieski, J., Stojkoska, B. R., & Trivodaliev, K. (2020, November). IoT based framework for air pollution monitoring in smart cities. In *2020 28th Telecommunications Forum (TELFOR)* (pp. 1-4). IEEE. 10.1109/TELFOR51502.2020.9306531

Kamruzzaman, M. M., Yan, B., Sarker, M. N. I., Alruwaili, O., Wu, M., & Alrashdi, I. (2022). Blockchain and fog computing in IoT-driven healthcare services for smart cities. *Journal of Healthcare Engineering*, *2022*, 2022. doi:10.1155/2022/9957888 PMID:35126961

Kannan, E., Trabelsi, Y., Boopathi, S., & Alagesan, S. (2022). Influences of cryogenically treated work material on near-dry wire-cut electrical discharge machining process. *Surface Topography : Metrology and Properties*, *10*(1), 015027. doi:10.1088/2051-672X/ac53e1

Karamitsos, I., Albarhami, S., & Apostolopoulos, C. (2019). Tweet Sentiment Analysis (TSA) for Cloud Providers Using Classification Algorithms and Latent Semantic Analysis. *J. Data Anal. Inf. Process.*, *07*(04), 276–294. doi:10.4236/jdaip.2019.74016

Karthik, S., Hemalatha, R., Aruna, R., Deivakani, M., Reddy, R. V. K., & Boopathi, S. (2023). Study on Healthcare Security System-Integrated Internet of Things (IoT). In Perspectives and Considerations on the Evolution of Smart Systems (pp. 342–362). IGI Global.

Karthik, S. A., Hemalatha, R., Aruna, R., Deivakani, M., Reddy, R. V. K., & Boopathi, S. (2023). Study on Healthcare Security System-Integrated Internet of Things (IoT). In M. K. Habib (Ed.), Advances in Systems Analysis, Software Engineering, and High Performance Computing. IGI Global. doi:10.4018/978-1-6684-7684-0.ch013

Karunanayake, Y., Thayasivam, U., & Ranathunga, S. (2019, November). Sinhala and tamil speech intent identification from english phoneme based asr. In *2019 International Conference on Asian Language Processing (IALP)* (pp. 234-239). IEEE. 10.1109/IALP48816.2019.9037702

Kasat, K., Rani, D. L., Khan, B., Kirubakaran, M. K., & Malathi, P. (2022). A novel security framework for healthcare data through IOT sensors. *Measurement. Sensors*, *24*, 100535. doi:10.1016/j.measen.2022.100535

Kaushik, K. (2023). Smart Agriculture Applications Using Cloud and IoT. *Convergence of Cloud with AI for Big Data Analytics: Foundations and Innovation*, 89-105.

Kavitha, C. R., Varalatchoumy, M., Mithuna, H. R., Bharathi, K., Geethalakshmi, N. M., & Boopathi, S. (2023). Energy Monitoring and Control in the Smart Grid: Integrated Intelligent IoT and ANFIS. In M. Arshad (Ed.), Advances in Bioinformatics and Biomedical Engineering. IGI Global. doi:10.4018/978-1-6684-6577-6.ch014

Kazemivash, B., & Moghaddam, M. E. (2018). A predictive model-based image watermarking scheme using Regression Tree and Firefly algorithm. *Soft Computing*, *22*(12), 4083–4098. doi:10.1007/s00500-017-2617-4

KazhuparambilS.KaushikA. (2020). Cooking Is All About People: Comment Classification On Cookery Channels Using BERT and Classification Models (Malayalam-English Mix-Code). doi:10.20944/preprints202006.0223.v1

Khan, A. N., & Yegnanarayana, B. (2001). Development of speech recognition system for Tamil for small restricted task. In *Proceedings of national conference on communication* (No. 3). Academic Press.

Kim, M., Yeo, J. H., & Ro, Y. M. (n.d.). Distinguishing homophenes using multi-head visual-audio memory for lip reading. *Proceedings of the AAAI Conference on Artificial Intelligence, 36*(1), 1174-1182. 10.1609/aaai.v36i1.20003

Kiran, R., Nivedha, K., & Subha, T. (2017, February). Voice and speech recognition in Tamil language. In *2017 2nd International Conference on Computing and Communications Technologies (ICCCT)* (pp. 288-292). IEEE.

Kochovski, P., Gec, S., Stankovski, V., Bajec, M., & Drobintsev, P. D. (2019). Trust management in a blockchain based fog computing platform with trustless smart oracles. *Future Generation Computer Systems, 101*, 747–759. doi:10.1016/j.future.2019.07.030

Koolagudi, S. G., & Rao, K. S. (2012). Emotion recognition from speech: A review. *International Journal of Speech Technology, 15*(2), 99–117.

Koshariya, A. K., Kalaiyarasi, D., Jovith, A. A., Sivakami, T., Hasan, D. S., & Boopathi, S. (2023). AI-Enabled IoT and WSN-Integrated Smart Agriculture System. In *Artificial Intelligence Tools and Technologies for Smart Farming and Agriculture Practices* (pp. 200–218). IGI Global. doi:10.4018/978-1-6684-8516-3.ch011

Koshariya, A. K., Khatoon, S., Marathe, A. M., Suba, G. M., Baral, D., & Boopathi, S. (2023). Agricultural Waste Management Systems Using Artificial Intelligence Techniques. In S. Kautish, N. K. Chaubey, S. B. Goyal, & P. Whig (Eds.), Advances in Computational Intelligence and Robotics. IGI Global. doi:10.4018/978-1-6684-8171-4.ch009

Krishna, Gopinath, Lakshmanudu, Prasad, & Kuma. (2019). IoT Enabled Water Distribution system. *Journal of Emerging Technologies and Innovative Research*, 351-355. www.jetir.org

Krithika, L. B., & Lakshmi Priya, G. G. (2016). *Student Emotion Recognition System (SERS) for E-learning Improvement on Learners Concentration Metric*. Elsevier B.V. doi:10.1016/j.procs.2016.05.264

Kumar Mahata, S., Das, D., & Bandyopadhyay, S. (2021). Sentiment Classification of Code-Mixed Tweets using Bi-Directional RNN and Language Tags. *Proceedings of the First Workshop on Speech and Language Technologies for Dravidian Languages*, 28-35. Available: https://scikit-learn.org/stable/

Kumar Reddy, R. V., Rahamathunnisa, U., Subhashini, P., Aancy, H. M., Meenakshi, S., & Boopathi, S. (2023). Solutions for Software Requirement Risks Using Artificial Intelligence Techniques. In T. Murugan & N. E. (Eds.), Advances in Information Security, Privacy, and Ethics (pp. 45–64). IGI Global. doi:10.4018/978-1-6684-8145-5.ch003

Kumar, P., Sampath, B., Kumar, S., Babu, B. H., & Ahalya, N. (2023). Hydroponics, Aeroponics, and Aquaponics Technologies in Modern Agricultural Cultivation. In Trends, Paradigms, and Advances in Mechatronics Engineering (pp. 223–241). IGI Global.

Kumara, V., Mohanaprakash, T., Fairooz, S., Jamal, K., Babu, T., & Sampath, B. (2023). Experimental Study on a Reliable Smart Hydroponics System. In *Human Agro-Energy Optimization for Business and Industry* (pp. 27–45). IGI Global. doi:10.4018/978-1-6684-4118-3.ch002

Kumar, D., Mandal, N., & Kumar, Y. (2023). Fog-based framework for diabetes prediction using hybrid ANFIS model in cloud environment. *Personal and Ubiquitous Computing*, *27*(3), 909–916. doi:10.1007/s00779-022-01678-w PMID:33815032

Kumari, N., Yadav, A., & Jana, P. K. (2022). Task offloading in fog computing: A survey of algorithms and optimization techniques. *Computer Networks*, *214*, 109137. doi:10.1016/j.comnet.2022.109137

Kumar, J., Singh, P., Yadav, A. K., & Kumar, A. (2018). Asymmetric Cryptosystem for Phase Images in Fractional Fourier Domain Using LU-Decomposition and Arnold Transform. *Procedia Computer Science*, *132*, 1570–1577. doi:10.1016/j.procs.2018.05.121

Kumar, P. R., Meenakshi, S., Shalini, S., Devi, S. R., & Boopathi, S. (2023). Soil Quality Prediction in Context Learning Approaches Using Deep Learning and Blockchain for Smart Agriculture. In R. Kumar, A. B. Abdul Hamid, & N. I. Binti Ya'akub (Eds.), Advances in Computational Intelligence and Robotics. IGI Global. doi:10.4018/978-1-6684-9151-5.ch001

Kumar, S., Singh, B. K., & Yadav, M. (2020). A Recent Survey on Multimedia and Database Watermarking. *Multimedia Tools and Applications*, *79*(27–28), 20149–20197. doi:10.1007/s11042-020-08881-y

Kusiak, A. (2019). Fundamentals of smart manufacturing: A multi-thread perspective. *Annual Reviews in Control*, *47*, 214–220. doi:10.1016/j.arcontrol.2019.02.001

Lakkhanawannakun. (2019). *Speech Recognition using Deep Learning*. Academic Press.

Lalitha, S., Madhavan, A., Bhushan, B., & Saketh, S. (2014a). Speech emotion recognition. In *Advances in Electronics, Computers and Communications (ICAECC), International Conference on*. IEEE.

Lalitha, S., Madhavan, A., Bhushan, B., & Saketh, S. (2014b). Speech emotion recognition. *Proc. Int. Conf. Adv. Electron. Comput. Commun. (ICAECC)*, 1-4.

Lane, N. D., & Georgiev, P. (2015). Can deep learning revolutionize mobile Sensing? In *Proceedings of the 16th International Workshop on Mobile Computing Systems and Applications*. ACM.

Leng, J., Wang, D., Shen, W., Li, X., Liu, Q., & Chen, X. (2021). Digital twins-based smart manufacturing system design in Industry 4.0: A review. *Journal of Manufacturing Systems*, *60*, 119–137. doi:10.1016/j.jmsy.2021.05.011

Le, & Provost. (2013). Emotion recognition from spontaneous speech using hidden markov models with deep belief networks. In *2013 IEEE Workshop on Automatic Speech Recognition and Understanding*. IEEE.

Lewis, Peltier, & von Schneidemesser. (2018). *Low-cost sensors for the measurement of atmospheric composition: overview of topic and future applications*. Academic Press.

Li, G., Yang, Y., Qu, X., Cao, D., & Li, K. (2021). A deep learning based image enhancement approach for autonomous driving at night. *Knowledge-Based Systems*, *213*, 106617.

Li, J., & Liu, H. (2013). Colour image encryption based on advanced encryption standard algorithm with two-dimensional chaotic map. *IET Information Security*, *7*(4), 265–270. doi:10.1049/iet-ifs.2012.0304

Liu, Y., Yu, W., Dillon, T., Rahayu, W., & Li, M. (2021). Empowering IoT predictive maintenance solutions with AI: A distributed system for manufacturing plant-wide monitoring. *IEEE Transactions on Industrial Informatics*, *18*(2), 1345–1354. doi:10.1109/TII.2021.3091774

Li, W., Hu, X., Wu, J., Fan, K., Chen, B., & Wu, P. (2022). Dual-color terahertz spatial light modulator for single-pixel imaging. *Light, Science & Applications*, *11*(1), 191.

Li, X., Song, J., & Liu, W. (2020). Label-Attentive Hierarchical Attention Network for Text Classification. *ACM Int. Conf. Proceeding Ser.*, 90–96. 10.1145/3404687.3404706

Lkozma. (n.d.). http://www.lkozma.net/knn2.pdf

Lu, Y., Xu, X., & Wang, L. (2020). Smart manufacturing process and system automation–a critical review of the standards and envisioned scenarios. *Journal of Manufacturing Systems*, *56*, 312–325. doi:10.1016/j.jmsy.2020.06.010

Maguluri, L. P., Ananth, J., Hariram, S., Geetha, C., Bhaskar, A., & Boopathi, S. (2023). Smart Vehicle-Emissions Monitoring System Using Internet of Things (IoT). In Handbook of Research on Safe Disposal Methods of Municipal Solid Wastes for a Sustainable Environment (pp. 191–211). IGI Global.

Maguluri, L. P., Ananth, J., Hariram, S., Geetha, C., Bhaskar, A., & Boopathi, S. (2023). Smart Vehicle-Emissions Monitoring System Using Internet of Things (IoT). In P. Srivastava, D. Ramteke, A. K. Bedyal, M. Gupta, & J. K. Sandhu (Eds.), Practice, Progress, and Proficiency in Sustainability. IGI Global., doi:10.4018/978-1-6684-8117-2.ch014

Maguluri, L. P., Arularasan, A. N., & Boopathi, S. (2023). Assessing Security Concerns for AI-Based Drones in Smart Cities. In R. Kumar, A. B. Abdul Hamid, & N. I. Binti Ya'akub (Eds.), Advances in Computational Intelligence and Robotics. IGI Global. doi:10.4018/978-1-6684-9151-5.ch002

Maheswari, B. U., Imambi, S. S., Hasan, D., Meenakshi, S., Pratheep, V., & Boopathi, S. (2023). Internet of Things and Machine Learning-Integrated Smart Robotics. In Global Perspectives on Robotics and Autonomous Systems: Development and Applications (pp. 240–258). IGI Global. doi:10.4018/978-1-6684-7791-5.ch010

Mahmud, R., Ramamohanarao, K., & Buyya, R. (2020). Application management in fog computing environments: A taxonomy, review and future directions. *ACM Computing Surveys*, *53*(4), 1–43. doi:10.1145/3403955

Malibari, A. A. (2023). An efficient IoT-Artificial intelligence-based disease prediction using lightweight CNN in healthcare system. *Measurement. Sensors*, *26*, 100695. doi:10.1016/j.measen.2023.100695

Mantri, R., Raghavendra, K. R., Puri, H., Chaudhary, J., & Bingi, K. (2021, July). Weather prediction and classification using neural networks and k-nearest neighbors. In *2021 8th International Conference on Smart Computing and Communications (ICSCC)* (pp. 263-268). IEEE. 10.1109/ICSCC51209.2021.9528115

Mariyam, M. A., Althaf, S. K., Basha, H., & Raju, S. V. (2023). Long Document Classification using Hierarchical Attention Networks. *International Journal of Intelligent Systems and Applications in Engineering, 2,* 343–353. Available: www.ijisae.org

Math. (n.d.). http://www.math.le.ac.uk/people/ag153/homepage/KNN/KNN3.html

Mehta, R., Rajpal, N., & Vishwakarma, V. P. (2018). Robust image watermarking scheme in lifting wavelet domain using GA-LSVR hybridization. *International Journal of Machine Learning and Cybernetics*, *9*(1), 145–161. doi:10.1007/s13042-015-0329-6

Metaxa, S., Kalkanis, K., Psomopoulos, C. S., & Stavros, D. (2019). A review of structural health monitoring methods for composite materials. *Procedia Structural Integrity, 22*, 369-375.

Mishra, R., Boopathy, S. R. G., Ravikiran, M., Kulkarni, S., Mukherjee, M., Ganesh, A., & Banerjee, K. (2023, September). Revisiting Automatic Speech Recognition for Tamil and Hindi Connected Number Recognition. In *Proceedings of the Third Workshop on Speech and Language Technologies for Dravidian Languages* (pp. 116-123). Academic Press.

Mishra, S., Khouqeer, G. A., Aamna, B., Alodhayb, A., Ibrahim, S. J. A., Hooda, M., & Jayaswal, G. (2023). A review: Recent advancements in sensor technology for non-invasive neonatal health monitoring. *Biosensors & Bioelectronics: X*, *14*, 100332. doi:10.1016/j.biosx.2023.100332

Mishra, S., & Sharma, S. K. (2023). Advanced contribution of IoT in agricultural production for the development of smart livestock environments. *Internet of Things : Engineering Cyber Physical Human Systems*, *22*, 100724. Advance online publication. doi:10.1016/j.iot.2023.100724

Mohammed, B. A., Al-Shareeda, M. A., Manickam, S., Al-Mekhlafi, Z. G., Alreshidi, A., Alazmi, M., Alshudukhi, J. S., & Alsaffar, M. (2023). FC-PA: Fog computing-based pseudonym authentication scheme in 5G-enabled vehicular networks. *IEEE Access : Practical Innovations, Open Solutions*, *11*, 18571–18581. doi:10.1109/ACCESS.2023.3247222

Mohanty, A., Jothi, B., Jeyasudha, J., Ranjit, P. S., Isaac, J. S., & Boopathi, S. (2023). Additive Manufacturing Using Robotic Programming. In S. Kautish, N. K. Chaubey, S. B. Goyal, & P. Whig (Eds.), Advances in Computational Intelligence and Robotics. IGI Global. doi:10.4018/978-1-6684-8171-4.ch010

Morabito, G., Sicari, C., Ruggeri, A., Celesti, A., & Carnevale, L. (2023). Secure-by-design serverless workflows on the Edge–Cloud Continuum through the Osmotic Computing paradigm. *Internet of Things : Engineering Cyber Physical Human Systems, 22*, 100737. doi:10.1016/j.iot.2023.100737

Morello, R., Ruffa, F., Jablonski, I., Fabbiano, L., & De Capua, C. (2022). An IoT based ECG system to diagnose cardiac pathologies for healthcare applications in smart cities. *Measurement, 190*, 110685. doi:10.1016/j.measurement.2021.110685

Morshed, A., Jayaraman, P. P., Sellis, T., Georgakopoulos, D., Villari, M., & Ranjan, R. (2017). Deep Osmosis: Holistic Distributed Deep Learning in Osmotic Computing. IEEE Cloud Computing, 4(6), 22-32. doi:10.1109/MCC.2018.1081070

Mourtzis, D., Angelopoulos, J., & Panopoulos, N. (2021). Smart manufacturing and tactile internet based on 5G in industry 4.0: Challenges, applications and new trends. *Electronics (Basel), 10*(24), 3175. doi:10.3390/electronics10243175

Mudaliar, N. K., Hegde, K., Ramesh, A., & Patil, V. (2020). Visual Speech Recognition: A Deep Learning Approach. *2020 5th International Conference on Communication and Electronics Systems (ICCES)*, 1218-1221. 10.1109/ICCES48766.2020.9137926

Murugesan, S. (2008). Harnessing green IT: Principles and practices. *IT Professional, 10*(1), 24–33. doi:10.1109/MITP.2008.10

Mustapha, U. F., Alhassan, A.-W., Jiang, D.-N., & Li, G.-L. (2021). Sustainable aquaculture development: A review on the roles of cloud computing, internet of things and artificial intelligence (CIA). *Reviews in Aquaculture, 13*(4), 2076–2091. doi:10.1111/raq.12559

Naik. (2023). Iot Based Air Pollution Monitoring System. *International Journal of Scientific Research & Engineering Trends, 9*(3).

Najafi, E., & Loukhaoukha, K. (2019). Hybrid secure and robust image watermarking scheme based on SVD and sharp frequency localized contourlet transform. *Journal of Information Security and Applications, 44*, 144–156. doi:10.1016/j.jisa.2018.12.002

Nanthini, K., Sivabalaselvamani, D., Chitra, K., Mohideen, P. A., & Raja, R. D. (2023, March). Cardiac Arrhythmia Detection and Prediction Using Deep Learning Technique. In *Proceedings of Fourth International Conference on Communication, Computing and Electronics Systems: ICCCES 2022* (pp. 983-1003). Singapore: Springer Nature Singapore. 10.1007/978-981-19-7753-4_75

Nassif, Shahin, Attili, Azzeh, & Shaalan. (2019). Speech recognition using deep neural networks: A systematic review. *IEEE Access, 7*(19), 143-165.

Niresi, Zhao, Bissig, Baumann, & Fink. (2023). *Spatial-Temporal Graph Attention Fuser for Calibration in IoT Air Pollution Monitoring Systems*. Intelligent Maintenance and Operations Systems (IMOS) Lab, EPFL.

Nishanth, J., Deshmukh, M. A., Kushwah, R., Kushwaha, K. K., Balaji, S., & Sampath, B. (2023). Particle Swarm Optimization of Hybrid Renewable Energy Systems. In *Intelligent Engineering Applications and Applied Sciences for Sustainability* (pp. 291–308). IGI Global. doi:10.4018/979-8-3693-0044-2.ch016

Norouzi, B., Seyedzadeh, S. M., Mirzakuchaki, S., & Mosavi, M. R. (2013). A novel image encryption based on row-column, masking and main diffusion processes with hyper chaos. *Multimedia Tools and Applications*, *74*(3), 781–811. doi:10.1007/s11042-013-1699-y

NPTEL. (n.d.). *Introduction to Hybrid and Electric Vehicles*. Academic Press.

Nugraha, F. A., Purwadi, A., Haroen, Y., & Heryana, N. (n.d.). The calculation of electric motor and Lithium battery capacity on Cikal Cakrawala ITB electric car. *Power Engineering and Renewable Energy (ICPERE), IEEE International Conference on*, 1-6.

Okokpujie. (2018). A smart air pollution monitoring system. *International Journal of Civil Engineering and Technology, 9*(9), 799–809.

Omar, A., & Abd El-Hafeez, T. (2023). Quantum computing and machine learning for Arabic language sentiment classification in social media. *Scientific Reports*, *13*(1), 1–18. doi:10.1038/s41598-023-44113-7 PMID:37828056

Pachiappan, K., Anitha, K., Pitchai, R., Sangeetha, S., Satyanarayana, T. V. V., & Boopathi, S. (2023). Intelligent Machines, IoT, and AI in Revolutionizing Agriculture for Water Processing. In B. B. Gupta & F. Colace (Eds.), Advances in Computational Intelligence and Robotics. IGI Global. doi:10.4018/978-1-6684-9999-3.ch015

Palaniappan, M., Tirlangi, S., Mohamed, M. J. S., Moorthy, R. S., Valeti, S. V., & Boopathi, S. (2023). Fused Deposition Modelling of Polylactic Acid (PLA)-Based Polymer Composites: A Case Study. In Development, Properties, and Industrial Applications of 3D Printed Polymer Composites (pp. 66–85). IGI Global.

Pallewatta, S., Kostakos, V., & Buyya, R. (2022). QoS-aware placement of microservices-based IoT applications in Fog computing environments. *Future Generation Computer Systems*, *131*, 121–136. doi:10.1016/j.future.2022.01.012

Pallewatta, S., Kostakos, V., & Buyya, R. (2023). Placement of Microservices-based IoT Applications in Fog Computing: A Taxonomy and Future Directions. *ACM Computing Surveys*, *55*(14s), 1–43. doi:10.1145/3592598

Pandey, V., Sircar, A., Bist, N., Solanki, K., & Yadav, K. (2023). Accelerating the renewable energy sector through Industry 4.0: Optimization opportunities in the digital revolution. *International Journal of Innovation Studies*, *7*(2), 171–188. doi:10.1016/j.ijis.2023.03.003

PappasN.Popescu-BelisA. (2017). Multilingual Hierarchical Attention Networks for Document Classification. Available: http://arxiv.org/abs/1707.00896

Pathak, S., & Arun, K. (2011). Recognizing emotions from speech. *Electronics Computer Technology (ICECT), 3rd International Conference on, 4*.

Pendyala, Rodda, Mamidi, & Vangala. (n.d.). *IoT-Based Smart Agricultural Monitoring System.* Academic Press.

Perez-Pinal, F. J., Nunez, C., Alvarez, R., & Gallegos, M. (2006). Step by step design procedure of an Independent-Wheeled Small EV applying EVLS. *IEEE Industrial Electronics, IECON 2006-32nd Annual Conference on*, 1176-1181.

Petajan, E., Bischoff, B., Bodoff, D., & Brooke, N. M. (1988). An improved automatic lipreading system to enhance speech recognition. *Proceedings of the SIGCHI conference on Human factors in computing systems*, 19–25. 10.1145/57167.57170

Philipos. (n.d.). *Loizou Speech Quality Assessment.* Academic Press.

Phuyal, S., Bista, D., & Bista, R. (2020). Challenges, opportunities and future directions of smart manufacturing: A state of art review. *Sustainable Futures : An Applied Journal of Technology, Environment and Society, 2*, 100023. doi:10.1016/j.sftr.2020.100023

Plageras, A. P., & Psannis, K. E. (2023). IOT-based health and emotion care system. *ICT Express, 9*(1), 112–115. doi:10.1016/j.icte.2022.03.008

Poorjam. (2019). *Quality Control in Remote Speech Data Collection.* Academic Press.

Pramila, P., Amudha, S., Saravanan, T., Sankar, S. R., Poongothai, E., & Boopathi, S. (2023). Design and Development of Robots for Medical Assistance: An Architectural Approach. In Contemporary Applications of Data Fusion for Advanced Healthcare Informatics (pp. 260–282). IGI Global.

Pramila, P. V., Amudha, S., Saravanan, T. R., Sankar, S. R., Poongothai, E., & Boopathi, S. (2023). Design and Development of Robots for Medical Assistance: An Architectural Approach. In G. S. Karthick & S. Karupusamy (Eds.), Advances in Healthcare Information Systems and Administration. IGI Global. doi:10.4018/978-1-6684-8913-0.ch011

Prathibha, S. R., Hongal, A., & Jyothi, M. P. (2017). IoT Based Monitoring System in Smart Agriculture. *2017 International Conference on Recent Advances in Electronics and Communication Technology (ICRAECT),* 81-84. 10.1109/ICRAECT.2017.52

Qiu, T., Chi, J., Zhou, X., Ning, Z., Atiquzzaman, M., & Wu, D. O. (2020). Edge computing in industrial internet of things: Architecture, advances and challenges. *IEEE Communications Surveys and Tutorials, 22*(4), 2462–2488. doi:10.1109/COMST.2020.3009103

Qu, Y., Ming, X., Liu, Z., Zhang, X., & Hou, Z. (2019). Smart manufacturing systems: State of the art and future trends. *International Journal of Advanced Manufacturing Technology, 103*(9-12), 3751–3768. doi:10.1007/s00170-019-03754-7

Radha, V., & Vimala, C. (2012b). A review on speech recognition challenges and approaches. *doaj.org, 2*(1), 1-7.

Radhakrishnan, V., & Wu, W. (2018). IoT Technology for Smart Water System. *2018 IEEE 20th International Conference on High Performance Computing and Communications; IEEE 16th International Conference on Smart City; IEEE 4th International Conference on Data Science and Systems (HPCC/SmartCity/DSS),* 1491-1496. 10.1109/HPCC/SmartCity/DSS.2018.00246

Radha, V. (2012a). Speaker independent isolated speech recognition system for Tamil language using HMM. *Procedia Engineering, 30*, 1097–1102. doi:10.1016/j.proeng.2012.01.968

Raghib, Sharma, Ahmad, & Alam. (2018). *Emotion Analysis and Speech Signal Processing.* Academic Press.

Rahamathunnisa, U., Subhashini, P., Aancy, H. M., Meenakshi, S., Boopathi, S., & ... (2023). Solutions for Software Requirement Risks Using Artificial Intelligence Techniques. In *Handbook of Research on Data Science and Cybersecurity Innovations in Industry 4.0 Technologies* (pp. 45–64). IGI Global.

Rahamathunnisa, U., Sudhakar, K., Murugan, T. K., Thivaharan, S., Rajkumar, M., & Boopathi, S. (2023). Cloud Computing Principles for Optimizing Robot Task Offloading Processes. In *AI-Enabled Social Robotics in Human Care Services* (pp. 188–211). IGI Global. doi:10.4018/978-1-6684-8171-4.ch007

Rahamathunnisa, U., Sudhakar, K., Padhi, S. N., Bhattacharya, S., Shashibhushan, G., & Boopathi, S. (2023). Sustainable Energy Generation From Waste Water: IoT Integrated Technologies. In A. S. Etim (Ed.), Advances in Human and Social Aspects of Technology. IGI Global. doi:10.4018/978-1-6684-5347-6.ch010

Raheja, N., & Manocha, A. K. (2023). An IoT enabled secured clinical health care framework for diagnosis of heart diseases. *Biomedical Signal Processing and Control, 80*, 104368. doi:10.1016/j.bspc.2022.104368

Rahman, M. S., Safa, N. T., Sultana, S., Salam, S., Karamehic-Muratovic, A., & Overgaard, H. J. (2022). Role of artificial intelligence-internet of things (AI-IoT) based emerging technologies in the public health response to infectious diseases in Bangladesh. *Parasite Epidemiology and Control, 18*, e00266. doi:10.1016/j.parepi.2022.e00266 PMID:35975103

Rajendra. (2021). Prediction of diabetes using logistic regression and ensemble techniques. *Computer Methods and Programs in Biomedicine, 1.* . doi:10.1016/j.cmpbup.2021.100032

Rajendran, S. & Doraipandian, M. (2019). Construction of Two Dimensional Cubic-Tent-Sine Map for Secure Image Transmission. *Communications in Computer and Information Science, 1116 CCIS*, 51–61. doi:10.1007/978-981-15-0871-4_4

Rajendran, S., Krithivasan, K. & Doraipandian, M. (2020). *Fast pre-processing hex Chaos triggered color image cryptosystem.* Academic Press.

Rajendran, S., Krithivasan, K., & Doraipandian, M. (2021). A novel cross cosine map based medical image cryptosystem using dynamic bit-level diffusion. *Multimedia Tools and Applications, 80*(16), 24221–24243. doi:10.1007/s11042-021-10798-z

Rajendran, S., Mathivanan, S. K., Jayagopal, P., Venkatasen, M., Pandi, T., Sorakaya Somanathan, M., Thangaval, M., & Mani, P. (2021). Language dialect based speech emotion recognition through deep learning techniques. *International Journal of Speech Technology*, *24*(3), 625–635. doi:10.1007/s10772-021-09838-8

Ramudu, K., Mohan, V. M., Jyothirmai, D., Prasad, D., Agrawal, R., & Boopathi, S. (2023). Machine Learning and Artificial Intelligence in Disease Prediction: Applications, Challenges, Limitations, Case Studies, and Future Directions. In Contemporary Applications of Data Fusion for Advanced Healthcare Informatics (pp. 297–318). IGI Global.

Ramudu, K., Mohan, V. M., Jyothirmai, D., Prasad, D. V. S. S. S. V., Agrawal, R., & Boopathi, S. (2023). Machine Learning and Artificial Intelligence in Disease Prediction: Applications, Challenges, Limitations, Case Studies, and Future Directions. In G. S. Karthick & S. Karupusamy (Eds.), Advances in Healthcare Information Systems and Administration. IGI Global. doi:10.4018/978-1-6684-8913-0.ch013

Rani, S., & Srivastava, G. (2024). Secure hierarchical fog computing-based architecture for industry 5.0 using an attribute-based encryption scheme. *Expert Systems with Applications*, *235*, 121180. doi:10.1016/j.eswa.2023.121180

Rashmi, Guruprasad, & Shambhavi. (n.d.). *Sentiment Classification on Bilingual Code-Mixed Texts for Dravidian Languages using Machine Learning Methods*. Academic Press.

Rastogi, R., & Bansal, M. (2023). Diabetes prediction model using data mining techniques Measurement. *Measurement. Sensors*, *25*(February). doi:10.1016/j.measen.2022.100605

Ratmele, A., & Thakur, R. (2022). OpExHAN: Opinion extraction using hierarchical attention network from unstructured reviews. *Social Network Analysis and Mining*, *12*(1), 1–16. doi:10.1007/s13278-022-00971-z PMID:36217360

Ravi, R., Surendra, U., & Shreya, N. (2020). *Comparative analysis of various techniques of IOT in Electric vehicle (No. 4500)*. Easy Chair.

Ravisankar, A., Sampath, B., & Asif, M. M. (2023). Economic Studies on Automobile Management: Working Capital and Investment Analysis. In C. S. V. Negrão, I. G. P. Maia, & J. A. F. Brito (Eds.), Advances in Logistics, Operations, and Management Science. IGI Global. doi:10.4018/978-1-7998-9213-7.ch009

Raza, S., Wang, S., Ahmed, M., & Anwar, M. R. (2019). A survey on vehicular edge computing: Architecture, applications, technical issues, and future directions. *Wireless Communications and Mobile Computing*, *2019*, 2019. doi:10.1155/2019/3159762

Razuri, J. G., Sundgren, D., Rahmani, R., Moran, A., Bonet, I., & Lars-son, A. (2015). Speech emotion recognition in emotionafeedback for human-robot interaction. *International Journal of Advanced Research in Artificial Intelligence*, *4*(2), 20–27.

Reddy, M. A., Gaurav, A., Ushasukhanya, S., Rao, V. C. S., Bhattacharya, S., & Boopathi, S. (2023). Bio-Medical Wastes Handling Strategies During the COVID-19 Pandemic. In C. S. V. Negrão, I. G. P. Maia, & J. A. F. Brito (Eds.), Advances in Logistics, Operations, and Management Science. IGI Global. doi:10.4018/978-1-7998-9213-7.ch006

Reddy, M. A., Reddy, B. M., Mukund, C. S., Venneti, K., Preethi, D. M. D., & Boopathi, S. (2023). Social Health Protection During the COVID-Pandemic Using IoT. In F. P. C. Endong (Ed.), Advances in Electronic Government, Digital Divide, and Regional Development. IGI Global. doi:10.4018/978-1-7998-8394-4.ch009

Reddy, S. B., & Kishore Kumar, T. (2018). Emotion Recognition of Stressed Speech using Teager Energy and Linear Prediction Features. *IEEE 18th International Conference on Advanced Learning Technologies.*

Rehman, A., Saba, T., Haseeb, K., Singh, R., & Jeon, G. (2022). Smart health analysis system using regression analysis with iterative hashing for IoT communication networks. *Computers & Electrical Engineering*, *104*, 108456. doi:10.1016/j.compeleceng.2022.108456

Ren, J., Zhang, D., He, S., Zhang, Y., & Li, T. (2019). A survey on end-edge-cloud orchestrated network computing paradigms: Transparent computing, mobile edge computing, fog computing, and cloudlet. *ACM Computing Surveys*, *52*(6), 1–36. doi:10.1145/3362031

Revathy, G., & ... . (2022). Investigation of E-voting system using face recognition using convolutional neural network (CNN). *Theoretical Computer Science*, *925*, 61–67.

Rudrakar, S., & Rughani, P. (2023). IoT based Agriculture (Ag-IoT): A detailed study on Architecture, Security and Forensics. *Information Processing in Agriculture*, 1–18. doi:10.1016/j.inpa.2023.09.002

Sadeeq, M. M., Abdulkareem, N. M., Zeebaree, S. R., Ahmed, D. M., Sami, A. S., & Zebari, R. R. (2021). IoT and Cloud computing issues, challenges and opportunities: A review. *Qubahan Academic Journal*, *1*(2), 1–7. doi:10.48161/qaj.v1n2a36

Saeed, U., & Dugelay, J.-L. (2010). Combining edge detection and region segmentation for lip contour extraction. In *International Conference on Articulated Motion and Deformable Objects.* Springer. 10.1007/978-3-642-14061-7_2

Sajid, N. A. (2023). A Novel Metadata Based Multi-Label Document Classification Technique. *Computer Systems Science and Engineering*, *46*(2), 2195–2214. doi:10.32604/csse.2023.033844

Saksamudre, S. K., Shrishrimal, P. P., & Deshmukh, R. R. (2015). A review on different approaches for speech recognition system. *International Journal of Computer Applications*, *115*(22). Advance online publication. doi:10.5120/20284-2839

Samikannu, R., Koshariya, A. K., Poornima, E., Ramesh, S., Kumar, A., & Boopathi, S. (2022). Sustainable Development in Modern Aquaponics Cultivation Systems Using IoT Technologies. In *Human Agro-Energy Optimization for Business and Industry* (pp. 105–127). IGI Global.

Sampath, B. (2021). *Sustainable Eco-Friendly Wire-Cut Electrical Discharge Machining: Gas Emission Analysis*. Academic Press.

Sampath, B., Pandian, M., Deepa, D., & Subbiah, R. (2022). Operating parameters prediction of liquefied petroleum gas refrigerator using simulated annealing algorithm. *AIP Conference Proceedings*, *2460*(1), 070003. doi:10.1063/5.0095601

Sampath, B., Sureshkumar, T., Yuvaraj, M., & Velmurugan, D. (2021). Experimental Investigations on Eco-Friendly Helium-Mist Near-Dry Wire-Cut EDM of M2-HSS Material. *Materials Research Proceedings*, *19*, 175–180.

Sankar, K. M., Booba, B., & Boopathi, S. (2023). Smart Agriculture Irrigation Monitoring System Using Internet of Things. In G. S. Karthick (Ed.), Advances in Environmental Engineering and Green Technologies. IGI Global. doi:10.4018/978-1-6684-7879-0.ch006

SantiD. P.MishraK.MohantyS. (2023). Quantum Text Classifier — A Synchronistic Approach Towards Classical and Quantum Machine Learning. Available: http://arxiv.org/abs/2305.12783

Saqlain, M., Piao, M., Shim, Y., & Lee, J. Y. (2019). Framework of an IoT-based industrial data management for smart manufacturing. *Journal of Sensor and Actuator Networks*, *8*(2), 25. doi:10.3390/jsan8020025

Saranya, S., & Bharathi, B. (2023, September). SANBAR@ LT-EDI-2023: Automatic Speech Recognition: vulnerable old-aged and transgender people in Tamil. In *Proceedings of the Third Workshop on Language Technology for Equality, Diversity and Inclusion* (pp. 155-160). Academic Press.

Saravanan, M., Vasanth, M., Boopathi, S., Sureshkumar, M., & Haribalaji, V. (2022). Optimization of Quench Polish Quench (QPQ) Coating Process Using Taguchi Method. *Key Engineering Materials*, *935*, 83–91. doi:10.4028/p-z569vy

Sarmadi, H., Entezami, A., & De Michele, C. (2023, March). Probabilistic data self-clustering based on semi-parametric extreme value theory for structural health monitoring. *Mechanical Systems and Signal Processing*, *187*, 109976. doi:10.1016/j.ymssp.2022.109976

Sarvakar, K., Senkamalavalli, R., Raghavendra, S., Kumar, J. S., Manjunath, R., & Jaiswal, S. (2023). Facial emotion recognition using convolutional neural networks. *Materials Today: Proceedings*, *80*, 3560–3564. doi:10.1016/j.matpr.2021.07.297

Satav, S. D., Lamani, D. G, H. K., Kumar, N. M. G., Manikandan, S., & Sampath, B. (2024). Energy and Battery Management in the Era of Cloud Computing. In Practice, Progress, and Proficiency in Sustainability (pp. 141–166). IGI Global. doi:10.4018/979-8-3693-1186-8.ch009

Satav, S. D., Hasan, D. S., Pitchai, R., Mohanaprakash, T. A., Sultanuddin, S. J., & Boopathi, S. (2024). Next Generation of Internet of Things (NGIoT) in Healthcare Systems. In B. K. Mishra (Ed.), Practice, Progress, and Proficiency in Sustainability. IGI Global. doi:10.4018/979-8-3693-1186-8.ch017

Scherer, K. R. (2005). What are emotions? and how can they be measured? *Social Sciences Information. Information Sur les Sciences Sociales*, *44*(4), 695–729.

Schmidhuber, J. (2015, January). Deep learning in neural networks: An overview. *Neural Networks*, *61*, 85–117.

Schuller, B. W. (2018). Speech emotion recognition: Two decades in a nutshell, Benchmarks, and ongoing trends. *Communications of the ACM*, *61*(5), 90–99.

Sekaran, S. A. R., Lee, C. P., & Lim, K. M. (2021, August). Facial emotion recognition using transfer learning of AlexNet. In *2021 9th International Conference on Information and Communication Technology (ICoICT)* (pp. 170-174). IEEE. 10.1109/ICoICT52021.2021.9527512

Selvakarthi, D., Sivabalaselvamani, D., Wafiq, M. A., Aruna, G., & Gokulnath, M. (2023, March). An IoT Integrated Sensor Technologies for the Enhancement of Hospital Waste Segregation and Management. In *2023 International Conference on Innovative Data Communication Technologies and Application (ICIDCA)* (pp. 797-804). IEEE. 10.1109/ICIDCA56705.2023.10099836

Selvakumar, S., Adithe, S., Isaac, J. S., Pradhan, R., Venkatesh, V., & Sampath, B. (2023). A Study of the Printed Circuit Board (PCB) E-Waste Recycling Process. In Sustainable Approaches and Strategies for E-Waste Management and Utilization (pp. 159–184). IGI Global.

Selvakumar, S., Shankar, R., Ranjit, P., Bhattacharya, S., Gupta, A. S. G., & Boopathi, S. (2023). E-Waste Recovery and Utilization Processes for Mobile Phone Waste. In *Handbook of Research on Safe Disposal Methods of Municipal Solid Wastes for a Sustainable Environment* (pp. 222–240). IGI Global. doi:10.4018/978-1-6684-8117-2.ch016

Sengeni, D., Padmapriya, G., Imambi, S. S., Suganthi, D., Suri, A., & Boopathi, S. (2023). Biomedical Waste Handling Method Using Artificial Intelligence Techniques. In P. Srivastava, D. Ramteke, A. K. Bedyal, M. Gupta, & J. K. Sandhu (Eds.), Practice, Progress, and Proficiency in Sustainability. IGI Global. doi:10.4018/978-1-6684-8117-2.ch022

Sengupta, T. N. (2008). S.: Lip localization and viseme recognition from video sequences. *Fourteenth National Conference on Communications*.

Senthil, T., Puviyarasan, M., Babu, S. R., Surakasi, R., Sampath, B., & Associates. (2023). Industrial Robot-Integrated Fused Deposition Modelling for the 3D Printing Process. In Development, Properties, and Industrial Applications of 3D Printed Polymer Composites (pp. 188–210). IGI Global.

Senthil, T. S., Ohmsakthi Vel, R., Puviyarasan, M., Babu, S. R., Surakasi, R., & Sampath, B. (2023). Industrial Robot-Integrated Fused Deposition Modelling for the 3D Printing Process. In R. Keshavamurthy, V. Tambrallimath, & J. P. Davim (Eds.), Advances in Chemical and Materials Engineering. IGI Global. doi:10.4018/978-1-6684-6009-2.ch011

Seo, J. M., Yoo, H., Yun, K., Kim, H., & Choi, S. I. (2018, September). Behavior recognition of a person in a daily video using joint position information. In *2018 IEEE First International Conference on Artificial Intelligence and Knowledge Engineering (AIKE)* (pp. 172-174). IEEE. 10.1109/AIKE.2018.00040

Shaikh, N., Kasat, K., Godi, R. K., Krishna, V. R., Chauhan, D. K., & Kharade, J. (2023). Novel IoT framework for event processing in healthcare applications. *Measurement. Sensors*, *27*, 100733. doi:10.1016/j.measen.2023.100733

Shamayleh, A., Awad, M., & Farhat, J. (2020). IoT based predictive maintenance management of medical equipment. *Journal of Medical Systems*, *44*(4), 1–12. doi:10.1007/s10916-020-1534-8 PMID:32078712

Shankaracharya, S. (2017). *Diabetes risk prediction using machine learning: prospect and challenges*. Bioinform., Proteom. Imaging Anal.

Shanmugavadivel, K., Sathishkumar, V. E., Raja, S., Lingaiah, T. B., Neelakandan, S., & Subramanian, M. (2022, December). Deep learning based sentiment analysis and offensive language identification on multilingual code-mixed data. *Scientific Reports*, *12*(1), 21557. Advance online publication. doi:10.1038/s41598-022-26092-3 PMID:36513786

Sharma, P., Abrol, V., Sachdev, A., & Dileep, A. D. (2016). Speech emotion recognition using kernel sparse representation based classifier. *2016 24th European Signal Processing Conference (EUSIPCO)*, 374-377.

Sharma, D. M., Venkata Ramana, K., Jothilakshmi, R., Verma, R., Uma Maheswari, B., & Boopathi, S. (2024). Integrating Generative AI Into K-12 Curriculums and Pedagogies in India: Opportunities and Challenges. In P. Yu, J. Mulli, Z. A. S. Syed, & L. Umme (Eds.), Advances in Higher Education and Professional Development. IGI Global. doi:10.4018/979-8-3693-0487-7.ch006

Shaw, R., Howley, E., & Barrett, E. (2022). Applying reinforcement learning towards automating energy efficient virtual machine consolidation in cloud data centers. *Information Systems*, *107*, 101722. doi:10.1016/j.is.2021.101722

Shenoy, J., & Pingle, Y. (2016, March). IOT in agriculture. In *2016 3rd International Conference on Computing for Sustainable Global Development (INDIACom)* (pp. 1456-1458). IEEE.

Shruthi, G., Mundada, M. R., Supreeth, S., & Gardiner, B. (2023). Deep learning-based resource prediction and mutated leader algorithm enabled load balancing in fog computing. *International Journal of Computer Networks and Information Security*, *15*(4), 84-95.

Sicari, S., Rizzardi, A., & Coen-Porisini, A. (2022). Insights into security and privacy towards fog computing evolution. *Computers & Security*, *120*, 102822. doi:10.1016/j.cose.2022.102822

Singh, A. K., Dalal, A., & Kumar, P. (2014). Analysis of induction motor for electric vehicle application based on drive cycle analysis. In *Power Electronics, Drives and Energy Systems (PEDES), IEEE International Conference* (pp. 1-6). IEEE.

Singh, A., Maheskumar, R. S., & Iyengar, G. R. (2022). A Diagnostic Method for Fog Forecasting Using Numerical Weather Prediction (NWP) Model Outputs. *Journal of Atmospheric Science Research*, *5*(4), 10–19. doi:10.30564/jasr.v5i4.5068

Singh, G., & Mittal, A. (2014). Various image enhancement techniques-a critical review. *International Journal of Innovation and Scientific Research*, *10*(2), 267–274.

Singh, G., Nagpal, A., & Singh, V. (2022). Text Classification using Improved IWO-HAN. In *Procedia Computer Science* (pp. 1184–1195). Elsevier B.V. doi:10.1016/j.procs.2023.01.097

Singh, G., Nagpal, A., & Singh, V. (2023). Optimal feature selection and invasive weed tunicate swarm algorithm-based hierarchical attention network for text classification. *Connection Science*, *35*(1), 2231171. Advance online publication. doi:10.1080/09540091.2023.2231171

Singh, N., Gunjan, V. K., Chaudhary, G., Kaluri, R., Victor, N., & Lakshmanna, K. (2022). IoT enabled HELMET to safeguard the health of mine workers. *Computer Communications*, *193*, 1–9. doi:10.1016/j.comcom.2022.06.032

Singh, N., Sasirekha, S. P., Dhakne, A., Thrinath, B. S., Ramya, D., & Thiagarajan, R. (2022). IOT enabled hybrid model with learning ability for E-health care systems. *Measurement. Sensors*, *24*, 100567. doi:10.1016/j.measen.2022.100567

Sisodia. (2018). Prediction of Diabetes using Classification Algorithms. *Procedia Computer Science, 132*, 1578-1585. doi:10.1016/j.procs.2018.05.122

Sivabalaselvamani, D., Nanthini, K., Selvakarthi, D., Niranchan, V. M., Kumar, L. S., & Swetha, P. (2023, September). Skin Melanoma Detection Using Image Augmentation. In *2023 4th International Conference on Smart Electronics and Communication (ICOSEC)* (pp. 1624-1630). IEEE. 10.1109/ICOSEC58147.2023.10275944

Sivabalaselvamani, D., Selvakarthi, D., Yogapriya, J., Thiruvenkatasuresh, M. P., Maruthappa, M., & Chandra, A. S. (2021, January). Artificial Intelligence in data-driven analytics for the personalized healthcare. In *2021 international conference on computer communication and informatics (ICCCI)* (pp. 1-5). IEEE.

Sivabalaselvamani, D., Selvakarthi, D., Rahunathan, L., Eswari, S. N., Pavithraa, M., & Sridhar, M. (2021, January). Investigation on heart disease using machine learning algorithms. In *2021 International Conference on Computer Communication and Informatics (ICCCI)* (pp. 1-6). IEEE. 10.1109/ICCCI50826.2021.9402390

Social Work Education BD. (n.d.). https://socialworkeducationbd.blogspot.com/2017/08/definition-of-emotion-and-its.html

Songhorabadi, M., Rahimi, M., MoghadamFarid, A. M., & Haghi Kashani, M. (2023). Fog computing approaches in IoT-enabled smart cities. *Journal of Network and Computer Applications*, *211*, 103557. doi:10.1016/j.jnca.2022.103557

Sreenivas, K., & Kamkshi Prasad, V. (2018). Fragile watermarking schemes for image authentication: A survey. *International Journal of Machine Learning and Cybernetics*, *9*(7), 1193–1218. doi:10.1007/s13042-017-0641-4

Srinivas, B., Maguluri, L. P., Naidu, K. V., Reddy, L. C. S., Deivakani, M., & Boopathi, S. (2023). Architecture and Framework for Interfacing Cloud-Enabled Robots. In *Handbook of Research on Data Science and Cybersecurity Innovations in Industry 4.0 Technologies* (pp. 542–560). IGI Global. doi:10.4018/978-1-6684-8145-5.ch027

Suhasini, S., & Bharathi, B. (2023, September). ASR_SSN_CSE@ LTEDI-2023: Pretrained Transformer based Automatic Speech Recognition system for Elderly People. In *Proceedings of the Third Workshop on Language Technology for Equality, Diversity and Inclusion* (pp. 161-165). Academic Press.

Sun, A., & Li, Y.-J. (2017). Using facial expression to Detect Emotion in E-learning System: A Deep Learning Method. Springer International Publishing AG.

Sundaramoorthy, K., Singh, A., Sumathy, G., Maheshwari, A., Arunarani, A. R., & Boopathi, S. (2023). A Study on AI and Blockchain-Powered Smart Parking Models for Urban Mobility. In B. B. Gupta & F. Colace (Eds.), Advances in Computational Intelligence and Robotics. IGI Global. doi:10.4018/978-1-6684-9999-3.ch010

Su, Q., Wang, G., Lv, G., Zhang, X., Deng, G., & Chen, B. (2017). A novel blind color image watermarking based on Contourlet transform and Hessenberg decomposition. *Multimedia Tools and Applications*, *76*(6), 8781–8801. doi:10.1007/s11042-016-3522-z

Suresh Kumar, Subhash, Tamilselvan, Sudhakar, & Vignesh. (2019). Automated water Distribution System in Metro's using IOT. *International Journal of Innovative Technology and Exploring Engineering, 8*(6), 207-211.

Swapna, G., Soman, K. P., & Vinayakumar, R. (2018). Automated detection of diabetes using CNN and CNN-LSTM network and heart rate signals. *Procedia Computer Science*, *132*, 1253–1262. doi:10.1016/j.procs.2018.05.041

Swetha, K., Kumari, E. V., Reddy, V. A., & Gupta, K. G. (2023, August). Visual Weather Analytics-Leveraging Image Recognition for Weather Prediction. In *2023 Second International Conference on Augmented Intelligence and Sustainable Systems (ICAISS)* (pp. 800-804). IEEE. 10.1109/ICAISS58487.2023.10250605

Syamala, M., Komala, C., Pramila, P., Dash, S., Meenakshi, S., & Boopathi, S. (2023). Machine Learning-Integrated IoT-Based Smart Home Energy Management System. In *Handbook of Research on Deep Learning Techniques for Cloud-Based Industrial IoT* (pp. 219–235). IGI Global. doi:10.4018/978-1-6684-8098-4.ch013

T, S. A., Jose, J., G, R., & Reddy, R. M. (2015). An E-learning System with Multiracial Emotion Recognition using Supervised Machine Learning. *International Journal of Recent Technology and Engineering, 8*(4), 4449.

Tabrizchi, H., & Kuchaki Rafsanjani, M. (2020). A survey on security challenges in cloud computing: Issues, threats, and solutions. *The Journal of Supercomputing*, *76*(12), 9493–9532. doi:10.1007/s11227-020-03213-1

Talaat, F. M. (2022). Effective prediction and resource allocation method (EPRAM) in fog computing environment for smart healthcare system. *Multimedia Tools and Applications*, *81*(6), 8235–8258. doi:10.1007/s11042-022-12223-5

Tamilselvan, G. M., Ashishkumar, V., Jothi Prasath, S., & Mohammed Yusuff, S. (2018). IoT Based Automated Water Distribution System with Water Theft Control and Water Purchasing System. *International Journal of Recent Technology and Engineering, 7*(4).

Tan, X., Chen, W., Zou, T., Yang, J., & Du, B. (2023). Real-time prediction of mechanical behaviors of underwater shield tunnel structure using machine learning method based on structural health monitoring data. *Journal of Rock Mechanics and Geotechnical Engineering, 15*(4), 886-895. doi:10.1016/j.jrmge.2022.06.015

Teoh, Y. K., Gill, S. S., & Parlikad, A. K. (2021). IoT and fog computing based predictive maintenance model for effective asset management in industry 4.0 using machine learning. *IEEE Internet of Things Journal.*

Thanda, A., & Venkatesan, S. M. (2016). *Audio visual speech recognition using deep recurrent neural networks. In IAPR workshop on multimodal pattern recognition of social signals in human-computer interaction.* Springer.

Thilak, R. A., & Madharaci, R. (2004). *Speech recognizer for Tamil language*. Tamil Internet.

Thingspeak. (n.d.). https://thingspeak.com/pages/learn_more

Tiwari, S., Dhanda, N., & Dev, H. (2023). A real time secured medical management system based on blockchain and internet of things. *Measurement. Sensors*, *25*, 100630. doi:10.1016/j.measen.2022.100630

Toomula, S., Paulraj, D., Bose, J., Bikku, T., & Sivabalaselvamani, D. (2022). IoT and wearables for detection of COVID-19 diagnosis using fusion-based feature extraction with multikernel extreme learning machine. In *Wearable Telemedicine Technology for the Healthcare Industry* (pp. 137–152). Academic Press.

Torfi, Iranmanesh, Nasrabadi, & Dawson. (2017). 3d convolutional neural networks for cross audio-visual matching recognition. *IEEE Access, 5*(22), 81-91.

Tran-Dang, H., Bhardwaj, S., Rahim, T., Musaddiq, A., & Kim, D. S. (2022). Reinforcement learning based resource management for fog computing environment: Literature review, challenges, and open issues. *Journal of Communications and Networks (Seoul)*, *24*(1), 83–98. doi:10.23919/JCN.2021.000041

Tuppad, A., & Patil, S. D. (2022). Machine learning for diabetes clinical decision support: A review. *Advances in Computational Intelligence*, *2*(2), 22. doi:10.1007/s43674-022-00034-y PMID:35434723

Ugandar, R. E., Rahamathunnisa, U., Sajithra, S., Christiana, M. B. V., Palai, B. K., & Boopathi, S. (2023). Hospital Waste Management Using Internet of Things and Deep Learning: Enhanced Efficiency and Sustainability. In M. Arshad (Ed.), Advances in Bioinformatics and Biomedical Engineering. IGI Global. doi:10.4018/978-1-6684-6577-6.ch015

Umamaheswari, P., & Ramaswamy, V. (2023, March). A Novel Modified LSTM Deep Learning Model on Precipitation Analysis for South Indian States. In *International Conference on Deep Sciences for Computing and Communications* (pp. 189-201). Cham: Springer Nature Switzerland. 10.1007/978-3-031-27622-4_15

Umamaheswari, P. (2022). Water-Level Prediction Utilizing Datamining Techniques in Watershed Management. In *Handbook of Research on Evolving Designs and Innovation in ICT and Intelligent Systems for Real-World Applications* (pp. 261–275). IGI Global.

Umamaheswari, P., & Ramaswamy, V. (2022). Optimized preprocessing using time variant particle swarm optimization (TVPSO) and deep learning on rainfall data. *Journal of Scientific and Industrial Research*, *81*(12), 1317–1325.

Ungurean, I., Gaitan, N. C., & Gaitan, V. G. (2014, May). An IoT architecture for things from industrial environment. In *2014 10th International Conference on Communications (COMM)* (pp. 1-4). IEEE. 10.1109/ICComm.2014.6866713

Vanitha, S., Radhika, K., & Boopathi, S. (2023). Artificial Intelligence Techniques in Water Purification and Utilization. In *Human Agro-Energy Optimization for Business and Industry* (pp. 202–218). IGI Global. doi:10.4018/978-1-6684-4118-3.ch010

Veeranjaneyulu, R., Boopathi, S., Kumari, R. K., Vidyarthi, A., Isaac, J. S., & Jaiganesh, V. (2023). Air Quality Improvement and Optimisation Using Machine Learning Technique. *IEEE Explore*, 1–6.

Veeranjaneyulu, R., Boopathi, S., Kumari, R. K., Vidyarthi, A., Isaac, J. S., & Jaiganesh, V. (2023). Air Quality Improvement and Optimisation Using Machine Learning Technique. *IEEE-Explore*, 1–6.

Veeranjaneyulu, R., Boopathi, S., Narasimharao, J., Gupta, K. K., Reddy, R. V. K., & Ambika, R. (2023). Identification of Heart Diseases using Novel Machine Learning Method. *IEEE Explore*, 1–6.

Veeranjaneyulu, R., Boopathi, S., Narasimharao, J., Gupta, K. K., Reddy, R. V. K., & Ambika, R. (2023). Identification of Heart Diseases using Novel Machine Learning Method. *IEEE- Explore*, 1–6.

Vempalli, S. K., Ramprabhakar, J., Shankar, S., & Prabhakar, G. (2018). Electric Vehicle Designing. *Modelling and Simulation (Anaheim)*, 1–6.

Venkateswaran, N., Vidhya, K., Ayyannan, M., Chavan, S. M., Sekar, K., & Boopathi, S. (2023). A Study on Smart Energy Management Framework Using Cloud Computing. In 5G, Artificial Intelligence, and Next Generation Internet of Things: Digital Innovation for Green and Sustainable Economies (pp. 189–212). IGI Global. doi:10.4018/978-1-6684-8634-4.ch009

Venkateswaran, N., Kumar, S. S., Diwakar, G., Gnanasangeetha, D., & Boopathi, S. (2023). Synthetic Biology for Waste Water to Energy Conversion: IoT and AI Approaches. In M. Arshad (Ed.), Advances in Bioinformatics and Biomedical Engineering. IGI Global. doi:10.4018/978-1-6684-6577-6.ch017

Venkateswaran, N., Vidhya, R., Naik, D. A., Raj, T. M., Munjal, N., & Boopathi, S. (2023). Study on Sentence and Question Formation Using Deep Learning Techniques. In *Digital Natives as a Disruptive Force in Asian Businesses and Societies* (pp. 252–273). IGI Global. doi:10.4018/978-1-6684-6782-4.ch015

Vennila, T., Karuna, M., Srivastava, B. K., Venugopal, J., Surakasi, R., & Sampath, B. (2022). New Strategies in Treatment and Enzymatic Processes: Ethanol Production From Sugarcane Bagasse. In Human Agro-Energy Optimization for Business and Industry (pp. 219–240). IGI Global.

Very Well Mind. (n.d.). https://www.verywellmind.com/an-overview-of-the-types-of-emotions4163976

Villari, M., Fazio, M., Dustdar, S., Rana, O., Jha, D. N., & Ranjan, R. (2019). Osmosis: The osmotic computing platform for microelements in the cloud, edge, and internet of things. *Computer*, *52*(8), 14–26. doi:10.1109/MC.2018.2888767

Villari, M., Fazio, M., Dustdar, S., Rana, O., & Ranjan, R. (2016). Osmotic computing: A new paradigm for edge/cloud integration. *IEEE Cloud Computing*, *3*(6), 76–83. doi:10.1109/MCC.2016.124

Vimala, C., & Radha, V. (2015). Isolated speech recognition system for Tamil language using statistical pattern matching and machine learning techniques. *Journal of Engineering Science and Technology*, *10*(5), 617–632.

Vogt, T., & André, E. (2005). Comparing feature sets for acted and spontaneous speech in view of automatic emotion recognition. *Multimedia and Expo. ICME 2005. IEEE International Conference on. IEEE*, 474-477.

Vuyyuru, V. A., Rao, G. A., & Murthy, Y. S. (2021). A novel weather prediction model using a hybrid mechanism based on MLP and VAE with fire-fly optimization algorithm. *Evolutionary Intelligence*, *14*(2), 1173–1185. doi:10.1007/s12065-021-00589-8

Wang, B., Tao, F., Fang, X., Liu, C., Liu, Y., & Freiheit, T. (2021). Smart manufacturing and intelligent manufacturing: A comparative review. *Engineering (Beijing)*, *7*(6), 738–757. doi:10.1016/j.eng.2020.07.017

Wang, J., Zhang, J., Honda, K., Wei, J., & Dang, J. (2016). Audio-visual speech recognition integrating 3D lip information obtained from the Kinect. *Multimedia Systems*, *22*(3), 315–323. Advance online publication. doi:10.1007/s00530-015-0499-9

Wang, Z., Chen, J., & Hoi, S. C. (2020). Deep learning for image super-resolution: A survey. *IEEE Transactions on Pattern Analysis and Machine Intelligence*, *43*(10), 3365–3387.

Xia, F. (2022). Label Oriented Hierarchical Attention Neural Network for Short Text Classification. *Acad. J. Eng. Technol. Sci.*, *5*(1), 53–62. doi:10.25236/AJETS.2022.050111

Xiang, R., Yang, H., Yan, Z., Mohamed Taha, A. M., Xu, X., & Wu, T. (2022). Super-resolution reconstruction of GOSAT CO2 products using bicubic interpolation. *Geocarto International*, *37*(27), 15187–15211.

Xu, H., Kang, X., Chen, Y. & Wang, Y. (2019). Rotation and scale invariant image watermarking based on polar harmonic transforms. *Optik*, *183*(December), 401–414. doi:10.1016/j.ijleo.2019.02.001

Xue, J., Huang, S., Song, H., & Shi, L. (2023). Fine-grained sequence-to-sequence lip reading based on self-attention and self-distillation. *Frontiers of Computer Science*, *17*(6), 176344. doi:10.1007/s11704-023-2230-x

Xu, M., Toosi, A. N., & Buyya, R. (2020). A self-adaptive approach for managing applications and harnessing renewable energy for sustainable cloud computing. *IEEE Transactions on Sustainable Computing*, *6*(4), 544–558. doi:10.1109/TSUSC.2020.3014943

Yamashita, K., & Markov, K. (2020). Medical image enhancement using super resolution methods. *Computational Science–ICCS 2020: 20th International Conference, Amsterdam, The Netherlands, June 3–5, 2020 Proceedings*, *20*(Part V), 496–508.

Yamni, M., Daoui, A., El ogri, O., Karmouni, H., Sayyouri, M., Qjidaa, H., & Flusser, J. (2020). Fractional Charlier moments for image reconstruction and image watermarking. *Signal Processing*, *171*, 107509. doi:10.1016/j.sigpro.2020.107509

Yang, H., Kumara, S., Bukkapatnam, S. T., & Tsung, F. (2019). The internet of things for smart manufacturing: A review. *IISE Transactions*, *51*(11), 1190–1216. doi:10.1080/24725854.2018.1555383

Yi, C., Wang, J., Cheng, N., Zhou, S., & Xu, B. (2020). Applying wav2vec2. 0 to speech recognition in various low-resource languages. *arXiv preprint arXiv:2012.12121*.

Yuvaraj, N., & SriPreethaa, K. R. (2017). Diabetes prediction in healthcare systems using machine learning algorithms on Hadoop cluster. *Cluster Computing*, *22*(S1), 1–9. doi:10.1007/s10586-017-1532-x

Zamil, A. A. A. (2019). Emotion Detection from Speech Signals using Voting Mechanism on Classified Frames. In *2019 International Conference on Robotics, Electrical and Signal Processing Techniques (ICREST)*. IEEE.

Zear, A., Singh, A. K., & Kumar, P. (2018). A proposed secure multiple watermarking technique based on DWT, DCT and SVD for application in medicine. *Multimedia Tools and Applications*, *77*(4), 4863–4882. doi:10.1007/s11042-016-3862-8

Zekrifa, D. M. S., Kulkarni, M., Bhagyalakshmi, A., Devireddy, N., Gupta, S., & Boopathi, S. (2023). Integrating Machine Learning and AI for Improved Hydrological Modeling and Water Resource Management. In *Artificial Intelligence Applications in Water Treatment and Water Resource Management* (pp. 46–70). IGI Global. doi:10.4018/978-1-6684-6791-6.ch003

Zhang, Y., & Rao, Z. (2020). Hierarchical attention networks for grid text classification. *Proc. 2020 IEEE Int. Conf. Inf. Technol. Big Data Artif. Intell. ICIBA 2020*, 491–494. 10.1109/ICIBA50161.2020.9277489

Zhang, Y., Xu, X., Liu, A., Lu, Q., Xu, L., & Tao, F. (2019). Blockchain-based trust mechanism for IoT-based smart manufacturing system. *IEEE Transactions on Computational Social Systems*, *6*(6), 1386–1394. doi:10.1109/TCSS.2019.2918467

Zhu, Y., Dai, Y., Han, K., Wang, J., & Hu, J. (2022). An efficient bicubic interpolation implementation for real-time image processing using hybrid computing. *Journal of Real-Time Image Processing*, *19*(6), 1211–1223.

Zonta, T., Da Costa, C. A., da Rosa Righi, R., de Lima, M. J., da Trindade, E. S., & Li, G. P. (2020). Predictive maintenance in the Industry 4.0: A systematic literature review. *Computers & Industrial Engineering*, *150*, 106889. doi:10.1016/j.cie.2020.106889

Zou, Qu, Luo, Yin, Ju, Tang. (2018). *Predicting diabetes mellitus with machine learning techniques*. Academic Press.

About the Contributors

G. Revathy has around 14 years of teaching experience. she has published around 35 international journals, 9 books and 5 book chapters. Her area of interest includes wireless networks, machine learning and computer vision.

* * *

Sam B. completed his undergraduate in Mechanical Engineering and postgraduate in the field of Engineering Design. He completed his Ph.D. from Anna University, Chennai, Tamil Nādu, India.

Sampath Boopathi is an accomplished individual with a strong academic background and extensive research experience. He completed his undergraduate studies in Mechanical Engineering and pursued his postgraduate studies in the field of Computer-Aided Design. Dr. Boopathi obtained his Ph.D. from Anna University, focusing his research on Manufacturing and optimization. Throughout his career, Dr. Boopathi has made significant contributions to the field of engineering. He has authored and published over 160 research articles in internationally peer-reviewed journals, highlighting his expertise and dedication to advancing knowledge in his area of specialization. His research output demonstrates his commitment to conducting rigorous and impactful research. In addition to his research publications, Dr. Boopathi has also been granted one patent and has three published patents to his name. This indicates his innovative thinking and ability to develop practical solutions to real-world engineering challenges. With 17 years of academic and research experience, Dr. Boopathi has enriched the engineering community through his teaching and mentorship roles. He has served in various engineering colleges in Tamilnadu, India, where he has imparted knowledge, guided students, and contributed to the overall academic development of the institutions. Dr. Sampath Boopathi's diverse background, ranging from mechanical engineering to computer-aided design, along with his specialization in manufacturing and optimization, positions him as a valuable asset in the field of engineering. His research contributions, patents, and extensive teaching experience exemplify his expertise and dedication to advancing engineering knowledge and fostering innovation.

Sivabalaselvamani D. has 15 years of experience in teaching. He obtained his Master's degree with First Class and Distinction from Anna University, Chennai, and a Ph.D. degree from the same university. Since 2010, he has been working as an Associate Professor in the Department of Computer Applications at Kongu Engineering College, located in Perundurai, Erode, Tamil Nadu, India. Moreover, Dr. Sivabalaselvamani has published numerous research papers in various international journals and conferences. His area of expertise includes Vehicular Ad-Hoc Networks (VANET), MANET, Internet of Things (IoT), Artificial Intelligence, Machine Learning, Deep Learning, and Blockchain Technologies.

Manivannan Doraipandian received his B.E in Electrical and Electronics Engineering from Bharathidasan University, Tiruchy, Tamilnadu, India (1996), M.Tech in Computer science and Engineering (2002) from the SASTRA University, Tamilnadu, India. Currently he is working as Senior Assistant Professor of Computer Science Department, School of Computing at SASTRA University, Tamilnadu, India. His area of interest in academic research is cryptography, security in Embedded Systems, Wireless Sensor Networks using ARM processors and embedded communication systems. In the past few years, his research interests have been focused on platforms capable of handling low power processor for Wireless Sensor Node and applications in distributed embedded platform, as well as information security related topics in the embedded systems domain.

Durga Karthik obtained Ph.D from SASTRA University in the year 2018. Research Area includes chemometrics, image processing and data analytics. Life time member of ISTE.

S. Meganathan completed his Ph.D. in 2013 at SASTRA Deemed University. He works as an Associate Professor in the Department of Computer Science & Engineering at Srinivasa Ramanujan Centre, SASTRA Deemed University, Kumbakonam. Four research scholars are pursuing Ph.D. programme under his guidance in data mining and its applications. Their research focuses on tropical cyclone prediction, electrical consumption prediction based on climate data, patient diagnosis systems on medical data, and improved D.S.S. systems on medical database systems. There are 32 research articles published in SCOPUS-indexed journals and 8 in SCI/SCIE indexed journals. He has experience in consultancy projects in the area of Video and Image Analytics for the Mahamaham Festival 2016, held at Kumbakonam,

Tamil Nadu. This project extended to various festivals conducted by the HR&CE departments and the Revenue Departments of the government of Tamil Nadu. The student projects for B. Tech, M.Sc., and M.C.A., programmes in meteorological data have been guided for the past 20 years.

Umamaheswari P. received M.Tech in Computer Science from SASTRA Deemed University, Thanjavur, Tamil Nadu, and India in 2011 and M.B.A. from Alagappa University, Karaikudi, Tamil Nadu, and India in the year 2006. She is pursuing a doctoral degree in Computer Science and Engineering from SASTRA Deemed University. She has 20 years of teaching experience for UG and PG courses in Computer Science and presently working as an Assistant Professor in the department of computer science and engineering at SASTRA University, SRC Campus, and Kumbakonam. Her research interest is in Data Mining, Machine Learning, and Deep learning. She published research papers in Book chapters, International Conferences, Scopus and Science Citation Indexed Journals.

A. Ramalingam completed his MCA and Ph.D (CSE) at Puducherry Technological University formerly called as Pondicherry Engineering College, Puducherry, M.Tech(IT) at AAI-DU, Allahabad and M.Phil (CS) at Periyar University, Salem. He has been working as a Professor and Head in the Department of Computer Applications (MCA Programme), Sri Manakula Vinayagar Engineering College (Autonomous), Puducherry since 2002. He has published more than 25 papers in International Journals, 30 papers in International/National conferences, 2 International and 5 National patents, authored and co-authored for 6 books, 2 book chapters and Invited speakers for reputed institutions. He is a Life member in the professional association of ISTE and CSI.

Index

P

R

S

T

V

W

Z

www.ingramcontent.com/pod-product-compliance
Lightning Source LLC
LaVergne TN
LVHW080631011026
849160LV00014B/1179